AUTHENTIC ITALIAN

AUTHENTIC ITALIAN

The Real Story of Italy's Food and Its People

DINA M. DI MAIO

ISBN-13: 978-0-9996255-0-7

To all *senza patria*, may you find a place that welcomes you.

CONTENTS

INTRODUCTION

Laurinburg, North Carolina, is a small town in southeastern North Carolina less than ten miles from the South Carolina border. The county seat of Scotland County, the town was incorporated in 1877 but dates to 1785.[1] Scottish Highlanders founded the Laurinburg Presbyterian Church in 1859, still in operation today.[2] For a while, the textile industry was a source of employment for the townsfolk.[3] Then the railroads were built and shipped cantaloupes and watermelons from nearby towns.[4] Laurinburg's history reads like any other Main Street USA with Fourth of July parades and downtown shops, an idyllic place, sort of like Andy Griffith's Mayberry. With a current population of almost sixteen thousand[5] people, it's not a place that often makes the news. But in 1972, it did.

It made the news for its most famous tourist attraction of the time, a mummy called "Spaghetti." However, the story of the mummy started 61 years before, in 1911. That year, a traveling carnival went through McColl, a small town in northeastern South Carolina. One of the workers was an Italian musician whose name is thought to be Concetto Farmica. (There are conflicting names on record for this man. One is Frezzo Connsceppo, although this name doesn't appear to be a correct spelling of an Italian name. Others are Forenzio Concippio or Giuseppe Camiola. His grave marker reads "Cancetto Farmica," but Cancetto is not a traditional Italian male name.) He was beaten with a tent stake by another carnival worker during a fight. He died at the closest hospital, which was in Laurinburg. On April 28, his remains were brought to the local McDougald Funeral Home. Concetto's father was also a carnival worker working for another company elsewhere. He didn't have the money to pay to move his son's body. Through an interpreter, he worked out a payment plan with the funeral director for embalming. He paid about $15-20[6] and left, promising to return with payment and burial instructions. Months later, the funeral owner received a letter from the family in Italy, requesting the body be sent back to Italy and that it was not to be buried in a non-Catholic cemetery. The funeral director wrote the family with the cost of shipping the body to Italy and got no response. The funeral owner kept the body, at this point a mummy, for 30 years in case the family returned. According to Christine Quigley in *Modern Mummies: The Preservation of the Human Body in the Twentieth Century*, in 1939, the Italian government offered him $500 for burial expenses but he turned it down.[7] An old newspaper clipping on "the mummy" from 1936 says McDougald had offers to buy the mummy but kept him because it was good advertising.[8] The next generation of the funeral home kept him for another 30 years. Farmica's body was kept in an open box where it could be viewed. Word got around and his mummy became a spectacle, referred to as "Spaghetti" because he was Italian. In 1972, Congressman Mario Biaggi of New York heard about it. He complained that Farmica should be buried. The current owner of the funeral parlor, Beacham McDougald, claimed in an article by Tim Bullard in *SCNow* that Biaggi was looking for votes in an election year and that is why "he picked up on this Spaghetti thing as being derogatory to Italians."[9] Finally, in a Catholic ceremony performed by a local priest, Farmica was laid to rest in Laurinburg.

A thirty minutes' drive from where I grew up.

In 1986, my parents moved from the New York Tristate area to a town not unlike Laurinburg. At the time, I didn't know the story of Farmica, but I would soon come to understand the racism, ethnicism, and classism that allowed a human being to be hanging in a closet as a carnival oddity and referred to as "spaghetti," a derogatory term for Italians used in the early nineteen hundreds. The moment I started sixth grade in August 1986, I knew I wasn't in Kansas anymore. There was always talk of the three races: "white, black, and Indian." (The Indians refer to the Lumbee Indian tribe, who preferred being called "Indian" to "Native American.") In sixth grade, I remember the rumor that the Ku Klux Klan was coming to steal a blond white girl as a sacrifice. Because the kids were scared, my teacher locked the door. I didn't know where I fit in but I learned very quickly that I was not white. I remember my teacher checking the "Other" box for my race on an official school document. Suddenly, all the things I took for granted—the "o" at the end of my name, my dark hair, my dark eyes, the hair on my arms, the food I ate, the religion I grew up with, the place I came from, the music I listened to, the holidays I celebrated made me something different, made me the "Other," defined me.

My parents opened an Italian pizzeria in North Carolina. They used the freshest, best-quality American-made Italian products they could find. They had an extensive menu with many Italian-American specialties. Customers would call asking for Domino's Pizza or Pizza Hut, hanging up when we explained we were "Di Maio Pizza." My parents made their own

Italian sausage, but people preferred and requested those frozen sausage pellets used by many commercial pizzerias. People didn't order much beyond pizza and spaghetti (they requested "'getti with meat sauce," the meat sauce they wanted being a spicy ground beef concoction similar to chili that makes me wonder if it doesn't evolve from Cincinnati chili sans cheese or a diner spaghetti) and sausage sandwiches, so my parents pared down the menu to these items (though not changing our family's sauce recipe to suit local taste). Our best customers were lawyers who worked at the nearby courthouse or local teachers and professors. It's no surprise to me that today, North Carolina is number four on *PMQ Pizza Magazine*'s top ten list of states with the fewest pizzerias per ten thousand people, according to Peter Genovese in *Pizza City: The Ultimate Guide to New York's Favorite Food*.[10]

Life was different, a culture shock to me. We could no longer get Italian bread to go with dinner on Sunday. No Italian pastries at the bakery. No more fish from the fish market on Christmas Eve. I missed these familiar foods and relished every opportunity to visit my relatives for a taste of *cannoli*, *sfogliatelle*, *pasticciotti*, *capocollo*, *soppressata*, sausage bread, *biscotti* (the hard bread, not the popular cookies). (Many of these Italian foods are laborious to prepare, and most Italians get them at specialty stores and do not make them at home.)

In my new home, my religion was condemned and disliked by many people who asked me if I worshipped statues, who looked at me funny and avoided me. The first question they'd ask me is "What church do you go to?" When they found out, they would invite me to their church. I learned quickly that unless I converted, I'd be alienated. Many asked if I was born in Italy. I guess they couldn't tell my accent was a New York one. In high school, our class officers had to represent every race: white president, black president, Indian president; white treasurer, black treasurer, Indian treasurer and so forth. Again, where did I fit in?

Only a few years ago, I got a freelance assignment for a magazine in Raleigh, North Carolina, to write a piece about a local business. I interviewed the owner at what I considered to be a normal and cordial interaction, wrote my article, and sent it in to the editor. Later, the editor called me asking if anything unusual happened during the interview because he said the owner had told him he wanted someone "local" to write the piece—not me. After many years' experience in the South, I knew what that meant.

It was also around this time, in 2009, that the local news channel in Raleigh, North Carolina, WRAL-TV, aired a segment about "Spaghetti," on its show hosted by Scott Mason, The Tar Heel Traveler.[11] Mason's show features his journeys across the state, finding the "fascinating places and colorful characters."[12] It's a local travel and human interest show about the state of North Carolina. The feature on "Spaghetti" was told as if this were a cute, whimsical little tale of local color. It even featured a black and white photo of a smiling man pictured next to the hanging corpse. And the funeral director said that when he was in high school, he heard that the pledges at a fraternity at UNC had to go to Laurinburg and ask for "Spaghetti." He goes on to say, "Without this, he would have just probably passed on and no one knew where he was or who he was . . . ." This show is how I found out about "Spaghetti."

In moving to North Carolina, my parents were ignorant of the cultural differences and didn't know it would be such a drastic change. They both grew up in Italian neighborhoods. They had relatives in Manhattan, Brooklyn, and the Bronx and took the tubes, as they called the trains, to other Italian neighborhoods. One of my grandfathers was a carpenter who worked in Brooklyn and the other was a truck driver who mostly delivered in New York City. Their world was Italian, yet it was also diverse with the diversity of cultures that make up New York City. My grandmother's best friend outside the family (Italians back then didn't have too many friends outside the family) was Armenian. My grandfather's best friend was African American. My grandmother worked for Jews where she learned to say "Oy vey" along with her "Mannaggia." My dad's neighborhood was also Polish and he went to many Polish weddings. My mom had German and Irish friends who taught her how to use mayonnaise and make more diverse foods like potato salad. In short, my parents didn't really notice that they were Italian because so many people were, and there were so many different types of people there with them. They were protected by the Tristate area bubble.

But I was free floating in a larger America, one with a lot more space, white-specked fields of cotton, green-yellow tobacco, and red-bricked buildings frozen in time. A place still fighting the Civil War, still distrustful of Yankees.

Before I go on, I want to clarify that this book isn't about me.

It's about spaghetti. No, not the man called Spaghetti that I mentioned before, his name born of prejudice.

No, this book is about another spaghetti, spaghetti and meatballs, the ubiquitous dish that so many Italian and non-Italian chefs, writers, businesses, and organizations claim is not Italian. Many of these authorities claim that spaghetti and meatballs is an Italian-American dish, one created because there was an abundance of beef in America when the early immigrants arrived here. These same Italian food authorities claim that the Italian food in America was created here on American soil, that it is not the true food of Italy. One article goes so far as to say that while Italian cuisine has ancient origins, "pasta with red sauce" was invented in the United States by poor immigrants.[13] On April 13, 2017, the U.S. Consulate General in Naples posted on its Twitter and Facebook pages that the *pizza fritta* was "arriving" in New York's Little Italy and "preparing to conquer the hearts of New York" because contemporary Neapolitan pizzaiolo Gino Sorbillo was going to be making it there.[14] Didn't it arrive 100 years ago when the Italian immigrants settled Little Italy and didn't it already conquer the hearts of America, let alone New York, as the *calzone*? Even well-meaning chefs like Rich Torrisi of Torrisi Italian Specialties said the food in his restaurant was "American" because he used Polly-O, Progresso, and Stella D'oro.[15] Because I write a food blog devoted mostly to Italian food and New York, I often read *Eater*. Columnist Robert Sietsema wrote many articles on different types of "Italian-American" food. He went so far as to claim that it was created in Brooklyn.[16] Ah, not only was Italian-American food created in America, we now have the exact latitude.

I didn't—and don't—believe that Italian-American food was created in America. I don't believe it is a blend of Italian and American food. I believe that the food of Americans of Italian descent is Italian food. So I set out to write a scholarly work about spaghetti and meatballs—and "Italian-American" food. I researched every book on the subject that I could find. That journey led me to the history of Italians in the United States. And that history included the story of the man called "Spaghetti." What did I find? That the story of one "spaghetti" cannot be told without the story of the other. Together, the story of Concetto Farmica and spaghetti and meatballs make up the story of the Italian people in the United States. And that's who and what this book is about.

It's about the 16 million[17] people who left Italy over 100 years ago and the ones who settled in the United States, enduring horrible working conditions in many different fields from mining to factories to construction to restaurant work. They endured then—and still endure now—prejudice, discrimination, and alienation by a culture that didn't/doesn't want them and didn't/doesn't understand them. Despite this, so many of them and their descendants contributed to this country, creating new businesses, shaping the culture, and helping to make this country what it is today, but their stories are still not told to a wider audience. This book is also for their descendants who still experience racial, ethnic, and class discrimination. In addition, this book is about the Italians who didn't leave, the ones in Italy today who contribute so much to the worlds of science, technology, fashion, and food. For those who don't know, modern Italy is struggling financially. It has one of the highest unemployment rates in the European Union. Its young people are leaving in droves, moving abroad in search of work and opportunity like their cousins did 100 years ago. This book is also about them. They are the new Italian immigrants to the United States and elsewhere. In fact, according to *We the Italians*, there are 356,831 expat Italians living in the United States today, mostly in New York but also in Los Angeles and Miami.[18] That number is probably higher because, according to sources Italian journalist Maurizio Molinari talked to in his book, *The Italians of New York*, there are expat Italians who overstay their visa and become illegal immigrants. In fact, in 1994, the New York police found that the ethnicity with the most illegal immigrants was Italian.[19] And, finally, this book is about the people who are not Italian but who love Italian food and culture, the people who will pick up this book because they want to know more, who are given different messages in the media about what does or doesn't constitute Italian food and who the Italians really are. The negative stereotypes: gangsters, mobsters, mafia dons, mafia goons, ignoramuses, big-haired bimbos, gluttons. The stereotypes that aren't supposed to be negative: grandmas and mammas ceaselessly cooking in the kitchen, idle men singing and drinking wine in the countryside. Who are these people who fascinate the world? Who are the real Italians?

One thing is certain, Italians do take food very seriously, and that is why after reading countless articles on how Italian-American food is not "real" or "authentic" Italian food, I had to do some research of my own. And what I found is that Italian-American food is the soul of Italy, the soul that left the body over 100 years ago. It lives on different soil, thousands of miles away, but no less Italian, no less real, than the flesh and blood Italians themselves.

This book is meant to enlighten all those who love Italian food and to give them a broader picture and understanding of the cuisine they love. Another goal of this book is to facilitate understanding and dialogue between Americans of Italian descent and their brothers and sisters in Italy in the hopes of diminishing the elitism so prevalent in discourse on all things Italian. Not too long ago, I recommended a good Sicilian restaurant in the United States to an American professor whose ancestry was from Parma and Genoa. His response was, "Good Sicilian food is an oxymoron." At that moment, I knew I was doing the right thing in writing this book.

I realize this topic is a controversial one. My goal is to tell the story that is oft untold when referring to the Italian-American people and their foodways and culture. I don't use the term "Italian American" to describe these people but choose "Americans of Italian descent" instead. (I chose this term on my own, but I see that Alessandro Masi, the secretary general of the Dante Alighieri Society in Rome suggests, in *We the Italians*, using it to describe the descendants of the Italian immigrants in the United States.)[20] The reason for this distinction is that the very term "Italian American" when applied to food has become warped in society, has a hidden prejudicial meaning. I also condemn the use of "red sauce" to describe a restaurant serving the cuisine of Americans of Italian descent. And obviously, condemn any use of the term "dago red" to describe wine. Any such terminology is an affront to the hardworking people who have contributed so much to American culture, as Rep. Tim Ryan has learned.

In the PBS documentary *New York*, writer Pete Hamill said it best. When he heard his father crying at the kitchen table, he knew whatever he did in life had to honor that crying, that sacrifice that the immigrant generation had gone through for us.[21] My great-great-grandfather died a pauper at the

Staten Island Farm Colony in Staten Island, New York. My great-grandfather lost his wife, daughter, and mother in the same year, and lived his last years and died in a tenement on Manhattan's Bowery that would, only a few years later, become the Palace Hotel flophouse, where CBGB's later stood. This book is the moment of their sacrifice. This book is my attempt to honor the crying of those who came before me, of the 16 million souls who left Italy, and the country who lost roughly a third of its population because it was struggling for an identity, as it, its citizens, and its American children still are today.

CHAPTER 1: What Is "Italian" Food?

When Carlo Collodi—the author of the children's classic *Pinocchio*, first encountered pizza from Naples, he said: "The blackened aspect of the toasted crust, the whitish sheen of garlic and anchovy, the greenish-yellow tint of the oil and fried herbs, and those red bits of tomato here and there give pizza the appearance of complicated filth that matches the dirt of the vendor."[1]

Pizza is now an ubiquitous food, loved and devoured globally. However, and I know I'm going to get a lot of tomatoes thrown at me for this statement, pizza wasn't made famous by Italians. It was made famous by Italian Americans. Between the 1870s and the 1920s, more than 16 million Italians emigrated from Italy to other countries.[2] It is estimated that four million of those immigrants came to the United States. Every source seems to conflict as to the exact number of Italian immigrants that left Italy and where they settled. Also, the range of years is always different, so it's hard to know how many came at what time. The lowest number I've seen is four million. The highest, 20 million. According to Samuel Baily in *Immigrants in the Lands of Promise: Italians in Buenos Aires and New York City, 1870 to 1914*, 14 million Italians left Italy between 1876 and 1915.[3] Author Maria Laurino's book, *The Italian Americans: A History*, says it's 16 million.[4] (If we go all the way to 1976, between 1876 and 1976, the number is 26 million.)[5] About 80 percent of these immigrants were from Southern Italy.[6] While some working-class Italians from Northern Italy settled in the United States in areas like St. Louis and California, Laurino says 85 percent of Italian immigrants in the United States were from Southern Italy, the majority departing Italy from Naples[7]— the same place where pizza was born.

There is, among Italians, a well-known bias of North against South, a fact I will write in more detail throughout the book. Collodi's description of

1

pizza is very telling of the Northern Italian bias against Southern Italians and could possibly be rewritten to describe the view of the Southern Italians themselves: "The blackened aspect of their dirt-covered faces, the whitish sheen of oil on their skin and hair, the greenish-yellowish tint of their poverty-ridden sicknesses, the red bits of tomato, the lingering smell of their garlic . . . . The Southern Italian gives the appearance of complicated filth." No, this is not what Collodi wrote, but this is the meaning behind his words and what he transferred to pizza. This inherent bias was the major reason 16 million[8] Italians, or one third of the Italian population, left their homeland.

As is evident in Collodi's quote, this bias is assigned to the foodways of Southern Italians. To see how this has evolved, one must understand what is meant by "Italian" food, a term that causes much confusion. That confusion arises for a number of reasons, one being that when speaking of Italian food, there are many distinctions to consider. The first distinction is that Italian cuisine is divided by North and South. There is Northern Italian (generally defined as north of Naples) versus Southern Italian (generally defined as Naples and south of Naples) cuisine. You've no doubt heard some of the basics regarding this distinction. In the North, the cooking fat of choice is butter. In the South, olive oil. In the North, they eat rice and polenta. In the South, pasta. The Northern diet is more meat-centric. The Southern diet is more vegetarian. For the most part, these basic points are true, but there is much more to the story, which I get to in the second distinction.

The second distinction is that Italian cuisine is regional. There are 20 regions of Italy, and each region has its own variations. This distinction is one that the contemporary food industry of Italy is marketing abroad in order to boost its economy and sell products from the different regions. For example, the preferred pasta in Puglia is *orecchiette*. In Rome, you will find the dish *cacio e pepe*. In Sicily, they eat pasta with sardines, couscous, chickpea fritters, cannoli, and *cassata*. In Calabria, you will find *'nduja* salami/sausage and chili peppers. In Sardinia, they eat *carasau* bread, *pecorino sardo*, *fregola* (a cross between couscous and pasta), *malloreddus* pasta, and *bottarga*. In Lombardy, they eat polenta. In the Piedmont, they eat cabbage and potatoes. So on and so forth. While it is true that there are regional delicacies in Italy as there are anywhere else, this distinction of 20 regions is the Italy of modern times. However, as I will write more later, Italy has been a united country only since 1861. So these regions came into existence in roughly the last 150 years. When it comes to cuisine, there is much overlap of certain regions. I would argue that many of the dishes of Southern Italy cross the different regions with only some variation. When I read through a cookbook on Sicily, Calabria, Basilicata, Puglia, Abruzzo, or Campania, I see similar dishes and ingredients to what my family traditionally cooked.

The third distinction made about Italian food is one of modernity. Simply, contemporary Italian cuisine versus older, more "traditional" Italian cuisine. Contemporary cuisine in Italian is today known as *cucina moderna*, or modern cooking. It differs from the traditional food in Italy. Note that this distinction is addressing only food in Italy, not in the United States or elsewhere where there are Italian people. However, *cucina moderna* is being marketed as "true" Italian cuisine along with the regional distinctions mentioned above.

Finally, the fourth and last distinction is Italian cuisine as it is known in the United States—in restaurants, cookbooks, television shows, and media—(produced predominantly for commercial purposes due to its popularity) for Americans of non-Italian descent versus Italian cuisine that Americans of Italian descent cook in their homes. (In addition to the four distinctions above, there is also Italian cuisine in Argentina, Brazil, Canada, Australia, Uruguay, and any other country Italians immigrated to during the great migration of 1880–1920. However, my argument is that these cuisines vary little from standard Italian fare unless they are a true fusion cuisine.)

And this last cuisine is one that is often unspoken of and unwritten about—and the most misunderstood and misrepresented—the Italian cuisine of the United States. What? *Unspoken of and unwritten about?* Aren't most cooking shows predominantly based on Italian foods? What about Lidia Bastianich? What about Rachael Ray? What about Mario Batali? What about Mary Ann Esposito? Aren't they cooking Italian-American food? What about the countless Italian cookbooks in the book store, the plethora of Italian cooking shows on TV?

If Italian-American food graces the cover of practically every glossy magazine, how can I say that the cuisine of Americans of Italian descent is often unspoken of and unwritten about? Because it's the truth. The majority of cookbooks, magazines, and TV shows geared for an American market are exactly that—geared for a *market*, to be sold as a *brand*. So then, what is this Italian-American cuisine? Is it American? Is it Italian? Or is it a combination of both?

I believe that there are two Italian cuisines in the United States, one cooked and eaten by the descendants of the Italian immigrants to the United States and one produced for the non-Italian, American public. Sometimes, these are one and the same. For example, a dish like eggplant parmesan is cooked at home and in restaurants and is featured on cooking shows and in magazines. I believe these dishes were popular with non-Italians and Italians alike and that is why they became so ubiquitous at Italian restaurants in the United States. However, there are many more dishes that Americans of Italian descent make at home that have not become popular and are not served in restaurants. Today, Italians from Italy are introducing some new Italian dishes and products to the American market as if they are a mystical revelation, when in actuality, Americans of Italian descent have known about these dishes and products and have used them for years. (*Some* of these dishes and products are indeed new and produced for the modern market.)

There are some dishes that confound Italians from Italy. They perceive these dishes as being Italian American, when in fact, they are not. I think the confusion comes from the fact that the dishes are completely American but are built around an Italian ingredient and get mistaken as being Italian. An example of an American dish like this is chicken spaghetti, a casserole made with spaghetti, condensed soup mix, an American type of cheese, and chopped peppers. The Pioneer Woman Ree Drummond has a recipe for this on her blog and the Food Network. The only thing Italian about this dish is the use of spaghetti, but it is entirely an American dish. Other dishes are trying to mimic real Italian dishes. An example is spaghetti with meat sauce where the meat sauce is made of ground beef and pepper where it resembles more of a chili sauce topping, popular in the Southern, Midwestern, and Western United States. Again, this dish somewhat resembles bolognese, but most likely stems from the Southern Italian tomato gravy on spaghetti (which is an Italian dish, although some Italians from Italy will argue that it is not). However, spaghetti with chili meat sauce is an American dish, as it is not how an American of Italian descent would prepare spaghetti. Another example of this is lasagna where cottage cheese is used instead of ricotta. There are many examples at Italian restaurant chains like Olive Garden where they are often creating Italian-sounding recipes that Americans of Italian descent have never heard of because they are exclusive Olive Garden dishes. (An example from the August 2016 menu is Pot Pie Italiano Chicken Con Broccoli or Pepperoni Fettuccine Alfredo.) Then, there are also dishes like Italian cream cake that are purely confounding. Italian cream cake is an American cake made with chopped pecans and coconut. It resembles a cake of the American South much more than it does anything Italian. It may fit into the mimic category if it was an American idea of an Italian rum cake that has the nuts coating the frosting. However, these dishes are marketed as if they are traditional recipes.

Italians from Italy have the impression that this cuisine is Italian American and that the Italians in the United States are eating these dishes as well. Would an American of Italian descent eat chicken spaghetti, spaghetti with chili meat sauce, or Italian cream cake? Possibly—and they might like it, but one thing is for sure. They would not call it Italian food. This is what I mean when I say this food is often misunderstood and misrepresented. Non-Italian Americans have one perception of Italian food that is based partly on historical biases and American taste preferences as well as modern marketing. Italians from Italy have a perception of Italian-American food based on many factors, including Northern versus Southern bias, contemporary Italian cuisine versus traditional, and American versus Italian-American cuisine. Are you confused? It is confusing because there is no one definition of Italian food, and also because contemporary Italians seeking to do business in the United States are sending a distorted message about what constitutes Italian food. Therefore, what I am saying is that Americans of Italian descent are cooking and eating Italian food with the methods and ingredients their ancestors used in Italy; in other words, what is known as Italian-American food is indeed Italian food.

Not only is it *inconceivable*, but it is also *ludicrous* to imply that one third of the entire country of Italy left and did not take its foodways, recipes, and traditions with it. It is this cuisine that is the subject of this book—as it is the goal of this book to prove that the cuisine of Americans of Italian descent in the United States is indeed Italian cuisine based on *real* dishes from Italy and not an amalgam of Italian and American ingredients morphing into some other, unknown-in-Italy cuisine. In addition, another goal of this book is to show that classifying or interpreting the cuisine of Americans of Italian descent in any other way but as "Italian" is discriminatory.

Much is known about the foodways of the Italians in the wealthy Northern city-states because it was written down.[9] Italian-American cuisine is the cuisine of Southern Italy, as it was handed down through millennia and brought to the United States during the great migration of 1880–1920, a cuisine based on oral history that one cannot find in a cookbook predating the modern era.[10]

Why is that? Many Southern Italians who immigrated to the United States couldn't read or write English, but they also couldn't read or write in their native language, Italian. In fact, according to Christopher Duggan in *A Concise History of Italy*, in 1860, only 2.5 percent of people could speak Italian, or the Tuscan form of Italian in use by the elite.[11] People spoke the dialects of their particular region. Therefore, it makes sense that there are conflicting numbers as to the literacy of early Italian immigrants. According to Laurino, at least 70 percent of Southern Italians were illiterate in 1901.[12] According to Peter G. Vellon in *A Great Conspiracy Against Our Race: Italian Immigration Newspapers and the Construction of Whiteness in the Early 20th Century*, 80 percent of Sicilians and Calabrians were illiterate while only 47 percent of Italian immigrants between 1899 and 1909 were.[13]

While many sources say that most early Italian immigrants were illiterate, there is much evidence to the contrary. There were many Italian language newspapers during the early period of Italian migration to the United States. In 1915, there were Italian newspapers in 35 states.[14] In 1920 in New York City, there were over 800,000 Italians and the Italian newspapers had a total circulation of over 240,000.[15] In 2012, I attended an exhibit at the Grolier Club in New York City entitled "Strangers in a Strange Land: A History of Italian-Language American Imprints, 1830-1945." The Grolier Club's press release for the exhibit described "a once thriving Italian-language

American book publishing industry that flourished in the U.S."[16] According to Duggan, by 1900, there was an overabundance of lawyers in Italy at twenty-four thousand and of doctors.[17] There was a problem of "intellectual unemployment"[18] much like the situation in Italy and the United States today. This fact suggests that many early immigrants to the United States were literate professionals. It is interesting to note that in ninth-century Salerno, witnesses to small property transactions—including women—could sign their name.[19] In the sixteenth century, in Udine in Northern Italy, a school was set up that taught all social classes how to read and write.[20] There were similar schools in other towns as well. My great-grandfather and grandfather could read and write in Italian. In fact, according to pages in their particular ship manifests and United States census records, most men could read and write Italian while most women could not. Albeit a page or two from a ship manifest is too small a representation of the immigrants to be considered the norm.

The spellings of some Italian words in the United States may be an indication that many of the early immigrants couldn't read or write. They spell some words phonetically using the English letters for sounds. For example, the word for conch in Neapolitan is *sconciglio*.[21] Neapolitans use a "g" sound for the "ci" sound, so that is where the "g" in *scungilli* comes from, as we spell a "g" sound with a letter "g" in English. In addition, "gli" has a "li" sound in Italian. In English, it would be a "li" spelling, not a "gli" spelling. Therefore, *sconciglio* is spelled *scungilli* if spelling an Italian word using English phonetics.

If the early immigrants were literate as some sources report, their recipes and their foodways were predominantly oral. In Italy, printed cookbooks were available in the fifteen hundreds, but they were available only to the upper classes, who could read and write.[22] By the eighteenth century, cookbooks were available to the middle class and to kitchen servants.[23] While some middle class may have utilized them, the tradition at the average inn was to have an oral menu.[24] Food historian Donna Gabaccia notes in *We Are What We Eat: Ethnic Food and the Making of Americans* that Jews, Poles, Ukrainians, Greeks, and Germans from Russia had many more written community cookbooks than Italians, African Americans, and Mexican Americans due to the latter groups' having a stronger oral tradition.[25] And it is an oral tradition that is passed down orally still by the descendants of those Italian-American immigrants. Their cuisine is completely, 100 percent, identifiable Italian food.

Since the Italian diaspora over 100 years ago, there has been much change in Italy—from World War I and II and their effects to the rebuilding of the Italian economy and its subsequent popularity abroad, i.e. "la dolce vita." The immigrants of the great migration may have experienced these changes through visits home or through contact with relatives. But it is likely that many did not. The Italian culture in Italy evolved as the new immigrants to the United States struggled to assimilate to the new culture in America. As a consequence of being marginalized in the United States, they held fast to their traditions—traditions of the late nineteenth- and early twentieth-century Italy. However, this group had been marginalized in its homeland of Italy as well, so even in Italy, oral history of its traditions was the only record of its existence. As Luisa Del Giudice, founder of the Italian Oral History Institute in Los Angeles, writes, "Oral history . . . not only supplements the historic record but may also create a historic record where none previously existed."[26] It certainly creates a history for those who were illiterate and/or purposely omitted from the written historical record due to socioeconomic class, political affiliations, or religious prejudice, as she mentions,[27] and this oral history can often tell a different story from the one previously held to be the only truth. "First-person oral historical narrative can frequently reveal alternative perspectives," notes Del Giudice.[28] The traditions of the Americans of Italian descent may seem archaic to Italian natives of today. This interpretation exists for a number of reasons, the main being that the Italian culture in Italy has evolved with the times and technology, as Italy struggles to this day for a national identity.

Even in the twenty-first century, Italian Americans in the United States are a marginalized group, encouraging an "Otherness." The "Other" is a term used in sociology to refer to that group—that group that is not the status quo, that group that is foreign, different, not like "Us." It is this "Othering," or being treated as the "Other," that leads many groups to clannishness—a clannishness borne of survival in an unwelcoming environment. This fact, coupled with the growing interest and new tools in genealogical research, is why Americans of Italian descent are longing to find out who they are. The foodways and gastronomic traditions of these people were handed down orally to their children and grandchildren, who are documenting it now and reaching a wide audience due to the advancements in technology with blogs and online video sites like YouTube. An example is *Cooking with Nonna*, an online cooking show started by Rossella Rago, an Italian American from Bensonhurst, Brooklyn, who cooks traditional recipes with her grandmother.[29] There are others like her who are using the Internet to showcase family recipes. Therefore, the traditions of the descendants of those early Italian immigrants to the United States are the historical record of these people, the Southern Italians, the Italians who created what is known worldwide as "Italian" food.

CHAPTER 2: The Italy They Left

My journey into the history of Italian-American food took me to the motherland, Italy. For without Italy and the Italian diaspora, there would be no Italian presence in the United States and its foodways. So a discussion about the food of Americans of Italian descent must start at the source—Southern Italy, from where the majority of early Italian immigrants to the United States came. And the story of their foodways must start with why they came. Their foodways are intertwined with their history.

I got my hand on every book on Southern Italian history written in English that I could find. In many ways, the books were pretty much the same. They each documented the history from the pre-Roman era, including that of the Etruscans of Tuscany, Umbria, and Lazio; Samnites in Campania, Abruzzo, and Molise; the Oscans in Campania; the Brutti of Calabria and Basilicata; the Lucanians in Basilicata; Daunii and Messapii in Puglia and other original Italic peoples of the peninsula. Then the books went on through Ancient Rome to present day. The history was confusing enough to follow because Italy was not a country until 1861. In order to study the history, I had to look at what was going on in different regions of Italy during different eras in time. My study included some information on Northern Italy as well. In a nutshell, the message is that different parts of Italy were ruled by different people, and it was constantly getting invaded by various groups. In this, most books are consistent. What I found was one particular picture—which I am going to convey to you here. However, with further study, I encountered a book by an Italian-born journalist named Pino Aprile. His book, *Terroni: All That Has Been Done to Ensure That the Italians of the South Became "Southerners,"* is a revisionist history of Southern Italy since the unification of Italy in 1861.[1] (*Terroni* is a derogatory term for Southern Italians that means they are ignorant and vulgar—of the earth.) It tells a different story from the one

9

traditionally told by historians. Given that so many Italians left their homeland at the same time in history so soon after the unification, I'm inclined to believe Aprile's version of the facts.

So as you read this chapter, please bear with me. Italian history is convoluted. For the purposes of this book, I'm not going into incredible detail but enough to give the reader an understanding of how this history pertains to the food history of the early Italian immigrants. There isn't much translated into English about the specific history of Southern Italy, so I had to take what I could get from mostly Anglo authors. Most of the books talk about Naples being a crowded, filthy, poverty-stricken city inhabited by happy-go-lucky, childlike, jovial, almost-moronic lower-class people contented with their lot because they didn't know any better. Was this true? I didn't think so, and thankfully, my research proved me right.

Southern Italians, especially those from parts of Basilicata (also referred to by its ancient name, Lucania), Calabria, and Puglia are among the oldest inhabitants of the Italian peninsula, with a culture dating back thousands of years.[2] The city of Matera is well known for its sassi, or stone caves carved into the rock. Until only recently, people had been living in these stone caves since the Paleolithic period.[3] The city's ancient look is one of the reasons it was chosen to represent Jerusalem in the film *The Passion of the Christ*.

The Latins in Rome began conquering neighboring areas. For example, the Greek settlement of Neapolis, or Napoli. The Neapolitans didn't put up a fight but chose to negotiate with the Romans and ultimately, submit. The Samnites, a group farther in the interior of south-central Italy, were great warriors with a developed civilization alongside the Roman one. They had three wars with the Romans, and eventually lost to them. The Romans knew they had a formidable enemy, so they committed a genocide of the Samnites. Many did survive because they were familiar with the interior mountains of Italy and could hide. Others blended in with Roman society. (Pontius Pilate was one of them). There is a famous battle, the battle of the Caudine Forks in 321 BC, where they defeated the Romans. The people from this area are still proud of this battle against the Romans. It is near the village where my grandfather was born, and I am a Samnite. Now, that was in 321 BC—a long time ago and yet I still identify with these people and this battle. As food writer Arthur Schwartz notes in *Naples at Table: Cooking in Campania*, the Samnites are called *I Sanniti* in Italian and have a name for their own cuisine, *cucina sannita*.[4] He considers this interesting because other Italians do not identify with the ancient peoples in the area. I think I know why people identify with their Samnite ancestors. It is because a genocide occurred, and it is very important to acknowledge that the Romans were not successful in killing the Samnites off.

As Rome rose to power, it was one of the most diverse places ever. Due to its position in the Mediterranean Sea, it was a center for trade. This fact brought many people from various parts of the ancient world to its shores. In addition, Rome would bring back people to be used as slaves from various places that it conquered. Slavery in Roman times was different from slavery in more modern times. Slaves could earn their freedom and many did, becoming part of the fabric of the Italian peninsula. The Western Roman Empire lasted over twelve hundred years, from 753 BC to its demise in AD 476.

Since that time, the Italian peninsula became a series of loosely defined regions made up of various ethnic groups, some mixed in with Germanic conquerors or "barbarians" like the Vandals, the Visigoths, the Huns, and the Ostrogoths, who invaded in the fifth century.[5] The Lombards invaded Northern Italy in the sixth century[6] and eventually took over Benevento and Salerno and parts of southern Italy.[7] Byzantium had control of parts of southern Italy for a time (especially in Puglia, Sicily, and Calabria).[8] These different groups left their mark on the foodways of Italy. The basic food of ancient Rome included bread, wine, and oil; the Germanic barbarian culture included meat, milk, and lard/butter.[9] (It sounds a lot like the distinction of Northern vs. Southern Italian food.) Arabs from North Africa invaded southern Italy, especially in Sicily and Puglia.[10] For 24 years in the eight hundreds, Bari was under Arabic rule.[11] The Franks had control of northern Italy in the eighth and ninth centuries.[12] There were also the descendants of the original inhabitants of the peninsula like the Lucanians in Basilicata and the Samnites in south-central Italy. Around the same time the Normans conquered England, they also conquered Italy, in the ten hundreds.[13] After the Turkish invasions of Albania in the fourteenth and fifteenth centuries, Christian Albanian refugees settled in southern Italy fleeing Islamic rule.[14]

During the Middle Ages, there was no Italy—only these regions. Christianity spread through the area and traditions of pagan Roman times mixed with Christian ideology to create new traditions. In the North, powerful city-states emerged like Florence, Padua, Modena, and Venice. These cities excelled in business, trade, art, architecture, science, and law. These cities gave us people like Leonardo da Vinci, Galileo, and Michelangelo.

But what often goes unnoted is that the South had an advanced culture during the Middle Ages as well. In about the ninth century, Salerno opened the first medical school.[15] (According to Barbara Kreutz in *Before the Normans: Southern Italy in the Ninth & Tenth Centuries*, the exact date is contested. It may have been the twelfth century, but there were Jewish doctors on record in the tenth century and the city was known for its medicine.)[16] A female professor there, Trotula, authored the first book on women's medicine in 1100.[17] In 1224, the emperor Frederick II created the University of Naples, still in operation today.[18] Thomas Aquinas was a student there. The university eventually had colleges of medicine and law. Tommaso Astarita notes in *Between Salt Water and Holy Water* that between 1400 and 1600, there were 900 law graduates, and in the seventeenth century, thousands.[19] In fact, lawyer Francesco D'Andrea wrote in the sixteen hundreds that "there is no city in the world in which talent is better rewarded, and where a man without other qualities than his own merit can rise to great charges and immense wealth, to supreme offices that govern the commonwealth, without needing either birth or money."[20] (Can this be said for the United States today?) According to Astarita, in 1496, Naples created the Annona, a governmental agency that licensed food makers like bakers and oversaw the food industry in the city.[21] So Southern Italy also had an advanced culture during this time.

Through the subsequent centuries, the peninsula continued to be invaded and dominated by various groups. In the seventeenth century, the Spanish got control of Naples and the lands to its south. This fact leads to yet another confusing part of Southern Italian history. It is contested whether or not the Spanish had a negative influence on Southern Italy. Naples was the largest city in the Spanish empire, with as many as four hundred thousand citizens by 1650.[22] The city would have grand celebrations with parades, fireworks, and feasting on the many celebrated feast days like the feast of St. John the Baptist in June.[23] At these parades, there would be grand arches made of salami and cheese to give to the populace that John Marino writes in *Becoming Neapolitan: Citizen Culture in Baroque Naples* were to show that Naples had great wealth to feed its people.[24] In the 1660s, macaroni was added to the menu at these celebrations.[25] In *The Italian Baroque Table: Cooking and Entertaining from the Golden Age of Naples*, Astarita mentions that a Neapolitan writer writing in the 1630s said that Naples was "the whole world."[26]

However, while there were some positive aspects to Spanish rule, the Spanish brought with them the medieval feudal system of land ownership and tenant farming that many scholars believe led to devastation in Southern Italy. The North and South evolved in disparate ways; while the North had many urban centers, the South was more rural with only one capital, Naples, and the surrounding rural areas.[27] While Spain was in power, Genoa was a major center for shipping and exporting, as well as finance, and aided Spain in its rise to power.[28] Henry Kamen notes in *Spain's Road to Empire: The Making of a World Power, 1492-1763* a Venetian ambassador in the sixteen hundreds who said that the Milanese were supporting Spain.[29] So Northern Italy may have had a financial impact on the South starting at this time. Critics, according to Kamen, felt that the Spanish were "transients" who were out of touch with what was going on locally.[30] Eighteenth-century political economist Paolo Mattia Doria wrote that the Spanish brought "ignorance, villany, disunion and unhappiness" to Southern Italy.[31] He likened the Spanish annihilation of the Indies to Southern Italy. He writes, "The Indies are not those in America; the true Indies are here in the kingdom of Naples."[32] The people of the South wanted the Spanish out. With the help of the French, in 1647, a Neapolitan fish seller, Tommaso Aniello, known as Masaniello, led a rebellion against the Spanish.[33] This rebellion led to the short-lived, months-long Republic of Naples. A similar rebellion occurred in Sicily.[34]

When Charles II, the last Habsburg King of Spain, died in 1700, the War of the Spanish Succession started to see who would take the throne.[35] A treaty called the Peace of Utrecht in 1713 ended the war and gave Naples and Sardinia to Habsburg Austria and Sicily to the House of Savoy of northwestern Italy/southeastern France.[36] In 1734, the Spanish/French Bourbon family, known as the Bourbons, later defeated the Austrians and rose to power in Southern Italy.[37] Napoleon defeated the Bourbons and took over Southern Italy from 1808-1815. After Waterloo, the Bourbons were restored to power and soon created the Kingdom of the Two Sicilies.[38] Various Northern city-states, especially Venice, as well as the papacy,[39] had long felt that Italy would be stronger against invaders if it were united. The seed of unification started to grow.

Elsewhere in eighteenth-century Europe, the concept of free trade became more than an idea. The idea of free trade, which is also what we would refer to as globalization today, took hold. The French Revolution paved the way for commercial reforms.[40] Prior to the eighteen hundreds, as Astarita writes, businessmen engaged in a particular trade were organized as a guild, such as a guild for macaroni makers, for bakers, etc.[41] These guilds were like a brotherhood, and they had a certain moral code based on Christian values.[42] They would do things like collect money for a member's sick relative, etc.[43] Guilds were disbanded when the idea of free trade came into practice.[44] Northern Italy subscribed to free trade, favoring investing and agricultural modernization.[45] The Lombards revamped agriculture to plant rice and corn and created textile plants of hemp, flax, and cotton.[46] Traditional history tells us the North had more economic development than the South, possibly because, as Astarita writes, Southern leaders rejected free trade ideas.[47] But Aprile's book says this isn't so—the South was economically developed in the eighteenth century and the North wanted its money and eventually took it for its own political and financial agenda.[48]

Sometime in the mid-eighteen hundreds, as the United States was setting the ground for its own Civil War, politicians from the North of Italy were striving to create a national identity, a united peninsula. This is where the history gets murky. Most of the history books tell a particular story of this time period. They speak of the destitution and oppression existing in the South prior to unification of Italy in 1861 that was brought on since Spanish rule. Count Cavour, known as Cavour, whose real name was Camillo Benso, a statesman from the Piedmont region in Northwestern Italy, was the driving force behind unifying Italy—although unification had been an idea that many had felt through the centuries. In 1860, that idea became a reality as the famous general Giuseppe Garibaldi led troops into Sicily and overtook the island.[49] He eventually won the rest of Southern Italy. Schoolchildren are taught this history. At the turn of the last century, they were taught patriotic songs hailing Garibaldi as a hero. (My grandmother sang such songs.)

Most history books would say that the Southern Italians were driven out of their homeland in the late eighteen hundreds for a number of reasons. These included thousands of years of suffering at the hands of countless "conquerors," a medieval feudal system[50] of sharecropping[51] that existed into the mid- to late eighteen hundreds where farmers had to give their landlord four-fifths of their crop[52] and no increase in wages in one hundred years.[53]

But there's *that other* story of the Italian unification, the one by Aprile that tells a story that until recently, had been hidden in memory. It is the story of the Kingdom of the Two Sicilies (Sicily, Naples, and Southern Italy), or *Regno delle due Sicilie*, as it is known in Italy, under Bourbon rule—one of a thriving place of culture, industry, and advancement. In fact, Aprile says that during Bourbon rule, Naples was the "third most important" city in Europe behind Paris and London.[54] He notes that in the 1856 Paris Exposition, the Kingdom of the Two Sicilies was "recognized as the most industrialized country in Italy," and "third in the world."[55] Taxes were low, as they had not been increased during the 126-year Bourbon rule, according to Aprile.[56] Goethe, the writer and statesman, had traveled to Naples in 1786–1787 and noted the plethora of food during the Christmas holidays.[57] He wrote, "Every year, an officer rides through the city, together with a bugler, and announces in every square and crossroads how many thousands of cows, veal, goat kids, lambs and pigs Neapolitans consumed. The populace pays great attention and rejoices for those numbers: everybody remembers, with satisfaction, the part they had in that delight."[58] Aprile notes the South was the first "to have a railway in Italy, use an electric telegraph, build iron suspension bridges, have gas lamps to light our cities."[59] He mentions the South had a robust agricultural trade with Northern and Central Europe.[60] The South had an enviable iron ore industry in Mongiana.[61] In 1832, a Basilicata native, Luigi Giura, designed Italy's first iron suspension bridge, the *Real Ferdinando sul Garigliano*.[62] Aprile notes the iron and steel industry had been in the South for nine hundred years up until a united Italy.[63] According to *The Pursuit of Italy* by David Gilmour, Naples had "the largest shipyards in Italy" and "the largest merchant marine in the Mediterranean."[64] He notes that it launched the first steamboat in Italy in 1818.[65] Naples also had an advanced and admired legal system, notes Gilmour.[66] According to Aprile, conditions for factory workers in Mongiana were better than their counterparts in England and elsewhere.[67] They had health insurance, a pension, and more reasonable hours (8 to 12 instead of 16).[68] In fact, during Bourbon rule, Naples was the third-largest city in Europe. Puglia, Aprile notes, had a prosperous olive oil industry, exporting olive oil to industrialized nations to be used as a lubricant in machinery.[69] They had "the most technologically advanced olive grove in the world" with a hydraulic press.[70] The Sannio Caudino (the Caudini tribe of Samnites) region near Benevento (where my grandfather comes from) has an ancient tradition of olive cultivation and oil production. This area is one of the natural habitats for olives to grow and its primary income comes from olive cultivation and oil production.[71] Calabria exported licorice, olive oil, wool, and *caciocavallo* cheese.[72] Aprile notes successful textile and paper mills (the largest in Italy) in the South.[73] He also mentions that until unification, there had been a thriving wool industry in Arpino since the Roman Empire that included a business run by Cicero's father.[74] Naples had an advanced educational system, according to Aprile, with 4,000 students, 14 middle/high schools and 32 conservatories.[75] Aprile quotes a writer who says that afterwards, there was one high school left with 60 to 70 students.[76]

The Italian and European perception of the Kingdom of the Two Sicilies as a place of poverty was far from the truth. Gilmour notes it was thought of as "a place of sloth and squalor, of grandeur and poverty, a place where landless labourers kept themselves just alive by scratching the parched soil of distant nobleman, where street urchins in the city picked the pockets of wealthy tourists and bands of brigands roamed with impunity in the hills outside, a land exploited and oppressed by an indolent monarchy, a frivolous aristocracy and a swarm of grasping clergy."[77] Aprile mentions a captain in the Italian army who thought he was going to save Southern Italy from poverty and corruption, but once he got there, he said the people wore "clothes and shoes, were industrialized, and had financial reserves. The average farmer had money. . . . Everyone lived happily in their financial situation. Now it is the opposite."[78]

The historical record always claims that the political leaders of the day wanted Italy united because of Italy's history of foreign invasion. They wanted a stronger Italy, one unsusceptible to being conquered. Or did they? Aprile cites Pier Carlo Boggio in 1859, a Cavour supporter, writing that the North had no choice but to go to war or go bankrupt.[79] "Piedmont is lost," Boggio writes.[80] According to Aprile, "The North repaid its debts in this manner, with the funds from the South."[81] The South contributed over 60 percent of the funds; Lombardy, 1 percent; and Piedmont, 4 percent.[82] According to Aprile, it is well known that during the time, in the Paris Stock Exchange, the government bonds of Piedmont were 30 percent less than their nominal value while the South's were 20 percent more.[83] After unification, i.e., in Aprile's words, after "thirty years of plundering and higher taxes," Naples still contributed 37 percent to Italy's economy.[84] Therefore, one can conclude only that Southern Italy was economically thriving and the

North wanted those financial resources for itself under the guise of a "united Italy." Cavour representative Farini writes, "In 7 million inhabitants of Naples there are not a hundred who want a united Italy."[85]

And this is the fact that is oft left out of history books—there were many Italians who did not support a unified Italy. Why? Maybe because Aprile's version of the facts is correct. Maybe they weren't suffering so much and perhaps they were even doing well. So rather than surrender to the Northern Italian army, the Southern Italians fought against it. This time period saw the birth of the Southern Italian "brigand," a term the government used to describe anyone who fought the North, referring to them as thieves, criminals, and guerrillas—not the freedom fighters many actually were. The two most famous brigands are Carmine Crocco and his lieutenant Ninco Nanco, who have become mythic legends, inspiring films. (One such film, *Li chiamarono ... briganti!* [*They called them brigands*] was released in 1999 and interestingly, it is difficult to find.[86] The movie depicts the Italian army killing men, women, children, and the aged.[87]) This terminology "brigand" leads to the controversy on what transpired during Italy's unification. Gilmour writes that there was a civil war going on, but that the government tried to keep it under wraps by calling it *il brigantaggio* (the brigandage) instead.[88] He cites a debate in Parliament in 1863 where the situation in Poland was being discussed but not the one in Naples.[89] At this debate, Benjamin Disraeli said, "True in one country the insurgents are called brigands, and in the other patriots; but, with that exception, I have not learned from this discussion that there is any marked difference between them."[90] In short, there was an unspoken, undocumented genocide against these "brigands" during a civil war after unification in the 1860s that killed anywhere from six thousand to sixty thousand[91] anti-unificationists and lasted nearly ten years.[92] The civil war occurred at the same time as the American Civil War, from 1861 to 1864.[93] Over 116,000 troops were used to squelch the anti-unificationists—a number that proves in itself that this was more than mere brigandage.[94] This was a bona fide civil war, and it took more than five years for half of the Italian Army to fight the anti-unificationists.[95] (This point in history would be affecting the lives of my great-great grandparents and was around the time my great-grandparents were born, yet none of this history was handed down from them.)

According to Aprile, there were a number of "wars" going on during and after unification in the early 1860s—"a war of invasion, one of armed resistance, a civil war between those who were invaded which was incited by the invaders, and a criminal one of plundering."[96] The North committed heinous atrocities, such as banning any weapons;[97] prohibiting farmers from having more food than was needed to feed a family for one day;[98] raping women; sentencing an eighty-eight-year-old woman to seven years in prison for aiding a "brigand";[99] imprisoning anyone who opposed the new regime;[100]

sentencing a woman to ten years in prison for having a picture of the Bourbon king;[101] killing a twelve-year-old shepherd for not surrendering his flock to the Northern army (*I Piemontesi*, to the Southern Italians); burning entire towns and churches (where documents were kept);[102] and perhaps worst of all, burning records and documents so they would be forever lost— so this story would be forgotten in the annals of history. Soldiers were told to shoot brigands in the back, because shooting in the back was reserved for criminals who were "beyond the pale of nationhood or humanity."[103] Often, the bodies of brigands were left out in the open or they were shot in the town square to send a message to the local people.[104] Aprile says the North aligned itself with the local mafia instead of helping the poor and uncorrupted.[105] Landowners and common people joined together to fight the Northern armies.[106] Prominent families joined together to reinstate the old government, but when it failed, they made deals with the North to keep their status while the brigands fighting for them took the fall.[107]

It must've been a terrifying time to be a Southern Italian. According to Jerre Mangione and Ben Morreale in *La Storia: Five Centuries of the Italian American Experience*, a history of Italian Americans, entire villages were burned if they were suspected of harboring or helping anti-unificationists.[108] One could be shot for insulting the flag or a portrait of the king.[109] The military was instructed to arrest anyone with the "face of an assassin."[110] In an effort to understand what was going on, the government studied why there were so many brigands and concluded that people respected "brigands" because they could get the "justice which the law fails to give."[111] Mangione and Morreale say that the Southerners were seen as inferior because they were "incapable or reluctant to accept the 'more modern and enlightened' northerners as liberators" bringing them the "benefits of democracy"[112] and could serve no other purpose than to be used for cheap labor.[113]

Did unification accomplish its goal of making a stronger Italy? To say that the Risorgimento was disorganized, and the Southern Italians felt that they didn't have a voice in this new unified Italy is an understatement. The Northern Italian government had no respect for the Southern Italians. The same year Garibaldi led his troops—1860—Vellon says an envoy of Cavour wrote about Southern Italy, "What barbarism! Some Italy! This is Africa: the bedouin are the flower of civilized virtue compared to these peasants."[114] Hardly the words of a liberator. (Astarita cites Carl August Mayer, a German who visited Naples only decades before in the 1830s and referred to Neapolitans as "big children .... [They are] not ... deformed by education."[115] William Gladstone and Nassau William Senior toured Naples and Sicily and the latter found Sicilians to have a "perverseness, a rashness, and a childishness which are not European, and can be accounted for only by the mixture of Saracenic blood."[116])

After unification, Aprile notes that the Italian government had 458 million dollars and used most of it to build roads, railways, schools, military, and ports in the North while only 3 million was used in the South. Where did they get the 458 million dollars? He explains, "These investments were made through to the beginning of the 1900s, as though a large inexhaustible gold mine had been discovered."[117] That inexhaustible gold mine he speaks of is the wealth of Southern Italy prior to unification. Basically, that money was taken from Southerners by the Northerners after unification and repurposed to pay debts and make improvements in the North. Therefore, one can conclude only that Southern Italy had been economically thriving before unification, and the North wanted those financial resources for itself, or under the euphemistic concept of a "united Italy."

Middle- and lower-class Southern Italians were heavily taxed—and unfairly—to pay for what they considered to be the North's war.[118] Mangione and Morreale cite an example of this unfair tax—that mules were taxed but not cows, the former belonging to the lower classes; the latter, the landlords.[119] They also point out that feudalism ended in 1806, but the peasants[120] working the land were still dependent upon the landlords, and in fact, their situation worsened after unification.[121]

During this time, according to the *Oxford History of Italy*, only two percent of the population owned property and had wealth and access to education.[122] According to Alberto Capatti and Massimo Montanari in *Italian Cuisine: A Cultural History*, it wasn't until the unification of Italy that "peasant" food began to be documented in an effort to "unify" Italy.[123] It was shortly after this period that millions of Southern Italians left Italy. It could be gauged that this addition of peasant traditions and foodways into the definition of Italian culture grew out of the tumultuous climate existing in Southern Italy.

Unfortunately, what happened in Southern Italy at the time was a consequence of a larger economic ideal. According to associate professor and coordinator of the Food Studies Program at New York's New School and author of *Al Dente: A History of Food in Italy*, Fabio Parasecoli, the idea that agricultural lands should be privatized took root during the French Revolution. He explains that economists called physiocrats said that people could amass wealth from agriculture and use that to reinvest in other things.[124] It was the origin of free trade and the ideals on which capitalism and the United States are founded. Astarita mentions that before the ideas of free trade came into being and practice, individual regions/countries/kingdoms would use their own system of taxing and providing for (or not) the lower classes.[125] These free market economic ideals were espoused by the leaders of the unification.[126] The agricultural lands of Southern Italy were ripe for the picking, no pun intended.

The French Revolution occurred from 1789 to 1799. In 1789, Charles Ulysses, a Swiss "naturalist," (I use quotations here as the goal of Ulysses's book seemed to be less on naturalism than on observing how Southern Italians could make better economic use of their land) traveled through Southern Italy and wrote of his experiences in *Travels through various provinces of the kingdom of Naples in 1789*, remarking on how the people there could be making much more money on the cotton they grew if they employed more modern methods of farming.[127] He writes, "It is incredible in what clouds of darkness the science of agriculture in this kingdom is enveloped, and still more incredible what feeble efforts are made to extricate it."[128] He also writes about the figs in Trani being cultivated with an ancient practice;[129] the *pecore gentili* breed of sheep used for wool and cheese since ancient times;[130] fertilizer in Puglia made from alga and dung that rots in an ancient way;[131] and excellent olive oil known since ancient times.[132] Ulysses notes that because cotton grew so well in Southern Italy, it should be the focal point for economic purposes.[133] "Italians! . . . ye are the spoiled, ungrateful, and degenerate favourites of nature," he writes.[134] Spoiled, ungrateful degenerates for not wanting to globalize and mass-produce for profit? Apparently, in addition to being degenerates, the Abruzzi are also "provincial apes, and half wild beauties" who "greedily" buy goods at the market and go back to their "nests in the rocks."[135]

When he asked them why they didn't make more use of their corn, oil, and silk industry so that it could bring more profit, they said they were doing things the way their ancestors did.[136] Oh! The horror of not skimping on quality and using newer, cheaper methods of doing things so the quality is degraded but the product can be mass-produced for a global market. It sounds like the issues of the modern era. However, the truth is that the issues of globalization and mass production and its effects on quality and environment have their origins in this history.

In the early eighteen hundreds, Southern Italy did make more use of its agricultural lands. Astarita notes that in 1821, the last branch of the Rothschild bank opened in Naples.[137] A lot of foreign investors came from Britain, France, Switzerland, and Germany, creating farms and factories.[138] He says they were growing higher-yield crops like corn, potatoes, and rice (much like the GMO corn and soy of today) and manufacturing goods like silk, leather, pasta, and tobacco.[139]

Feudalism had been abolished in 1806, but in its place, a bourgeoisie emerged, while a large part of the population remained poor and disadvantaged. This bourgeoisie had positions in local government and also owned land at the local level. In addition, land was also owned by foreign investors—not the people who had lived on it and farmed it for thousands of years. Later, after unification, Astarita says the lands of the Catholic Church were confiscated and sold to private owners, who kept the lower classes working the land in a feudal-like manner.[140]

Obviously, with this level of turmoil, one could see that this was a dangerous time. Historians and popular culture note the importance of family to Americans of Italian descent. The instability and fear of these times may have led to the familial secrecy and governmental distrust that historians attribute to early Italian immigrants in the United States. According to Aprile, at this time, the Italian government wanted to create a colony of Southern Italians somewhere in Africa or the Pacific Islands to get rid of them, and they sought the advice of the British who opposed that course of action as repugnant.[141] The unification of Italy led to complete devastation in Southern Italy—to unlivable conditions that eventually sparked what was, according to Ruth Ben-Ghiat and Stephanie Malia Hom, in the introduction to *Italian Mobilities*, the greatest voluntary mass emigration of any country in the world.[142] Alfredo Niceforo, an Italian sociologist wrote in 1900: "One of the two Italies, the Northern one, shows a civilization greatly diffused, more fresh, and more modern. The Italy of the South shows a moral and social structure reminiscent of primitive and even quasibarbarian times, a civilization quite inferior."[143] Aprile cites Giustino, a member of the Fortunato family that had helped the anti-unificationist Crocco and a journalist and supporter of Southern interests who believed in a united Italy.[144] However good this ideal sounded in theory, he found, as time went on and much devastation occurred, it was different in practice. He felt the Northern businessmen were "pigs that are far worse than the biggest of our own pigs"[145] and that the South had been better off under Bourbon rule.

In 1904, Lucania (present-day Basilicata) wanted to secede in order to take care of itself, as taxes were extremely high; at that time, according to Aprile, the North was taxed at 8.8 percent, while the South was taxed at least twice more.[146] The tide turned a bit in the next few years with tax breaks in the South and some improvements like the aqueduct of Puglia that Aprile says lasted until the start of World War I.[147] However, oral history of this time period teaches us otherwise—that Southern Italians were still being taxed to death. My great-grandparents owned an inn and were taxed on everything, including the brooms they owned. There was even a tax on emigrating.[148]

As Aprile writes, "When they realized that their armed resistance had failed, millions of them traveled across the ocean rather than be in the company of their greedy liberators."[149] He is speaking of the earliest immigrants to the United States and other countries. As conditions did not improve and only worsened, more left. It is important to note here that the peoples who were native to the Southern Italian peninsula had never left since they settled the area in ancient times. Even in ancient times, when the Greeks started arriving in Puglia, the natives moved farther out into Lucania but did not leave. For a third of the population of Italy to leave in the late eighteen hundreds—and the majority of the Southerners, conditions had to be unbearable. (It is important to note that there were working-class people in the North as well and many of them emigrated because of harsh working conditions. Australian Italian Gianfranco Cresciani, general manager of infrastructure development within the Ministry for the Arts in New South Wales as well as author and Italian migration historian, notes that in 1898, they rioted in Milan and the Italian Army shot and killed two hundred people at the bread line and injured one thousand.[150] Northern Italians predominantly immigrated to Argentina, other parts of South America, Australia, and the Western United States.)

The ones who stayed were doing so conditionally—to see if things would get better. They found their homeland in turmoil, struggling to define itself, with opposing forces in the North and South and influences by other European countries. The politicians in power had conflicting goals for the future of Italy. Some Italian statesmen believed in colonialism because it would make Italy a major European player and because France was doing it, so they sent Italian troops to Ethiopia to what became an embarrassing failure. Others believed in isolationism. The North started its plans of industrializing the South. A horrible problem with malaria developed in the South due to deforestation and excess water.[151] The lands that teemed with agriculture were now barren. There was much decay of buildings, crops, and fields.[152] In 1884, seven thousand people in Naples died from cholera.[153] Cresciani says that by 1887, deposits in Northern banks had about eight times the money in Southern banks.[154] During the nineteenth century, only 9.5 percent of the population were allowed to vote despite voting reforms, according to John Dickie in *Darkest Italy: The Nation and Stereotypes of the Mezzogiorno, 1860-1900*.[155]

The Southern Italian was again, as usual, less than an afterthought, and more of a nuisance, often referred to as "the problem of the South." As Carlo Levi wrote much later in *Christ Stopped at Eboli*, his 1945 book on Southern Italy written while in political exile for his being a Communist, the State is "the problem."[156] He expounded: "We can bridge the abyss only when we succeed in creating a government in which the peasants feel they have some share."[157] A member of the Chamber of Deputies, Ercole Lualdi said that Italians were leaving not to find riches in America but "in tears, cursing the government and the *signori*."[158] The Southern Italians did not want to leave but saw it as a means of escaping a situation that appeared to have no positive resolution for them. Descendant of Calabrian immigrants, Joseph Luzzi, writes it best: "My Ph.D. in Italian would be the passport to a cultural homeland that class, history, and society had all conspired to deny me and my family."[159]

The divide between North and South was likened to the divide between North and South in Great Britain and the United States by author

David Yeadon in *Seasons in Basilicata* in as late as 2004.[160] He says in Italy the divide "seems far more potent."[161] He speculates that it was either due to the fact that "Italy was essentially a batch of loosely related nation-states" until 1861 or the "striking economic disparities" with the North being industrialized and far richer than the undeveloped South.[162] Certainly, regional identity had a great deal to do with it. As Ben Morreale and Robert Carola mention in *Italian Americans: The Immigrant Experience*, the "early immigrants had no concept of being 'Italians.'"[163] They identified with particular regions like Campania or Sicily. When they moved to the United States, they moved to neighborhoods with people from the same regions or villages. Often in New York City, a city block would house people from the same town.

As Morreale and Carola point out, these early immigrants became "Italian" in America.[164] Unfortunately, they became Italians because they experienced an ethnic prejudice that lumped them all together because of their looks, their accents, their religious beliefs—an ethnic prejudice that still exists to this day. While the immigrants were seen as Italian to the non-Italian Americans, they still identified with their regions, and many do to this day. In Italy, this regional pride is called *campanilismo*. This idea is named for the tall bell towers, or *campanile*, in the city centers. During the Middle Ages, the *campanile* represented Northern Italy's "keeping up with the Joneses." Cities tried to have bigger *campanili* to outdo each other. In Italy today, this idea plays out as one of sport or fun, as mentioned in the BBC documentary *Two Greedy Italians* where two cities compete in a horse race.[165] It is not fun, however, when this regionalism is used to further marginalize the traditions of descendants of Southern Italians. There are some groups of Italians who feel strongly that their cultural ties to their region are stronger than their ties to a united Italy. For example, many Sicilian Americans (as well as Sicilians) would prefer that Sicily was not part of Italy. There are also many Southern Italians who still feel that they do not want to be united with the North because of the prejudicial history that continues to this day. A group exists in Southern Italy, the Neo-Bourbons, hoping to revive the Kingdom of the Two Sicilies. And then there is the Northern League, or *Lega Nord*, in Italian. It is a political party known for wanting to secede from Italy.[166] Currently, with the interest of genealogy, many Americans are learning more about the regions in Italy where their families are from, and identifying with the traditions and culture of those areas. In the United States, the descendants of Italian immigrants are collectively known as "Italians"; however, many still identify with the regions of Italy from where their families emigrated.

The Italy they left was a place that didn't want them. They fought to keep their traditions and their homeland with all the strength they had. In the end, it wasn't enough. The Northern Italian forces behind the Risorgimento won. If it weren't for the United States and employment opportunities in other parts of the Americas, would they have survived in a destitute Southern

Italy? No one will ever know. Because they came to America. They brought with them their traditions, including their foodways. Their foodways included the history of the regions of Italy, the indigenous foods to these areas, the introduction of foods from the Middle East and the Americas, socioeconomic factors, religious reasons, and scientific and health information of the time in question. In Italy, diet was also influenced by the church. The majority of Italians were Roman Catholic, and the majority of Italian immigrants to the United States were also Roman Catholic. They brought their religious dietary rules with them, such as abstaining from meat during Lenten Fridays, Ash Wednesday, and Good Friday—traditions that Americans of Italian descent still follow today. These dietary rules would influence what types of dishes were served during these holy times, such as the eggs with tomato sauce my grandmother made and I make on a Friday during Lent.

Without them, Italy moved forward, as they started a new life elsewhere. During the 1930s and the rise of Fascism, regional cuisine was documented and Southern Italy was represented, but this cataloging started 50 years after the first immigrants left Italy. The old ways of Southern Italy went with them to the New World.

CHAPTER 3: Is *Cucina Moderna* the True Food of Italy?

Modern Italians and chefs of Italian descent say there is a distinction between food in modern Italy, referred to as *cucina moderna*, and food made by Italian Americans. They say the Italian-American food is not Italian—that it was made by peasants who had no access to ingredients from their homeland—who made do with what was available in America—who created a different cuisine—something foreign—something not Italian.

Lidia Bastianich tells Italian journalist Maurizio Molinari that Italian-American cuisine is "another thing entirely."[1] She explains that it is "the product of the poor immigrants who when they arrived, cooked what they had by remembering the dishes from home and preparing them with what was locally available."[2] Molinari quotes her as mentioning "the abundance of peppers" and dishes like "chicken parmesan or pasta with meatballs" as part of this "new tradition."[3] According to Molinari, because of restaurants like Bastianich's Del Posto, Sirio Maccioni's Le Cirque, Tony May's San Domenico (SD26) and others like it, Americans can experience "real Italian cuisine."[4] He cites Bastianich's Del Posto as being "the exact opposite of Italian-American cuisine, because here Italian dishes aren't suffocated but rather enhanced by local ingredients . . . ."[5] Some dishes he mentions are pasta with spicy jalapeño, gazpacho, and steak "the way the cowboys of the West like it."[6] Hmm? Is Del Posto an Italian restaurant or a Mexican/American West one? Bastianich says, "These dishes show that Italian cuisine can maintain its own traditions, enriching them with new tastes from other traditions."[7] OK, but then it's not "real" Italian cuisine. Of course, Bastianich has other restaurants that serve Italian cuisine, and this is her vision for only Del Posto.

Eater food writer and critic Robert Sietsema writes that Italian-American cuisine was "invented" by Italian housewives in the late nineteenth century because they couldn't get Italian ingredients in New York.[8] He does mention this would eventually be "remedied" with imports.[9] He goes so far as to say that many "Italian-American" recipes were "created" in Brooklyn[10]—a claim that would be refuted by any American of Italian descent from the areas of New Jersey, Pennsylvania, Ohio, Chicago, St. Louis, New Orleans, or California, who made the same recipes, having never or only briefly set foot in Brooklyn.

Even scholar Simone Cinotto, author of *The Italian American Table: Food, Family, and Community in New York City*, refers to the cooking of Italians in America as "invented."[11] Although he is referring to restaurant cuisine, he says that immigrants adopted these dishes as their own, creating a new cuisine, and their own identity, in America.[12]

When posing the question "Italian cooking: where does it come from?" in her *Classic Italian Cookbook*, cookbook author and Italian food diva Marcella Hazan derives an answer in the regions of Italy with no mention of the immigrants who left the country.[13] In her autobiography, *Amarcord*, she is much less diplomatic. The "so-called Italian food" she finds when she moves to New York "resembled only occasionally in name, but never in appearance, taste, or intentions, what I had known at home."[14] Olive oil was a "coarse imitation" of what she had in Italy.[15] She recounts a tale from one of her cooking classes (which attracted celebrities like Danny Kaye and Burt Lancaster) of an Italian-American restaurant owner who wasn't familiar with the herb rosemary, "astonishing" everyone in the class with "how little she knew of basic Italian ingredients."[16] I am guessing Hazan had not read Italian-American author Helen Barolini's seminal work *Umbertina* lest she would know Italian Americans know what rosemary is. While this illustration is meant to astound the reader too, it does more to show what appears to be Hazan's inherent bias of Italian Americans and their cuisine by using this one restaurateur as representative of the whole.

She speaks of being "amused" by chef Joey Venezia and his "Italian-American habit" of dropping the last vowel in Italian words like mozzarella (mozzarel).[17] Dan Nosowitz's article for *Atlas Obscura* in November 2015, "How Capicola Became Gabagool: The Italian New Jersey Accent, Explained" is an interesting discussion on the Italian language, with which I do not completely agree.[18] Nosowitz calls "gabagool" a "mutation" of the word "capicola."[19] Capicola didn't become gabagool. It was always spelled capicola/capocollo and always pronounced gabagool by Southern Italians who immigrated to the United States over 100 years ago. In the dialects of Southern Italians, words are often pronounced this way—by leaving off the final vowel. By referring to this pattern of speech as a habit, Hazan is marginalizing the language of Southern Italians. Italian language has evolved today and the language is becoming more standardized—based on the Tuscan dialect, so the dialectic nuances of other regions are being lost. According to language teacher Filomena Fuduli Sorrentino in an interview for *L'Italo Americano*, the younger generation of Italians in Italy is using/incorporating more English words into Italian because of American influence.[20] This influence will change/is changing the Italian language. Another reason that the Italian-American variation is closer to the original dialects of Southern Italy than is the modern Tuscan form of Italian. In addition, "c" is pronounced like a hard "g," "r" can sound like "d," "o" can sound like "u." Writer and Southern Italian-cooking school operator Arthur Schwartz writes in *The Southern Italian Table: Authentic Tastes from Traditional Kitchens* that the Italian-American word for arugula, *rugala*, is "fossilized Southern Italian dialect, meaning it is a dialect word no longer in use in the homeland" and different from the term used today, *rucola*.[21] However, I think it is just being pronounced with the hard "g" instead of the hard "c" and standardized to Tuscan Italian. Nosowitz says "mozzarella" becomes "mutzadell," but it doesn't. It was pronounced mutzadell because the double zz is pronounced like "tz." He also says "ricotta" becomes "ree-goat" but it doesn't. He calls this consonant swapping, but it wasn't. It was the sound Southern Italians used and use for certain letters. In fact, his title suggests that this is unique to Italians from New Jersey when it is not. In addition, according to Luzzi, other languages and dialects still exist in Italy: a large group in Alto Adige speak German; 100,000 in Piedmont speak an ancient dialect, Occitanic, and Franco-Provençal; 50,000 in Veneto speak Slovene; 50,000 speak Ladin in the Dolomites; 30,000 speak Greek in the South; 15,000 speak Catalan in Sardinia; and 100,000 in Sicily speak Arbëresh (an Albanian dialect).[22] In his 2015 book, *The Italians*, journalist John Hooper says Piedmontese is spoken by 1.6 million Italians and Sicilian by 4.7 million.[23] He also mentions Venetian, Lombard, and Neapolitan as distinct dialects, but Giulia Casati of the Italian School of New Jersey, says these and Sicilian are different languages from Italian.[24] Hooper notes that Italians who are in the same region may use different words to mean the same thing.[25] When Rosa Turano, a nonna who cooks at Enoteca Maria, a restaurant in Staten Island, New York, that serves a different Italian grandmother's cooking each night, came to the United States from the Veneto region in northern Italy, she found the dialects of Sicilians and Neapolitans "stranger . . . than English."[26] UNESCO includes Sicilian and Neapolitan (South Italian) as endangered languages.[27]

Tommasella Perniciaro, in an article published by food and wine travel company Catavino, mentions the town of Alghero, in northeastern Sardinia, that was ruled by the Catalans from Spain from the fourteenth to eighteenth centuries.[28] The article says that sometime in the 1860s, a Sardinian activist who had traveled to Barcelona for a conference noticed the two cultures were similar.[29] In fact, as time went by, the people of Alghero forgot the roots of their language.[30] According to the article, they thought they were speaking their own dialect, but in fact, it was Catalan.[31] Today, Perniciaro notes, their dialect has official recognition as a variant of Catalan.[32]

Interestingly, it's not very well known that Italians settled in Mexico during the great migration of the late nineteenth century because there weren't many of them—only about three thousand from Northern Italy.[33] Many came to be farmers.[34] Some still live in cities founded by Italians like Chipilo where they speak a variation of the Venetian dialect.[35] While affected by Spanish, the Chipilo dialect still has grammatical structures that no longer exist in the version spoken in Italy, which has also evolved, according to Carolyn MacKay, linguistics scholar and professor of English at Ball State University whose research includes that of the Basso-Bellunese Veneto dialect in Italy and Chipilo.[36]

In Santa Cruz, California, the Genoese dialect is still spoken, according to the documentary, *Tra Ponente e Levante*.[37] Ligurian fishermen from the town of Riva Trigoso on the Ligurian coast settled there during the great migration.[38]

R.B., an Italian American who lived in Brazil, writes on Candida Martinelli's Italophile Site, that in Southern Brazil, there are towns where people speak the dialects of Lombardy and Trento, and those regions of Italy have financed schools in those areas of Brazil.[39] These two examples in Mexico and Brazil prove my point exactly that the descendants of the immigrants of 100 years ago are keeping the Italian traditions alive while Italy itself is evolving.

Cresciani writes in as recent as 2003 that during unification, "Italian, as a language, was a minority language (as indeed it is even today, most Italians preferring to speak their own dialect)."[40]

As we have seen, any means available are used to discredit the foodways of Americans of Italian descent, including attacking their language. Schwartz is kinder than modern native Italians and most other writers on Italian food. "Today, Italian-American food is often ridiculed as a bastard cuisine that is heavy and crude," he writes. "In truth, this new Italian-American cuisine was not that dissimilar from its prototype, and had a lot more finesse than it is given credit for."[41] He goes on to describe what is oft repeated—that Southern Italians were poor people who didn't eat much beyond vegetables and pasta while in Italy and that the availability of cheap meat and higher quality of life in the United States enabled them to create new dishes.

Chef Rocco DiSpirito also distinguishes Italian and Italian-American cuisine in his cookbook, *Rocco's Italian American*.[42] While his distinction is more positive, it still discounts the "Italianness" of Italian-American cuisine. He writes, " . . . the Italian-American food tradition is a cuisine in its own right. So, next time you hear some snotty food expert scoff at it, calling it 'inauthentic' or 'not really Italian,' scoff back that he could be so ignorant. It is not 'authentically' Italian; it is a cuisine that originated from the relocation of people and the new existence of a cuisine in a foreign land."[43]

In the introduction to restaurateur Romeo Salta's *Pleasures of Italian Cooking*, Myra Waldo says Salta came to America "looking for a good Italian meal, but all he could find were Italian-American restaurants featuring garish murals of the Bay of Naples, meat balls [sic] and spaghetti, and very loud jukeboxes."[44] So, Waldo says, he opened his own restaurant serving "authentic" Northern Italian food.[45] There are many recipes in his cookbook that are Southern Italian recipes and made in the homes of Americans of Italian descent, including eggplant parmigiana, baked clams, escarole and beans, pastina, meatball soup, macaroni and bean soup, baccalà, pasta with lentils, lasagna, spaghetti with tomato sauce, spaghetti with olive oil and garlic, steak pizzaiola, and veal scaloppine, to name a few in only half of the book. For his recipe for macaroni with ricotta, he allows the substitution of cottage cheese for ricotta,[46] which is definitely not authentically Italian. Many of the same recipes in Salta's cookbook also appear in John Scialdone's *Neapolitan Peasant's Cookbook*. Scialdone's parents were from Naples and he wrote his book so that their foodways wouldn't be lost in an ever-mobile and changing society.[47]

According to food writer John Mariani in *How Italian Food Conquered the World*, one of Romeo Salta's waiters, Felice Bastianich, opened restaurants in Queens along with his wife, Lidia.[48] Lidia Bastianich would become a famous chef, restaurateur, cookbook author, and TV personality known mostly by her first name, Lidia. In fact, the name Lidia became synonymous with Italian food in the United States, as she was called "the first lady" of Italian cuisine here. My grandmother used to enjoy watching Lidia's TV program to see how she would cook familiar dishes. Lidia is an excellent chef and certainly knows how to run a successful restaurant business. However, Lidia's background and experience isn't representative of the millions of Southern Italians who also came to this country and created successful food businesses and restaurants, serving the food of Southern Italy.

In an interview with Umberto Mucci in *We the Italians: Two Flags One Heart*, Lidia Bastianich (referred to as Bastianich in the rest of this book) said she began her culinary career at age 14 in a pastry shop in Queens owned by actor Christopher Walken's family.[49] She immigrated to the United States in 1958.[50] She is from Istria, now part of Croatia on the Balkan peninsula.[51] Croatia was part of the former Yugoslavia and has an interesting history that won't be detailed here, but Istria was part of Italy from 1919-1947.[52] Bastianich says her family escaped the Communist regime in 1956[53] to Trieste in Northeastern Italy in the Friuli-Venezia Giulia province, a province with much Germanic and Slovenian influence. It borders present-day Slovenia. While she thought it was the other way around, she found out on the PBS genealogy series *Finding Your Roots* that her maiden name is Motika, Italianized to Mattichio by the Italian government under Mussolini in 1930.[54] (At that time, in an abhorrent practice, the Fascist Italian government banned the Slavic language, requiring that Italian be spoken.[55] In addition, the government forced the change of Slavic surnames to Italian-sounding ones.[56]) The show also conducted a DNA test that showed her DNA is 63 percent Eastern European and 28 percent Italian and Greek.[57] Culturally, she was raised Italian.[58]

As Bastianich writes in the introduction to her cookbook, *Lidia's Italy*, Istria had been part of the Roman Empire and later, part of the Republic of Venice, so it has Italian influence.[59] It was also part of the Austrian Empire and has Germanic influence as well.[60] Bastianich is from Pula, in Istria County, Istria.[61] The Croatian Bureau of Statistics has 2011 census data for Istria County, listing 68 percent Croats and almost 7 percent Italians.[62] Given Istria's location, its Italian influences are similar to those areas of Italy that are closest to it—Friuli-Venezia Giulia and Veneto. As Hooper writes of the regional differences in Italy: "What is true of Sicily is unlikely to be true of Trieste."[63]

Lidia's Italy is broken into ten chapters on different cities or regions of Italy like Rome, Naples, Sicily, etc., with traditional dishes from those regions. She also includes a chapter on Istria. The chapter on Istria includes seafood dishes (Istria is a small peninsula so there's plenty of seafood); "*makaruni*" (macaroni) and pasta dishes; sauerkraut with pork which is served for every holiday; roast goose with *mlinzi* which are a type of dumpling—thin, cracker-like sheets that soak up the sauce when cooked; dessert crepes called *palacinke*, and a dessert quince soup.[64]

In the chapter on Trieste, one can see the Germanic, Hungarian, and Slavic influence with recipes like pork, sauerkraut, and bean soup called *jota*; use of potato gnocchi; beef goulash; sacher torte; and apple strudel.[65] The next chapter on Friuli includes dishes like polenta, potato gnocchi, pork chops with savoy cabbage, turnips and potatoes, and apple torte.[66] The fourth chapter includes dishes from Veneto, the province of Venice. It includes a type of pasta called *bigoli*, beans, polenta, risotto.[67]

These differences proved true for Bastianich as she experienced Italian culture in the United States. She wrote a cookbook on Italian-American cuisine, *Lidia's Italian American Kitchen* (2001), which came out six years before *Lidia's Italy*.[68] In her introduction, she says that she was "fascinated" by Italian-American cuisine that "although it was called Italian, [she] did not recognize."[69] She goes on to say that in her restaurant career, she strove to have a better understanding of this cuisine.[70] She says that when she opened restaurants, customers wanted this Italian-American cuisine,[71] and that eventually she was able to add things like gnocchi, polenta, and risotto, what she calls "traditional" dishes to the menu.[72]

Bastianich's family had moved to New York City where the Italian population is from Southern Italy and the Italian food is Southern Italian. And she says in *Lidia's Italy* that she first went to Naples in 1966 on her honeymoon,[73] so perhaps she wasn't exposed to Southern Italian cuisine before moving to the United States. That is most likely why she personally didn't recognize the dishes on the menu. However, there had been Northern Italian immigrants in the United States, in areas like California and St. Louis, and they were making and eating polenta, risotto, and gnocchi. In fact, there probably doesn't exist an American of Italian descent who hasn't eaten polenta or had a grandparent who made various dishes with it. While it is traditionally a Northern Italian food, Southern Italians eat it as well. (Although one branch of my family says that they didn't eat polenta or corn—that they used it for animal feed, but the other side ate it.) Adrift at sea in a raft for 47 days after a plane crash, famed World War II POW Louie Zamperini, an American of Northern Italian descent and subject of *Unbroken*, a movie directed by Angelina Jolie, recounted tales of his mother's gnocchi and risotto to his fellow GIs as motivation to stay alive.[74] So these foods that Bastianich remembers were also dishes of Americans of Italian descent.

She goes on to say that she "received many accolades for bringing traditional Italian cooking to [her] customers."[75] She writes that the *New York Times* recognized her restaurant for "true" Italian food.[76] She does mention that these accolades had repercussions on Italian-American cuisine.[77] "Italian-American cooking was being dismissed as an impostor by journalists and professionals alike," she writes.[78] She felt that there was "something real" in Italian-American cuisine and that she would find out what this "phenomenon" was all about.[79] She questions where the early Italian immigrants got their Italian ingredients and "doubts" that they had "virgin olive oil, Parmigiano-Reggiano, fresh mozzarella, or ricotta."[80] According to Mariani, no one had "virgin" or "extra virgin" olive oil then, as it was a designation created to grade olive oils by the International Olive Oil Council (now the IOC) in the 1970s.[81] The IOC, created in Madrid in 1959 with oversight by the United Nations, resulted from a 1955 treaty on olive oil production.[82]

Her question is easily answered, however, if one looks to the history of any Italian-American neighborhood in the United States, and if one looks to the history of early immigration. Food writers and chefs imply that these immigrants were all "peasants." It is a fallacy to say or write that the early immigrants were "peasants." True, many had been tenant farmers, but many others were in the skilled trades as masons, stonecutters, carpenters, bakers, barbers, shoemakers, tailors, miners, and fishermen.[83] The town of Barre, Vermont, attracted Italian stonecutters who settled there in the late eighteen hundreds because of its granite industry.[84] Italians were also professionals like lawyers, accountants, teachers, pharmacists, and doctors.[85] In 1904, Yale and Columbia professor Gino Carlo Speranza, wrote that New York City had 115 Italian physicians, 63 pharmacists, 4 dentists, 21 lawyers, 15 public school teachers, 9 architects, 4 technical engineers, and 7 mechanical engineers.[86] In 1892, Frank Corrao, an immigrant from Palermo, became Brooklyn's first Italian lawyer.[87] Salvatore Cotillo, who emigrated from Naples as a child in 1895, became the first Italian to be in the New York State Assembly and Senate and the first to become a justice of the New York Supreme Court.[88] According to New York artist Walter Grutchfield, who documents historic sites in New York City, Italian immigrant Francis Avignone was in his early twenties when he purchased Stock Pharmacy in New York City's Greenwich Village and renamed it Avignone Pharmacy in 1898.[89] Cinotto notes that in the 1920s, Italian-American deposits were valued at more than $150 million in New York City's five largest banks, hardly a sum belonging to poor peasants.[90] In 1904, Amadeo P. Giannini established the Bank of Italy in San Francisco and would later create what is now Bank of America.[91] According to Miles Ryan Fisher in *Italian America* magazine, Giannini had the novel idea of loaning money to the working class, an idea previously rejected by the banking industry.[92] Giannini opened his own bank, the Bank of Italy, later changed to Bank of America.[93] The article says that after the San Francisco earthquake struck in 1906, he was able to rescue some bags of money.[94] In a horse-drawn cart, he went to the docks, set up his bank on barrels and wooden boards, and began loaning money to those who had lost houses and belongings.[95] He later said that all the loans had been repaid.[96] According to Joseph P. Kahn in *Inc.*, Lena Realmuto, whose father co-founded the Roman Macaroni Company in 1894, graduated Columbia University and helped her father with accounting.[97] (She would marry Joseph Pellegrino, CEO of Prince Macaroni Company.)[98] Molinari mentions Lucio Noto, who was the director of the Mobil Corporation and a child of Sicilian immigrants.[99] He earned a degree in physics and then went on to get an MBA from Cornell University.[100] Joseph Calabro, who founded Calabro Cheese Corporation in 1953, was a Sicilian immigrant with a Ph.D. in physics and mathematics.[101] According to the Andy Boy website, in the early nineteen hundreds, Sicilian immigrants Andrea and Stefano D'Arrigo came to the United States, learned English, and earned engineering degrees before founding the successful produce company, Andy Boy, still in existence today.[102] According to his foundation's website, Generoso Pope immigrated to New York from Italy at 15 years old.[103] His first job was as a water carrier in construction.[104] From there, he built successful construction and publishing businesses.[105] His construction company helped build Rockefeller Center and Radio City Music Hall.[106] He was influential in politics and the media.[107] The father of writer and activist Daniela Gioseffi, Daniel Donato Gioseffi, was an immigrant from

Puglia who came to the United States through Ellis Island as a child in 1913.[108] According to Gioseffi in the documentary of her life, *Author and Activist: The Daniela Gioseffi Story*, he worked his way through college with odd jobs like selling newspapers, attending parking lots, and shining shoes.[109] After earning a Phi Beta Kappa honor at Union College, he went on to graduate from Columbia University.[110] He became a chemical engineer and invented soft light.[111] These are only a few examples of early Italian immigrants who had advanced education and successful businesses and careers. Dismissing all Italian immigrants to America as "peasants" allows a prejudice and elitism to perpetuate.

Monica Cesarato, owner of a food tour company and cooking class in Venice, says in the *Local*'s "Ten 'Italian' Dishes That Don't Actually Exist in Italy," "People don't realize that the Italians who emigrated to the States and the UK were mostly impoverished farmers who couldn't afford certain ingredients."[112] The article calls this phenomenon by the popular term "cucina povera" (i.e., "poor kitchen"), which means "using readily available ingredients and leftovers" and is oft used to describe the "peasant" or "poor people's food" that originated in Naples.[113]

However, while many poorer classes of Italians immigrated to the United States and worked in agriculture and mining in places like West Virginia, Ohio, Texas, and Louisiana, many more settled in the larger cities, establishing neighborhoods and communities.[114] These immigrants were an economically diverse group, and many were middle class with professions, skilled trades, and business skills. The early immigrants opened groceries, butcher shops, and markets, importing products from Italy just like Bastianich does now with the Italian specialty store, Eataly, that she owns along with her son and well-known chef Mario Batali as B&B Hospitality Group, Oscar Farinetti, and the Saper brothers. Ironically, Batali's great-grandfather was one such Italian-American immigrant, opening an import business in Seattle in 1900.[115] (The business is still open but now owned by Bruce Biesold and his wife, Phyllis.)[116]

Schwartz notes the Italian immigrants opened food businesses "soon" after they came to the United States, importing olive oil, cheeses, and macaroni from Italy.[117] John Mariani, an Italian-American food writer and critic, along with his wife, Galina, write in *The Italian American Cookbook: A Feast of Food from a Great American Cooking Tradition* that the early immigrants opened stores in their own neighborhoods importing goods from Italy.[118]

The history of Italian imports in the United States is a complicated one of economic issues, tariffs, competition, and war. According to Cinotto, the heyday of Italian imports to the United States was 1890 to 1920.[119] He notes that the Italian government established chambers of commerce in cities to which Italians immigrated.[120] The first was opened in 1887 in New York and funded for decades by the Italian government.[121] As Cinotto says, the purpose of these chambers of commerce was to create an import relationship.[122] Ercole Locatelli, whose name many may recognize from cheese still available today, led the New York chamber of commerce during the 1930s.[123] (As noted, while Locatelli cheese is still available today, since 1998, it is owned and produced by the French Lactalis dairy group that also owns and produces other brands like Galbani. Locatelli was owned by Nestle Group from 1961 to 1998.)[124] According to Cinotto, in 1910, pasta imports were 55,903 tons; olive oil, 10,586 tons; cheese, 9,270 tons; and tomato products, 12,471 tons.[125] During this time, the United States imposed various tariffs and duties on Italian imported products. Cinotto notes that, in 1909, the duty on tomato products from Italy was 40 percent of the value.[126] He also mentions that from 1906 to 1909, the United States banned imports of fresh fruit from the Mediterranean.[127]

These new Italian immigrants were eating Italian foods. In the introduction to *The Italian American Cookbook*, John Mariani cites Donna R. Gabaccia's book *We Are What We Eat: Ethnic Food and the Making of Americans* that describes a small Italian neighborhood in Wisconsin with a daily diet consisting of "polenta, vegetable soups, wild greens, eel, dried codfish, offal, baby lamb, *cassatta* [sic] cake, and Italian cookies."[128] However, this is not a completely accurate reading of the passage in Gabaccia's book on Madison, Wisconsin's ten-block Greenbush neighborhood occupied by Italians.[129] Gabaccia doesn't describe *all* of these foods as foods in the *daily* diet but that some of these foods were eaten *seasonally*.[130] She describes the eel, lamb, offal, dried codfish, and *cassata* as well as other foods as being eaten during Italian festivals and holidays like Christmas and Easter.[131] Their daily diet consisted more of polenta, vegetable soups, cheese, and wild greens.[132] Many had gardens and ate the vegetables they grew.[133] Americans of Italian descent still eat these things, not on a daily basis because they include modern foods like those found in modern supermarkets, but they are part of the diet of Americans of Italian descent. Novelist Adriana Trigiani writes about her grandmother canning her own tomatoes, a tradition many Americans of Italian descent still do.[134] Some Americans of Italian descent still have gardens with fig trees and grow their own vegetables. Many still eat the same special occasion foods as the Italian settlers of Greenbush.

As Jane Ziegelman, food historian and author of *97 Orchard: An Edible History of Five Immigrant Families in One New York Tenement*, points out, Italians took food and cooking very seriously and wanted products that "grew from Italian soil" and imported from Italy "whenever possible."[135] In 1890, Jacob Riis, author of *How the Other Half Lives*, wrote about an Italian fish stand in New York that was "full of slimy, odd-looking creatures, fish that never swam in American waters, or if they did, were never seen on an American fish-stand,"[136] suggesting that fish was being brought in from somewhere besides the United States as well. According to Oretta Zanini De Vita in the

Encyclopedia of Pasta, during the early twentieth century, Italian immigrants in the United States imported the most pasta from Sicily and Naples.[137] Mariani notes that by 1938, there were over 10,000 groceries run by Americans of Italian descent, and there was "good trade" in importing from Italy both "canned and bottled goods."[138] Indeed, Cinotto notes, in the mid-1930s in New York City alone, Italians owned 10,000 groceries, 2,000 bakeries, 875 butcher shops, and 757 restaurants.[139] The Vaccaro brothers came to the United States from Contessa Entellina, Sicily, in the mid-eighteen hundreds.[140] In 1899, they started the Standard Fruit and Steamship Company, importing fruit such as coconuts and bananas from Honduras.[141] As time went by, their business grew to include the ice business, supplying ice during World War I, according to the National Italian American Foundation (NIAF).[142] Eventually, the company they started would become part of Dole Food Company.[143] In 1870, Luigi Pastene, an Italian immigrant, opened an Italian grocery importing products from Italy that eventually became the Pastene Corporation.[144] In 1879, Gabaccia says Italians in California imported 300,000 gallons of olive oil and 1,500 tons of figs.[145] She also mentions in 1884, A. Canale from Genoa opened a business in Charleston, South Carolina, importing "foreign" fruit.[146] (By 1910, she notes, 10 percent of Charleston's produce market owners were Italian and Greek.)[147] In 1895, current owner Peter Longo's grandfather started selling coffee, tea, dried mushrooms, and olive oil at his store that would become the Porto Rico Importing Co. in New York City's Greenwich Village in 1907, according to his interview with authors and photographers James and Karla Murray.[148] In July 2016, writer Paul Biasco reported on a discovery made in an old building being torn down in Chicago.[149] It was the city's oldest importer, Vincenzo Formusa Co., started in 1898 and now still selling products under the Marconi Foods name, according to Biasco.[150] (The article says Forumusa but the accompanying photo has "Formusa" clearly written on the store's awning and window.)[151] The old building had much memorabilia, including old cans of olive oil.[152] Biasco says the owners used to import pasta, olive oil, cheese, and tomatoes from a family in Italy.[153] Author Sheryll Bellman mentions in *America's Little Italys: Recipes & Traditions from Coast to Coast* that in 1905, Vincent Taormina and Company opened an importing company in New Orleans, selling olive oil and tomatoes from Italy.[154] Eventually, this company would merge with another to become the famous Progresso.[155] During the height of the infamous Black Hand in the first decade of the nineteen hundreds, a cheese importer in Little Italy was bombed, so they were importing cheese at this time.[156] Gabaccia notes the founders of the La Rosa Company imported olive oil from Sicily beginning in 1907.[157] In 1915, the Jewish Teitel Brothers opened an Italian grocery on Arthur Avenue in the Bronx (still family-owned and operated today), importing food from Italy.[158] According to the Mezzetta website, in 1935, Italian immigrant Giuseppe Luigi

Mezzetta opened a store in San Francisco selling imported Italian peppers, olives, and other products.[159] Today, the business he started is a fourth-generation family business.[160] In 1919, A. G. Ferrari Foods opened in San Jose, California.[161] The original owner of New York's Di Palo's was an immigrant from Basilicata who opened a dairy and eventually sold imported products from Italy.[162] Gabaccia says that in the 1930s, C. Granucci and Sons imported Italian cheeses, Italian and French dried mushrooms, tomato paste, Italian and European canned fish and sardines, and olive oil from Lucca, Italy.[163] Di Bruno Bros. in Philadelphia began importing products from Italy in the 1960s.[164] According to Raleigh historian Ernest Dollar, around 1900, Antonio Dughi opened a grocery store selling fresh seafood and produce in downtown Raleigh, North Carolina, a location atypical for early Italian immigrants.[165] The maker of Ragù pasta sauce, Giovanni Cantisano started as an importer.[166] In the 1910s, my great-grandparents and great-uncle had separate butcher shops where they also imported products from Italy. *Godfather* novelist Mario Puzo grew up poor in New York City's Hell's Kitchen but remembers his mother and father buying imported olive oil, cheeses, and fruit.[167] And it appears that the imported products were being used by non-Italian Americans. At American-themed restaurant, Harry Carpenter's Sandwich Stands, located in Los Angeles, "genuine Italian spaghetti" with "imported cheese" was on the menu in 1938, as depicted in *Menu Design in America: A Visual and Culinary History of Graphic Styles and Design 1850-1985*.[168]

According to Hugh Shankland in *Out of Italy: The Story of Italians in North East England*, even in the North East of England, where a small number of Italians had settled in the late eighteen hundreds, they had opened groceries and ice cream shops, where they imported Italian food items and "surely stocked Italian produce."[169] (The *Oxford Companion to Italian Food* notes that in the United Kingdom, Italian immigrants were known for their ice cream and fish-and-chip shops.)[170]

Italians were not only importing Italian products, but they were also importing products from other European countries, as well as Mexico, South America, Canada, and Africa. Cinotto cites *Feeding the City*, a study by the Federal Writers' Project of New York during the Great Depression, that noted the products sold in an Italian grocery in Harlem: "North Italian Pignoli seeds; Cape Cod stock-fish, Dalmatian sour cherries for making red wine; Oregano from Northern Italy and Greece, used for seasoning; California garlic; Newfoundland cod-fish; Spanish and Italian olive oil in 6 gallons [sic] tins; bags of Mexican fave bean, Chile lentils for soups and macaroni, and domestic split peas for soups; two pans of Greek and Italian black olives; can of Brazilian raw green coffee for roasting; two cans of Abyssinian coffee, roasted, ready for demitasse; two silver-wrapped balls of Albanian Mizritha cheese for eating and grating; Provoloni cheese, used for eating, from Northern Italy; Gorgonzola cheese, imported from Rome, the aristocrat of Italian cheese; four varieties of Caciocavallo (Sicilian style) cheese used for grating and eating, and imported from Ragusa, Italy; imported Roman cheese used for grating; imported Parmesan cheese from Italy, used for grating, canned Italian *caponata*, a mixture of eggplant and vegetable, American-made Brioschi Effervescenti, California tuna fish in olive oil and Italian peeled tomatoes, two cans of Italian olive oil; Locatelli brand of *provolonina* cheese imported from Naples, Chicago-made Salami, Sicilian style; Provoloncini cheese made in Wisconsin; Genoa-style Salami made in Chicago and used with *antipasta* [*sic*], which is a mixture of peppers, olives and anchovies."[171]

According to Aprile, in the first quarter of the nineteen hundreds, Northern Europe and the United States became "great consumers of fresh fruit" and imported them from Italy[172] (except for the years 1906–1909 in the United States when they were banned[173]). Why? What sparked this change in Northern Europe and the United States and who was importing this fresh fruit? I would say Italian immigrants in those countries.

The majority of Americans of Italian descent lived in communities with other Italians in larger cities like New York, Boston, Chicago, and Philadelphia. Those who lived farther from these urban areas would stock up on supplies when they visited or would have items mailed to them by a relative. Former *New York Times* restaurant critic Frank Bruni described his grandmother sending Italian food care packages to them when they moved to San Diego.[174] Novelist Adriana Trigiani's family moved from Roseto, Pennsylvania, to Big Stone Gap, Virginia. She jokes that her mom would "'import' ricotta from the north."[175] Her father would stock up on things like prosciutto.[176] Therefore, immigrants had access to and preferred imported products from Italy.

In addition to importing products, early Italian immigrants also created the foods they had eaten in Italy. According to a 1961 Polly-O cookbook, Giuseppe Pollio settled in Brooklyn in 1899 and began making ricotta and mozzarella in Coney Island, "using the traditional method prevalent in Italy at that time."[177] At the writing of that book, the Pollio family had been making these cheeses for 150 years.[178] Alleva Dairy, still in operation today in New York City's Little Italy, opened in 1892.[179] Di Palo's dairy shop opened there in 1910 and is now an Italian deli and grocery.[180] According to Cinotto, domestic production of Italian products grew during World War I and imports continued to decline.[181] He notes that the Fascist government in Italy tried to persuade American Italians to buy Italian products as a sign of patriotism.[182] However, their allegiance was to the United States.[183]

During the 1930s, American-produced Italian products soared, well over Italian imports, notes Cinotto.[184] And not only in the United States.

American-produced Italian products reached Latin America and Great Britain.[185] Maybe this was in response to the Hawley-Smoot Tariff Act of 1930, as Cinotto mentions, which upped the duties on cheese and tomato paste to 35 and 50 percent of the value, respectively.[186] World War II saw a nosedive for Italian imports, as the United States did not import food from Italy.[187] This continued to allow American producers of Italian products to grow and flourish. Italians used California olive oil, Gabaccia says, although they deemed its quality "only fair."[188] Another example is the pounds of cheese produced throughout the decades. In the 1920s, Cinotto notes that American producers of Italian cheeses were at less than two million pounds.[189] In 1940, 25 million pounds; in 1943, 45 million; and in 1946, 75 million.[190]

Not only did these early Italian immigrants import food and create American-made Italian products, they created other food businesses and opened restaurants. In 1885, Gabaccia says Giovanni Savarese created a fishing business near Tampa, Florida, and by 1920, there were 20 such businesses in the area owned by Italians.[191] In 1906, Amedeo Obici founded Planters Nut & Chocolate Company after he successfully sold peanuts at his fruit market.[192] In the early nineteen hundreds, Joseph Di Giorgio, a Sicilian immigrant, successfully re-created the European model of auctioning produce that had been shipped nationwide, the beginnings of the Di Giorgio Corporation, according to Gabaccia.[193] Mariani does mention that Americans of Italian descent thought that home cooking was superior to restaurant food,[194] but he says that "none" of the early immigrants had "any experience eating in or running a restaurant."[195] Mariani mentions that Italian restaurants were first opened by Southern Italians in their own neighborhoods using their home cooking as a model.[196] I disagree that none of the early immigrants had experience eating in or running restaurants. According to Parasecoli, restaurants on the Italian peninsula date back to ancient Roman times where there were a number of types of restaurants, including take out counters, al fresco dining, taverns, and inns.[197] There were pizzerias in eighteenth-century Naples and by mid-century, they had tables and chairs for customers to sit and eat, according to Carol Helstosky in *Pizza: A Global History* and Antonio Mattozzi in *Inventing the Pizzeria: A History of Pizza Making in Naples*.[198] In nineteenth-century Naples, Mattozzi writes that there are records of licensed businesses, including pizzerias, trattorias, and taverns.[199] These businesses were classified into seven tiers for fee purposes.[200] The first and second class producers and wholesalers paid a higher fee than the other classes.[201] But while pizzerias were among shops in the seventh class, trattorias were in the third.[202] At the time, a trattoria was what we would call a restaurant now.[203] In the 1840s and 1850s, it was common that pizzerias had a dual license as a trattoria.[204] According to Capatti and Montanari, there were Italian immigrants who owned inns in Italy (such as my great-grandparents), and inns were predecessors of the modern Italian restaurant, as they served food and had their own menus.[205] Mattozzi cites an 1898 article in *Napoli Nobilissima* magazine by a Neapolitan historian named Alfonso Fiordelisi, "Where our grandparents ate," that discusses food establishments of the early eighteen hundreds, including trattorias that catered to various social classes.[206] According to Mattozzi, other authors wrote about "taverns, trattorias, osterias, and inns" in "centuries past."[207]

Bastianich quotes Mangione and Morreale that men came alone to the United States and that the modern "Italian-American restaurant most likely had its birth" from the boarding houses where they stayed.[208] (Philadelphia's oldest Italian restaurant, Dante & Luigi's Corona di Ferro, opened in 1899 with a boarding house for newly arrived immigrants.)[209] This argument is not a fully correct statement, however, as many of the early Italian immigrants came over with their families; were middle class; had businesses, skills, and professions; lived in large cities in communities with other Italians; and opened restaurants in their own neighborhoods for themselves. And some opened restaurants in non-Italian communities. According to Gabaccia, by 1910, in Charleston, South Carolina, there were five restaurants operated by Italians.[210] (Greeks ran 17.)[211] One named "Geuiseppe Savarese" had a spaghetti special called the "Italian Plan."[212] Paul Moses, author of *An Unlikely Union: The Love-Hate Story of New York's Irish and Italians*, writes that in New York, Vincent Saulino, an immigrant from a town near Rome, came to the United States in 1880 and opened a restaurant with his wife that well-known, respected police detective Joseph Petrosino used to frequent, and eventually, he married their daughter.[213]

Mariani writes that Italian-American cuisine "grew into a genre all its own"[214] and that it was "born in the early twentieth century,"[215] "so distinct" from the cooking of Italy.[216] In fact, he refers to this cuisine as a "genre" a number of times in *The Italian American Cookbook*'s preface and introduction. He goes on to say, "We have also been frequent critics of the mediocrity of so many Italian-American restaurants that cut corners, use inferior ingredients, and never evolve beyond the clichés of a genre that had become cloyed with 'red sauce' and fried foods."[217] Bruni writes that "red-sauce" Italian restaurants were the only kind when he was growing up.[218] He says, "A bottomless bowl of pasta: *now that's Italian!* Or so we were all led to believe, and I didn't pay enough attention during my first spin through Italy in my early twenties to be disabused of that myth."[219] The use of the term "red sauce" by people of Italian descent is disconcerting to say the least and one wonders if it stems from a subconscious peer pressure. In order to be a restaurant critic, one must eat out at five-star restaurants and "hob-knob" with the elites of the restaurant and hospitality industry, many of whom are already denouncing the cuisine of Italian Americans as inferior or false. Since the elites have this ingrained prejudice against Southern Italian cuisine, do food writers of Italian descent feel that they have to distance themselves from it just for career survival? It is a known fact that restaurant critics bore easily. In their line of work, they are always looking for the standout dish, the new technique, something fresh and exciting to write about. Perhaps critics of Italian-American restaurants are only expressing boredom with the familiar food, but I would argue that there is a way to do so without denigrating a culture's foodways, which I don't think is the intent of most food writers and chefs, but it can be an effect of their words.

It's important to note here that most restaurants in the United States that serve Italian food are catering to a non-Italian palate and audience. Ziegelman quotes a newspaper reporter, who visiting Italian restaurants at the beginning of the twentieth century, noted, "The Italian taste in cookery is not always such as pleases the native American palate."[220] Therefore, to an extent, the ingredients and methods used reflect that. Beppe Severgnini, an Italian journalist, writes in his memoir on living a year in the United States, *Ciao, America!: An Italian Discovers the U.S.*, that "non-Italians don't deserve the old caricatures of Italian cuisine, with their palate-scarring hot sauces and meat drowning in thick gravy."[221] The cuisine he is referring to is "Italian-American," and the versions of Italian-American cuisine in American restaurants is often inauthentic (as is most cuisine when compared to home cooking or haute cuisine). Many of these restaurants are businesses, and like any other business, have concerns for the bottom line, and use lesser-quality ingredients because it makes financial sense to do so. Also, many of these restaurants are owned by people who are not of Italian descent. For example, American Italian restaurants are often owned by Greek Americans, evident by additional offerings like Greek salad, gyros, or spaghetti sauce spiced with cinnamon. Gabaccia notes that in 1975, Connecticut had 482 pizzerias, 40 percent of them with Greek owners.[222] (This comment is not speaking on their quality but on their authenticity.)

The argument that Italian-American food is one of quantity versus quality repeats itself over and over in books on this topic. Creating a gimmick, like an unlimited bowl of pasta or family-style multiple courses creates the image they are trying to sell of the Italian family sitting around the table, eating for hours. The truth is a meal like that occurs, traditionally, only on Sundays and holidays in households of Americans of Italian descent—and what people do not realize is there is a lot of "in between" in these meals. There's the antipasto, which everyone picks at while the dinner is still cooking. Then there's the first course—pasta. The second course—meat—is one most people rarely even eat because they are full. There are also salad and vegetables. And people stop to nibble on fennel as they sit around the table and talk. Finally, in the evening, there is coffee and dessert.

Italian restaurants are not the only restaurants guilty of this quantity versus quality problem. Many restaurants offer buffets—like Chinese,

Southern, breakfast—that are cheap and filling but not so healthy or tasty, but again, it is a style of restaurant that many Americans enjoy because they can feed their family affordably.

While some Italian restaurants may use inferior ingredients, in their home cooking, I would argue that most Americans of Italian descent use high-quality and Italian ingredients. Mariani notes that Italian immigrant food started out as "poor people's food," with the usual characteristics of "poor people's food": cheap, plentiful, and highly caloric.[223] Mariani writes that before the 1970s, olive oil was in "one-gallon tin cans" and mostly of "mediocre or inferior quality."[224] He writes that "first-rate" ingredients like balsamic vinegar and extra-virgin olive oil made an appearance after the 1970s and 1980s when "northern" Italian restaurants popped on the scene.[225] The use of "first-rate" here implies that the ingredients Americans of Italian descent had been importing to their shops from Italy in various cities around the country (New York, Boston, Philadelphia, Chicago, San Francisco, New Orleans, St. Louis, to name the largest) or making on their own were "second-rate" or at least inferior.

How could Americans of Italian descent be making inferior ingredients when they have been using the same processes since ancient times? Archaeological scholars say that the people of Southern Italy have been making cheeses since the early Hellenistic period (370–230 BC), over two thousand years ago.[226] The fact that these people moved to a new country would not preclude them from carrying on a millennial-old tradition. Writing in his 1979 cookbook, restaurateur Alfredo Viazzi noted that "excellent" Parmesan cheese was being made in Wisconsin and Argentina.[227] Today, the Italians in Italy would take exception to his statement, as they are trying to promote "Made in Italy" products. According to Antonio Verde, Consul General of Italy in L.A., interviewed at the Mediterranean Diet Roundtable in L.A. in 2016, "Made in Italy" products are ones deemed by Italian law to be 100 percent made in Italy, including design, production, and packaging.[228] The widely used term for food products that are not "authentic" is "Italian sounding." According to the *New York Times*, Italian-sounding products garner over $60 billion a year.[229] That's a lot of money and no wonder the Italian food industry has waged war against "Italian-sounding" products, as well it should, if those products are, indeed, inferior, such as Parmesan cheese made from wood pulp. However, a Parmesan-style cheese from Wisconsin would fit in this category, even if it were made of good quality, as would Kraft Parmesan cheese. Parmesan cheese is from Parma in Emilia-Romagna. There is no comparison of real Parmesan cheese from Parma to Kraft Parmesan cheese. But there are/were also Italian cheeses of exceptional quality made in the United States. The problem lies in when the local Italian-American businesses became corporations or died out because of competition from corporations and quality subsequently degraded (e.g., grocery-store ricotta) or when non-Italian-American businesses and/or corporations create "Italian-sounding" food of lower quality (e.g., chain pizza). But just because something is "Made in Italy" or an Italian-branded product does not automatically make it a superior product. I would prefer the cheeses made from any Italian-American dairy to commercial Italian cheeses found in the grocery store today. For example, Galbani's tag line is "Authentic Italian Cheese" yet its ricotta has added gums in it, although, recently, the company created a "3 simple ingredients"[230] version without gums.

The same can be said for winemaking. Mariani says that "the history of Italian wine may be ancient, but until the mid-twentieth century, the wines in question were not of very high quality."[231] He says winemaking dates back to the ninth century BC, the "vast majority" from "small plots by peasants who had little knowledge of how to get the best from whatever grapes grew on their land."[232] I find this confusing. He is saying that these peasants made wine this way for thousands of years but had no idea what they were doing? Parasecoli notes that in the seventh century BC, the Etruscans had developed better methods of cultivating grapes and they established wine trade with the Romans and Celts.[233] During ancient Roman times, wine was a major commodity. The wines from the Southern Italian regions of Naples and Sicily had gained repute, and a wine from Basilicata was also popular, according to Parasecoli.[234] While Mariani says that winemaking outside of monasteries "languished" during the Dark Ages,[235] Kreutz says in the ninth century, Campanian wineries were still using ancient Roman techniques for growing grapes.[236] A booklet entitled "The Wines of Italy" published by the Italian Trade Commission in 2002 says that winemaking didn't employ the same advanced techniques of the Romans until the seventeenth and eighteenth centuries when more scientific methods of production were used, a comment which seems to support Mariani's idea of the Dark Ages.[237] In 1789, Ulysses had "excellent wine" made with "superior skill and judgment" in Southern Italy.[238] The Trade Commission booklet also notes that the nineteenth century saw advanced winemaking and shipping.[239] As the late Joel Dalmas of Valdese, North Carolina, and part owner of the Waldensian Heritage Wines, said to me, "If you have French or Italian blood, you know how to make wine."[240] According to Mauro Battocchi, Italian Consul General in San Francisco, interviewed by Mucci in *We the Italians*, Italian immigrants practically created the wine industry in California.[241] Brothers Peter and Robert Mondavi, whose parents were immigrants from Northern Italy, were instrumental in building California's wine business, as were brothers and sons of immigrants, Ernest and Julio Gallo.[242] Mariani discusses the history of the evolution of the current wine market in Chapter 10 of *How Italian Food Conquered the World*.[243] In my opinion, that's what the current wine market is, a wine *market*. It is my opinion and belief, that the classic wines of Italy were denounced in the market as inferior in order to create a *global* wine market.

Mariani mentions a wine tasting that he attended that Lucio Caputo, the then-Italian Trade Commissioner of New York, had set up to showcase Sicilian wines to New York wine writers.[244] The writers were not impressed with the wine, which they found to be "musty, oxidized, even rank."[245] Mariani says the Sicilian wine makers were affronted, explaining that their wines were made with traditional methods for centuries and they tasted how they should.[246] (Interestingly, the *Local* reported in August 2017 that researchers found archaeological evidence that Sicilians have been making wine for six thousand years, that is three thousand years longer than originally thought.)[247] Caputo then told them that in order to compete in a global market, they would have to change the wines because they were "flawed"; some didn't change their methods, while others did, according to Mariani, "learn[ing] a great lesson."[248] What is the lesson, exactly, that they learned? If Ulysses found the wines of Southern Italy to be excellent in the seventeen hundreds, what was wrong with them in present day? Is it the association with Southern Italy itself? Did the wine industry need to distance itself from the history of the Southern Italian "peasant" to be considered more marketable?

In fact, this notion that any food originating in Southern Italy is peasant food is ludicrous. Humans in Southern Italy evolved from hunter-gatherers to farming and producing food in the Neolithic period around 4000 to 2500 BC, although it may have been as early as 7000 BC in Puglia.[249] According to the *Oxford Companion to Italian Food*, eight thousand years ago, migrating tunny and bonito (fish) were so plentiful, the Greeks and Italians could predict a large amount of fish at certain times of the year.[250] This most likely led to the drying of fish so it could be eaten at times when fish were not migrating.[251] The Italians have been producing cheeses, dried and cured meats, pickled vegetables, and wine since those times. And not only producing—perfecting—crafting—taking the time needed to create the most flavorful taste experience. Poor peasants who need to eat would not take a year to age a food, opening a window or measuring wind and light and temperature to find the ideal conditions to produce that food so that it reaches its peak of flavor. According to *We the Italians*, Calabrian DOP *salumi, pancetta, soppressata,* and *capocollo* are created using a time-tested process that involves salting and seasoning for as much as 45 days.[252] But many sources will say that cured and dry meats are peasant food because they needed something to last them through the winter. It seems likely that without refrigeration in those days, everyone would eat these foods—not only the poor. And these foods were ideal for journeys and pilgrimages, of which all classes partook. Now, this is not to be confused with the class system that existed—the upper classes and monarchs, as aforementioned, could read and write and wrote their recipes down in cookbooks. And in Sicily, there existed a high and low cuisine. This high cuisine was popular in Naples and other areas of Italy as well. The chefs who cooked for the royalty and nobles were referred to as *Monzu*, a Neapolitan form of the French word *monsieur*, a term that represented the courtly cuisine of the Bourbons, according to Louis Inturrisi in *Savoring Italy*.[253] In *Naples at Table*, Schwartz notes that French cuisine was the rage among the elite, and the aristocracy wanted a *Monzu*, a family cook trained in French cooking.[254] He also includes a *Monzu* recipe for mushroom pate.[255] He notes that the upper classes preferred food that was beige and white in color while the lower classes ate more colorful foods.[256] Perhaps the most famous *Monzu* recipe today is the *timballo* or *timpano* featured in Stanley Tucci's *Big Night* movie, a large pie filled with pasta, meats, cheese, and vegetables.[257] Another term for the high cuisine is *cucina alto-borghese*.[258] The low cuisine was popular food, eaten by everyone else—not only peasants.

According to Mariani, until well into the twentieth century, until the Italian government stepped in and created DOC and DOCG designations in the 1960s, Italian wine couldn't compete with the quality of French and German wines.[259] He says the Italians weren't making the same technological advances as the other two countries were and there was much devastation of land after the wars.[260] This perspective is a wholly commercial one. Americans of Italian descent had been drinking wine from Italy and making their own wine with those thousand-year-old traditions. Mariani cites Luigi Veronelli who thought that in order to compete with the higher standards of haute cuisine (which at the time was only French), Italian wine had to be given a DOCG (*denominazione d'origine controllata e garantita*) designation.[261]

Unlike the restaurants based on the cuisine of Southern Italy, Mariani describes new Italian restaurants as "serious" and "refined," words, to me, that exude classism and elitism more than a description of cuisine.[262] I understand Mariani means that Italian food was "elevated" to be considered "fine" dining, and I do not ascribe classism and elitism to Mariani but to the words "serious" and "refined," words I think he uses to impress upon the hospitality industry that Italian food is on par with say, French cuisine. However, these words are reminiscent of medieval cookbooks and their description of the differentiation between the rich and the poor and how peasants were too stupid and coarse to understand good taste.[263]

And, as aforementioned, referring to the cuisine of Americans of Italian descent as "peasant" cuisine is derogatory. Peasant is a fifteenth-century[264] term that, according to Merriam-Webster, has two definitions. The first is "a member of a European class of persons tilling the soil as small landowners or as laborers."[265] The second is "a usually uneducated person of low social status."[266] An older Webster's dictionary I have also includes "a person regarded as boorish, ignorant."[267] In Italian history, peasants were described with terms like stupid, coarse, and vulgar. Use of this term as it has been applied to Italian food history and discourse implies that a) there is something inferior about people in a lower socio-economic class and b) that all the 16 million immigrants of the great migration were an inferior group, i.e., they (and in turn, their children) were/are stupid, coarse, and vulgar.

In the late nineteenth century, a sense of altruism for the poor began to emerge, especially when books like *How the Other Half Lives* showed the deplorable living conditions of the tenements of New York City. Prior to that time, the prevailing thought was that there was something inherently lacking in the character of peasants to make them be in a lowly station. According to Capatti and Montanari, when discussing the taste of sugar, fourteenth/fifteenth-century writer Gentile Sermini wrote, "Make sure that the peasant does not taste sweetness but only sour things. Rustic he is; rustic he will remain."[268] Peasants were seen as vulgar and uncouth, not deserving of anything "refined" because they couldn't "appreciate" it, note Capatti and Montanari.[269] They say that the underlying message was that "each person eats in the manner prescribed by his social class."[270] This belief system, while appearing archaic now, is arguably still held in the modern world, as foods deemed to be healthier like fresh fruits and vegetables and less fatty cuts of meat are more expensive and processed foods with chemical additives are cheaper and more available for the poorer classes.

Why are sources constantly referring to Italian-American cuisine as "peasant" food? The reason may be a simple one, as Italy tries to gain ground with its "Made in Italy" campaign: competition. Perhaps the history of pasta production is the best illustration. The early Italian immigrants to the United States imported macaroni from Italy. When they first started making macaroni to sell in the United States, they did so in small shops, but they soon branched out to larger operations. According to Kahn, in 1894, Pietro Realmuto created Roman Macaroni Co. which had annual sales of $300,000 by the 1920s.[271] In 1912, three Italian immigrants, Michele Cantella, Gaetano LaMarca, and Giuseppe Seminara, opened the Prince Macaroni Manufacturing Co. in Boston's North End.[272] (Prince would later be run by Joseph Pellegrino, a Sicilian immigrant, who coined "Wednesday is Prince Spaghetti Day" and led Prince to become a multimillion-dollar company.)[273] According to Zanini De Vita, Sicilian-American Vincent La Rosa's pasta company in the United States "would offer serious competition to the Italian imports."[274] Gabaccia says that by 1930, he had 300 workers and made $3-5 million annually.[275] Newer technologies made the operation grow exponentially. In 1924, two brothers, Italian immigrants from New York, Guido and Aurelio Tanzi, patented a machine called *fusilla* for making *fusilli* pasta.[276] Before their invention, Zanini De Vita notes, it wasn't possible to commercially produce *fusilli*.[277] Macaroni production in the United States soon outpaced Italian production.[278] According to the Academia Barilla, in 1951, then-owner of Barilla pasta, Pietro Barilla, took a trip to America that influenced his work for the company, including technological advancements.[279] This fact may hit on the crux of the entire discussion—

perhaps modern native Italians see the success of the Italian-American businesses as economic competition and in turn, create in the media the perception that these Italian-American products are "inauthentic" in the goal of driving business for Italian imports? After all, in 2012, the *New York Times* reported that Eataly accounted for almost a third of the $250 million yearly sales of the Batali & Bastianich Hospitality Group.[280]

The question then would be, what is an "authentic" Italian product? As we have seen, according to native Italians, it is one produced in Italy. But how authentic are Italian products? According to *Two Greedy Italians*, the Mottolini Company of Valtellina, in the Northern region of Lombardy, uses beef from cows raised in South America and other parts of Europe to make the region's famous *bresaola*, a cured meat.[281] According to its website, Mottolini has been making *bresaola* since 1986.[282] According to an article in the *We the Italians* newsletter, the earliest record of *bresaola* making dates back to the fifteenth century but it is older than that.[283] There is a Protected Geographical Indication (PGI) trademark for genuine *bresaola della Valtellina*.[284] This *bresaola* must be produced in a certain manner and in this area because the local climate affects its taste.[285] Nowhere does the article mention that it must be made from cattle raised in Italy or raised locally;[286] however, one would think that that would contribute to making the product genuine.

What has Italy been doing to ensure that consumers are getting authentic products? Despite the effects of capitalism and an expanding global market, the country is on the forefront in protecting the established, traditional methods of producing food products. According to Parasecoli, such food products carry the Italian Ministry of Agriculture and Forestry logos as well as the European Union mark for Protected Denomination of Origin.[287] The Italian government passed these laws in the 1950s as a guarantee that food products claiming to come from particular regions in Italy really did so, as Liz Barrett notes in *Pizza: A Slice of American History*.[288] According to the *Oxford Companion to Italian Food*, the designations DOC (*denominazione di origine controllata* or Controlled Designation of Origin), DOP (*denominazione di origine protettata* or Protected Designation of Origin), IGP (*indicazione geografica protetta* or Protected Geographical Indication) and SGT (*specialità tradizionale garantita* or Traditional Specialty Guaranteed) serve as a guarantee that the products were produced in a specific manner according to a set definition.[289] It notes that the designations are based on the geographic region where the item is produced, the environmental conditions, and the methods used to produce it.[290] DOC and DOP have the strictest standards. IGP means that products made in a particular region can also contain ingredients from other places.[291] SGT means a traditional method was used to create the product.[292] Some examples of Italian foods that have a DOC include *Parmigiano-Reggiano* and *aceto balsamico tradizionale di Modena*, foods with ubiquitous imposters, says the *Oxford Companion to Italian Food*.[293] According to *We the Italians*, the DOP *salumi* from Calabria are made from pigs raised and slaughtered in Calabria, fed a diet of barley, field beans, corn, acorns, and chickpeas.[294] These *salumi* include *capocollo di Calabria* DOP, *pancetta di Calabria* DOP, *soppressata di Calabria* DOP, and *salsiccia di Calabria* DOP, all made under painstaking, careful processes.[295]

A DOC or DOP designation can work against the producer of some traditional products, though, because the definition is so strict and doesn't allow for any variation. This unfortunate ramification can keep certain products off the market. Organizations like Slow Food are advocates for these "other" foods that do not meet the DOC/DOP designations, according to the *Oxford Companion to Italian Food*.[296] The Slow Food movement started by Italian Carlo Petrini in 1986 began as opposition to McDonald's opening near Rome's Spanish Steps.[297] It is now a global movement, advocating the production and consumption of local foods with natural and sustainable methods.

The DOC/DOP designations give consumers faith in Italian products. However, today, Italy is also a victim of food globalization. Restaurants in the Italian Riviera city of Portofino in the Northern province of Liguria serve frozen fish from China.[298] According to David Gentilcore in *Pomodoro*, between 1870 and 1893, American Alexander Livingston created or improved 13 varieties of tomatoes.[299] He says some of these varieties were sold in Parma, Italy, because they were suitable for concentrate production.[300] Also, he notes that after World War II, "self-supporting, determinate plant varieties . . . were imported from the United States."[301] According to Capatti and Montanari, Argentina had been exporting poultry and beef to Italy during the twentieth century.[302] They also mention that Argentina is expanding its production of "imitation" Italian specialties with their original Italian names but at lower prices.[303] In 2015, the *New York Times* reported that a bacterium, *Xylella fastidiosa*, killed olive trees in Puglia, hurting the olive oil industry.[304] How did the bacteria arrive in Italy? From plants imported from Costa Rica.[305] The article also mentions that California and Brazil have a history of problems with this bacteria. It costs California $104 million a year.[306] (Although this type of thing is not unheard of. Stephen A. Briganti, president and CEO of the Statue of Liberty-Ellis Island Foundation in New York, mentions in an interview with Mucci for *We the Italians* that his grandfather's brother, who was an agriculture professor, developed a cure for an olive tree disease in Basilicata.)[307] A 2015 article in *Fanpage* reported that police found a large landfill under a broccoli field in my grandmother's town outside Naples; toxic and hazardous waste had been buried there and reached the root level of the broccoli.[308]

In 2015, the *New York Times* published a few interactive graphic pieces by illustrator and art director Nicholas Blechman called "Food Chains" with a focus on a few different Italian food products: "Extra Virgin Suicide," "The Mystery of San Marzano," "Code Name Parmigiano," and "Planet Pasta."[309] The short pieces show how each product is made in today's world. Unfortunately, it's not a pretty picture. Olive oil is often mislabeled as coming from Italy when it is made from olives grown in other countries or it is degraded with inferior quality oils.[310] San Marzano tomatoes are also often mislabeled as coming from Italy when they come from elsewhere.[311] He also mentions that tomato paste is made from tomatoes grown in China and imported to Italy.[312]

According to an article in the *Guardian*, the British supermarket chain Asda had this problem with tomato puree provided by a supplier in Southern Italy.[313] In order for tomatoes grown in China to get a "Produced in Italy" label under European Union law, the article says they must be processed into a different form.[314] It notes that Asda's supplier was only adding salt and water and arguing that that constituted sufficient processing to be labeled "Produced in Italy."[315] Antonino Russo, in charge of AR Industrie Alimentari who supplied the tomatoes, was convicted of fraud and the court said the minimal processing didn't satisfy the processing requirement for labeling the tomatoes "Produced in Italy," according to the article.[316] Russo says 90 percent of his tomato product is exported—not used in Italy.[317] Maybe that's why the food in Italy tastes so good.

Blechman finds that *Parmigiano-Reggiano* is still produced with the same methods as 100 years ago, but that authenticity comes with a hefty price tag—$26.80 a pound.[318] He is disappointed after touring the Barilla factory because it is a huge sterile factory run by computers.[319] At a Roman trattoria that makes homemade pasta, he sees boxes of Barilla in the kitchen.[320]

While the graphics are cute and the concept is entertaining, "Food Chains" shows the sad state of affairs in Italy today. Despite the Slow Food movement and other food protections, the country has already fallen prey to globalization and all its ills, like the production of counterfeit, poorer-quality or misleading products.

In addition, Italians themselves are falling prey to the marketing tactics so pervasive in today's ever-expanding capitalistic culture. Reported in a Winter 2015 article in the Sons of Italy *Italian America* magazine, Italians, French, and Spanish are drinking less wine than they used to.[321] The numbers are startling. The article says that in the 1970s, an Italian consumed 29 gallons a year to only 13.6 gallons now.[322] It quotes Jancis Robinson, the wine critic of the *Financial Times* who told *Newsweek* a reason for this decline in consumption: "Wine—so much part of tradition and the past in these countries—is seen as an old person's or peasant's drink, whereas heavily advertised beers, spirits, and sodas are seen as more youthful and modern."[323] It sounds as if the Italians, French, and Spanish are playing right into the advertisers' hands. According to Vinepair's United States of Alcohol map, beer is the most popular alcoholic drink in the United States.[324] Is American influence to drink beer and soda creating this perception?

Mariani says that Italian-American cooking "continues to evolve each year, not only getting closer to the original sources in Italy but incorporating the best American ideas and products into the mix, so that one can speak of the new Italian-American cuisine as one of the major food cultures of the world."[325] What about the millions of Southern Italian immigrants who brought their foodways with them to America? *They* were closer to the original sources in Italy than anyone is today, especially in our modern world where corporations and governments have much more influence over food production. And Italian-American cuisine, or the cuisine of the Southern Italian immigrant to America is one of the two most popular cuisines in the world (along with Chinese). According to Severgnini in *La Bella Figura: A Field Guide to the Italian Mind*, 42 percent of interviewees preferred Italian cuisine followed by Chinese.[326] One could argue which cuisine is more popular, but no one would argue that Italian and Chinese are the top two cuisines in the world. And not only is Italian one of the two top cuisines in the world, the "red sauce" variety of the Southern Italian immigrants is the most popular Italian cuisine in the world. Schwartz writes, "The food of Southern Italy is still today 'the Italian food the whole world knows as Italian,' in the words of the late, venerated food writer Waverly Root."[327]

At the end of the introduction, Mariani writes a seemingly contradictory statement, "Not for a moment are we suggesting that the new Italian-American cuisine is superior to the great traditional regional cooking in Italy or to the immigrant food that established the genre in the first place."[328] It is unclear what he means by "new Italian-American cuisine." Is it the cuisine started in the 1970s incorporating Northern Italian elements and gravitating toward a wealthier, urban class in cities like New York? Or does it include the "impostor" dishes so synonymous with Italian food like spaghetti and meatballs or eggplant parmigiana? Eggplant parmigiana, according to Astarita, is "one of Naples' most beloved dishes and greatest contributions to world cuisine."[329] Mariani goes on to say that there is a "great deal of snobbery in food these days,"[330] yet some of the things he writes seem to perpetuate this snobbery. And coming from a respected food and restaurant authority of Italian descent, his words can be more damaging. His ethnicity lends credibility to the idea that the food of the Americans of Italian descent is not "true" Italian cuisine. Mariani does say that Italian-American food " . . . sets the standards for Italian-style food in the rest of the world."[331] I agree with this statement, but I believe the food of the descendants of the early Italian immigrants is not "Italian-American" or "Italian-style." It is the *true* food of Italy, one the early immigrants brought with them to their new homeland that *continues* to be cooked, eaten, and enjoyed by their children and grandchildren today.

CHAPTER 4: They Came to America

The views expressed by food writers and chefs, essentially questioning the "validity" of the cuisine and foodways of Americans of Italian descent, much like Collodi's, whether intended or not, serve to further an inherent bias against the Southern Italian in Italy where they suffered persecution since Roman times and in the United States where they continue to be discriminated against in media, politics, business, the professions, educational institutions, religious institutions, and social organizations and maligned as ignorant, low-class, stupid, and criminal. The most obvious example of this is the portrayal of Italian Americans in entertainment, such as in shows like HBO's *Sopranos* and MTV's *Jersey Shore* where they are gangsters or "guidos," a slang term for young Italian-American men. According to *Italian America* magazine, Joe Bastianich, son of Italian chef Lidia Bastianich and host of *Master Chef* and *Master Chef Junior*, appeared in an episode of the latter dressed in a jogging suit with an undershirt and gold chain around his neck.[1] He was riding a scooter for persons with disabilities that sported an Italian flag.[2] When asked why he was dressed like that, with a New York accent, he said, "Because this is what all old Italian American men look like."[3] A popular video game about violent criminals, the *Mafia* series, has Italian-American characters.[4] A third installment of the game was released in October 2016.[5] Another example, in the field of academia, is the discrimination Italian Americans were subjected to at the City University of New York, of which I will discuss more in Chapter 10. In history, the contributions of Italian Americans are often forgotten like the case of Luigi Del Bianco, who the National Park Service had refused to acknowledge as the chief carver of Mount Rushmore until May 4, 2016, when it posted on its

Facebook page that Del Bianco was the chief carver, according to the *New York Times*.[6] The article says Del Bianco was responsible for carving the lifelike expressions into the faces, the most distinctive and critical part of the project.[7] Antonio Meucci is still not recognized as the inventor of the telephone despite the fact that the U.S. House of Representatives passed a resolution in 2002 to recognize his achievement.[8] (In Meucci's patent infringement case, described in a pamphlet by Bonnie Heather McCourt for the Garibaldi-Meucci Museum, he used an English translator, and Alexander Graham Bell's lawyer picked apart what the translator was saying in an effort to make Meucci look incompetent. He succeeded, as the judge, William Wallace, ruled in Bell's favor because he thought Meucci wasn't capable of inventing the telephone.)[9] Quite often, when an Italian enters politics, he is alleged to be in the mafia. The *New York Post* reported that in 2015, New York State Supreme Court, Queens County Justice Duane Hart, allegedly asked an Italian plaintiff in a property dispute case if he had mafia ties.[10] The article says the judge also allegedly said the case reminded him of *Goodfellas* and that he and one of the attorneys were the only people involved in the case whose names did not end in a vowel.[11] The Associated Press reported that two Italians who came to the United States legally as children in the 1960s, Paula Milardo and Arnold Giammarco (a U.S. Army veteran) were deported in 2011 and 2012, respectively, over prior convictions, Milardo for felony theft and Giammarco for drug possession and misdemeanor theft.[12] The article says both were deported despite having turned their lives around and paying restitution.[13] A group of Yale University students is currently suing the federal government for failing to process Giammarco's citizenship application, according to the article.[14] i-*Italy NY* says that the Metropolitan Opera House in New York only began adding Italian subtitles to operas in 2012, due to the efforts of the Italian Consul General Natalia Quintavalle and Italian-American groups.[15] As Severgnini writes, Italians are referred to as "Eye-talians" just as they had been 100 years ago.[16] "Nothing has changed," writes Severgnini.[17] He notes that even a president, Jimmy Carter, introduced the late New York governor Mario Cuomo as an "Eye-talian" at a convention.[18] Severgnini writes, "Any illusion we might have that Italy counts for something in this world is quickly crushed. In the twinkling of an Eye (-talian)."[19] Americans of Italian descent continue to struggle to fit into American society.

Those who study Italian history and culture are aware of the Northern and Southern differences and the Northern bias against the South. To fully understand the treatment of Southern Italian cuisine in the culinary world, one must understand the political climate of Italy in the eighteen hundreds mentioned earlier in this book. In addition to studying the climate from which these immigrants come, one must understand the climate in the United States and what the early Italian immigrants faced in their new country. In essence, they left one country that didn't want them and sought refuge in another country that didn't want them.

Italians were often not considered white like other European immigrants or even as Northern Italians. According to Vellon, after 1905, the U.S. Immigration Commission classified Italians as two races: Northern and Southern.[20] They were considered inferior to earlier, Anglo-Saxon immigrants.[21] Laurino cites Edward Alsworth Ross, a sociologist who taught at Cornell and Stanford, who wrote that Northern Italians had "much Northern blood—Celtic, Gothic, Lombard, and German" whereas Southern Italians had "Greek, Saracen, and African blood."[22] Ross said the "frequency of low foreheads, open mouths, weak chins, poor features, skew faces, small or knobby crania, and backless heads" of Neapolitan ship passengers made it impossible for them to "take rational care of themselves."[23] Roberto Paulucci di Calboli, writing about the Italians in England, said, "Even the most superficial observer could not fail to note the prevalence in these wandering peoples of broad cheek bones, over-developed lower jaws, thick hair, abnormally long arms, the surly look in their eyes."[24] He goes on to mention their tattoos and that tattoos are a sign of "primitive nomadic man in the wild."[25] In fact, the English in England were worried about the influx of Italian immigrants there, saying they were "idle," "vicious," "slovenly," and "never improve" because they had "innate" habits that would "work great injury" against the British in time.[26] They were "far less intelligent than the old [immigrants of Anglo-Saxon stock]" reported the U.S. Immigration Commission.[27]

In 1890, Riis wrote *How the Other Half Lives*, enlightening the well-to-do on the situation in the tenements of New York. By today's standards, the book is offensive to many races and cultures. However, at the time, it was the prevailing thought. Riis writes that the Italian follows his "natural bent," "comes in at the bottom . . . and is content to live in a pig-sty."[28] While the book is insulting, it also aided the immigrants by exposing their innumerable hardships, including the *padrone* system. The *padrone* was an agent who "helped" the Italian secure a job in America, but these *padroni* often cheated the immigrants who didn't speak English or have any other assistance or recourse from the Italian or American governments. According to writer Ferdinando Fontana, in the late nineteenth century, Italy was partially to blame for the suffering of the Italian immigrant, but the United States also "let the proprietors of those hovels earn formidable incomes, keeping the factories in the condition of primitive caves."[29] Speranza mentioned Italian farm workers in the United States who "had been bound to a mule and whipped to work like slaves" and who "bore the marks of brutal abuse committed by cruel bosses with the consent of their superiors."[30] While Riis is trying to convey a sociological portrait of the newly arrived Italian immigrant, his prose is one of ignorance and misunderstanding. He describes Italians hanging out in the streets, conducting business in the streets, "lovemaking" in the streets, obvious criticism of the Italian propensity for being outside.[31] The Italians were simply carrying on life as they had lived it at home, going to the markets and strolling in the streets for social purposes, known as *passeggiata*, a custom still carried on in Italy today.

Riis complained that Italians came to New York at a "tremendous rate."[32] Mangione and Morreale note that Southern states like South Carolina, North Carolina, and Alabama enacted legislation that allowed only "white citizens of the United States, and citizens of Ireland, Scotland, Switzerland and France together with all other foreigners of Saxon origin" to live in their states.[33] According to the blog of author Susan Taylor Block, a developer from Wilmington, North Carolina, Hugh MacRae, created immigrant colonies in North Carolina, including immigrants from Italy, and later Romania, Poland, Hungary, Germany, Eastern Europe, and Belgium.[34] J. Vincent Lowery, assistant professor of humanistic studies and history at the University of Wisconsin at Green Bay, notes that the Italian colony was one of the most successful but when speaking at a legislative hearing to promote these immigrant colonies, MacRae didn't mention the Italian colony because he thought it would dissuade support for more immigration.[35] In 1882, Congress enacted the Chinese Exclusion Act to stop what was considered undesirable immigration.[36] Lowery says in later years, quota systems would be used to keep out southern and eastern European immigrants.[37] The concept of selective immigration came into being, meaning the classification of immigrants based on "desirability"—that is, racial and ethnic desirability.[38] MacRae's interest was in agriculture, and he argued that quotas shouldn't apply to farmers who were much needed in the agricultural South, notes Lowery.[39]

The Italian colony was created in 1906 in St. Helena, North Carolina, outside of Wilmington.[40] The Italians were from the Veneto area in northeastern Italy.[41] The Southern United States was particularly prejudiced against Italian immigrants. They didn't know how to racially classify Italians. Vellon notes that Southern newspapers referred to them as "Dagoes" or "white" or "black as the blackest Negro in existence."[42] He says that in 1906, a school district in Mississippi was unsure if Italian children should go to white-only schools or if they fell under Jim Crow laws.[43] When the Italians were lynched in New Orleans, the headline in an 1899 newspaper in New York said, "Italians in Louisiana: Lynch Law Applied to Italians Alone Among White Men Because They Are Classed Somewhere Between White Men and Negroes."[44] That same year, the *Richmond Planet,* an African-American newspaper, listed by race all those lynched.[45] The races listed were "white," "colored," and "Italian."[46] According to Vellon, an Italian man in Mississippi was beaten trying to advocate that Italians were white.[47] Cinotto notes a case in 1922 where an African-American man was acquitted of miscegenation because his partner was Sicilian, i.e., not white to the court.[48] (Interestingly enough, in 1980s North Carolina, this issue still existed, as I was classified as "Other" in the race category on an official school document.) Italian immigrants confounded Southern whites, who didn't know how to classify them racially and who couldn't understand how they could live with, work with, and do business with African Americans.[49] In 1899, an article in the *New York Sun* reported that Italians "seem wholly destitute of that anti-negro prejudice which is one of the distinguishing features of all the white races in the South."[50]

As Ziegelman points out, rather than aid these immigrants or facilitating communication to understand them and their culture, leaders of the day criticized them as being "clannish," which is a symptom itself of any group that is marginalized and discriminated against.[51] The solution the Commission found was to examine ways to reduce immigration and decided that a literacy test was the most efficient, according to Baily.[52] Congress passed the Literacy Bill in 1917 in an effort to keep Southern Italians out of the United States.[53] Prohibition was instituted for many reasons. Anti-immigration was definitely one of the reasons, not only directed at Italians but at other immigrants of the time like Germans.[54] It is probably no coincidence that immigrants created successful Napa Valley wineries forty years before Prohibition.[55] These immigrants were of varied ethnic backgrounds, including the Prussian Charles Krug, the Hungarian Agoston Haraszthy (who also supported Chinese immigration), and the Finnish Captain Gustave Niebaum, all pioneers of the California wine industry.[56] Italians also made their mark, creating successful wineries in the late eighteen hundreds, such as Seghesio, Simi, Sebastiani, Foppiano, Giuseppe Magliavacca, Secondo Guasti of the Italian Vineyard Company, and Andrea Sbarbaro of the Italian Swiss Colony, according to wine writer Dick Rosano.[57] He notes that Prohibition disabled the industry, but once it was repealed, many Italians reopened vineyards.[58] Before Prohibition, states kept enacting laws aimed at restricting Italians' ability to earn a living. Baily says that in 1915, New York made citizenship mandatory to get licenses to be cartmen, junk dealers, and peddlers, jobs held by many Italians.[59] An example of the preference for Anglo-Saxon immigrants was in the National Quota Act of 1924.[60] Baily notes the annual quota for Germans was dropped from 69,330 to 45,700 whereas the quota for Italians was dropped from 40,000 to 3,660.[61]

Italians met with significant prejudice and hardships. Italians were lynched in places like Louisiana, Florida, West Virginia, Colorado, Mississippi, Arkansas, and Illinois as well as murdered in North Carolina.[62] With slavery abolished, some workers lived in a state of peonage, or what is known as debt slavery, where they owed a debt to their bosses and had to work to pay it off, according to PBS.[63] For example, if the boss fronted the money for the train ticket to the jobsite, the workers had to reimburse him. However, in practice, this was very unfair, as the workers had to work long and hard for very little money and sometimes could not pay it back, as PBS notes.[64] In those instances, they would receive very little food.[65] Mangione and Morreale detail one well-known case that occurred in 1906 involving Italian railroad workers in Winston-Salem, North Carolina, who had no money to buy food and were on the brink of starving.[66] They nonverbally communicated this to the company's superintendent who misinterpreted it as a death threat.[67] The superintendent and deputy sheriff organized a group to invade the Italians' tents, note Mangione and Morreale.[68] Two were killed in the fighting, and nine were jailed.[69]

In 1891, eleven Italians were lynched in New Orleans.[70] They had been accused of killing a police detective there and when they were found not guilty, an angry mob lynched them.[71] According to Moses, Theodore Roosevelt thought it was "rather a good thing" and referred to Italians with the term "dago" in a letter to his sister.[72] As mentioned, other lynchings of Italians occurred in Louisiana, West Virginia, Mississippi, Arkansas, Florida, Colorado, and Illinois in the late eighteen hundreds and early nineteen hundreds, amounting to 46 lynchings, according to Vellon.[73] He also reports that in 1901, three Italian workers in Mississippi were shot at their home in the middle of the night for allegedly stealing cattle.[74] (They were also discriminated against in other countries that they immigrated to like France.[75] According to Cresciani, in 1893, 50 Italians were killed by their French mining co-workers.[76])

The most famous case of prejudice against Italians in the United States is the case of Nicola Sacco and Bartolomeo Vanzetti, who were both executed by electrocution in 1927 for an alleged murder and robbery.[77] They maintained their innocence and had many supporters who protested on their behalf, including the writer Dorothy Parker.[78]

In his autobiography, *The Story of a Proletarian Life*, Vanzetti described his working experiences. He had trained for six years in Italy at pastry shops and bakeries.[79] He was a caramel maker, but he did not like it because of the awful working conditions.[80] When he came to the United States, through an agent, he found a job as a dishwasher at an Italian restaurant.[81] He worked at two other restaurants and he was fired from both.[82] Later, he found out that these agents paid the restaurant owners for every worker they hired, so it made sense for a restaurant to fire and rehire new employees.[83] He described his experience at one of the restaurants: "The pantry was horrible. There was not a single window in it. When the electric light for some reason was out it was totally dark, so that one couldn't move without running into things. The vapor of the boiling water where the plates, pans and silver were washed formed great drops of water on the ceiling, took up all the dust and grime there, then fell slowly one by one upon my head as I worked below. During the working hours the heat was terrific. The table leavings amassed in barrels near the pantry gave out nauseating exhalations. The sinks had no direct sewerage connection. Instead the water was permitted to overrun to the floor. In the center of the room there was a drain. Every night the pipe was clogged and the greasy water rose higher and higher and we trudged in the slime."[84] Vanzetti's experience sheds light on the deplorable conditions of restaurant workers in New York at the time. His situation can be likened to the conditions Mexican and Chinese restaurant workers endure today, although there are more safeguards because of regulations and inspections. His last words transcend ethnicity and are as applicable now as they were then: "If it had not been for these thing, I might have live out of my life, talking at street corners to scorning men. I might have die, unmarked, unknown, a failure. Now we are not a failure. This is our career and our triumph. Never in our full life can we hope to do such work for tolerance, for justice, for man's understanding of man as we now do by dying. Our words, our lives, our pains—nothing! The taking of our lives—lives of a good shoemaker and a poor fish peddler—all! That last moment belongs to us—that agony is our triumph!"[85]

With all the discrimination suffered by the early Italian immigrants, it is no surprise their foodways would also be suspect by American society. Bellman notes that when the early immigrants came to America, the American diet was very "meat and potatoes."[86] Milk was touted as a health food. The Italian diet was high in vegetables.[87] According to Mangione and Morreale, Southern Italians relied heavily on lentils, split peas, fava beans, escarole and wild chicory, fruit, and bread.[88] According to Ziegelman, the prevailing thought in America was that early Italian immigrants had low character and weren't as physically adept because they subsisted on "stale bread, macaroni with oil, and . . . a handful of common garden weeds."[89] Riis described their bread as "stale," "disgusting," and "baked not in loaves, but in the shape of big wreaths like exaggerated crullers" with a negative connotation rather than one of an objective observer trying to understand a foreign custom.[90] He relates a story that gave the Elizabeth Street police a "laugh"—a dead goat that had been reported was later missing because an Italian had taken it away.[91] If Riis had bothered to ask the Italian immigrants about it, he might have learned that they had a natural respect for the animals and used all parts of an animal in their cooking so as not to be wasteful (which is what the majority of cultures do when slaughtering animals). He also cites "big, awkward sausages, anything but appetizing" but says he didn't have the courage to ask what they were.[92] Perhaps if he had had the courage, he could have dispelled the vile rumors and prejudices against the Italian immigrants and helped to make their transition to American life an easier one. Instead, his book perpetuated biases already felt by Americans. Laurino notes that social workers of the day thought the Italians had poor nutrition because they were smaller in stature than Anglo Americans.[93] Moses cites

Congressman Melbourne Ford of Michigan, who even used their foodways in his argument to curb immigration. " . . . the food they eat is so meager, scant, unwholesome, and revolting, that it would nauseate and disgust an American workman, and he would find it difficult to sustain life upon it."[94] According to Ziegelman, immigrant organizations created pamphlets "educating" predominantly Jewish and Italian immigrant women on how to healthfully feed their families.[95] She mentions that, at that time, fruits and vegetables were thought to have little nutritional value while milk was touted as a major health food.[96] Immigrant women were taught to make cocoa, white sauce, oatmeal, boiled potatoes, and cooked apples, she notes, instead of their macaroni, olive oil, deli meats, and pickles.[97] It wasn't until the 1950s that the health benefits of the Mediterranean diet, including the diet of Southern Italians, consisting of vegetables, grains, and healthy fats was discovered by Ancel Keys, who had researched the low incidence of heart disease among Italians.

The early Italian immigrants were not happy with the food they found in America. And food was no less important to these immigrants than it had been in Italy. There were Italian men who came to the United States to work in agriculture, mining, and similar trades who lived in boarding houses, as mentioned earlier. But even this group of Italians (who would most likely be termed "peasants") was particular about food. According to Ziegelman, other ethnic groups ate whatever food the employers provided, but the Italians "demanded" food from Italy.[98] She says they mostly ate bread and macaroni, but also ate rice, sausage, corned beef, cod, sardines, beans, peas, lentils, fatback, tomatoes, sugar, and coffee.[99]

Baily notes that both in the United States and in Argentina, Italian immigrants spent more than half of their income on food.[100] Parasecoli says from 1881-1886 in Italy, Italians spent 80 percent of their income on food.[101] According to Baily, in New York City, 65 percent of Italian families lived below the American standard of living, living in overcrowded conditions and going without necessities like clothing, but still spent half of their income on food.[102] These statistics support how important food was and is to the Italian people.

They quickly brought over their own products. Morreale and Carola mention that as early as 1885, these immigrants were growing Italian varieties of vegetables like peppers, zucchini, eggplant, fennel, and broccoli.[103] Peppers and zucchini are native to the Americas, but Italians had varieties of them like the *cucuzza*, a squash originating in Italy. Ziegelman says they imported seeds from Italy.[104] According to the *Woman's Day Encyclopedia of Cookery*, Italians brought broccoli seeds to the United States and grew broccoli in their own gardens "long before the vegetable was known throughout the country as a whole."[105] It wasn't until 1920 that broccoli was grown commercially.[106] Gabaccia says Santo Ortolano, an Italian farmer from California, claimed that he introduced broccoli in the United States in 1902.[107] She notes that he also grew *cucuzza*, the long Italian squash.[108] Now a popular vegetable in high-priced gourmet salads because of its candy cane-striped interior, the Chioggia beet, named after the fishing village near Venice where it was first created, was brought to the United States in the nineteenth century by Italian immigrants, according to David Kamp and Marion Rosenfeld in *The Food Snob's Dictionary: An Essential Lexicon of Gastronomical Knowledge*.[109] Immigrants from Northern and Southern Italy settled near Walla Walla, Washington, and went into the produce business.[110] According to Jens Lund's article, "Walla Walla Sweets: Onions and Ethnic Identity in a Pacific Northwest Italian Community," in *Columbia Magazine*, in 1900, Pete Pieri, from Corsica, first grew the "French onion," and by the 1920s, Italian immigrants John Arbini and Tony Locati were growing what would later be known as the "Walla Walla Sweet" onion.[111] Susan Taylor Block mentions that in the early nineteen hundreds, Calabrian immigrant James Pecora from the St. Helena colony in North Carolina brought a variety of broccoli and introduced other vegetables to the state.[112] According to the *San Francisco Chronicle*, Italian immigrants from Genoa established the Colombo Market selling produce from their farms around San Francisco in 1874.[113] (Unfortunately, the article states that they were known to be an insular community, not even employing Italians from other regions of Italy.)[114] Andrea and Stefano D'Arrigo, founders of the famous produce company Andy Boy, were the first to ship broccoli on a refrigerated railway car across country in 1926, according to Andy Boy's website.[115] Bellman writes " . . . it was the Italians who introduced vegetables, tomatoes, zucchini, peppers and the like to the American palate."[116] Writer and television host Burt Wolf, in the "Coming to America" episode of his *Travels & Traditions* show, credits the Italian immigrants with making fruits and vegetables staples of the American diet.[117] Moses mentions that, in his 1906 memoir, New York City Police Commissioner William McAdoo noted the vegetables he saw in Little Italy near his office.[118] McAdoo writes, "It is one of the singular sights of Little Italy to see an array of most excellent-looking vegetables generally a week or two earlier than they appear in other parts of the city . . . . I could never ascertain where these vegetables came from, but they looked very inviting."[119] According to an article in *L'Italo Americano*, Giuseppe "Joe" Desimone came to the United States from Naples in 1897 with 50 cents, worked on pig farms, and eventually went to Seattle, where he became a successful farmer.[120] He bought Pike Place Market in 1941 and owned it until he died in 1946.[121] His son ran it until 1974 when he sold it to the city.[122]

Modern food writers and chefs, among others, fail to mention this history—that these early immigrants brought foods from Italy to the United States—that they carried on Italian traditions here in the United States—that they introduced Americans to Italian food. These people were the kind that would be classified as "peasant," yet they were exhibiting the same nuances of palate as the wealthier class of nobles back in Northern Italy. (Betty Boyd Caroli notes in *Italian Repatriation from the United States, 1900-1914*, that even repatriating Italians traveling home by ship in third class had to have Italian cheese "of good quality.")[123] Mariani also mentions that a social worker said the Italian immigrants were not "Americanized, still eating Italian food,"[124] which shows the immigrants were eating Italian food in America—not American food. He notes that his own grandmother cooked the "kind of dishes she had eaten back" in Italy.[125] Elizabeth Vallone writes in "Food! Glorious food! Italians are what they eat" in *L'idea* magazine that broccoli and zucchini are "words borrowed from the Italian language."[126] Her use of the word "borrowed" implies that these words are used by English speakers not of Italian descent. However, the reason Americans use the words "broccoli" and "zucchini" are because early Italian immigrants brought these vegetables to the United States and introduced them to Americans. There was no borrowing because these early immigrants were from Italy and spoke Italian. (As mentioned before, zucchini are native to the Americas, but Italians had varieties of them.)

In the United States, as mentioned earlier, Americans of Italian descent planted vegetables and tended to their own gardens. Rooftop gardens are the hipster trend in Brooklyn today, but Italian immigrants started it over 100 years ago. They had gardens in window sills and empty lots—wherever they could grow something, they did. Foraging is another trend. Ziegelman mentions the Italian women who foraged for dandelions in empty lots.[127] While growing up in Brooklyn, Schwartz saw Italians foraging and gardening.[128] DiSpirito mentions his family's garden where they grew "escarole, arugula, romaine, red and white onions, broccoli, carrots, rutabagas, parsley, basil, tomatoes, green bell peppers, Cubanelle peppers, chili peppers, zucchini, eggplants, cucumbers, garlic, cabbages, cauliflower, peas, apricots, grapes, peaches, plums, sour and sweet cherries, and more."[129] His family "rarely" frequented a supermarket.

When Hazan first lived in New York, she shopped at Grand Union supermarket and reminisced about Italy where she shopped from seafood and produce markets.[130] However, they existed in New York. She says they were on Ninth Avenue—not where she lived—and "that involved subways and buses and the carrying of heavy packages up and down many steps and through crowds."[131] (At the time, Italian markets existed in many other places in New York besides Ninth Avenue. I feel that there had to have been markets closer to her.) She did make it out to these stores, but it sounds like the vendors "did not respond with the warmth I had expected when addressed in Italian."[132] She goes on to say, "Not infrequently, they slipped into a dialect corrupted by dialecticized English that was incomprehensible to me. One of the men was so irritated by my failure to understand him that he ended by insulting me: '*Ma vai, non sei mica italiana, tu*' ('Go on, you are not Italian'), he said, offensively using the familiar 'tu' form of address."[133] I have recently bought produce from a Neapolitan man in the United States who used the "tu" form of address when talking to me. I wasn't offended. I was flattered. My perception of her based on her book and her stories like this one is that *she* had an air of snobbery. First, she seems to imply that she is too good? or too delicate? or too above? taking public transportation and carrying groceries home—so much so that she'd rather imply that these markets did not exist rather than shop at them. And second, because the vendors didn't treat her with the respect she felt she deserved, or maybe fawn all over her, their stores weren't worth supporting. I'm skeptical of her because of her tendency to generalize—one unfriendly Italian-American market owner or one Italian American who wasn't familiar with rosemary isn't representative of the whole.

Privately owned specialty markets still exist—although that existence is threatened. Hazan begs the question why good produce isn't available in the United States. "Why aren't we showing the people who raise our produce how to be better farmers?" she asks in her 2008 memoir, *Amarcord*.[134] Agriculture has a long, deep history in the United States, and her comments could be perceived as insulting to farmers nationwide. Produce that is mass-produced and shipped worldwide is often picked before it is ripe so that it will last the long journey. Much produce in American supermarkets is mass-produced and often, unripe and not very flavorful, and much of it is from a country other than the United States. At my grocery store now, vegetables that during my adolescent and young adult years came from the United States are now from other places. The tomatoes, cucumbers, salad greens, and avocados come from Mexico and as far away as Holland. Italy is now participating in this globalized produce market. In recent decades, it has become the largest producer of kiwi fruit, a fruit introduced in Italy only decades ago, according to Parasecoli.[135] And they are no more delicious than any other kiwi fruit that has to be picked before ripe to travel thousands of miles. When produce is grown by small farmers in the United States and sold at local farmers' markets, it is of better quality than the produce grown elsewhere and transported. However, there are many factors that affect how produce is grown, including soil, water quality, etc. Italian produce is prized because of a combination of volcanic soil and sea winds and a number of such factors. Volcanic soil is rich in minerals, producing exceptional fruits and vegetables.[136] Schwartz notes that much of the fertile areas in Italy are around volcanoes like Mount Vesuvius in Naples and Mount Etna in Sicily.[137] I can confirm that Italian produce is exceptional. I have tasted Sorrento lemons that have such a sweet, fresh lemon flavor. I have tasted delicious strawberries and oranges from Sicily. I have tasted wonderfully sweet and flavorful *annurca* apples from the Benevento area of Italy. And the tomatoes grown in Italy have an amazing flavor and a beautifully rich red color. The oregano that grows from the ancient hills of Mount Taburno is like no other I've ever tasted. While Italy produces exceptional fruits and vegetables, the United States has the potential to as well.

Today, with apples being engineered to shine and grapes being engineered to be sweeter, there is much technological interference in the natural growth of food. It sounds like Hazan's argument should be more anti-globalization than an inherent failing in American farmers' ability to grow produce. I have had amazingly delicious oranges, strawberries, and grapefruits grown locally in Florida and blueberries, peaches, and tomatoes from New Jersey. In fact, the best orange I ever tasted was from a tree in my friend's backyard in Orlando, Florida. Grocery store produce does not compare. Wherever food is grown holistically on a local level in the right conditions, it is delicious. A good example of this globalization is that of lentils. In the United States, most grocery stores carry green lentils. However, my mother remembers lentils being brown and having to be heavily rinsed. Schwartz mentions Southern Italian lentil dishes in his book and they call for European brown lentils.[138] In the United States, consumers used to have more variety before globalization decided to allow only the varieties that are the easiest and cheapest to produce. In addition, the population of the United States is over 325 million;[139] the population of Italy is almost 61 million.[140] The United States has five times as many people to feed, and it exports a lot of what it grows.

Hazan does bring up a good point about vegetables—that they require very simple preparations to taste good and that Italians eat them because they are tasty.[141] What might have shocked her is that Americans of Italian descent already know this and have been growing their own vegetables for generations and have been cooking and seasoning vegetables in the way they were taught by their grandparents since the great migration. I am partly alluding to her shock at the Italian American who didn't know the herb rosemary but also to her conclusion that all Americans are satisfied and happy with the packaged and tasteless produce at the grocery store.

Italian immigrants didn't only plant their own vegetables and fruits. According to Parasecoli, they also raised pigs and chickens in their basements, much like they did in Italy.[142] Gabaccia says in New York, they also raised goats in their tenement kitchens and basements.[143] In fact, there are many sources that mention Italians living with animals, especially when writing about the Sassi caves in Matera, Basilicata, as if this were a horrid example of abject poverty. However, it was perfectly natural as a part of the lifestyle to live around animals. The Italians had a healthy respect for animals, as many cultures do, and raised the animals that would then be used for slaughter to feed the family. In fact, Cinotto mentions an immigrant couple who reported that the thing they missed most about Italy was living with their animals.[144]

The early Italian immigrants suffered a profound prejudice and discrimination that transcends generations, a prejudice their descendants contend with still. And it is so deep that it continues to pervade all aspects of their existence—including the food they eat.

C H A P T E R 5: Spaghetti and Meatballs

S
o today, these myths about Southern Italian cuisine get disseminated by food writers of native Italian and non-Italian descent and serve only to discredit the Southern Italian-American immigrant. Robert Sietsema, *Eater* food writer and critic, writes in an article on hero sandwiches that Italian-American bakeries started to make baguettes when they became fashionable in the 1920s, added cold cuts, and created something that did not exist previously in Italy.[1] I disagree. Bread baking is a long-time Italian tradition—since pre-Roman times—and indeed even the cookbook author Pellegrino Artusi, who is considered the foremost authority on Italian cuisine, speaks of long loaves.[2] Cinotto says that Italian bread was baked into a "great variety of traditional shapes."[3] In *The Italian Baker*, Carol Field mentions Como bread of the past, or *pane di Como antico*, now known as *pane francese*, or French bread, in Italy, that is shaped like a "fat cylinder."[4] She also mentions that *calzoni* means "pant legs" in Italian and were not the filled pockets we know today but were long and narrow breads encasing salami and sausage.[5] The pinnacle of bread baking, according to Field, was during the reign of Augustus with 329 bakeries in Rome where they made breads in various shapes, including "the long, thin sandwich bread molds that are still in use today."[6] Travel and food writers Jane and Michael Stern note that as early as 1902, Italian immigrant Giovanni Amato made sandwiches for dockworkers in Portland, Maine, using long loaves of bread.[7]

The shape of bread aside, one of the biggest controversies, if not the biggest, of the Italian versus American food debate is spaghetti and meatballs.

"Oh God!" exclaims Monica Cesarato, sighing, in an article entitled "10 'Italian' Dishes That Don't Exist in Italy," in the *Local*. "Well, this is definitely not Italian."[8]

According to an article by Judy Buchenot in the *Aurora-Beacon News*, Gaetano DiBenedetto, an Italian chef from Sicily who owns an Italian restaurant in Illinois, says, "We don't serve spaghetti and meatballs because it is not Italian."[9] The article says DiBenedetto's restaurant was recognized by the Italian government as Ospitalità Italiana, an authentic Italian restaurant.[10] There are only six hundred restaurants with this designation.[11]

An article by Eva Sandoval in *Fodor's Travel* says that chefs in Italy "give credit [for spaghetti and meatballs] to Disney's 'Lady and the Tramp' or Middle American 'Little Italies' for the inspiration."[12]

Shaylyn Esposito writes in the *Smithsonian Magazine* that "large meatballs, doused in marinara over spaghetti are 100 percent American."[13]

Spaghetti with meatballs is Italian-American "mythology," according to an article by Alessia Gargiulo in *Swide*, the Dolce & Gabbana luxury magazine. She writes, "Although we were moved by the kissing scene in **Lady and the Tramp** and we found **Catherine Scorsese** cooking spaghetti with meatballs for her son Martin adorable, they don't exist in Italy."[14]

Oh, yes, meatballs existed—even in recipe books, as Artusi wrote about them in his cookbook. But Artusi was a literate Northern Italian who didn't venture into the wilds of Italy's toe, instep, and heel. In his 2009 book, *The Southern Italian Table*, Schwartz says "it's a fallacy that Italians never serve meatballs with pasta."[15] He notes that in Puglia, Basilicata, and Calabria, tiny meatballs are served with pasta and sauce,[16] which is what he said in his 2004 *New York City Food* book that only very small meatballs are served with pasta and large ones, "after a pasta course"[17] but updates his 1998 *Naples at Table* where meatballs "are never put on the same plate as spaghetti," noting they are in Puglia.[18] According to Capatti and Montanari, in 1570, Bartolomeo Scappi references them in his cookbook.[19] Artusi reprints a 1694 recipe for tripe meatballs served with tomato sauce and Parmesan cheese.[20] Lidia Bastianich ate meatballs, but they were more like meat patties and weren't served with tomato sauce and pasta.[21] The fact that her family made them into patties and served them without tomato sauce sounds like a regional difference. In many countries on the Balkan peninsula, ground meatballs and patties called kofta are served in a variety of ways, including without tomato sauce. In fact, meatballs are a popular and ancient food, first appearing in the Punjab region of Northern India around four thousand years ago, according to Vera Abitbol in the *196 Flavors* blog.[22] They are very prevalent in European, Middle Eastern, North African, and Asian cuisine, with numerous cultures having their own variation of them (Romanian *chiftele*, Pakistani *kofta*, Swedish meatballs come to mind). Artusi says it would be "pretentious" of him to instruct his readers on how to make meatballs; he jokingly claims the "jackass" taught humans how to make them.[23] Italian food writers and chefs say that the Southern Italians didn't have a diet high in meat because they couldn't afford it, so a gravy made with meat or spaghetti with meatballs would be implausible. Sietsema says the meatball was "born" because of the plethora of ground beef in the United States and that early Italian immigrants didn't have access to ingredients from Italy.[24] Italian meatballs, however, are often made with a mix of beef, pork, and veal. Massimo Montanari, professor of medieval history and the history of food at the University of Bologna, says in *Italian Identity in the Kitchen, or Food and the Nation* that "southern peasants" in America "invented" spaghetti and meatballs, the "prototypical Italo-American dish."[25]

In Naples, there is a famous character called Pulcinella, or Punchinella, which has older origins but was made famous in the *commedia dell'arte* theatrical tradition by actor and playwright Silvio Fiorillo. He is a comic, mischievous character. According to Gentilcore, in 1632, Fiorillo wrote a play in which Pulcinella calls the Spaniards in Naples the "enemy of macaroni,"[26] meaning they are the enemy of Naples. In a work written in 1774 or 1775 by Francesco Cerlone, Pulcinella says, "I dream (the power of love!) I dream of a big plate of maccheroni with meatballs on top. I stretch my hand, I grab the maccheroni and meatballs, I adjust and wrap them, I am about to put them in my mouth and . . . I wake up with my heart pounding and I start crying like a baby" [my translation].[27] If one believes that art imitates life, the Neapolitans were eating meatballs with spaghetti/macaroni/pasta at least as early as 1774.

There is a painting that I saw in the North Carolina Museum of Art's permanent collection that dates from 1725 to 1730 by Alessandro Magnasco entitled *The Supper of Pulcinella and Colombina*, depicting the pair engaging in their typical theatrical behaviors backstage.[28] The painting utilizes various shades of brown, gray, and cream to impart detail.[29] Interestingly, Pulcinella is eating from a plate of spaghetti that arguably has one to three distinct round shapes atop it that could possibly be meatballs, as the round shapes are delineated with different coloring.

Food writers consistently say that the peasant diet was one of grains and vegetables, with only occasional meat—on holidays. Under Napoleon, from 1807 to 1811, the French researched local economic and social conditions and had locals in the field like doctors and lawyers write reports, the *Statistica murattiana*, according to Gentilcore.[30] He notes they asked about eating habits and found that the poor mostly subsisted on vegetables.[31] With advancements in archaeological methods in recent years, according to Parasecoli, scholars can now use archaeological evidence to add to the record about the diet of peasants and the lower class, confirming what scholars already knew that peasants ate grains, vegetables, and greens; raised pork and made cured and dried meats; and made dairy products from goats and sheep and ate their meat.[32] What is surprising to the record is that peasants not only used cow's milk for cheese, they also ate beef—and not only the old, tough meat, notes Parasecoli, because, for a time during the Middle Ages, he adds, peasants were allowed to hunt and fish on their landlord's property.[33] According to Gentilcore, in the mid- to late sixteen hundreds, John Ray, a gardener, theologian, and naturalist wrote that tomatoes in Italy were prepared with marrows, pepper, salt, and oil.[34] Astarita mentions Latini, in *The Modern Steward*, written between 1692 and 1694, who says that ox and cow are "very nutritious and benefits especially men who perform strenuous work all the time, as it produces abundance of blood."[35] One can infer here that the men performing strenuous work are of the working class, not nobles. Recall Goethe's experience in Naples in 1786–1787, cited by Parasecoli, where the average citizens of Naples partook in the eating of cows and veal.[36] In 1789, naturalist Ulysses mentions that the forests of Naples were home to cattle,[37] that cattle was the main object for sale at a market in the Abruzzo region,[38] that cattle was a staple in Basilicata[39] and horses and cattle were part of a fair in Salerno.[40] The Neapolitan General Pietro Colletta mentioned the fact that Basilicata "abounds in . . . cattle" in his preeminent history of the Kingdom of Naples.[41]

Zanini De Vita mentions Emilio Sereni, an Italian Jew who was an anti-Fascist member of the Italian Communist Party, who wrote on political and agricultural issues in Italy during the years preceding and during World War II.[42] She cites his writing about the negative impact Spanish rule had on the Neapolitan diet, saying that the Neapolitans had been "mangiafoglia" or "leaf eaters" and became "mangiamaccheroni" or pasta eaters "with these carbohydrates their only resource."[43] When he says mangiafoglia he says "mangiafoglia with a fine fat broth made with plenty of meat."[44] Perhaps this broth was the predecessor of the meat sauce or gravy made by the Southern Italians, and once they were released from an economically repressive regime, they could return to eating meat in abundance. Southern Italy was under Spanish rule from 1559-1713, 150 years; Naples, from 1503.[45] Claudia Roden notes in *The Food of Spain* that the first cookbook to mention tomatoes was *Lo Scalco alla Moderna* by Antonio Latini, published in Naples in 1692.[46] The book includes only a few tomato recipes, all with "alla spagnola" in the name, suggesting that the Spanish used tomatoes in cooking and introduced it to the Neapolitans.[47] Gentilcore notes that Latini has a recipe for *salsa di pomodoro alla spagnola* which is a tomato sauce.[48] The Spanish have a dish of *albondigas* (meatballs) in tomato sauce, which, according to Roden, is Catalonian.[49] (In Brazil, according to the *Flavors of Brazil* blog, these are called *almôndegas ao molho de tomate*.[50] Brazil has many European culinary influences, so I'm not sure if the Italians or the Portuguese or another group brought these there. There are a large number of Campanian immigrants to Brazil.[51] The *Flavors of Brazil* blog says it is an Italian dish.[52]) According to Astarita, by this time,

Southern Italy had a long history of a relationship with Catalan cuisine.[53] Since the Neapolitans ate macaroni in abundance, maybe they married pasta with *albondigas* and other meats to create the Neapolitan meat sauce. Gentilcore mentions Vincenzo Corrado, a monk and cook, who included recipes for tomato sauce in his 1773 cookbook, including a tomato sauce that can be used over meat like mutton.[54] Luigi Bicchierai was a Tuscan innkeeper in the early nineteenth century who learned how to cook from Neapolitan friars at a local monastery, according to Gentilcore.[55] He adds that Bicchierai had written a recipe for a meat sauce that includes tomatoes and meatballs.[56]

There is evidence of meatballs in tomato sauce in Neapolitan cuisine. In Arturo Iengo's *Cucina Napoletana*, written in association with I.R.V.A.T., the Institute for the Protection and Promotion of Regional Products, Neapolitan food was "greatly" influenced by Catholic convents and monasteries.[57] They had gardens and sold produce as well as created recipes that have become the fabric of local cuisine.[58] Meatballs in tomato sauce, or *polpette alla Napoletana*, is a recipe that originates from the convents, according to Iengo.[59] In the book, the meatballs include ingredients like pine nuts and raisins,[60] ingredients that Americans of Italian descent often put in their meatballs but are never found in commercial meatballs.

Tomato sauce, as most people know, is a Southern Italian tradition. The tomato, from North America and brought to Italy from Spain after Columbus's voyage to the Americas, is ubiquitous in Southern Italian cooking. Tomatoes had a slow history in Europe. Initially, as Roden says, they were considered poisonous.[61] She writes that in the sixteenth century, they were grown in Spain and only gained more widespread use about 200 years later.[62] According to Astarita, Latini had a recipe for "Spanish-style tomato sauce" made with roasted tomatoes, chopped onions, chili, herbs, salt, oil, and vinegar to be used "over boiled meat and other dishes."[63] Gentilcore notes that in the mid-eighteen hundreds, taverns in Naples served pasta with a meat or tomato sauce, with grated cheese on top.[64] An anonymous text from 1817 Naples, notes Astarita, included a recipe for *maccheroni* with cheese and a tomato sauce in the "Neapolitan style" that though having tomatoes, was more of a rich meat sauce.[65] Artusi did write about this Neapolitan meat sauce, *maccheroni alla Napoletana*, and notes that it is cooked with tomato sauce, the sauce is used for the macaroni and the macaroni is served with cheese, "as is done in Naples"[66]—just how Americans of Italian descent serve it today. The meat is served on the side. He even describes *braciole*, the beef roll-up wrapped in string that is synonymous with Italian-American cuisine.[67] Ironically, he says, "People who like their pasta swimming in sauce will find this dish especially appealing."[68] But I thought only modern Italian Americans serve pasta with a lot of sauce—well, that's what the modern food media would have us believe. Iengo also mentions classic slow-cooked meat and tomato sauce, or *ragù di carne*.[69] He describes it as a nineteenth-century dish made for nobles because of its high meat content.[70] These recipes are exactly how Americans of Italian descent make a sauce or "gravy," serving the sauce with the macaroni (cheese on top) and the meat on a platter to be eaten after the macaroni. Although they may add different meats like neck bones, pork, beef, meatballs, or sausage. And in fact, Southern Italian cooking became synonymous with this "red sauce," which is nowadays used in a derogatory manner to describe cuisine of traditional Italian-American restaurants. But Italian-American immigrants who didn't speak English cooked this tomato sauce or "gravy," especially on Sundays. The sauce included various meats, one of which was meatballs, and this was done by people who had little interaction with American people and lived in Italian-only neighborhoods. Marie Vitarelli, whose parents came to America from Calabria, recalls her mother's Sunday gravy with meatballs (among other meats) in an oral history videotaped by her granddaughter and played on YouTube.[71] In *The Brooklyn Cookbook*, written by Lyn Stallworth and Rod Kennedy, Jr., Carol Alvino tells the story of her Sicilian grandmother, who arrived in the United States in 1903 and taught her and her mother how to cook spaghetti and meatballs.[72] Two commenters following the online version of the *Smithsonian Magazine* article referenced earlier in this chapter write that their grandparents emigrated from the Molise region of Italy in 1910 and 1920 and also made spaghetti and meatballs, eggplant parmesan, and lasagna.[73] Schwartz recalls childhood neighbors who, fresh off the boat from Naples, made spaghetti and meatballs.[74] Chef Rocco DiSpirito writes, "The pasta sauce was ragù or 'gravy'—marinara sauce in which several types of meat had been braised all day. We ate the meat separately, a tradition from Southern Italy. Over time, in Italian-American restaurants, that gave way to pasta as a side order with meat."[75] My grandparents and great-grandparents were from towns and villages in Campania and made meatballs (along with other meats) in a tomato gravy. My great-grandparents, specifically, never learned English, did not intermingle much with non-Italians once in the United States, and rarely left their Italian neighborhood. And in fact, Americans of Italian descent eat courses. Antipasto is the first course. The primo, or first course, is the pasta. The secondo, or second course, is the plate of meat that had cooked in the tomato gravy. During this meal, most people do not progress to the meat course because they are full from pasta. But some do, and also a salad is served after as well. Mariani writes, "Pasta *alla marinara*, which might be combined with golfball [sic] -size meatballs, was a staple of those southern Italian immigrants who had lived along the coast in Italy."[76] Americans of Italian descent also serve golf-ball-size meatballs in their homes, unlike the "giant" meatballs food writers speak of in American restaurants serving Italian food. Chef DiSpirito's mother emigrated from Naples and could not write English or Italian.[77] However, she cooked. Her giant meatballs became famous—as a signature item that helped to promote her son's restaurant.

Other writers speak of tiny meatballs, or *polpettine*, that are found in Italy. I've read they are served in a brodo, or broth.[78] My grandmother made soup with tiny meatballs, so Americans of Italian descent do not traditionally make gargantuan-size meatballs. Ziegelman writes that meatballs and the Neapolitan ragù were not part of the peasant diet but were part of the diet of the Italian middle and upper classes, many of which, as has been mentioned previously, immigrated to the United States in great numbers.[79]

In the introduction to Ada Boni's *Talisman Italian Cook Book*, Mario A. Pei writes that meat is used for two purposes, one as a broth for soup and "the meat sauce for macaroni."[80] He goes on to say that the "ragout beef of Puglia, whose by-product supplies a rich meat sauce for macaroni, is a rewarding experience in taste. Meatballs and meat loaves (polpette and polpettoni) are also widely used," and they are made from a mix of beef and pork.[81] Chef and cookbook author Gennaro Contaldo, born in 1949 near Salerno and raised there, writes about his family eating the "traditional beef ragù and homemade pasta" for Christmas lunch, and he also shared a memory with Jamie Oliver of his father teaching him how to make spaghetti and meatballs.[82] My relatives living in Italy today eat meatballs for Christmas.

Meatballs were not, in fact, "invented" in America, but existed throughout Europe and the Middle East and were a novelty to the non-Italian American because of their round shape. Restaurateurs either simplified the Neapolitan meat sauce with macaroni for Americans of non-Italian descent in American restaurants, serving spaghetti with only meatballs, or non-Italian Americans focused on the meatballs because they were a novelty. Mariani cites William Grimes in *Appetite City*, who wrote that in the 1850s, Caffè Moretti in New York served "huge bowls of boiled spaghetti in 'beef gravy' with grated Parmesan cheese," a dish that Americans were not familiar with and did not know how to eat.[83] Mariani points out that it was served with beef gravy, not tomato sauce. But I think it still could have been tomato sauce/gravy. The term "beef gravy" is in quotation marks in the original quote, which could mean that it was a beef gravy, but not a traditional beef gravy—maybe it was made from tomato sauce and just called "gravy" because that term would be in the frame of reference of the Anglo-American culture of the time—a culture that didn't identify with a tomato-based gravy for their beef and meat. The dish eventually caught on, and as early as 1908, a recipe for "Spaghetti and Meat Balls" appeared in the *Chicago Tribune*, according to Ziegelman.[84] Therefore, this dish is not unknown in Italy as the food literati would have one believe but was a dish eaten in Italy and subsequently brought to America by the early Italian immigrants.

In his Scandinavian cooking show, contemporary Norwegian chef Andreas Viestad mentions people telling him he must not like eating all that potato sausage in Norway.[85] He didn't know what they were talking about because he hadn't had potato sausage in Norway.[86] After researching, he found that potato sausage was a food that was prevalent in Norway in the nineteenth century and subsequently brought to America by Norwegian immigrants.[87] This saga of potato sausage mimics that of spaghetti and meatballs, except that spaghetti with meatballs is still eaten in Southern Italy.

Boni includes two recipes for spaghetti and meatballs.[88] The forward in her book says that a few recipes are from "Italo-American" restaurants, but the collection itself is described as "an Italian, not an Italo-American cookbook."[89]

Cookbook author Maria Luisa Taglienti hails from a noble family from Campania.[90] Born and raised in Rome,[91] she set out to create a cookbook for the American homemaker,[92] and indeed, created one of the most inclusive and respectful Italian cookbooks. For her cookbook, *The Italian Cookbook*, she took a three-month trip to Italy in 1952 to research Italian food, including out-of-print cookbooks, old manuscripts, and top restaurants.[93] She referred to the cuisine and dishes in her cookbook as Italian, saying, "This is a collection of recipes from *all* sections of Italy."[94] Her book includes a recipe for spaghetti and meatballs with a tomato sauce (although the balls are referred to as "patties.")[95] In addition, her cookbook of Italian cuisine includes dishes often labeled as "Italian-American" like manicotti, cannelloni, lasagna, spaghetti carbonara, veal marsala, veal pizzaiola, and eggplant parmigiana. Many of her other recipes are recognizable to Americans of Italian descent as ones they cook at home. The only distinction Taglienti's cookbook makes is that some of the recipes "are much more common over here than in Italy."[96]

By the 1930s, spaghetti was a part of American culture, and American restaurants served their own versions of it. Examples are the grilled steak spaghetti served at Chili Bowl in Los Angeles in 1934, depicted in *Menu Design in America*.[97] Or the Mexican spaghetti or hamburger steak with chili beans, spaghetti, and French fried potatoes served at El Coyote Spanish Café in Los Angeles in 1935.[98] Or the spaghetti with chili at Whitney Bros. Pie Shop in San Francisco in 1933.[99] Interestingly enough, in 1934, chicken *tagliarini* appeared on the menu of Topsy's Roost in San Francisco.[100] *Tagliarini*, or *tajarin* in dialect, is a traditional pasta from the Piedmont region of Italy. The Italian immigrants to San Francisco were predominantly from the Piedmont and Liguria regions.

The evidence clearly shows that spaghetti and meatballs is Italian. Native Italians and Italian expats in America may not be aware of the history of spaghetti and meatballs because it comes from Southern Italy. In addition, Italy and Italian food businesses are trying to market "Made in Italy" products in the United States and want to rebrand Italian food in America to include those products. But Italy didn't make Italian food popular—Southern Italian immigrants to the United States did. And their cuisine is arguably the most popular food in the country and the world.

CHAPTER 6: Italian Food in America

If you ask the average family what they want for dinner, they will probably say pizza. If they are going out to eat, it will probably be to a pizzeria or Italian restaurant for classic Southern Italian food. Why are the dishes of Southern Italian immigrants so popular? The answer is very simple. They taste good. But not only do they taste good, they are easy to prepare. Severgnini calls the cooking of the early immigrants "a stroke of genius."[1] He notes that this was home cooking and that the home had been a "laboratory" for centuries.[2] He says this cooking was "honest, practical, and working-class."[3] Speaking of Americans of Italian descent and native Italians, he, unlike many other native Italians and expats, uses the all-inclusive word "Italian" to describe both groups: "In fact, it was further proof that we Italians are good when we don't try to complicate things."[4] Unfortunately, he still uses the word "working-class" to describe Southern Italian cuisine, a phrase that conjures the old definition of peasant. But at least his words are a step in the right direction. His statements acknowledge that the Italians who settled in the United States 100 years ago made the foods they had made in their native Italy.

And they made them well. We've already discussed the numerous food businesses Italians created across the country. Their impact was so great that their cuisine eventually became one of the most popular—if not the most popular. Some dishes garnered more attention than others like spaghetti and meatballs and pizza and were served regularly at restaurants. Less popular dishes or dishes that had religious symbolism were made at home or for celebrations or holy days. Maybe some other dishes fell out of fashion for unknown reasons. Or maybe they just didn't taste as good as the classics like spaghetti and meatballs, pizza, eggplant parmesan, etc.

If we liken Italian food to American food, we can better understand the evolution. For example, a menu in the 1880s might include turtle soup or boiled mutton—a far cry from a menu now—but it might also include roast beef and mashed potatoes, foods still enjoyed at home or in restaurants. (One can still find mutton on the menu at Keens Steakhouse in New York City.) Food in every part of the world evolves as time goes on due to advancements in food technology and science, environmental changes and concerns, political and legal influences, and changing demographics and immigration influences. The late nineteenth century and early twentieth century was a time of rapid technological advancement. These advancements carried over to the kitchen. Refrigeration brought about a food revolution.[5] This had a huge impact on food production and storage and gave birth to the TV dinner, changing the way everyone ate worldwide. Food traveled and was available out of season.[6] We already discussed political and legal influences, such as import taxes and boycotting products during wartime. We only briefly touched on environmental impact at this time with such things as deforestation in Southern Italy leading to a malaria problem and eventually, the dislocation of a whole people. An example of environmental impact is "soil fatigue," the condition where the soil has been used so much that it lacks the nutrients needed for plants to grow, according to an article by L. Volosciuc and V. Josu in *Soil as World Heritage*.[7] According to *We the Italians*, soil fatigue was one of the reasons the *carota novella di Ispica* PGI, a type of new carrot, began being cultivated in Italy in the 1950s because it matures early and has crunch and flavor.[8] Italians in Italy today may be used to making dishes with this carrot, but many Americans of Italian descent might not know it because the carrot didn't exist when their ancestors left Italy and the United States had its own varieties of carrots in the twentieth century. Of course, each new addition of immigrants to the United States changed the foodways. We've already seen the impact Italian immigrants had on the food industry in the United States after they immigrated. So the foodways of both Italy and the United States were influenced by these factors.

In addition, food in different parts of the United States is different. One will find the menu of a five-star New York restaurant like Per Se or Daniel is very different from the menu of a country restaurant in one of the Southern states. In fact, it would be correct to say that while the food media (books, magazines, television) focus on trends, the restaurants and the home cooks in the "heartland" of America are cooking, eating, and serving food from recipes that are traditional and handed down. One could argue that chicken and pastry is a much more American dish than any served in a five-star New York City restaurant today. Just because a dish doesn't appear on a menu in California or New York doesn't mean it wasn't eaten in Nebraska or

North Carolina. The same can be said for Italy. Just because a dish doesn't appear on a menu in Florence doesn't mean it wasn't eaten in Potenza. Therefore, just because recipes do not appear in Italian cookbooks published and written in prior centuries or on menus doesn't mean these recipes didn't exist. Many Southern Italians were illiterate and beyond marginalized, so why would any Northern aristocrat want to eat the food they cooked? This question is fundamental and it is the reason that food of the Southern Italian wasn't written down until modern times.

When we look at Italian culinary history, the first cookbooks were usually written by household stewards (kitchen managers) or the "lady of the house" of the wealthier upper class, note Capatti and Montanari.[9] Because they were made for a wealthier audience, these books would not reflect the cuisine, taste, or available products of the peasant class. In addition, these books were often very regional, so they would reflect the cuisine only of the area in which they were written. And some were written in Naples, reflecting Southern Italian cuisine, though not peasant cuisine. In the Middle Ages, Montanari notes, vegetables, garlic, and onions were considered peasant food, but as time went by, in the Renaissance, these foods appear in recipes of the upper classes, so borrowing from peasant cuisine had to have taken place.[10] Montanari points out, "'popular' recipes did not enter elite cuisine in their original form" because the wealthy had to elevate dishes to what was appropriate for their class.[11] He writes that Renaissance Italian cookbooks, "and the alimentary models proposed by them, express a broad social culture" because the wealthy "encountered" peasants in everyday life and as household servants.[12] He thinks that one can rely on these cookbooks to make a composite of Italian cuisine, "because the written tradition, the expression of an elite cuisine, over the centuries represented and transmitted a culture in which everyone could recognize fragments of his own identity."[13] However, *does* this mean that everyone on the Italian peninsula and surrounding islands could recognize parts of his or her own culture in these books? And is a "fragment" of the middle class or peasant class enough to consider them inclusive of the whole of Italy or Italian cuisine—are a few fragments here and there enough to tell the story of the tenant farmer or the innkeeper?

As Parasecoli notes, in 1634, Giovan Battista Crisci wrote about the cuisine of Southern Italian villages and rural areas.[14] However, these areas are "dominated by landowners and nobles," so it's hard to know if he was writing about cuisine of the lower classes or of the landowning nobles of the South.[15]

Later, in 1891, Artusi published *La scienza in cucina e l'arte di mangiare bene* (*Science in the Kitchen and the Art of Eating Well*). Artusi is recognized as the first person to compile a cookbook of regional Italian cuisine and is therefore the authority on it. Those who wish to create an argument whether or not something is considered Italian food often cite Artusi's book. However, the farthest South he goes is Naples (most likely not leaving the city's borders to discover the cuisine of the areas of the mountainous interior and those rural areas that make up most of Campania, for example), completely bypassing Basilicata, Puglia, and Calabria and including only three Sicilian recipes, according to Capatti and Montanari.[16] They ask, and so do I, how can this book be an authority on Italian cuisine when it leaves out almost half of the country's cuisine?

The answer is simple: it is not. The inherent bias of Northern Italy (i.e., wealthy Italy) against Southern Italy (i.e., its poor relation) allows this fallacy to perpetuate, and American chefs/restaurateurs/those in the food industry support the perpetuation of this bias by consistently and constantly discrediting the cuisine of the Southern Italian-American immigrant. How many times have you heard the word "red sauce" or saw it in a review? The very term connotes other terms—dago, spaghetti bender, greasy eye-talian, wop. Red sauce=Southern Italian immigrant. The celebrated Italian restaurants today serve what has become classified as "Northern" Italian cuisine or the new trend of "regional" Italian cuisine, which often translates to Northern Italian cuisine, i.e., no "red sauce." Indeed, the idea of Northern cuisine in American restaurants is a fallacy. Modern Italian cuisine, when served in the United States, is lumped under the category of "Northern" in addition to cuisine that is traditionally Northern Italian, but it is much more a reflection of *cucina moderna* than regional cuisine.

Again, the early Italian immigrants came to the United States, many enduring hardships and suffering, many unable to read and write in Italian, let alone English, the language of their new country. Their children learned English and the later generations wrote these recipes down. With the advent of the Internet and the easy and instant connection people have with each other, the discussion of Italian-American foodways has exploded. Many writers, some who are native Italians, some Italian Americans, and others of non-Italian descent write articles discrediting the cuisine of Italian Americans as being some kind of fantasy creation that Italian Americans dreamed up out of thin air to claim some kind of identifying factor with the homeland. A humongous billboard sponsored by the Italian Trade Agency (ITA) in Times Square depicts Italian cheeses, dried meats and pasta, tomato sauce, olive oil, and rice with the headline: "Buy Authentic Italian," as if the Italian food Americans have been eating isn't authentic Italian. The ITA is a trade organization sponsored by the Italian government to help Italian companies do business worldwide.

Born and raised in Tuscany, Claudia Baroncelli, editor at *Swide*, writes in "Feast of the Seven Fishes: the Italian American tradition not all Italians know," that the Feast of the Seven Fishes is an "ancient" yet "Italian-American" celebration "confined to the States."[17] Well, it can only be one or the other—is it ancient or is it Italian American? Domenick Rafter writes in the *Queens Tribune* that it is "more of an Italian-American tradition than an

Italian one."[18] However, he adds that it was celebrated in Puglia, Calabria, and Campania.[19] Indeed, some Americans of Italian descent have never heard of it, just like Baroncelli mentions Italians never hearing of it, even though Americans of Italian descent eat fish on Christmas Eve. Most likely, the origin of the seven fishes is a regional one and that is why not all Americans of Italian descent know the tradition by name or the requirement of seven fishes. According to the *Oxford Companion to Italian Food*, there are seven or nine fishes, and the tradition is celebrated in Puglia and Abruzzo.[20] Right there, we have four regions in Southern Italy that celebrate it. It stands to reason that the tradition is of Southern Italian origin and one celebrated by Americans of Italian descent because their ancestors come from Southern Italy. While there are regional differences to the tradition, it is still a tradition of Southern Italy. My cousins in present-day Southern Italy eat fish-only dishes on Christmas Eve.

In the United States, holidays are often the time when Americans of Italian descent make traditional dishes. At Christmastime, they make cookies like *strufoli/struffoli* (also known as *pignolata*) and fried bows. *Struffoli* are a Neapolitan treat—fried dough balls in honey syrup decorated with pine nuts, sprinkles, or dried fruits. Bastianich says of *struffoli*, " . . . here is one dish that made it intact from the old country to the new."[21] Bows are another fried dough treat that cross many cultures. In Italy, they are made in many regions and have many names like *chiacchiere, cenci, cartellate, galani, bugie, frappe, donzelli, donzelline, crostoli, farfellate* or "wandi," which I think is *guanti* or "gloves" in Italian. It may be "*vanti*" because in Neapolitan dialect, "v" is pronounced like "w" and "t" sounds a bit like "d." *Vanti* are boasts and since these cookies are also called "*bugie*," or "lies," they could be called boasts as well. They can be sprinkled with powdered sugar or honey syrup. In Puglia, there's a variation called *cartellate* in a circular shape drizzled with a honey syrup or *vincotto* (cooked wine syrup). *Anginetti* cookies, also known as knot cookies, are a popular Italian cookie. Anise cookies are made with anise flavor. Similar in taste to licorice, anise is a flavor that appears often in Italian foods. *Mostaccioli* are diamond-shaped Neapolitan chocolate spice cookies. Tri-colored rainbow cookies are a favorite as well. Sesame cookies are finger-shaped cookies coated with sesame seeds. *Cucidati/cuccidati* are fig cookies from Sicily. These cookies, when made by hand, are labor intensive. Pizzelles are originally from the Abruzzo region of Italy and most likely predate the Roman Empire. Years ago, families had irons to create this waffled cookie, and the iron included a family crest or design. *Pignoli* cookies are popular Italian cookies made with pine nuts. Many of these cookies like *struffoli*, bows, sesame cookies, and pizzelles have their origins in ancient times but are still prepared by Americans of Italian descent. During the Christmas season, Italian families also roast chestnuts and snack on nuts like hazelnuts. They drink liqueur like anisette or Galliano.

For Fat Tuesday, Neapolitans would make large meatballs with raisins, which some still make in the United States today. For Lent, many Americans of Italian descent who are Roman Catholic refrain from eating meat on Ash Wednesday, Fridays, Good Friday, and Holy Saturday, as this was a Roman Catholic tradition. They serve meatless dishes on these days, including things like *pasta fagioli*, rice with eggs and cheese, eggs with tomato sauce, or fish dishes.

For Easter, Americans of Italian descent eat traditional foods like lamb. The Neapolitans eat *pizza chiena*, or *pizza rustica*, a meat- and cheese-filled savory torte. They also eat *pastiera* or *pizza grano*, a sweet wheat and ricotta pie. In the Benevento area of Italy, this pie is made with rice instead of wheat and Italian Americans from this area of Italy make the pie this way today. Neapolitans also eat an Easter bread called *casatiello*, which can be made sweet or savory. The dough is wrapped around hard-boiled eggs in various shapes. The savory bread has meats and cheese and is somewhat peppery. Some Italian Americans still eat *sanguinaccio*, a chocolate pudding made with pig's blood. *Sanguinaccio* is available at Italian bakeries in New York City in the weeks preceding Easter.

Besides the popular Christian holidays, many Italians celebrate saints' days as well. Each town in Italy has its own patron saint, and these feast days are celebrated with great splendor. They often include a processional of a statue of the saint, along with music from a band. There are often interesting feats like the *Giglio* in Brooklyn where men carry the statue on their shoulders. Of course, there is food. Every Italian street fair has zeppole, a fried ball of dough served with powdered sugar, as well as pizza, cannoli, sausage and pepper sandwiches, Italian ice and gelato, clams, calamari, and more. These festivals are usually sponsored by a local church or Italian organization. There are also traditional foods served only on these particular occasions.

March 19 is St. Joseph's Day. St. Joseph, or San Giuseppe, is the husband of Mary, the mother of Jesus, and the patron saint of workers and pastry chefs. For St. Joseph's Day, Neapolitans make *zeppole di San Giuseppe*, different from the feast zeppole. This zeppole is a kind of cream puff, a choux pastry filled with custard cream, sometimes topped with a cherry (or not). Sicilians make *sfinci/sfinge*, also a type of cream puff with a more rounded shape and a ricotta filling. Italian Americans whose families come from the Molise and Abruzzo regions of Italy make a chickpea-filled fried pastry called calzone, pronounced *cavazoon* in dialect, according to Bob Batz, Jr., in the *Pittsburgh Post-Gazette*.[22] He notes these were traditionally given free to friends, not sold.[23] The article says restaurateur Rezero "Rizzi" DeFabo, owner of Rizzo's Malabar Inn in Pittsburgh, Pennsylvania, makes these on St. Joseph's Day to give to anyone who wants them.[24] Sicilian Americans celebrate St. Joseph's Day with a parade and a St. Joseph's Day table, a spread of symbolic foods like fava beans that helped the Sicilians live through famine and *cuccidatta*, fig-filled cakes.[25] St. Joseph's Day tables are popular in New Orleans where there were more Sicilian immigrants.

Like these holiday traditions, there are also the everyday pantry staples and dishes of Americans of Italian descent that indeed have roots in the Italian peninsula. Here, I will briefly discuss a few.

Olive oil

Olive oil is the first thing that comes to mind, as it is a staple of Italian cooking and eating. People in the Mediterranean have been using olive oil since at least 6000 BC.[26] Olive oil, often referred to as liquid gold, *is* gold to the people of the Mediterranean and is used predominantly in Southern Italy. (Northern Italians tend to use butter or lard as the primary cooking fat.) Americans of Italian descent (as well as their Southern Italian counterparts) have a pantry stocked well with olive oil, as it is used on salads, in the preparation of vegetables, on breads, for frying and cooking, even some baking. (Yes, olive oil has a low smoke point, but it is used for frying.)

Olive oil counterfeiting has made headlines lately. Tests have shown that olive oils sold in the grocery store contain a mixture of olive and other inferior oils like soybean. These tests, conducted at UC Davis, were sponsored by the California olive oil industry, an obvious competitor of Italian olive oil.[27] However, counterfeiting most likely does occur, and it's not surprising because this phenomenon is nothing new. My great-grandfather imported products from Italy in his store back in the 1920s–1950s, and he encountered the same problem. As Cinotto notes, in the 1930s, olive oil counterfeiting was big business with oils such as cottonseed, peanut, corn, or sesame along with artificial coloring used instead of olive oil.[28] A 1939 Locatelli cheese cookbook for housewives warns of counterfeit olive oil made from inferior oils such as these and to look for tins labeled "Packed in Italy" for the best quality.[29] Store owners caught selling counterfeit olive oil were fined and given jail time, according to Cinotto.[30] It still goes on today where olive oil is mixed with other oils like soybean, sunflower, or palm oil and colored green with chlorophyll.[31] And what were once Italian olive oil brands are now Chinese.[32] In 2014, China's government-owned Bright Food bought a majority stake in Salov, an Italian olive oil producer with recognizable brands like Filippo Berio and Sagra, the *Local* reports.[33]

Extra virgin olive oil from Tuscany tends to be greenish in color and has a peppery bite. I was always taught that good olive oil was gold in color. Food snobs will scoff at this, preferring the green of the Tuscan oils. The Sannio oils of Benevento are golden in color. Schwartz mentions the "pleasant, fruity flavor" of the golden olive oil produced in Campania.[34] And he says that good Puglian olive oil does not have that peppery bite.[35]

It is important to note that "extra virgin" olive oil is a fairly new term. It refers to the first pressing of the olives, also referred to as cold pressed. The term "extra virgin" was created in the 1960s, and prior to that, olive oil had been created for thousands of years in the Mediterranean using ancient methods without that designation.[36] What happened in the 1960s to inspire this change? New technology, of course. An expensive stainless steel milling technique, according to NPR, and that in order to counteract costs of this new technology, some producers skimp and add inferior quality oil[37] like soy, canola, or nut oils to the olive oil. This may be true, but as I mentioned before, cheap, inferior, fake, counterfeit olive oil was around before extra virgin came into being.

60 Minutes recently did an exposé entitled *Agromafia* about the Italian police going after the mafia for taking cheaper grades of olive oil and sometimes mixing them with other oils and selling them as extra virgin olive oil.[38] As a result of this counterfeit trade, according to Jerry Finzi of *Grand Voyage Italy*, Italy is investigating seven olive oil producers.[39] *60 Minutes* also pointed out that police found forty-two thousand gallons of regular red wine to be sold as Brunello Di Montalcino in Tuscany,[40] lest anyone think the Tuscans or Northern Italians are immune from engaging in illegal or fraudulent behavior. (Unfortunately, unethical behavior abounds in businesses all over the world, especially in the BIG FOOD and BIG PHARMA industries. We hear stories in the news on a regular basis how these two industries dupe or manipulate the public to protect their profit margins. Much of the questionable behavior being "legal" according to the law, but perhaps unethical or against the natural law, such as corporations putting cheaper ingredients in pretty much all American food products for decades and now successfully lobbying to keep GMOs from being labeled on food packages; high fructose corn syrup as the cheap substitute for sugar until the public noticed; the use of soy in many forms, as soybean oil, soy flour, soy protein, and soy lecithin [an emulsifier] in practically every packaged product on the market and in animal and fish feed and in vegetable wax; and the marketing of pharmaceutical drugs with long lists of harmful and potentially deadly side effects.)

Olive oil does have a DOP or PDO seal and a blue IGP or PGI seal guaranteeing its preparation, processing, and production was done in a particular region, notes Finzi.[41] In early 2016, ANSA reported that the Chamber of Commerce of Bari created an olive oil identification system called In Oleo Veritas.[42] The article says the system includes testing for chemical and pesticide residue and any changes to the oil during the production process.[43] The Chamber will pay the 500-euro cost of the testing for each olive oil producer.[44] Each producer will get a QR code to put on the product so information about the olive oil can be accessed using a smartphone.[45]

Despite these issues with some Italian olive oil producers, Italian olive oil is still the gold standard. According to the *Olive Oil Times*, in 2016, Italy got 109 awards from the New York International Olive Oil Competition, competing against 25 other countries.[46]

Pizza

Pizza is probably the most popular food worldwide. Why? Because Italian Americans made it such. When the first Italian immigrants opened pizzerias in the United States, they opened them for themselves in their own neighborhoods. Pizza at that time was very different from what it is today. One could get only a plain cheese pizza with what is now called "thin crust" or a slice with onion that was thicker, resembling the Sicilian slice. The popularity of this cheap and delicious food reached the non-Italian American. Through the years, pizza evolved to include toppings like pepperoni, olives, mushrooms, and more, and in the modern day, there are any number of concoctions like ham and pineapple. The majority of pizza in the United States is fast food or delivery and not of very good quality. Americans of Italian descent know the difference between a good pizza and a bad pizza. In the United States, the early pizzerias were coal-fired, a sign of the times. But the early Italian immigrants, like my grandmother, remembered wood-fired pizza from Naples.

Ancient foods

According to Capatti and Montanari, the following foods are found in ancient Roman texts: sausages, eels, sea urchins, shellfish, a plethora of cheeses, onions, cardoons, broad beans, lentils, stuffed olives, olive oil, semola wheat, breads and sweets, salt, and wine.[47] In any Italian-American household, one will find the above-mentioned foods, thus showing that Italian-American cuisine dates back to ancient times. I don't think modern food historians/Italian chefs/restaurateurs will argue against this. What they will argue is that particular, specific dishes are not Italian, but that the individual ingredients may be.

Parasecoli says the Phoenicians, ancestors of today's Lebanese, had trading posts throughout the Mediterranean, including Sardinia and Sicily.[48] There isn't much evidence as to the Phoenician diet, Parasecoli says, but they did eat grains with cheese and honey, and a fish sauce similar to the Roman *garum*.[49] There are a number of recipes in *The Lebanese Kitchen* by Salma Hage that are very similar to recipes that native Italians and Americans of Italian descent make in their homes, such as a wheat berry and pomegranate dessert and an orange and onion salad.[50] In fact, Bastianich includes a recipe for orange and red onion salad in the chapter on Sicily in *Lidia's Italy*.[51] This salad

81

is eaten by Neapolitans as well, as it was a favorite of my grandmother and is a favorite of mine. These recipes serve as an example of the cross-cultural sharing that took place thousands of years ago.

Ricotta and mozzarella

Varro, an ancient Roman scholar, wrote about men making ricotta from ewe's milk in 37 BC. In the early nineteenth century in Sorrento, a new process was used to make ricotta from whole milk. According to a 1961 Pollio cookbook, the Pollio family (of Polly-O) had been making ricotta and mozzarella for about 100 years when Giuseppe Pollio came to the United States from Italy in 1899 and started making these cheeses in the traditional way—a kettle on an iron tripod lit by an open flame.[52] The Polly-O company eventually modernized its methods.[53] (Now, the company is owned by Kraft Foods.) However, this example shows that the early Italian immigrants were using the traditional methods used in Italy to create foods in the United States.

Specialty foods

According to Capatti and Montanari, other Italian cookbooks in the Middle Ages, Renaissance, and post-Renaissance periods name various products used in Italian cooking like "oranges from Naples," "honey from Sicily and Taranto," and "chestnuts from Taranto."[54] These foods are eaten in Italian-American households. Oranges are used in salads or eaten fresh. Honey is used in traditional dishes like *struffoli*. Chestnuts are roasted during the winter. Native Italians will argue that American produce is not the same because the sea breezes of the Italian coast and the volcanic soil are the ideal conditions for growing perfect produce and grains.

Salads

In the Middle Ages, Italian cookbooks had a plethora of vegetable recipes, note Capatti and Montanari. In fact, they say Italy was known for having a diet heavy with vegetables, herbs, and plants, i.e. "salads"—unlike its other European counterparts.[55] They cite Castelvetro, who wrote a book about Italian gastronomy in 1614 and said salad should be "well salted, with little vinegar and lots of oil."[56] While the ratio of oil and vinegar is his particular preference, this is the dressing used by Americans of Italian descent—oil, vinegar, and salt. This dressing is not to be confused with "Italian dressing" found in American restaurants and supermarkets, which is an American creation—not what Americans of Italian descent use to dress their salad.

Zeppole

Short story writer Giambattista Basile writes in the sixteen hundreds that he misses the zeppoli of Naples, according to Capatti and Montanari.[57] Americans of Italian descent still make these fried treats for religious holidays like St. Joseph's Day, church festivals, and street fairs.

Vegetables

In their book, Capatti and Montanari list ingredients used in Italian cooking and discuss their origins. Spinach, citrus fruits, cane sugar, eggplant, and artichokes come from the Middle East.[58] The eggplant was considered food eaten by "people of a lowly station or by Jews" because it was considered "vulgar."[59] The Southern Italian immigrant had many eggplant dishes, only one of which is eggplant parmigiana. The book also lists green beans, cauliflower, and fennel.[60] Speaking of fennel, they say it is "always served at the end of the meal, as is the custom in the south of Italy even in our own time."[61] Americans of Italian descent also serve fennel at the dinner table.

Tomatoes

Everyone associates the tomato with Italian cuisine yet it comes from the Americas. It didn't become popular in Italian cuisine until the eighteen hundreds;[62] it was seen as a "poisonous" plant, although it was used by peasants since it was brought to Italy.

Gentilcore mentions Neapolitan doctors Achille Spatuzzi and Luigi Somma who wrote in the late eighteen hundreds about a working-class dish— tomato salad eaten with raw tomato, onion, and oregano.[63] Americans of Italian descent make a raw tomato salad with onion, oregano, and olive oil. In fact, I grew up on this salad—it was a summer favorite.

Potatoes

The potato, also from the Americas, was pushed on Italian peasants, especially for baking. There is a Neapolitan pie made with mashed potatoes that is still made by Americans of Italian descent today in the United States.

Sorbet

Sorbet was made in Italy. Astarita says it was called snow and in 1722, there was a guild for snow vendors.[64] Early Italian immigrants brought their ice confection-making traditions to the United Kingdom, as was mentioned earlier, and to the United States. They made a treat that became known as Italian ice in the United States. And Burt Wolf also credits the Italians for bringing ice cream to the United States.[65] According to Bellman, in the 1770s, an Italian immigrant, Giovanni Basiolo, opened the first gelato shop in the United States, in New York City, paving the way for future ice cream shops.[66] In 1896, Italo Marcioni (Anglicized to Marchiony) sold homemade lemon ice in glasses from a pushcart wagon on Wall Street.[67] The glasses had a tendency to break or to not be returned, so he invented an edible cone to hold the ice.[68] In 1903, he patented a cone-making machine and sold ice cream from cones in his shop at 219 Grand Street in Hoboken, New Jersey, until a fire destroyed it in 1934.[69]

Fish

Americans of Italian descent use anchovies in their sauces just like how it was done in Italy.[70] Artusi mentions salt cod, or baccalà, which is prepared and eaten by Americans of Italian descent today.

Polenta, rice, cheese, cured meat, and soup

Capatti and Montanari write that polenta, rice, cheese, cured meats, preserves, and soup were food for the poor.[71] Polenta dates back to Roman times when it was made from other types of grains. Once corn was introduced to Italy from the Americas, it was made from corn.[72] Americans of Italian descent are always making soups—escarole and beans, lentil soup, vegetable soups, chicken soups, soup with polenta. And they also make dishes with polenta, polenta with tomato sauce, fried polenta, cooked polenta. An old Neapolitan pie made with rice is still made in the United States by Americans of Italian descent. As early as the Middle Ages, Parmesan cheese took precedence and is the cheese of choice for Italian food in America. However, Southern Italians prefer *pecorino romano*, and Italian Americans often use it in place of Parmesan. According to Capatti and Montanari, cured meats were seen as peasant food because they could last long.[73] Americans of Italian descent brought the tradition of curing meat with them to the United States. It's interesting to note that in Italy between 1931 and 1969, 30 percent of cured meats disappeared due to various factors, say Capatti and Montanari.[74] In essence, Italian food in Italy has changed and evolved with technological advancements, different methods of farming, and other socio-economic factors. Today, as I previously mentioned, on the program *Two Greedy Italians*, a butcher in Northern Italy gets its beef from Argentina to be made into cured meats. The mullet roe delicacy, *bottarga*, so beloved in Italy is most likely coming from Brazil these days, according to the *Flavors of Brazil* blog.[75] The blog notes that while the Italian mullet was overfished, Brazil is teeming with mullet known as *tainha*.[76] The Fuck family (yes, that *is* how their name is spelled) started a business processing the mullet roe and sell it by the name Bottarga Gold, the blog adds.[77]

Pasta e fagioli, a pasta and bean soup, is a staple of Italian and Italian-American cooking, often seen on restaurant menus.

Pasta

The origins of pasta are often debated. Most modern writers think the theory of Marco Polo bringing it back from the East is a myth and will now say that the Arabs introduced the Sicilians to their way of drying pasta. This view is the most widely accepted, but even it is hard to believe because pasta isn't a staple of Middle Eastern cooking. If they invented it, why don't they still eat it? Zanini De Vita says that there are documents that prove Italians were eating pasta at least a century before Marco Polo traveled east.[78] An Italian calendar I had said that pasta initially came from Basilicata. An Etruscan tomb from 400 BC depicts a scene where pasta is likely being made, according to Bellman.[79] In Roman times, the Romans ate a dish called *lagana*, predecessor of the modern lasagna, with large, long pasta served with other ingredients.[80] Bellman notes that, in the twelve hundreds, Genoa and Pisa sold dried pasta.[81] Capatti and Montanari say a fourteenth-century Neapolitan recipe collection, the *Liber de coquina*, has a recipe for lasagna layered with grated cheese.[82] The earliest mention of *maccheroni* being produced is in a 1509 edict in Naples, according to Astarita.[83] Pasta had been served with grated cheese for centuries, according to Capatti and Montanari.[84] They cite Artusi who writes with aversion to seeing plates of macaroni being sold in Naples with "a great deal of pepper and sharp cheese."[85] Pasta being al dente is more of a Southern Italian tradition, note Capatti and Montanari.[86] That's how it is served in the homes of Italian Americans—topped with grated cheese.

According to Capatti and Montanari, pasta was served as a side dish in wealthier homes in Italy, while the peasant and middle class served it as a main dish.[87] They cite Girolamo Cirelli, who wrote in 1694, that "[peasants] imagine they are putting on a big show when they invite a friend to eat and serve him lasagne or macaroni."[88] Therefore, a plate of pasta as the main course of a meal is a Southern Italian tradition, one carried over to America by Southern Italian immigrants.

And it is important to note that there are many shapes and varieties of pasta. Some of these are native to certain regions of Italy. However, pasta shapes predominantly have to do with the type of sauce or preparation of the pasta. For example, pastas that go with a lighter sauce or ones that can withstand a heavier sauce or those used in soup. Americans of Italian descent know many of these varieties and made them in their homes long before corporations like Barilla published books outlining pasta shapes. Americans of Italian descent have used more pasta shapes than spaghetti, linguine, penne, ziti, rigatoni, and lasagna, arguably the more well-known shapes. (And I will add these shapes are well known because Italian Americans served them in their restaurants.) In fact, some of my favorites that my family prepared are *fusilli*, *perciatelli*, and *cavatelli*—pasta shapes you wouldn't find in restaurants before the modern era of *cucina moderna*. My great-grandparents and grandparents made *strozzapreti*.

Technology in the seventeenth century made the production of pasta easier and cheaper, so it became a more popular food in Naples, note Capatti and Montanari.[89] They say Neapolitans and Sicilians were known as "the macaroni eaters"[90] in their native Italy, and I would add, it's much like their derogatory nickname in their new country, "spaghetti benders."

The food blog, *This Italian Life*, posted an article on *scrippelle*, a crepe dish made in the Abruzzo region.[91] The blog's author, Phyllis Macchioni, an American living in Italy, had never heard of them until she read about them on an Italian-American Facebook page in a post by a woman in Philadelphia.[92] Yet another example of Americans of Italian descent as guardians of the gastronomic legacy of early Italian immigrants.

Tortes

Many areas of Italy make large savory tortes or pies with fillings of meat, fish, cheese, and/or vegetables. In Naples, the torte is called a pizza (not to be confused with pizza, the flatbread with tomato sauce and cheese). An example of this is a *pizza chiena* or *pizza rustica*, often served during Easter in Italian-American homes.

Meat

According to Capatti and Montanari, beef began to replace pork as the most popular meat in Italy in the Middle Ages for the more elite classes in the cities.[93] They also note that veal was more popular in Italy than elsewhere in Europe as a nutritious food.[94] These meats are eaten by Americans of Italian descent, and all three are combined to make meatballs.

Capatti and Montanari mention a painter eating "half a head of kid" in the sixteenth century.[95] Some Italian Americans eat this—*cappozelle*—today, if they can stomach it. It is one traditional dish that is going out of fashion, as the majority of people do not gravitate toward offal.

Antipasto

Another tradition Americans of Italian descent continued when they came to America was that of antipasto. Antipasto consists of small plates, like Spanish tapas or Middle Eastern mezze, served before the meal. They can include peppers, olives, cheeses, and cured meats. The antipasto has its origins dating back to the sixteenth century, according to Capatti and Montanari.[96] They say it was popular with the lower and middle classes.[97] While it gained popularity with a wider audience in the 1930s, note Capatti and Montanari, it had its critics that the spice would ruin the palate.[98]

*

"Do not be fooled by the Italian-American meal," writes Vallone for *L'idea* magazine.[99] "It is more American than Italian. It is not bad, it is different and definitely not what the locals are eating in Venice, Padua, Lucca, Bari and Taranto."[100]

This quote speaks to three distinctions made earlier. One, Italian cuisine for Americans of non-Italian descent versus Italian cuisine of Americans of Italian descent. In addition, it also speaks to contemporary Italian cuisine versus traditional Italian cuisine. And, finally it speaks to regional Italian cuisine. The food that is created for Americans not of Italian descent uses Italian ingredients to create dishes that are unknown in Italian cuisine. A prime example of this are the menus of Italian restaurant chains, as most of the dishes are unrecognizable to Americans of Italian descent. Perhaps it is this fact that has native Italians scoffing at the American idea of Italian food. But the native Italians can rest easy, as Americans of Italian descent know that this is not real Italian food as well and many of them refuse to eat at restaurants such as these. According to Italy's Ministry of Agriculture and Forestry, 82 percent of Italians will spend more to know where their food is coming from, says an article by the Polli Cooking Lab.[101] The article says six out of ten Italians read product labels.[102] Eighty-nine percent of Italians make DOP purchases, the article adds, and the "Italianness" of a product is important to 71 percent of Italians.[103] As Severgnini writes, it takes only "one glance" for Italians to know if a food is good or not.[104] I can assure him that Americans of Italian descent also have this keen gastronomical sense, and if they were given such a survey, the numbers would be similar to those of their cousins in Italy.

There are a number of dishes that are easily identified as "concoctions" or "creations" and not "authentic" or "traditional" Italian food. Some are the result of the restaurant industry's playful experimentation with Italian ingredients. However, they have become synonymous with Italian food and are often served at Italian-themed restaurants. These include dishes like Caesar salad, a dish created in 1924 by Italian immigrant and successful restaurateur Caesar Cardini[105] (served at Joe Bastianich's Becco now);

fettuccine Alfredo—a creation from a restaurant in Italy (although based on a dish eaten by Italians); penne alla vodka—a restaurant creation from the early 1970s (Lidia Bastianich calls this an "American-Italian" dish[106] which I think is a good description as it is an American creation not served traditionally in homes of Americans of Italian descent); shrimp scampi—a restaurant creation probably based on a method of cooking scampi, Italian langoustines;[107] garlic bread—an American creation probably from the restaurant industry; mozzarella sticks—a contemporary American restaurant industry creation; lobster ravioli—American restaurant creation of the 1990s; chicken parmesan—an American creation although probably based on eggplant or veal parmesan which is Italian; Italian dressing—an American creation (Italians and Americans of Italian descent use olive oil and vinegar to dress their salad); and Philly cheesesteak—invented in the 1930s by Pat and Harry Olivieri.[108] Tiramisu is a popular Italian dessert found in Italian restaurants in the United States; however, it was created by Alba Campeol at her restaurant, Le Beccherie, in Treviso in 1971, according to Bellman.[109]

It is said that Salvatore Lupo, a Sicilian immigrant, created the New Orleans *muffuletta* in 1906 at his grocery store, known as Central Grocery.[110] However, there is a bread from Sicily called *moffoletta*. Elena of *La Montagna Incantata* blog says *moffoletta* predates the Roman Empire.[111] She describes it as a round bread with sesame seeds, identical to the bread used for *muffuletta*.[112] It is served differently, however. *Moffoletta* in Sicily is served with olive oil, anchovy, and cheese, according to Elena.[113] RAI TV did a segment on the *muffuletta*'s origins in Sicily's *moffoletta*.[114] The program states that the ingredients in the sandwich are what make the New Orleans *muffuletta*—it has an olive salad, mortadella, salami, *prosciutto cotto*, provolone, and Emmentaler cheese.[115]

In the 1970s, Silvio Maccioni of Le Cirque, created another dish, spaghetti primavera, according to *Food & Wine*, now known as pasta primavera and synonymous with Italian-American food.[116] Worthy of mention, "macaroni" or "spaghetti" became "pasta" to elevate it to a newer, more elite status. San Francisco's famous *cioppino*, a stew made from tomato and wine and local seafood like clams, mussels, shrimp, whitefish, and crab, according to Serena Renner in *AFAR* magazine, originates from the Genoese stew named *ciuppin* brought to San Francisco by fishermen who settled in the mid- to late eighteen hundreds.[117]

Fettuccine Alfredo was invented by Alfredo Di Lelio in 1908 at his mother's Roman restaurant, according to his granddaughter, Ines, who wrote me through my blog.[118] In 1914, he opened his own restaurant, Alfredo.[119] As the story goes, his wife couldn't eat while she was pregnant, so he created this dish as nourishment.[120] Fettuccine Alfredo is fettuccine in a creamy butter and Parmesan "sauce." At this point in time, this dish existed as a basic pasta dish, pasta with butter and cheese, already eaten by Italians and Americans of

Italian descent on any kind of pasta, and it is still eaten by Italians and Italian Americans today. Pasta with butter and cheese is not something one would typically find at a restaurant. It is something that is eaten at home. In fact, one can omit the cheese and just have pasta with butter as well. It's usually eaten when you are sick or when you want a quick, easy meal or don't have ingredients on hand for something else, as Alessia Gargiulo mentions in her *Swide* article, "17 Italian foods that aren't Italian at all."[121] The typical Italian/Italian American doesn't use this much butter or cheese when making this dish. So the novelty of Alfredo's dish is that it contained a lot of butter—which makes sense because he was trying to nourish his pregnant wife who was having digestive problems. (Using butter to nourish women who had just given birth or sick people was not unique to fettucine Alfredo. There's an Iranian porridge called *kaachi* that is made from butter and flour and served for the purpose of nourishing women who just gave birth, according to Bita at *Honest & Tasty* blog.[122])

The difference between the Italian and American versions is that in the Italian version, only butter and Parmesan are used, and together, they create a silky butter sauce. According to Kimberly Kohatsu for the *Huffington Post*, Douglas Fairbanks and Mary Pickford ate fettuccine Alfredo at Alfredo's in 1920 while honeymooning and brought the dish back to America.[123] In the American version, heavy cream is also used to get a creamier, saucy consistency. This, however, is not how the dish was intended.

There are also foods that are obviously American creations like buffalo wings (created by Italian American Teressa Bellissimo at the Anchor Bar in Buffalo, New York).[124] Mariani calls these a regional "style of Italian food,"[125] like the toasted ravioli of St. Louis, but I think they are more appropriately labeled American food because they are an American food created by a person of Italian descent. According to Calvin Trillin's account of buffalo wings for the *New Yorker*, they are made with hot sauce and served with blue-cheese dressing.[126] Both of these are American condiments. Nina Picariello, one of the nonnas who cooks at Enoteca Maria in Staten Island and who is from Italy, refers to "spicy chicken wings" as "uniquely American."[127] We wouldn't say orange juice is an Italian-style food just because Anthony Rossi founded Tropicana and created a process to pasteurize fruit juice.[128] Or that peanuts are an Italian-style food because Amedeo Obici, a Venetian immigrant, founded Planters Nuts.[129] Granted, peanuts and orange juice are stand-alone foods and not food creations like buffalo wings and toasted ravioli.

Mariani mentions a formal dinner by Mrs. Julia Cooley Altrocchi (an Irish American with an Italian-American husband) in *The American Hostess* in 1948 consisting of a frozen tomato salad with crackers and *pollo alla cacciatora* with Burgundy wine, cranberry jelly on orange slices, fried artichoke hearts, wild rice with mushrooms, slices of French bread, zabaglione, cupcakes, coffee, and candies.[130] He says, " . . . for most Americans, this *was* Italian food."[131] This example is not the best one to illustrate his point because it is *not* characteristic of what most non-Italian Americans think of as Italian food. Instead, better examples of Italian food prepared by "most" non-Italian Americans would be lasagna made with cottage cheese instead of ricotta, or spaghetti made with a chili sauce.

Mariani writes, "I have, over the past four decades, been an attentive witness to the rise in status of Italian food from a low-class, coarse ethnic food to the most recognizable, stylish, and influential cuisine in the world."[132] He notes that the "'red sauce' dishes" of Italian-American cooking—rather than the dishes of all the regions of Italy—defined Italian food.[133] These "red sauce dishes" of Italian-American cooking that he speaks of are dishes of Southern Italians—the majority of immigrants to the United States.

He also mentions that in the 1970s there was "some improvement" in Italian restaurants, and that "food got better as the owners and chefs attempted to persuade customers that Italian food was not all spaghetti with red sauce and fettuccine with cream sauce."[134] However, he uses restaurants like Patsy's in the Theater District, Amerigo's in the Bronx, and Coppola's as examples, which all make those same Italian-American dishes.[135] As Mariani himself says, "The fact is that most Americans who went out for Italian food expected it and *wanted* it to be those entrenched clichés of Italian-Americana."[136] Yes, the food of the Southern Italian immigrant is *the* most popular Italian food.

Are there bad Italian restaurants in America? YES! Little Italy in Manhattan had many good Italian restaurants that my family spoke highly of, but I had the worst lasagna of my life at one. These days, many restaurants cut corners to survive financially, and, much of the food that is produced in the United States is made with fillers, chemicals, and inferior ingredients. Mariani quotes Marcella Hazan who said, that "of course, no one expects that the Italian way of eating can be wholly absorbed into everyday American life. Even in Italy it is succumbing to the onrushing uniformity of an industrial society."[137] What people fail to realize with comments like these is that the United States may have started the trend of commercially mass-produced food, but at one time, even in the United States, there was fresh and wholesome food. There was a time not too long ago that I remember where one got real yogurt instead of the sugary corn starch-gelatin-gum concoction that passes for yogurt in most grocery stores and where produce was seasonal, not available year-round. With ever-changing technology, the one constant in a capitalistic society is the idea of feeding more for less, benefitting shareholders, not consumers. And it is a trend that Americans do not like any more than anyone else, as is evident by the growing trend of buying local, community-supported agriculture, farmers' markets, farm-to-table, small food purveyors, etc.

Despite living in a capitalistic country, Americans of Italian descent are keeping traditional foodways alive. They make those Italian dishes in their homes. Iengo's cookbook includes recipes that one would find in contemporary Naples today, including the region's classics.[138] Ironically, many of these recipes are ones found in the homes of Americans of Italian descent—white bean and escarole soup, cannellini bean soup, *fusilli* with ricotta, spaghetti with tomatoes and basil (the classic Neapolitan sauce), pasta and chickpeas, linguine with clams and tomatoes, meat and tomato ragù, pasta with pumpkin, vermicelli (or spaghetti) with garlic and oil, rice with tomato and basil, lamb with eggs and cheese, meatballs in tomato sauce, *baccalà*, *baccalà* with olives, eggplant parmigiana, calzones, *pastiera*, zeppole, *baba*, *struffoli*, and more.[139] Maybe these are not recipes found in Italian restaurants in the United States, but one can be assured, they are cooked in the homes of Americans of Italian descent. *Struffoli* and *sfogliatelle* were mentioned in the seventeenth century in Latini's cookbook, according to Astarita.[140] And Italian Americans are always eating sausage sandwiches with peppers and onions at home and at feasts and fairs. Schwartz says, "In the Sila Grande Mountains of Calabria, there are roadside stands that tuck wood-grilled sausages into rolls, sometimes with sautéed onions and peppers, exactly as Italian sausages are served at American fairs."[141] Schwartz's cookbook *Naples at Table* is filled with recipes served in contemporary Naples;[142] however, many of these dishes are served by Americans of Italian descent. My family makes them. His book includes recipes that are oft forgotten or left out of Italian cookbooks. I think this is because most people have the impression that Americans of Italian descent only cook a small repertoire of dishes that are found in Italian restaurants in America—spaghetti and meatballs, baked ziti, lasagna, eggplant parmesan, etc. However, that is not the case. A number of recipes in *Naples at Table* are recipes prepared by my family and other Italian-American families—and not just families of Neapolitan descent, as many recipes are found in other parts of Southern Italy. Some of these recipes from *Naples at Table* include Genovese sauce (a sauce made from onions and beef), *cotica* in gravy (Schwartz mentions this pig skin dish and calls it *cotica* though we called it *cotenna*), macaroni with cheese and eggs, macaroni with ricotta and tomato sauce, lamb with cheese and eggs (we call this lamb with peas).[143]

In a small valley of rolling hills in western North Carolina, there is a city named Valdese that was founded in 1893 by a group of Protestant Italians known as the Waldensians.[144] Though founded that year, Valdese's history dates back to the twelfth century and a wealthy merchant in Lyons, France, named Peter Waldo (or Valdes), who gave up his riches to preach the Bible.[145] The Poor of Lyons, as his followers were called, became a group known as the Waldensians, who lived in the Cottian Alps in Italy, bordering France. Through the centuries, the Roman Catholic Church declared the Waldensians heretics because they preached the Bible—only priests were allowed to do so—and because they allowed individual interpretation of the Bible. The group lived through persecution, including massacres, and survived in the harsh mountain region eating staples like potatoes and cabbage. Due to the ever-changing European political climate, the Waldensians lived in constant turmoil. They were banished from their homeland but fought through much hardship to return in 1689.[146] Under Napoleon, they were given equality, but after his reign, their harassment continued. With the Edict of 1848, King Charles Albert of Sardinia granted the Waldensians certain religious freedom—the ability to emerge from the mountains and attend schools and universities and conduct business.[147] By the late nineteenth century, the number of Waldensians was high.[148] The overcrowding led some to seek a new home elsewhere, as did many Italians in that era.

The owner of the Morganton Land and Improvement Company in Morganton, North Carolina, had a wealthy aunt in Europe who sympathized with the Waldensians' plight. He offered them ten thousand acres of land.[149] A small fraction of the twenty-five thousand Waldensians came to North Carolina in 1893, 207, founding the town of Valdese (Italian for "Waldensian").[150] Today, there are nearly two thousand descendants of the original settlers.[151]

Interestingly enough, the land in which they settled was a foothill area similar to their native Italian home. The soil in Valdese was also not optimal for farming. A few men left town to work in textile mills and returned to open their own in 1901.[152] Waldensian Hosiery Mills thrived. In 1928, Alba Hosiery Mills opened and soon after, other businesses grew.[153] Ten years later, Valdese was named the "Fastest Growing Town in North Carolina."[154] Today, Valdese is host to a theater production about the Waldensians. There is also a museum about the history of the people and the town. There are bocce courts, wineries, Italian flags, and traditional masonry on the homes of Waldensian families. And there are Waldensians, some of whom speak French or Patois, a French-Italian dialect of the now dead Provençal language spoken by the city's first settlers in 1893.[155]

The late Italian born-and-bred British chef Antonio Carluccio was from the Piedmont area of Italy, just as the Waldensians. In 2001, the Waldensians of Valdese, North Carolina, published the Waldensian cookbook, including American and traditional Waldensian recipes.[156] In Carluccio's *Italia: the recipes and customs of the regions*, text copyrighted in 2005, there is a section with a few recipes from the Piedmont area.[157] One recipe is for the famous Piedmontese dish, *bagna cauda*, an anchovy-olive oil vegetable dip.[158] This dip is included in the Waldensian cookbook.[159] Carluccio also includes a recipe, *tajarin all'Albese*, a *tagliolini* pasta cooked with chicken livers and optional white truffles.[160] In the Waldensian cookbook, there is a recipe for "*tagliarini* con fegatini," noodles with chicken livers, with basically the same ingredients—olive oil, tomatoes, and Parmesan cheese.[161] Carluccio lists *zabaione* as the dessert from the Piedmont.[162] The Waldensian cookbook has two recipes for it, including eggs, sugar, and Marsala wine—the same ingredients as Carluccio's.[163] Parasecoli in *Al Dente* (published in 2014) writes that the Waldensians made a cheese and bread soup called *barbet*.[164] In the Waldensian cookbook, there is a dish made from cheese, bread, and broth called "La Souppa."[165] And finally, there is *soutisso*. *Soutisso* is sausage that is made in Valdese, North Carolina, that usually consists of ground pork, nutmeg, garlic, and black pepper.[166] This sausage is still made and eaten in the Waldensian Valleys in the Piedmont of Northern Italy.[167]

The Waldensian immigrants came to North Carolina in 1893—over 100 years before they published this cookbook—and they are making the exact same recipes with pretty much the same ingredients as their ancestors did in the Piedmont and that Italians in the Piedmont are still making in contemporary Italy today. Why? The reason is that these recipes were passed down through an oral tradition. The Waldensians were a more insular community—as there were no other groups of Italians in North Carolina. Their traditions, religious beliefs, and foodways were different from the majority of Italian-American immigrants to the United States, who were for the most part, Roman Catholics from Southern Italy. Because Waldensians didn't immigrate to the United States in great numbers, their foodways are not as well known as that of the Southern Italian immigrants. The dishes of the Waldensians survived over 100 years for one reason—they are family recipes that the families made in their homes and passed on orally to each subsequent generation.

Italy is bringing a concept to the United States—that there is more to Italian food than what can be found at traditional Italian-American restaurants. This is true—and it is something that Americans of Italian descent have known. As mentioned before, there are many dishes that Italian Americans make at home that are not served at Italian restaurants in the United States. I don't know if native Italians do not know this or if they just want to scoff at Italian-American food so that they can market their *cucina moderna*. *Cucina moderna* translates to "modern cooking" or "modern kitchen," and that is indeed what it is—modern Italian food. If you visit a restaurant in the United States that serves *cucina moderna*, you will most likely see *bresaola*, *cotechino*, and *lardo*. You will see pasta in a variety of shapes that were previously not served in Italian-American restaurants. Some of these pasta shapes are new—as cuisine has evolved. Some of them have been known to Americans of Italian descent but just not served in Italian-American restaurants. Examples are *strozzapreti*, which translates to "strangle the priest" or the Puglian pasta *orecchiette* or the small *cavatelli*. This pasta can be found on many a *cucina moderna* restaurant menu, but it is a pasta that the old Italian immigrants used as well—it just wasn't served on Italian-American restaurant menus, so it was not so well known. You may see pasta black from squid ink. Instead of traditional lasagna with tomato sauce, you will see on the menu *lasagna verde*, the dish from Emilia-Romagna, layers of green lasagna noodles and a béchamel sauce with ground beef. You will even see meatballs, but they will be called *polpette* or *polpettine* and come only with a tomato sauce, not pasta. You will see *scamorza* and *burrata* cheeses. You will see *branzino* and sea urchin. You will see pastas in wild boar, duck, veal, or lamb ragù. You will see *gnudi*, ricotta dumplings. Instead of eggplant parmesan, you will see eggplant *involtini*, rolled eggplant stuffed with cheese with tomato sauce, a dish my grandmother made.

Much of *cucina moderna* focuses on regional specialties like '*nduja*, spicy salami/sausage from Calabria, *orecchiette* pasta from Puglia, *malloreddus* pasta from Sardinia or *burrata* from Campania, to name a few. And in fact, regional restaurants are all the trend these days. It's an interesting trend, and one I also enjoy, as it introduces diners to foods they might not have known about before and also to the regional differences in Italian cuisine. However, while the restaurants are regional and include a few regional specialties and ingredients, they are still examples of *cucina moderna*, those classics revisioned in a new way to reflect the modern tastes of Italy. In Manhattan, there are Neapolitan restaurants like the Soho- and Noho-area Sessanta and Song e Napule; Obica, the mozzarella bar featuring Campanian *mozzarella di bufala*; the Puglian restaurant I Trulli and a new Sicilian pizzeria in Hell's Kitchen, Filaga. I've eaten at all of them. While I enjoyed my meals at each restaurant, I probably would not rate any above three stars, as in New York, a restaurant really has to be exceptional to garner a four- or five-star review. (This is not to say that other restaurants specializing in regional cuisine wouldn't get a four- or five-star rating from me.) Again, many of the dishes are dishes of Americans of Italian descent, so they were familiar to me while they may not be to someone who is not of Italian descent. For example, from a recent dinner menu at I Trulli: *cavatelli* with broccoli rabe (they add almonds); spaghetti with meatballs and tomato; penne with ricotta, tomato and basil; eggplant parmigiana; veal *milanese*; chicken parmigiana; broccoli rabe with pepperoncino, and more. The owner of Obica, Silvio Ursini, wanted to present Italian food in the same way he saw sushi presented at sushi bars in Tokyo, fresh and *modern*.[168] His restaurant serves DOP *mozzarella di bufala* from Campania along with other Italian dishes. In an interview, Ursini mentions there being a lot of "pseudo" Italian food in the market.[169] While this is a true statement because there are a lot of restaurants serving subpar Italian food, being a native-born Italian, he was probably including the food of Italian Americans in this definition of "pseudo" although I'd have to ask him to really know. I think that native-born Italians do think they are bringing something unique to the American restaurant scene, when in actuality, Americans of Italian descent have been eating/creating/importing these foods for themselves and serving them in restaurants. And in addition, some of these new restaurants are just as average in taste, presentation, and service as any average "Italian-American" restaurant.

Cucina moderna advocates fresh pasta as opposed to dry, as if fresh is superior or what the majority of Italians eat. According to Astarita, the majority of pasta historically eaten in Italy was dry.[170] According to Giuseppe Di Martino, the owner of Pastificio G. Di Martino pasta company, in business for over a century, "Pasta was invented to be a food store—to last—so it was meant to be dry, not fresh."[171] Indeed, some recipes are specific to dry pasta, as fresh pasta might not be able to withstand the sauce.

As I mentioned, a lot of *cucina moderna* is the home cooking of Americans of Italian descent. Much of it is also the food of modern Italy. Some of it is delicious—some of it varies from American tastes—some of it is umami—some of it is not. Some of it is made from centuries- or millennial-old traditions. Some of it is cheapened with modern methods for a mass audience—in much the same way native Italians criticize American Italian restaurants. Some of it uses modern culinary techniques like the mozzarella stretched and injected with tomato essence that Carluccio and Contaldo eat at a contemporary restaurant in Campania in their *Two Greedy Italians* series.[172]

In addition to Italian food in restaurants, Americans can find Italian food products here in the United States at local supermarkets, specialty grocers, and even mail order from Italian food purveyors like Fratelli Carli that sells products from Italy like olive oil, the Easter *Colomba* (like a *panettone*), cookies like *amaretti* and *cantuccini*, jam preserves, and honey. It is true, as Mariani says, that the FDA regulations banned certain products like prosciutto in the 1950s.[173] Who can forget the movie, *Lady Liberty* (*La Mortadella*, in Italy), where Sophia Loren tries to enter the country with a *mortadella* but is prohibited by customs? It is one my family and I still laugh about whenever *mortadella* comes up in conversation. Mariani says that in 2000, the USDA allowed *mortadella*, speck, and others.[174] Nowadays, there is a plethora of Italian food to be found. But how much of it is Italian? Remember in Chapter 3, I mentioned "Italian-sounding products"? These Italian-sounding products are ones that the Italian government wants to ban. To the Italian government, these products are not "authentic" Italian products. But are products from Italy superior?

Food bloggers have had an ongoing love affair with Nutella. But the Nutella from Italy tastes different from the one sold in the United States. As Carrie Vasios Mullins wrote in *Serious Eats*, the former is more hazelnutty; the latter, more sugary.[175] What about Galbani ricotta and mozzarella that is currently being advertised in the United States? Well, the ricotta is no different from commercial ricotta available in the United States. It also has carrageenan and gums. Galbani is owned by the Lactalis American Group, a division of the French dairy corporation, and largest in the world, Groupe

Lactalis.[176] According to an article by David Robinson in the *Buffalo News*, Groupe Lactalis bought the Italian-American Sorrento brand founded in 1947 by Louis Russo, an Italian immigrant from Sorrento, and instead of marketing it under the Sorrento name—with the goodwill of this product, it marketed it under the name of the Italian brand it bought, Galbani.[177]

"Goodwill" is a term in trademark law that refers to intangible aspects of a company's trademark. It has a lot to do with a company's reputation. A company puts out a product with a certain level of quality and then it invests its money, energy, and time in advertising this product. Because of this investment, a company may get repeat customers over time or in a specific geographic area that the company may be targeting. That consumer loyalty that a company builds up has value, as consumers will choose to buy a product based on the reputation of that brand. Usually, this concept comes into play when there has been some kind of trademark infringement where one company tries to gain customers by "trading on the goodwill" of another company. Of course, in this example of Sorrento and Galbani, there is no infringement. When companies merge, and the new company buys the trademark rights of the old company, they are also buying the goodwill in the trademark(s), which has a monetary value. Groupe Lactalis bought Sorrento. It also owns Galbani. It is making a choice to use the Galbani name *instead of* the Sorrento name to attract consumers in an American market that was familiar with the goodwill of the Sorrento brand. I've seen it in stores labeled Galbani Sorrento with the Galbani tagline—"Italy's Favorite Cheese Brand." Was this decision made to follow a trend that has started that Italian products are superior to Italian-American ones? I don't know the details of this particular case, so I don't know the monetary value of the Sorrento and Galbani trademarks. Without thinking of monetary value, in the United States, the name Sorrento was more recognizable than Galbani. It was associated with a good-quality ricotta and an Italian-American company. Of course, in general, these corporate-made products should not be confused with products made in Italy or elsewhere using traditional and centuries-old methods or products. A cheese made by a corporation cannot compete with one made in a more traditional manner without added gums.

Every grocery and specialty food store has a section of Italian products, some new and some already known by Americans of Italian descent. As I mentioned before, many of the established Italian-American brands have become corporations or have been sold to corporations and their products are no longer the quality products they once were. Often, one sees soybean oil used in jarred vegetables and sauces instead of olive oil; soy flour in breadcrumbs; gums in dairy products; and other inferior ingredients that are part of a larger, more global food production debate. It is unfortunate and it is here where I agree with the Italians in Italy that food should be produced with high-quality ingredients with traditional, time-tested methods. The Italian government food labeling helps consumers to know when a product is produced in such a manner. But, as I mentioned, it is important to note, that just because a product is from Italy doesn't mean it was produced with these high standards. And just because a product was made in the United States doesn't mean it wasn't.

When I peruse the grocery store aisles, I see many familiar and unfamiliar brands of Italian food. Being of Italian descent, I can, most of the time, distinguish if a product is Italian American or Italian and whether or not it is corporate or privately owned. I like to think of myself as a discerning connoisseur, and I've been schooled to look for the best-quality products from my Italian grandparents, parents, and my fellow connoisseurs and friends, Florie and Barney Seligman. Not to mention living in New York City and taking full advantage of the delights of Balducci's, Dean and DeLuca, and the like. I *always* read labels and investigate unfamiliar ingredients. But that's me. I realize not everyone has time or interest to do so and may just pick up a jar of tomato sauce or a bottle of olive oil without thinking twice. Or other consumers may want to buy quality products but do not know what to buy because they are unfamiliar with the type of products. That's where the Italian-sounding products can be influential in their decision.

As I mentioned, Italian-sounding products sold $60 billion annually. According to an article in *We the Italians*, there are nine Italian chambers of commerce in North America, five in the United States, three in Canada, and one in Mexico.[178] The article says these chambers keep tabs on Italian-sounding products in local markets.[179] It discussed a survey conducted by the Assocamerestero (the Association of the Italian Chambers of Commerce Worldwide) and financed by the Italian Ministry of Economic Development regarding Italian-sounding food products.[180] The survey was obviously translated from its original Italian, as it was not very clearly conveying its message. However, I understood the gist of it—that while Italian food exports went up by two percent in the past 15 years, there is still much competition from Italian-sounding products.[181] Some of the products named include those of BelGioioso, Stella D'oro, and Mama Francesca.[182] According to its website, BelGioioso was founded in the United States in 1979 by Italian immigrant Errico Auricchio whose great-grandfather had created a cheesemaking company.[183] Stella D'oro was founded by Italian immigrants Joseph and Angela Kresevich in 1930 and were very popular cookies.[184] My family and I have fond memories of them. The company was sold to Nabisco in 1992 and then to Lance in 2009.[185] I was not familiar with Mama Francesca. According to its website, it is owned by Cheese Merchants of America, a wholesale cheesemaker that specializes mostly in Italian-type cheese brands.[186] The ingredients for Mama Francesca's Parmesan cheese includes cellulose powder, and interestingly, on the Cheese Merchants website, it says its imported Parmesan comes from Argentina.[187] *We the Italians* says brands like these have product packaging that uses the Italian flag, Italian coloring, or imagery; uses words like "Contadina" described in the article as meaning "peasant" in Italian; misspells Italian products like "sopressata" instead of "soppressata"; or uses product names as they are in Italy, such as *panettone, cantuccini,* or *grissini.*[188]

This phenomenon should not be a surprise, as the immigrants of 100 years ago brought their foodways with them from their native country and created food businesses here in the United States. They made the same dishes and taught their children how to make those dishes. In turn, their children made those food products and sold them. Because of Italian-American food purveyors and restaurateurs, Italian food gained in popularity to become one of the two favorite cuisines in the country. The corporate machine also cashed in on its popularity by creating Italian food products and making it one of the two most popular cuisines in the world. Italy didn't do this—Italian America did.

The Italian government wanting to ban "Italian-sounding" food products is at least, unfair, and at most, egregious. "Italian sounding" and the word "Italian" does not belong to Italy alone. The millions of Italians who settled around the world are ethnically Italian and have been known as "Italian" in their birth countries. The food they cook, eat, and produce is Italian. In the present day, Italy does not have the right to piggyback on the goodwill they created for the past 100 years in trademarks and businesses in their respective countries any more than it does to disallow them from making the products that are inseparable from their identity.

As a food lover and connoisseur, I want to make clear that I recognize there are many inferior-quality products these days. And I am not disputing that Italy has superior food products. Unfortunately, there is a larger issue going on in food production today than I want to discuss in this book. One is hard-pressed to find any products that are produced as they naturally should be. Dairy products are one of the biggest offenders. Ice cream isn't ice cream anymore—it's milk and gums, like the new tara gum I saw on a recent label. Heavy cream isn't cream anymore, it's cream and gellan gum, and even if you do find it without gums, it still has a thinner, more watery consistency than it used to. I am a proponent of the Slow Food Movement, but I also like the days when high-quality delicacies were flown in from France and Italy to be made into wonderful creations at New York's top restaurants. More and more I am seeing food labels with "produced with genetic engineering" on the label, including American staples like good, old-fashioned country grits, for example. In a time when BIG FOOD is degrading food quality with the reasoning of "feeding the world," it is good to know there are governments supporting nourishing, wholesome food—if that is what they are doing. Swapping one inferior product made in America for one inferior product made in Italy is not a reason to buy something "Made in Italy" or Italian-branded.

I'm a discerning shopper, so I look for the best possible quality when I shop. And I don't think some of the products coming from Italy are the best. In fact, many are no better than the American alternatives. I recently saw a jar of marinated artichokes that were labeled "Product of Italy" in English and Italian. They were not marinated in olive oil but sunflower oil and also contained MSG.

Many of the wonderful Italian-American food companies were bought out by larger corporations, and now their products are produced cheaply with gums, fillers, and soy ingredients. Or I'm sure many had to change with the times to stay afloat and use cheaper ingredients like soy oil instead of olive oil. These are not the ingredients their predecessors used. Many of the early immigrants and their children used high-quality ingredients to make their products. In general, only in recent years has the quality of food in America degraded to what it is now. I think that is why young Italian expats think the food in America is so off-putting—because they are experiencing it for the first time *now*. I have never had better ricotta cheese than I did in the small town my grandfather left almost ninety-something years ago. And yes, the *bufala* mozzarella in Napoli is spectacular. But I also have had wonderful ricotta and mozzarella here in America. And not all food in Italy is superior. Grocery stores there are full of products with the same inferior ingredients as here in the United States. Just as in America, one has to seek out to find the food produced in the best manner.

In addition to Italian food products, New Yorkers had access to Italian food experts at their home as an anniversary promotion run by Eataly, according to its website, through Amazon's Amazon Prime service in 2017.[189] One could "Order in an Eatalian"—a real live Italian food *expert*—not an Italian person, for a private class.[190] While Eatalian doesn't refer to an Italian person, and it is a clever play on words for their idea, it still has the ring of stereotype, however distant, the "eating Italian" or is even reminiscent of the "eye"-talian.

*

Italians from Italy do love to ridicule what they consider Italian-American food. There's even a Facebook group called Degrado Italo-Americano.[191] It translates to "Italian-American degradation/corruption." It posts photos of Italian food products and dishes that have degraded the image of Italian food. Examples are hoagie sandwiches filled with spaghetti and tomato sauce, a pizza labeled "Margherita" with nothing but mozzarella and sliced sandwich tomatoes on it, Prego bacon and provolone sauce, Buitoni's herb chicken tortellini, pizza with tortellini on top, and more. (The site depicts food products from places like Colombia and Asia as well.) While this group refers to this food as "Italo-Americano," any American of Italian descent would recognize this food as inauthentic and commercial representations of Italian food. If the group wants to show depictions of commercialized Italian food, then it needs to rename itself to reflect that. Picturing these foods in association with Italian Americans is disrespectful to the early immigrants and their descendants, who know, cook, and eat authentic Italian foods. Now and again, the group will post a photo of an authentic Italian-American dish, such as the manicotti with tomato sauce it posted on February 10, 2016.[192] Now, Schwartz writes that manicotti is another dish, like spaghetti and meatballs, that is unheard of in Italy.[193] (However, we have learned, and so has Schwartz, that spaghetti and meatballs *is* found in Italy.) According to Enoteca Maria nonna Christina Narisi Carrozza, born near Palermo of Sicilian parents, manicotti come from the South and are filled with cheese and cannelloni are from the North and are filled with meat.[194] The poster on Facebook said, "In the U.S., they call 'cannelloni' manicotti."[195] He wants to know why. Commenters respond: "I think it is a problem due to Italian Americans, who can not [sic] speak either in Italian or American,"[196] "Note, also in this case, the sauce thrown on the food by way of plaster for walls, as is traditional,"[197] "The name is the last issue with that dish,"[198] "'rogues' would be [a] more appropriate [name] given the repeated damage inflicted on the good taste,"[199] "for me just to phonetic preference: cannelloni would be more difficile [sic] to pronounce for an American,"[200] "are not cannelloni and that is not pasta, so they might also be called mushy tubes with sauce, would be fine,"[201] "So they can say to have them [sic] invented them."[202] The word "manicotti" means "sleeves" in Italian. That is why one person says it should be called "rogues" instead. These comments are quite insulting, implying that Italian Americans cannot even speak "American," a language that doesn't even exist, as they speak English.

Another example that Italians are intent upon rewriting the history of Italian food in the United States is the IACC, Italy-America Chamber of Commerce. From its Miami branch website: "Unioncamere (the Association of Italian Chambers of Commerce) with the support of the Italian Government, have constituted the certification 'Marchio Ospitalità Italiana – Ristoranti Italiani nel Mondo' – a seal of quality that is conferred annually to authentic Italian restaurants around the world."[203] Note only "authentic" restaurants get the IACC seal of approval. There are 300 restaurants in the United States with the IACC seal of approval.[204] The 2016 awards ceremony in Miami included winning restaurants Al Dente Ristorante (San Juan), Antica Mare (Miami), Baraonda (Atlanta), Bologna Café (Osprey), Cibo Wine Bar Fort Lauderdale (Fort Lauderdale), Farinelli 1937 (Coconut Grove), Il Forno (Doral), Il Nuovo Mercato (San Juan), La Cucina di Ivo (San Juan),

Limoncello Italian Restaurant Bar & Lounge (Aventura), Sette Bello (Fort Lauderdale), Vino & Tigelle (Miami), and Zona Blu (Weston).[205] This list is a very small sampling of member restaurants. The executive chef and chef at Zona Blu are from Sardinia and Sicily, respectively.[206] The owner of Sette Bello's family are more recent émigrés from Sicily.[207] I couldn't find the owner for a few of these, but it would be interesting to see who the owners and chefs are for all Marchio Ospitalità Italiana restaurants and how many are Americans of Italian descent, or more importantly, descendants of Italian-American immigrants of 100 years ago. Now, because I say this does not mean that I do not think these restaurants are good or worthy of recognition. I have not dined at any of these, so I cannot judge. I have dined at some of the restaurants on the New York list and of the ones I dined at, I found them to be average with the exception of two. From the Ospitalità Italiana preamble on the official website: "Italian cuisine is the result of a centuries-old historical process of Italian society, always leading to significant moments of human civilization. For an innate inclination to the attention of the Italians to human relationships and the quality of life, the culture of the table has become in the course of time the symbol of hospitality and welcome, the food has taken on a value like art and music. For these reasons, the Italian food should be considered a contribution to the heritage of humanity and should be defended and protected from adulteration and falsification to preserve its history, culture, quality and authenticity."[208] My argument is with the term "authentic" used to describe the style of Italian food. If they are protecting the image of Italian food against the effects of multinational corporations and globalization, then, yes, I agree with this statement. I think it is surely one of the reasons because I do not want ricotta made with gums either. However, I think one of the reasons is to disassociate from the Italian immigrants of 100 years ago. That's why I think a more appropriate phrase to describe food from Italy is "the cuisine of modern Italy." This language is more appropriate than "authentic" because the cuisine of Americans of Italian descent is authentic Italian cuisine. This language would not offend the immigrants and their descendants.

As we have seen, native Italians are bringing the cuisine of the new Italy to America. Some of the dishes are the dishes of the early immigrants of 100 years ago—the dishes that Americans of Italian descent cook at home or serve in restaurants. Some of the dishes of the new Italy are reinvented classics. Most are completely new, reflecting Italy's own evolution in the last 100 years since it lost a large part of its population. Others are just chef creations using Italian ingredients.

The food of the new Italy is good, but ironically, most of these restaurants fall back on the very dishes they criticize as being Italian American—the food of the old Italy—of the early Italian immigrants. Why? Americans eat Southern Italian food because it is delicious. It became popular because it is delicious. And it sells because it is delicious. It represents the struggle of the early immigrants, yes, but it also represents their ingenuity, their business sense, their motivation and determination to succeed and to prove Italy and the United States wrong—that they are worth something, that they can achieve given the opportunity, that they have something to offer. Their food cannot be rebranded—it is timeless and classic. Unless I be misunderstood, there is no question that the food of the new Italy is good, and a food that will be embraced in the United States for what it is—food of the new Italy. But the old is forever. Wild boar ragù will never replace spaghetti and meatballs.

CHAPTER 7: Pizza

While spaghetti and meatballs is a very popular dish, the quintessential Italian dish the world over is pizza. Pizza hails from Naples, but Italy didn't make pizza famous. America did. More specifically, Italian immigrants to the United States over 100 years ago brought this dish with them. At the time, pizza was not a popular food in Italy and existed only in Southern Italy. If you recall *Pinocchio* writer Carlo Collodi's description of pizza from Chapter 1, you can tell how the upper classes and Northern Italians viewed pizza. Samuel Morse, inventor of the telegraph and a developer of the Morse Code, had pizza in Naples in 1831 and said it was "a species of most nauseating cake . . . covered over with slices of pomodoro or tomatoes, and sprinkled with little fish and black pepper and I know not what other ingredients, it altogether looks like a piece of bread that had been taken reeking out of the sewer," according to Helstosky.[1] She says it was known as "peasant" food of Naples eaten by the *lazzaroni*, the then-term for the city's poor, as writer Alexandre Dumas (famous for *The Count of Monte Cristo* and *The Three Musketeers*) noted, in his travel guide *Le Corricolo*, in 1843.[2] The pizza could be eaten at any meal, including breakfast. It was served with different toppings, such as oil, lard, tomatoes, fish, or cheese[3] and was sold with prices that varied with size. According to Helstosky, Dumas concluded that pizza was a "gastronomic thermometer of the market," meaning it was a gauge of the local economy, what the people were producing and eating.[4] He wrote this book in 1843, almost 20 years prior to Italy's unification and ensuing civil war, when the seeds of change were being sown. In fact, Dumas lived in Italy and supported the unification movement.[5] Therefore, I would assume that his earlier travelogue on Italy was really a book about the state of its economy.

However, pizza was a food eaten way before Dumas's time. It was not a reflection of the nineteenth-century economic climate so much as it was a reflection of the people of Southern Italy, a people who enjoyed good-tasting, simple pleasures in life. This very Italian concept of enjoying good simple food is the prevailing view on foodways and cooking today. Simply, Italians ate pizza in the nineteenth century for the same reason they and the world eat it now—because it was a whole food and it tasted good.

In ancient times, people of the Mediterranean ate different kinds of flatbreads with toppings on them like olive oil, herbs, cheese, and fish. Indeed, types of flatbreads existed all over the globe. Helstosky notes that the Etruscans in Italy made a flatbread they used to sop up sauce.[6] She adds that the Greeks baked the toppings on top of the bread and served it as a main course.[7] Also, she mentions, the Romans ate a flatbread called *placenta* (unfortunate name) topped with cheese, honey, bay leaves, and oil,[8] that according to Field sounded "focaccialike" in Cato's description.[9] Pizza was made in Pompeii in expertly designed pizza ovens and sold in pizzerias.[10] Field writes that during the time of Augustus, Virgil wrote about a flatbread in Naples called *moretum*, covered with a pestolike sauce.[11] According to Italian food blogger Anna Pernice, in the sixteenth and seventeenth centuries, Italians made a pizza now lost to antiquity with basil, lard, cheese, and pepper called *mastunicola*.[12] Legend has it that this pizza was created by a woman for her laborer husband and named after him, "Master Nicola," according to Enrico Volpe in *I Piatti Tipici della Cucina Napoletana e Lucana*.[13] Afterwards, he notes, pizza with small fried fish became popular.[14]

When did the flatbread become a pizza? The evolution occurred at the point where the flatbread became the meal in itself, says Helstosky.[15] Schwartz thinks the word pizza is "obviously related to" the word pita.[16] To others, it's not so clear. Helstosky says some people think the word "pizza" comes from the verb *pizzicare*, meaning "to pinch" because one pinches the dough to make a pizza.[17] She says some think it evolves from Greek, Arabic, or Hebrew words for flatbread (like *pita*)[18] or from the Latin words *picea*, meaning "of pitch," Helstosky says refers to the texture or color of baked bread or pizza.[19] Volpe notes that pizza could derive from the combination of two words: *pezzo*, meaning "piece," or *pazzo*, meaning "crazy."[20] Some scholars think the Lombard word for "a mouthful," *bizzo* or *pizzo* may be the origin of pizza.[21] According to Field, many sources think "pizza" is *picea* in Neapolitan dialect.[22] I have my own theory—that the word derives from the Greek word *pitta*, or *pita*. I'm basing this on a comparison with the city of Pozzuoli outside of Naples. Pozzuoli was founded by ancient Greeks, but the Romans moved there in 194 BC.[23] The name of the town in Latin was Puteoli.[24] According to a 1789 book of Neapolitan dialect, the Neapolitan name of the town is Pezzulo.[25] The volcanic sand in the area is known as pozzolana.[26] In Latin, it was *pulvis puteolanus*, "dust of Puteoli."[27] So I'm wondering if the "t" sound became double z's, and if the same happened to the word pita=pizza. Ed Levine says in *Pizza: A Slice of Heaven* that food writer Ed Behr writes that "pizza is an alternation of the Greek word *pitta*, which was introduced to southern Italy during the Byzantine conquest of the sixth century."[28] Food writer Nancy Verde Barr writes that Calabrians use the word "pitta" for filled pizza like a type of *pizza chiena* or *rustica*.[29] Levine notes that the earliest mention of the word "pizza" is from a Latin text from southern Italy in AD 997 called the *Codex Cajetanus*, a type of historical book on the area of Gaeta.[30] According to an article by Martin Maiden, linguistics professor at the University of Oxford, the book states that a tenant must give a bishop 12 pizzas every Christmas.[31] If only we still paid our rent in pizza.

The history isn't clear when pizza finally started to be pizza or resemble modern pizza. One thing is certain: it happened after the tomato was introduced to Italy, which is some time after Columbus's voyage to the Americas. The Associazione Verace Pizza Napoletana (AVPN, or VPN in the Americas), a nonprofit organization created in 1984 to protect and promote Neapolitan pizza, says pizza marinara was created in 1734, as its website and Helstosky note.[32] Pizza marinara, as defined by AVPN, is a pizza with only tomato, oil, oregano, and garlic.[33] There were pizzerias in Naples prior to this date, such as "n'tuno," opened in 1725 (or 1732, sources conflict on the date) by Domenico Testa and Zi'Ciccio's that opened in 1727.[34] Antica Pizzeria Port'Alba opened a pizza stand in 1738 and a restaurant in 1830, which is still open today, Barrett notes.[35] As Helstosky notes and I concur, Artusi's book, the preeminent Italian cookbook, doesn't mention pizza.[36] This fact is not a surprise, given that Artusi's cookbook bypassed most of the South with only a sprinkle of recipes from Naples and Sicily. He does mention a recipe for *pizza alla napoletana*, but it's not pizza as we know it. It's a ricotta custard pie.[37]

The most famous story of pizza is that of Queen Margherita, the queen of the newly united Italy. She and the king, Umberto I, visited Naples in 1889. Pizzaiolo Raffaele Esposito of Pizzeria Brandi, the oldest pizzeria in Naples, prepared a number of pizzas for her. One had lard, *caciocavallo* cheese, and basil. Helstosky notes one had "little fish,"[38] which I think were probably anchovies. And the final one had tomatoes, mozzarella, and basil in the colors of the Italian flag, red, white, and green. (Interestingly, the patriotic use of red and green coloring in food existed before unification, as, according to Field, after political unrest in 1821, red cherries and green citron were used in *panettone*.[39] The red, white, and green or tricolor flag was used in different form from the present-day Italian flag in areas of Northern Italy during the late eighteenth and early nineteenth centuries.[40]) This pizza would later be known as pizza Margherita, although, according to Pernice, documents exist that confirm this type of pizza was made at least as early as the mid-eighteen hundreds.[41] It was no mistake that Queen Margherita chose the latter pizza with its patriotic coloring, at a time when Southern Italians were just starting to leave the country in droves because the Southerners felt they had been swindled by the Northern invaders and a united Italy brought them nothing but devastation and taxation.

Despite this questionably mythic tale, pizza did not garner much attention in Italy. It remained a regional dish from Naples. According to Helstosky, a 1938 restaurant guide to the Naples area mentioned a number of pizzerias, but none in the rest of the country.[42] In fact, she says that from 1922 to 1945, it was "ignored by much of Italy."[43]

From the time of Queen Margherita's first taste of pizza to the end of World War II, pizza may have been ignored by the whole of Italy outside of Naples, but it wasn't ignored by the millions of Southern Italians who emigrated from Italy to the United States and other countries. In 1905, Gennaro Lombardi opened the first pizzeria in the United States, Lombardi's in New York's Little Italy, still in operation today.[44] At age 17, he bought a bakery and got the first license to sell pizza in New York City, according to Peter Genovese in *Pizza City: The Ultimate Guide to New York's Favorite Food*.[45] As Genovese mentions, other pizzaioli trained with him and went on to open their own shops: John Sasso, who opened John's on Bleecker Street in 1929; Patsy Lancieri of Patsy's in East Harlem, who then taught his nephew, Patsy Grimaldi, who owned Grimaldi's in Brooklyn; and Anthony Pero, who opened Totonno's in Coney Island in 1924.[46] (Current owner and granddaughter of Anthony Pero, Louise "Cookie" Ciminieri, says, in an interview with Genovese, that her grandfather "created pizza in this country" while working as a pizza maker for Lombardi.)[47]

To bake a pizza, the oven one uses must be able to reach very high temperatures. These first pizzerias in New York City had coal-fired ovens. Prior to that, in Naples, pizzas had been baked in wood-fired ovens. According to AVPN, "Verace Pizza Napoletana," or "original Neapolitan pizza," must be baked in a wood-fired oven.[48] Both types of ovens impart a smoky flavor, and the coal-fired oven makes great pies with black-bottomed crusts. Barrett says there was a return to wood-fired ovens in the United States in the 1980s.[49] Wolfgang Puck says wood-fired ovens make "crisp, delicious crust scented with a deep smoky flavor."[50] Personally, my experience with wood-fired pizza in the United States hasn't been what he describes. The pizzas are usually soggy in the middle—and these are pizzas that are served immediately. I am a proponent of coal-fired pizza, what is known in the United States as old New York pizza or New Haven pizza. People divide these into two distinct styles, but I do not.

At the same time as pizzerias were opening in New York City, they were opening in Italian enclaves across the country. Claiming to be the second-oldest pizzeria after Lombardi's is O'Scugnizzo's in Utica, New York, which was opened in 1914 by an Italian immigrant named Eugeno Burlino.[51] Burlino started with tomato pies, defined by O'Scugnizzo's website as pizza without mozzarella.[52] Joe's Tomato Pies in Trenton, New Jersey, opened in 1910, and though called "tomato pies," the pizza has mozzarella.[53] Joe Papa from Naples worked at Joe's and opened Papa's Tomato Pies in 1912, according to Barrett.[54] Mario's Restaurant on Arthur Avenue in the Bronx opened in 1919, selling pizza, notes Levine.[55] Frank Pepe opened in New Haven, Connecticut, in 1925.[56] Pizzeria Regina opened in Boston in 1926, according to Genovese.[57] Salvatore and Chiarina Marra, immigrants from Naples, opened Marra's pizzeria in Philadelphia in 1927.[58] Also that year, in Buffalo, New York, Neapolitan immigrant Fioravante Santora opened a pizzeria.[59] Aloy's in Poughkeepsie, New York, opened in 1929.[60] In New Haven, Connecticut, in 1932, Dominic Zuppardi opened Salerno's Bakery, making bread and pizza.[61] In 1947, according to Zuppardi's website, his son changed the name to Zuppardi's Apizza and focused on pizza.[62] According to an article in the *East Boston Times-Free Press*, the Santarpio family in Boston opened a bakery in 1903 that changed into a café in 1933 and into a pizzeria in 1966.[63] In Illinois in 1933, Sicilian immigrant Guy Alongi opened Alongi's that started as a bar and later became more of a pizzeria.[64] So did Pizzi Café, opened in 1934 in Ohio by Tony Pizzi, an immigrant from Italy, who sold square pizzas.[65] In 1939, after a trip to Boston to visit relatives, he learned of round-shaped pizzas and began making them at his own shop.[66] According to Pizzi Café's website, he is credited with bringing round-shaped pizza to Ohio.[67] Sciortino's opened in Perth Amboy, New Jersey, in 1934.[68] Also in 1934, an Italian American in New Haven, Connecticut, started what is now Modern Pizza.[69] According to DeLucia's website, in 1917, an Italian immigrant named Costantino DeLucia opened a bread bakery in Raritan, New Jersey, that began selling pizza in the 1930s and became pizza exclusively in the 1950s.[70] Jennie's in Monroe, Connecticut, was established in 1935 by the DeSimones, Neapolitan immigrants who had previously had a bakery since 1918.[71] The Cantalupo family, immigrants from Naples, opened Lupo's (called Tommaso's since 1971 when the Cantalupo family sold it to Tommy Chin, a Chinese American, who then changed the name to an Italian version of his name) in San Francisco in 1935.[72] Since 1973, it has been owned by Agostino Crotti.[73] According to its website, it was the first pizzeria with a wood-fired oven on the West coast.[74] Nicola Bevacqua opened the Reservoir Tavern in Boonton, New Jersey, in 1936, selling pizza and Italian food.[75] Also, in 1936, DeLorenzo's Tomato Pies opened in New Jersey.[76] In 1938, Salvatore Consiglio opened Sally's Apizza in New Haven, Connecticut.[77]

I'd also like to point out that all of these pizzerias are still in operation today. If you read about the oldest pizzerias in the United States, you will find these pizzerias listed. They oft appear in pizza histories, books, and articles. However, there were other pizzerias created by early Italian immigrants and Italian Americans that have closed through the years. My great-aunt and uncle had a pizzeria in the 1920s and '30s that has since closed. (My grandmother worked there, and this is where my grandfather came to court her.) Since the cult of pizza is fairly a new one—especially within the past ten years with the popularity of food blogs and online food sites—the documentation of pizzerias has only recently begun to happen. And that documentation includes the pizzerias that are in operation today or that closed not too long ago. There were other pizzerias, restaurants, and bakeries in cities that were inhabited by early Italian immigrants and their descendants, and it would take a lot of research to uncover these all across the country.

One of the earliest peddlers of pizza in the United States was Frank Pepe. Pepe, an Italian immigrant, began selling what pizza writers refer to as "white pizza" with olive oil, oregano, and anchovies from a street cart and then opening Pepe's in New Haven in 1925. I think Frank Pepe's white pizza was simply a variation of pizza that had been eaten in Naples and that he brought with him to the United States. It was a very old variation of pizza as it had been eaten in Naples before the tomato arrived.

I also feel this way about the Trenton tomato pie (which is found at other pizzerias besides the ones in Trenton, L&B Spumoni Gardens in Brooklyn is one, although it is different, arguably more like a *sfincione*, defined later in this paragraph) and the Sicilian pizza. Pizza writers and aficionados list anywhere from 10-14 different categories for pizza currently in the United States. These include separate categories for old New York pizza, New Haven pizza, Chicago pizza, the Jersey tomato pie. Adam Kuban, who wrote the popular pizza blog, SLICE, lists 30, which I think is entirely too many.[78] (One of the pizzas he lists is called *pizza di sfrigole* from the Abruzzo region of Italy that editor Carey Jones discovered.[79] Jones says it is made from lard, flour, salt, and "little pig bits" and has a pastrylike texture.[80] To me, this is not pizza. Although it is called pizza, it is in a different category—more like a bread. It is what we always called lard bread. Perhaps similar to a *ciccioli* bread or Neapolitan *casatiello*. This is a good place to mention that Italians use the word "pizza" to refer to a few different things. One is, of course, the pizza we all know. Others are pies, tortes, and as a generic word for dough, as in *pizza fritta*, or fried dough—also a phrase meaning calzone. While I have seen the *pizza di sfrigole* referred to as a focaccia, it is more breadlike than pizzalike.) While pizza "authorities" want to distinguish all these different styles, I believe that many of these categories are one and the same: the pizza that the Neapolitan, Sicilian, and Southern Italian immigrants brought with them to the United States. Nick Azzaro, owner of Papa's Tomato Pies in Trenton, New Jersey, was asked what the difference is between tomato pies and pizza. His response: " . . . sign makers charged by the letter, and 'PIZZA' is five letters shorter than 'TOMATO PIES.'"[81] This means that there is no difference, and I agree. Yes, with a tomato pie, the cheese is put on the dough first before the tomato. Does this create a variation in taste experience and texture? Absolutely. But I believe this was just a personal style of the pizzaiolo or a style that existed in a particular area of Naples and is pizza, just as Azzaro says. I also think Sicilian pizza derived from the Sicilian *sfincione*, as other pizza writers like Barrett, have noted.[82] The *sfincione* is similar to a focaccia with a rectangular shape and a thicker, more doughy texture. It's topped with tomato and minimal cheese. I would say that Sicilian immigrants who opened pizzerias created these and called it pizza because pizza was popular and easy to pronounce, unlike *sfincione*. And like Barrett says, mozzarella was added to suit American taste.[83] I would go further to say that areas of the country where square or rectangular, doughy pies gained popularity probably had more Sicilian immigrants opening pizzerias. I'm thinking of Detroit-style pizza. Perhaps these immigrants were from Puglia, as Schwartz writes that pizza in Puglia is in a sheet pan, not round.[84] Another style is the deep dish, often distinguished from the Chicago style and also distinguished from Giordano's, which has a top crust. I believe that these styles stemmed from the Italian *pizza chiena*, or *pizza rustica*, which is a double crusted pie filled with meats and cheese (though not filled with tomato or tomato sauce). Helstosky likens deep-dish pizza and tomato pie to the Renaissance Italian *torta*.[85] This may be so, but the Renaissance Italian *torta* can also be likened to the *pizza chiena*. In fact, I think that deep-dish pizza is more similar to the *pizza chiena*, which the early immigrants were making and eating. Another style of pizza I'd like to mention is St. Louis, known for its uncharacteristic use of Provel cheese. Barrett says Provel was created in 1947 by Costa Grocery (now Roma Grocery) and the Hoffman Dairy Company of Wisconsin (now with Kraft Foods) specifically for use on pizza.[86] She says it was supposed to melt without being stretchy like mozzarella.[87] She mentions it also has liquid smoke as an ingredient. Barrett theorizes that the liquid smoke is supposed to lend a smoky flavor similar to that of a wood-burning oven.[88] While she may be right, my theory is that it is supposed to taste like smoked provolone or possibly *scamorza*, smoked mozzarella. It is a blend of provolone, cheddar, and Swiss cheeses.[89] Provel doesn't contain mozzarella, the typical pizza cheese. But not all Neapolitan pizza had mozzarella. Remember one pizza that pizzaiolo Raffaele Esposito prepared for Queen Margherita had nothing but lard, *caciocavallo*, and basil. *Caciocavallo* is a Southern Italian cheese that tastes similar to provolone. And pizza in West Virginia, Ohio, and western Pennsylvania is made with only provolone like at West Virginia pizzeria Di Carlo's, established in 1945,[90] or with provolone mixed with mozzarella. According to Rebecca Caro in the *From Argentina With Love* blog, in Argentina, pizza is served with provolone as the only cheese or with a mozzarella and provolone mix.[91] While this may have nothing to do with Provel, I think perhaps some of the early immigrants put provolone on pizza because that's what they had done in Italy.

The early immigrants to the United States (and other countries) brought their foodways with them. Whatever they had been eating in their region of Italy, they also ate in the United States. Pizza is no exception. The early immigrants created the first pizzerias in the United States in Italian neighborhoods. Eventually, pizza, like spaghetti and meatballs, reached a wider audience and non-Italian Americans began opening their own pizzerias as well.

The prevailing thought in most books on pizza is that pizza became a popular food in the United States after American GIs discovered it in Italy while they were stationed there during World War II. This myth is repeated in every pizza book as well as other books on American food like the *Woman's Day Encyclopedia of Cookery*, published in 1966.[92] Helstosky's book also mentions this, but she goes on to say, " . . . but it is also true that Italian-Americans did their share to promote the food at street fairs and in family-friendly restaurants."[93] Bob Orkand writes in *The Item*, a Huntsville, Texas, newspaper, "Cristoforo Colombo of Genoa, Italy, didn't really 'discover' America, despite what we were all taught in second grade or thereabouts. But 450 years after Columbus' alleged discovery, American GIs returning from World War II campaigns in Italy brought with them a discovery which almost rivals that of the Italian explorer in its earth-shaking significance. They discovered pizza!"[94]

I disagree with this myth. American GIs didn't discover something that was already being produced and eaten by early Italian immigrants, their American children, and people who lived in or around Italian neighborhoods. Early Italian immigrants created the first pizzerias in the United States and like spaghetti and meatballs and other Italian foods, pizza gained in popularity as it moved out of Italian neighborhoods. Non-Italian Americans were discovering pizza in the United States prior to World War II. Moses cites a *New York Tribune* writer, who in 1903, described a "'pomidore pizza,' or tomato pie . . . with plenty of red pepper on top."[95] The article says, "Pie has usually been considered a Yankee dish exclusively, but apparently the Italian has invented a kind of pie."[96] Mariani cites the *New York Herald Tribune* food columnist, Clementine Paddleford, who wrote in 1939, "If someone suggests a 'pizza pie' after the theater, don't think it is going to be a wedge of apple. It is going to be the surprise of your life, . . . a nice stunt to surprise the visiting relatives, who will be heading East soon for the World's Fair. They come to be surprised, and pizza, pronounced 'peet-za,' will do the job brown."[97] Before the War, food columnists and reviewers were enlightening the general public about pizza. I'm wondering if the myth of the American GI bringing pizza to the States got started because of Ira Nevin, the creator of the first gas-fired pizza oven.

Prior to World War II, Nevin's family owned a business for which he worked that built and repaired brick ovens in New Rochelle, New York, according to Mariani.[98] Nevin was stationed in Italy during the war, notes Orkand.[99] Afterwards, he studied engineering under the GI bill. I've read conflicting reports of either an Italian-American pizza maker or an Italian pizza maker in Naples approaching him about a gas appliance that couldn't get a high enough temperature to bake pizza. In 1945, as Barrett notes, Nevin set to work and created a gas-fired pizza oven.[100] According to Barrett, this oven was cleaner and cheaper to use.[101] Before this invention, Barrett says, all ovens in the United States were coal-fired.[102] The coal-fired ovens in the old New York pizzerias could be about 12 x 12 feet, says Barrett.[103] And, Barrett notes, coal-fired ovens require much more maintenance to operate and take a long time to heat from cold.[104] With a coal-fired oven, Barrett says, coals sit in a compartment adjacent to the oven and can reach up to 2,000 degrees Fahrenheit.[105] Heat moves to the brick oven floor, she notes, creating a temperature of 600-1,000 degrees, and the domed top and brick walls retain and reflect heat.[106] She adds, in the modern coal-fired oven, gas burners ignite the coals.[107]

Within 20 years, Barrett notes, the gas-fired oven became the popular style of oven in pizzerias in the country.[108] Because it was cheaper and easier to use, it stands to reason that it brought down the costs associated with opening a pizzeria. The 1950s and '60s saw a boom in pizzerias as well as pizza innovation. And pizza moved out of the Italian neighborhoods and into the mainstream society. Helstosky notes that pizzamaking kits were available for home cooks in 1948.[109] Frozen pizzas, she adds, were available in the early 1950s.[110] Rose and Jim Totino opened a pizzeria in 1951 in Minneapolis, Minnesota, and created a frozen pizza company that they later sold to Pillsbury.[111] Gabaccia notes that Rose went on to work at Pillsbury and became its first female vice president.[112] Pizza Hut opened in 1958.[113] Popular culture reflected the opening of pizzerias across the country. Dean Martin was singing, "When the moon hits your eye like a big pizza pie, that's amore." On *The Andy Griffith Show*, Andy and Barney suggested taking Thelma Lou and Helen out for pizza. Ralph Kramden mentions pizza in *The Honeymooners*. Little Caesars was opened in 1959 in Garden City, Michigan, by Michael and Marian Ilitch.[114] In 1960, the owners of DomiNick's in Ypsilanti, Michigan, sold to brothers Tom and James Monaghan.[115] James sold his half to Tom, who then changed the name to Domino's and offered fast delivery.[116] In 1962, Pep Simek, who owned a bar near a cemetery in Medford, Wisconsin, created Tombstone Pizza.[117] He sold it to Kraft in 1986,[118] and Levine says, in 1995, Kraft made DiGiorno, the first frozen pizza with a rising crust Kraft developed with a patented process using "hydrophilic colloids for stability and surfactants to 'facilitate flour hydration and initial dough development.'"[119] Ed Levine and Jeffrey Steingarten tested various frozen

111

pizzas for *Pizza: A Slice of Heaven* and Steingarten concluded they were all "ca-ca."[120]

The proliferation of pizza meant one thing—the commercialization of pizza and its ultimate standardization in mainstream society. However, the old mom and pop places with their coal ovens were still producing pizza the traditional way—as a number of them still do today. Pizza quickly deviated from a quality product to one made with cheaper and inferior ingredients. People who grew up near Italian-American neighborhoods were exposed to authentic Italian pizza, but people who didn't usually had a Pizza Hut, Domino's, Pizza Inn, or Little Caesars. And these shops are to pizza what McDonald's and Burger King are to hamburgers. Levine makes a good point about these pizza chains. He says, "The pizza chains were all started by business people, as opposed to individuals interested in food."[121] He then outlines the three fundamental tenets of fast food restaurants: 1. A standardized product, 2. Competitive pricing, and 3. Cheap labor.[122] He says how this translated to the pizza at these chains is that the pizza was made at one facility and transported to the pizza shops to be baked.[123] To keep costs down, he notes, owners use lower-quality ingredients.[124] Because workers aren't paid well, he says, they don't have the extensive training and know-how of a pizzaiolo.[125] Levine himself taste-tested pizza at all of these chains.[126] I have had pizza at Pizza Hut, Pizza Inn, Domino's, Little Caesars, Papa John's, Godfather's Pizza, and Sbarro's. Some were worse than others, and like Levine,[127] I believe that all are not worth eating. Unfortunately, not only did mainstream America get their first taste of pizza at these places, so did the world, notes Helstosky.[128] According to its website, Pizza Hut has sixteen thousand stores in more than one hundred countries.[129] Helstosky says it was the first pizza chain to open in China, in 1988.[130] It also opened in Moscow in 1990 and in India in 1996.[131] John Schnatter opened Papa John's in 1984 and, according to Barrett, was the first pizzeria to offer online ordering across the country.[132] Helstosky says, "The value of America's culinary contributions to the pizza may be debatable, but the economic and technological contributions of the United States account for the tremendous global reach of pizza today."[133] It is true that the United States made pizza a globally loved food. Helstosky says, "Italian immigration facilitated pizza's popularity, American innovations in franchising and marketing, combined with a particularly creative or liberal approach to pizza-making, provided the momentum needed for pizza's global rise to power."[134] And it started because the early Italian immigrants brought their pizza recipes and methods with them to the United States, opening bakeries, pizzerias, cafés, and restaurants serving pizza.

It is important to note that emigrants from Italy opened pizzerias in the countries to which they immigrated. So non-Italians in these countries were getting a taste of pizza that wasn't the commercialized American variety. In Australia, Salvatore Della Bruna and Franco Fera opened Toto's Pizza

House in Melbourne in 1961.[135] According to Samantha Oster in *Cardinal Points: Mapping Adelaide's Diversity—People, Places, Points of View*, in 1956, Italian immigrant Lucia Rosella opened Lucia's Pizza Bar in Adelaide.[136] Pizza ovens first arrived in Canada in the 1950s, according to John Mackie in the *Vancouver Sun*.[137] Amy Pataki of the *Toronto Star* says Toronto's oldest pizzeria is Vesuvio Pizzeria & Spaghetti House, opened in 1957 by the Pugliese family, Italian immigrants to Canada.[138] Domenico Pugliese went to New York to learn the pizza trade, she notes.[139] Montreal's oldest pizzeria is Pizzeria Napoletana, opened in 1948 in the city's Little Italy and was first host to Italian immigrant workers, according to its website.[140]

Italian Americans made pizza famous. Helstosky says Italians in many areas outside of Naples weren't even eating it until after the 1960s,[141] meaning the Southern Italians brought it to the United States who in turn brought it back to Italy.[142] Mattozzi makes a distinction between pizza and Neapolitan pizza, saying that Neapolitan pizza was "the exclusive property of the city of Naples for over two centuries."[143] He quotes Neapolitan journalist, Roberto Minervini, who in 1956, wrote that "almost all" of the pizzaioli who opened up pizzerias outside of Naples were not successful.[144] "Outside of Naples" isn't defined, but it surely cannot include the United States, because by 1956, Italians in the United States had many successful pizzerias across the country, and in fact, they made pizza a globally loved food. Most of them were making Neapolitan pizza, especially on the East Coast in states like New York, New Jersey, Connecticut, Pennsylvania, Rhode Island, and Massachusetts. Mattozzi also says, "Even though some pizzerias had been opened in America by Neapolitan emigrants at the end of the nineteenth and the beginning of the twentieth century, they were isolated phenomenon that did not have much importance."[145] Was Lombardi's an isolated phenomenon? Pepe's didn't have much importance? *They* made pizza what it is today. *They* made pizza famous. He goes on to say that in the mid-twentieth century, pizza left the Naples's "city limits" to traverse the world.[146] I disagree. It was the Italian in America who made pizza a worldwide food, not the Italians in Naples.

Italians in Naples were obviously unhappy with the commercialized version of pizza they were seeing from American companies. As Helstosky notes in 1981, the *Associazione Pizzaioli Europei e Sostenitori* (APES), or the Association of European Pizza-Makers and Supporters, known since 1996 as the *Associazione Pizzaioli e Similari*, or the Association of Pizza-Makers and Such, was founded to improve the quality of pizza in response to its commercialization.[147] But the Neapolitans didn't end there. Helstosky says they wanted a protected DOC status for Neapolitan-style pizza, and in 1984, the AVPN formed to protect and promote Neapolitan pizza as the "true" representation of Neapolitan pizza, "Verace Pizza Napoletana."[148] Levine says restaurateur Peppe Miele founded the VPN in America in 1998.[149] Prof. Carlo

Mangoni, who teaches nutrition at Second University of Naples, devised the VPN in a 42-page book that outlines its history and production, according to Lucas Leigh in *PMQ* magazine.[150] Leigh says this book became the guideline for the Italian government, which, Helstosky notes, subsequently awarded Pizza Napoletana DOC status in 1997.[151] Helstosky defines DOC as *denominazione di origine controllata*, a legal "certification of regional authenticity."[152] She says pizzerias worldwide can become members of the AVPN and display the emblem that guarantees they are making "Verace Pizza Napoletana."[153] They exist now in many countries around the globe. The AVPN recognizes only two types of pizza: Margherita (tomato, olive oil, basil, grated hard cheese, and mozzarella or *fior di latte*) and marinara (tomato, olive oil, oregano, and garlic).[154] There are also other requirements in the ingredients and method of baking. Dough must be made with flour, salt, water, and natural yeast and kneaded in such a way where the dough doesn't overheat, notes Helstosky.[155] She adds it must be manipulated by hand and cooked on the surface of the wood-fired oven at 750 degrees.[156] In addition, the ingredients must be from Campania, Italy, and include either *mozzarella di bufala* or *fior di latte* (cow's milk mozzarella), San Marzano tomatoes from Campania, extra-virgin olive oil, and 00 (double zero) flour.[157] Adhering to the rules can be expensive, though, as Levine addresses the irony that a food that was started for the masses has become one legislated for the affluent.[158] Although, Miele says, according to Leigh, American products are acceptable, like California-grown plum tomatoes, premium flour, and fresh mozzarella.[159] It is also interesting to note that many of the owners of VPN restaurants worldwide are not of Italian descent, so in an ironic twist, the pizza deemed authentic Neapolitan pizza is being made by non-Italians.

There are many pizzerias that do not meet the strict requirements—even pizzerias in Naples, notes Helstosky, and I would add all the pizzerias opened by the early Italian immigrants to the United States.[160] Surprisingly, Levine notes, the pizzeria that allegedly served Queen Margherita in 1889, Pizzeria Brandi, doesn't qualify as having VPN.[161] Another pizzeria in Naples, Da Michele's, also doesn't qualify and, as Levine says, admittedly uses cheaper ingredients like vegetable oil instead of extra-virgin olive oil, cow's milk mozzarella, and San Marzano tomatoes that come from the Sarno Valley, not near Mount Vesuvius.[162] Levine says that the pizzeria uses "cheap oil."[163] I would have to say that I would not want a pizza made with vegetable oil in the United States, especially since most vegetable oils are made from 100 percent soy today and most likely, GMO soy, although I'm not sure if GMO soy is allowed in Italy. Writing in *Naples at Table* in 1998, Schwartz says most Neapolitan chefs use peanut oil for *frying*.[164] In 1998, soybean oil wasn't as prevalent, so I'm not sure if the use of peanut oil has changed in Italy today. In the United States, vegetable oil is from GMO soy. However, not all of these ingredients are necessarily lower quality and not all pizzerias without

VPN are using lower-quality ingredients. Some pizzas are just a different style. According to their website, the Condurro family of Da Michele's started making pizza in 1870.[165] Michele Condurro opened his pizzeria in 1906 and it has been at its current location since 1930.[166] There are only two types of pizza served there, the Neapolitan classics, marinara and Margherita. The pizzeria's website says it doesn't use "junk" to make its pizza, only "natural" ingredients.[167] In an article by Claudia Ausilio in *Vesuvio Live*, owners Francesco and Fabrizio Condurro say they use a blend of vegetable, peanut, and sunflower oils before they cook the pizza and then use olive oil on the pizza once it is cooked.[168] They say they do this because, at high temperatures, the olive oil leaves a burned taste to the dough.[169] In addition, they use *fior di latte* (cow's milk) mozzarella.[170] *Fior di latte* is cheaper than *mozzarella di bufala*, but I wouldn't necessarily say it's "cheap" or "bad" to use it. It is different and not as creamy or flavorful as *bufala mozzarella*, but it is still good. The Condurros say it bakes better.[171]

As Schwartz notes in *The Southern Italian Table*, " . . . every little locality likes to claim its own special variance on the Neapolitan model."[172] He says in Salerno, sixty miles south of Naples, they brag about crispy crust.[173] Puglia has a sheet-pan style.[174] Sicily has a plethora of pizza varieties besides Neapolitan-style.[175] So the Italian government is denying the cultural legacy of the Southern Italians still in Italy as well as those who came to the United States and other countries in the late nineteenth and early twentieth centuries by saying that they are not producing "true" Neapolitan pizza. Even when many pizza aficionados prefer different styles of pizza. Levine traveled to Naples and sampled pizza from 15 different pizzerias, and he thought they were all basically the same.[176] They had "bready" crusts that weren't crispy, and they were wet because the canned tomatoes weren't drained and there was moisture from the cheese.[177] My reasoning for this may not be the moisture from the tomatoes and cheese so much as the *doppio zero*, or double zero, flour used to make the pizza, or perhaps a combination of all three. I'm thinking perhaps the finer flour does not hold the ingredients as well as a stronger-grain flour. It may be the wood in a wood-fired oven, according to Frank Pepe's website, which says that coal does not produce the steam that wood does.[178] Regardless, Levine didn't seem to think it was a contest—he preferred the crisp, charred crust of the coal-fired oven pizza in the United States.[179] I have to say that I agree with Levine. I prefer the crispy crust of Sally's in New Haven or Grimaldi's in Brooklyn or John's of Bleecker or Lombardi's in Manhattan or, I would add, the New York-style of Di Fara's in Brooklyn. I have tried a few pizzas in Naples and felt that for the most part, the crust was more doughy and the center was more soggy, requiring a knife and fork to eat it, or if folded, the ingredients would slip off the inner edge. However, the ingredients themselves are superior to most ingredients found on American pizza. With a VPN designation, Gino Sorbillo's pizza is highly recommended. There is usually a huge wait to get inside, and they don't always give out numbered tickets. I fought my way in to try this pizza and felt it was good, but not great. I did, however, enjoy Sorbillo's Patrizio pizza with local onions, the ramata onion from Montoro (*cipolla ramata di Montoro* from Irpinia) and the Alife onion (*cipolla di Alife*), that were the most deliciously sweet onions I've ever tasted. I also tried pizza from Vesi, recommended to me by my cousins. Vesi was founded in 1921 and is also a VPN pizzeria.[180] Vesi makes a delicious pizza, and it was the least "soggy" of the ones I sampled. I enjoyed a *pizza portafoglio* from the cart at Donna Sophia on Via Tribunali. *Pizza portafoglio* is a pizza that is folded in quarters and eaten on the go. It was crispier and very delicious. Donna Sophia has an APN (*L'Associazione Pizzaiuoli Napoletani*, or the Association of Neapolitan Pizzaioli) designation which, unlike the VPN, does not certify the pizza but the pizzaiolo, the pizza maker. Some pizzeria owners, like Paolo Cavalli of Cavalli Pizza in Texas, think this is better because the certification travels with the pizzaiolo.[181] According to Scott Reitz in the *Dallas Observer*, Cavalli's criticism of VPN certification is lack of monitoring.[182] He says a representative from Naples came once to observe for an hour, gave the certification, and never returned.[183] Da Michele is also popular, and while it does not have a VPN, I thought it was a good pizza, albeit soggy. While I prefer the coal-fired New York-style and New Haven-style pizza, all of these Neapolitan pizzas are worlds better than any chain pizza and most run-of-the-mill pizzerias in the United States.

In addition to the VPN designation, the *Guardian* reported that Italy requested that Neapolitan pizza be made part of UNESCO's list of Intangible Cultural Heritage of Humanity for those things that are intangible unlike a building or natural site, which would be on UNESCO's World Heritage List, and in December 2017, it got its wish as the Art of the Neapolitan Pizzaiolo became part of UNESCO's list of Intangible Cultural Heritage of Humanity.[184] This list includes things like traditional dances, ceremonies, foods, and artwork created with a particular skill handed down through generations. Examples, according to the UNESCO website, are Spanish Flamenco and Chinese paper-cut.[185] There are other foods on the list like gingerbread craft from Northern Croatia, gastronomic meal of the French, and the Mediterranean diet.[186] In addition, the BBC reported that the Italian government recently proposed legislation that would require pizzaiolo to complete a 120-hour course and pass an exam to become a professional pizzaiolo.[187]

It is understandable why the Italian government and the Neapolitan pizzaioli would want to protect Neapolitan pizza, given the excess of commercialized products posing as pizza out there. I described my parents' experience in North Carolina where people preferred Pizza Hut and Domino's to the more authentic New York-style pizza my parents made.

What I object to is by creating the VPN and being on UNESCO's list, the Italian government is saying that the pizza produced by the early Italian immigrants was not pizza but in effect, was something different, not real, not authentic, not Italian. Again, the Southern Italian immigrant denied his history, denied his truth, denied his being.

Someone asked me, why do you care if Neapolitan pizza has this designation? I care because I am the descendant of that Southern Italian immigrant. It is my history, my truth, my being at question. Again, this is economic competition, the Italians versus the Americans, who can produce a globally loved pizza? Currently, according to Genovese, the pizza business brings in $35 billion annually—just in the United States.[188] And it's a global market. It can be found anywhere from Shanghai to Moscow to Kenya to Sydney. Helstosky notes that in 1982, Wolfgang Puck hired Ed LaDou as pizza chef at Spago.[189] He created barbecue chicken pizza, pizza with truffles, and smoked salmon pizza, essentially creating a new era of designer pizza and elevating pizza from a food for everyone to a food for the epicurean set.[190] She notes that Chef Alice Waters served pizza at Chez Panisse.[191] Pizza appealed to every income bracket. Levine notes that Chef Todd English has opened pizzerias named Figs and one can be found at the LaGuardia airport in New York.[192] Pizza was such a versatile food that each market added something a little different to suit the tastes of that region. In Romania, Helstosky notes, pizza is thin crust with scant cheese or sauce but a lot of fresh veggies like mushrooms, olives, and peppers.[193] She says in Brazil, pizza has little to no sauce and soft crust with hard-boiled eggs, hearts of palm, or sweetcorn.[194] In Kuwait, she says pizza has shawarma beef or chicken and sliced pickles.[195] Pizza is universally loved, and I think everyone wants his slice, pun intended. According to Dinfin Mulupi in *How we made it in Africa*, in Ethiopia, there are many Orthodox Christians who observe long fasting periods where they cannot consume dairy or meat.[196] The article says pizzerias like Cris's Pizza in Addis Ababa, have adapted, serving cheese- and meat-less pizzas.[197] Italianfood.net notes in 2015, Richard Wang, fresh food category manager at City Super Group gave the Italians advice on how to market to Chinese consumers.[198] He said that the Chinese buy American pizza "because they do not know that the best pizza in the world is Italian."[199] There are two VPN pizzerias in Shanghai now, according to the Associazione Verace Pizza Napoletana.[200]

To date, there are VPN members in 37 countries, including Italy, from the Philippines to New Zealand to the United Arab Emirates to Norway to Canada, to Brazil and Japan.[201] To make true Neapolitan pizza, all the pizza books say one must have a special brick oven. According to a 2015 article by Cara Giaimo in *Atlas Obscura*, in 2009, Paulie Gee in Brooklyn bought one custom-made from Stefano Ferrara, a third-generation oven-builder in Italy; the price of the oven, including transporting, customs, and installation was

$25,000.[202] (The current VPN rules are a bit more relaxed to accommodate situations where owners cannot have a wood-fired oven. If a pizzeria owner can prove they cannot have a wood-fired oven installed, they can use a VPN-approved gas oven.)[203] In addition, one must buy products like mozzarella and San Marzano tomatoes from Campania. All of this is business for Italy. And that is fine, but not at the price of the Southern Italian immigrant's history.

Naples isn't alone in blame. American capitalism is at fault as well. As it does with pretty much every product it makes, it degrades the quality and creates a misrepresentation in consumers' minds. The quality that was there 20 to 30 years ago is gone. It has changed, and any person who comes here now, in the twenty-first century, has the impression that food in the United States is lower quality and inferior. It is, but I'd like to stress that it didn't used to be. One used to be able to get full-fat creamy heavy cream, buttermilk, and ice cream. One could get oils that were something other than soy. Bread was made from wheat flour—not soy. Produce was sold seasonally and locally. Just name any product made by a large American corporation today. Yogurt, for one. An Israeli told me yogurt in Israel is real yogurt, not the yogurt in the United States. Cream cheese is made from whey protein and gums. Popular American chocolate tastes like a brown paste with an oily mouthfeel. Pizza has been no exception. Chain pizza is the standard pizza most people know, and it is made from inferior ingredients. Papa John's claim is better ingredients, and it is better than other chains, but, according to its website, its dough is made with soybean oil.[204] The part-skim mozzarella has modified food starch, whey protein concentrate, and sugarcane fiber.[205] The pizza sauce has mostly sunflower oil but also olive oil.[206] At Pizza Hut, according to its website, the pizza crust has soybean oil, the cheese has powdered cellulose (the wood pulp we heard about in the news) and modified food starch, and the garlic crust has soybean oil and vegetable mono and diglycerides and a lot of other stuff.[207] (Not to mention the pan oil has TBHQ.)[208] According to its website, Domino's pizza crust has soybean oil and L-cysteine,[209] an amino acid usually made from hog hair, hair swept up at Chinese salons, or poultry feathers, but I do not know the source of Domino's L-cysteine. The pizza cheese has modified food starch, whey protein concentrate, and cellulose.[210] The pizza sauce has soybean oil.[211] I couldn't find detailed ingredient information on Little Caesars's website. The only thing it writes is that it uses "100% Mozzarella and Muenster" cheeses and "vine-ripened California crushed tomatoes."[212] These pizza companies are the top four in sales, according to *Pizza Today* magazine in 2016.[213] When one reads their ingredients, one understands why the Italian government created the VPN.

These companies were responsible for the closing of many an Italian-American family-owned pizzeria. If there were no Pizza Hut or Domino's, I might be inheriting a family business today that would have probably put me through school. (Or not. As I mentioned, North Carolina wasn't the most welcoming place for an Italian-owned family business.) Levine interviewed House of Pizza and Calzone owner John Teutonico who closed his business in 2004 after a Domino's opened up in the Brooklyn neighborhood.[214] Unfortunately, pizza became mass-produced by big businesses. And a large majority of non-Italian Americans preferred this false, commercialized pizza to pizza created by Americans of Italian descent in their family pizzerias.

What the Italian government and the Italian people need to understand is that Southern Italian immigrants brought their tradition of pizzamaking to the United States and other countries where they settled. They created pizza with the whole, nutritious ingredients with which pizza should be made. The pizza made by the early Italian immigrants to the United States was no less Italian, no less Neapolitan, no less Sicilian, no less authentic, no less real, no less valid than the pizza made in Naples by VPN members with DOC designations today. Those families in the United States whose businesses have stood the test of time, who continue to run private businesses in a time when it is increasingly difficult to do so are the cultural legacy of the Italian Americans. Their pizza is our history. Eating commercialized pizza or "Verace Pizza Napoletana" can be enjoyable. Some of both of these types of pizzas taste good. However, neither is preserving the cultural heritage of Americans of Italian descent.

CHAPTER 8: Italian Food Around the World

The world over people associate Italian food with a certain lifestyle. That is, *la dolce vita*, literally translated to "the sweet life," popularized by the 1960 Fellini film of the same name, but meaning living the good life. As Mariani mentions in Chapter 6 of *How Italian Food Conquered the World*, this notion permeated to cars, fashion, travel, and of course, food.[1] The Italian elite in Italy wanted their representation of Italian food (not the Southern Italian cuisine of Americans of Italian descent) to be the standard definition of Italian food. They scoffed at what was considered the heavy-handed garlic in this American-Italian cuisine, which only perpetuated prejudice of Americans of Southern Italian descent as being "garlic-eaters" or smelling like garlic.

This garlic bias was one that went back to the Middle Ages, where, as Montanari notes, the upper class associated garlic, onions, and vegetables with peasants.[2] In fact, Southern Italian cooking, while it does utilize garlic a lot, uses it with a light touch to add flavor to dishes—not in the way it is overly used in some American restaurants. And any American of Italian descent would agree with this statement. As Severgnini says, "Like elegance, garlic should be present but should not intrude."[3] My belief is that Italians from Italy wanted to disassociate from their "lower-class" American brothers and sisters, denouncing the use of garlic and "red sauce."

In the decades following, Italy would be fighting to change its image in the American and global market. Perhaps this was due to the influx of post-World War II Italian immigrants. In the 1970s, restaurants opened serving Northern Italian cuisine, dishes like polenta and risotto, dishes with butter and cream, a simplified version of the cuisine of Northern Italy. And very often, these restaurants had to include those "Italian-American" dishes so loathed because those dishes were popular not just with the American people but with the global market. Schwartz also mentions that many of those restaurants had Southern Italian chefs.[4]

According to Mariani, in 1979, Tony May founded the Gruppo Ristoratori Italiani (GRI) to enhance the image of "authentic" Italian cuisine to "restaurants, US press, culinary schools, importers, distributors and general consumers with the intent to achieve a better understanding of Italian food and wine in North America"; Mariani says May had the food media visit Italy to see where the food was produced to be exposed to the "true flavors and culinary concepts of modern Italy."[5] Americans of Italian descent had been doing this for generations, many visiting Italy or with relatives in Italy still conducting business and importing. Mariani also mentions Lucio Caputo, who established the Italian Wine & Food Institute in 1983 to "promote and further improve the image of Italian wines and foods in the United States."[6]

Mariani says Piero Antolini, a food and travel writer who directed the official magazine of the Italian Federation of Cooks, *Il Cuoco*, "acknowledged that Italian-American food was better known abroad than Italian food."[7] Antolini said, "This Italian cuisine for export may have done damage to our culinary image; on the other hand, this probably could not have been avoided. The early Italian immigrants were in no position to behave differently."[8] This statement comes across as elitist and seems to ignore the role American commercialism played in exporting Italian-American food. His statement sounds like the same tired one of "peasant ignorance" when not all early Italian immigrants were peasants, and if some were peasants, it doesn't mean they didn't know good food. In fact, they made good food. American commercialism created chain restaurants and fast food that produced poorer-quality versions of their dishes and also warped the definition of Italian food for advertising and marketing purposes. This fact has little to do with the early immigrants and more to do with the American business model.

Mariani also quotes film producer Dino De Laurentiis, who, in 1981, said, "There really are no Italian restaurants in the United States," and then he opened his own.[9] Does this statement mean that Italian-American restaurants are not serving Italian food, and in fact, are "inauthentic," i.e., inferior to ones in Italy? If one is talking about restaurants in 1980s Italy, then this statement is most likely a true one. As the culture evolved in Italy through the decades since the great migration, Italians in the United States adhered to the culture their grandparents brought with them. Italian food in Italy changed while Italian food in the United States remained traditional.

In 1980s New York, this "Northern Italian/Tuscan" cuisine was preferred among trendy/elite circles. Tony May called it "modern *cucina italiana*"[10] which is a better description, as, as Mariani mentions, it encompassed a number of influences, technological advances, more access to diverse ingredients, and more regional mixing. May describes the cuisine as being lighter, it is assumed, than Italian-American cuisine. " . . . you didn't feel like you'd just eaten a cow when you left Palio," he says.[11] According to Mariani, the formerly known "Italian-American cuisine" was ignored as boring.[12] Hazan mentions that she was often told that Italian cooking from Italy would not be successful in America.[13] She says, "I was weary of the clichés of so-called northern Italian as I was of the garlicky, over-sauced, overflowing portions of presumed southern-style Italian. I was eager to prove that judiciously balanced classic dishes, based on genuine regional traditions, could win the game. I had the satisfaction, which I shall carry with me always, of knowing that they would have. I was ahead when the game was called."[14]

However, the popular style of Italian cuisine in the world was then and still is the cooking of Southern Italy as it was originally brought to the United States by Southern Italians during the great migration. Hazan is known for a tomato sauce made from fresh tomatoes, onion, and butter,[15] but this sauce is not the sauce of Italian Americans or Southern Italians. Real Italian tomato sauce is made with olive oil, and this is the sauce that is used the world over to make any kind of Italian food product that calls for tomato sauce. In addition, Southern Italians use canned tomatoes, either chopped or in puree form as well as tomato paste. Schwartz writes, "It's not only for their convenience, but also because they are generally better than fresh."[16] And historically, because they weren't available in every region. For example, the famous *bucatini all'amatriciana*, the dish from the 2016-earthquake-ravaged town Amatrice, calls for canned tomatoes because tomatoes were not grown locally in the mountainous area known for shepherding.[17]

A popular dish in foreign countries that did not gain popularity in the United States is spaghetti bolognese. However, Americans *not* of Italian descent do seem to add ground beef to their tomato sauce, and perhaps this style of spaghetti sauce has its origins in spaghetti bolognese in the United States as well. British-Italian chef Antonio Carluccio educates that this dish is not Italian.[18] "It is something you will find in a restaurant run by non-Italians or by Italians not in touch with genuine Italian food," he writes in his book, *Antonio Carluccio's Italian Feast*.[19] Bolognese sauce, from Bologna in the Emilia-Romagna province, he notes, is served with *tagliatelle*, not spaghetti, as most cookbooks confirm.[20] Hazan goes on to mention that bolognese ragù can be served with tortellini, rigatoni, ziti, *conchiglie*, and *rotelle*.[21] Hazan notes that when made correctly, a ragù will "cling" to the "folds of homemade noodles,"[22] of which all the pastas she names have, more or less. Perhaps this is why it is not recommended to be eaten with spaghetti, although one has to wonder if the association of Southern Italians with spaghetti is too strong for a sauce with a Northern geographic name.

Today, Italian food companies are marketing *cucina moderna*, modern Italian cuisine from Italy, as the "true," "authentic" Italian food—and the food of the Southern Italian immigrant as "American" food. According to the *Local*, in 2015, Forbes magazine named Eataly one of the 25 most "disruptive" brands meaning brands that "grow in leaps and bounds, changing the trajectory of consumers' viewpoint of the brand and the marketplace."[23] Customers shop there because some feel it is a way to experience "true Italian food" because " . . . there is so much 'fake' Italian stuff out there . . . ."[24] Ironically, Molinari notes that Farinetti of Eataly imported sperm from Piedmontese cattle to create a crossbreed in the United States because regulations forbid the importing of meat.[25] Isn't this straying from tradition and creating a "fake" food? Isn't this what native Italians accuse Italian Americans of doing? Not having access to food from Italy therefore using a substitution in the United States?

It is no secret that the economy of Italy is struggling. Recently, the *Telegraph* reported that Osama bin Laden's family bought the largest stake in a Carrara marble quarry.[26] In 2015, the *Guardian* reported that a Chinese company bought Pirelli tires.[27] It is no wonder Italy is trying to capitalize on its most popular and most marketable asset—its food. However, it is doing so by alienating itself from the children it abandoned a century ago. Those children were and are Italy's biggest competitors in the food business. In the 1920s, Ettore Boiardi started Chef Boyardee, selling pasta and tomato sauces. Contadina sold tomatoes. An Italian immigrant created the American Macaroni Company; another, Emanuele Ronzoni, from Genoa, created Ronzoni. The United States was the most successful producer of pizza.

All of this food is labeled or referred to as Italian food. However, Italy feels that it is not Italian food because it doesn't come from Italian soil. Parasecoli says Italian food companies like Barilla, Ferrero, and Buitoni are successfully marketing themselves worldwide.[28] But, he notes, Barilla gets its wheat from the United States, Canada, and Eastern Europe.[29] While Barilla can date its origins back to a baker from 1576, the modern company is a multinational corporation, having been sold to the American company Grace in 1970.[30] According to the Academia Barilla, Pietro Barilla regained a majority stake in 1979 and his sons run it today.[31] And Barilla pasta isn't produced only in Italy. The company has factories in Greece, Turkey, Mexico, and the United States (Iowa and New York).[32] Barilla Group owns Academia Barilla, "the first international center dedicated to the diffusion, promotion, and development of Italian gastronomic culture in the world."[33] They have a culinary center located in Parma and travel programs and cooking classes, as well as a library, historical menu collection, and more.[34] They published a series of cookbooks outlining Italian food. Much of it is *cucina moderna* with the occasional recipe based on tradition like Neapolitan Easter wheat pie, *taralli, chiacchiere*, crispy fish fritters, fried zucchini flowers, and various pasta dishes renamed or differing slightly from some traditional versions. These traditional recipes are still cooked today in homes of Americans of Italian descent.

Italy is also trying to promote "Made in Italy" labeling. However, "Made in Italy" labeling doesn't necessarily mean you are getting a product actually made in Italy by Italian craftsmen. There are many Chinese immigrants in Italy today. *New York Times* writer Jennifer 8. Lee notes in her book, *The Fortune Cookie Chronicles: Adventures in the World of Chinese Food*, that the city of Prato, 14 miles outside Florence, is 15 percent Chinese.[35] She says there are factories owned by Chinese there with Chinese workers, and the products made are labeled "Made in Italy."[36] In June 2015, an article in Fox News reported an Italian investigation regarding the smuggling of $5 billion out of Italy into China through a money-transfer service and that about half of that amount went through the Bank of China.[37] The money was the result of counterfeiting, prostitution, labor violations, and tax evasion.[38]

According to the U.S. Embassy & Consulates in Italy, annual trade between the United States and Italy was $80 billion in 2015.[39] According to an article in *We the Italians*, Italian food exports totaled 33 billion euros in 2013.[40] The article says Italy leads the world in the pasta market and has a healthy olive oil and wine business, but it is trying to rev business in other sectors like dairy, cheese, meat, coffee, canned goods, and fruit where right now, other countries take the lead.[41]

According to its website, the Milan Expo 2015 was an exposition hosted by Italy from May through October 2015 where more than 140 countries gathered to show the latest technologies in the global pursuit of feeding the world's population.[42] The site says it "examines human history through the lens of two aspects of food production: traditional cultural values and the use of new technologies."[43] The first Expo occurred in London in 1851[44]—before the Civil War in the United States and the unification of Italy but after the French and American Revolutions and after the physiocratic ideals of free trade and global agriculture took world dominance.

According to the *Guardian*, Milan won its position as host of the Expo in 2008, but it came with controversy.[45] Aprile notes that part of the controversy is the appropriation of funds for the Expo.[46] He says the funds that were supposed to be used for impoverished areas were spent on Milan's Expo Convention Center and other things like a "salvation mission for 100,000 wheels of *parmigiano* and *grana* cheeses that remained unsold."[47] The *Guardian* described the Expo as a "temporary theme park" with Epcot Center-like pavilions for each country.[48] Brazil created a tropical forest and Japan served a "virtual meal."[49] Also, the article says a number of people were arrested in corruption scandals in association with contracts for the Expo.[50] ANSA reported that the super grocery, Eataly, allegedly got a contract without bidding for two pavilions with 20 restaurants.[51] The article explains Raffaele Cantone, Italy's anti-corruption head, said there were no "irregularities" with the contract but that some "explanations" needed to be made.[52] Opening day of the Milan Expo 2015 saw violent protests in the streets.[53] The protestors shouldn't be dismissed as rowdy vandals, however, as there are valid concerns about the "globalization of food," and the eventual degrading of quality that does come with that, not to mention environmental impact and chemical contamination.

Even Pope Francis criticized the Expo, saying, "In certain ways, the Expo itself is part of this paradox of abundance, it obeys the culture of waste and does not contribute to a model of equitable and sustainable development," he said, noting that the Expo should concentrate on "the faces of the men and women who are hungry, who fall ill and even die because of an insufficient or harmful diet."[54]

Italy spent $2.8 billion[55] on the Expo—a high sum for a country struggling with a 42 percent unemployment rate.[56] According to Aprile, in the South, only 17 percent of fifteen- to twenty-four-year-olds are employed.[57] He notes that between 2002 and 2006, over one million jobs were created in Northern Italy and only forty thousand in the South.[58] According to *We the Italians*, Italy is predicted to increase its agrifood export market to seven billion euros by 2018.[59] Money was a motivating factor in the Milan Expo 2015.

In hopes of reversing Italy's downward spiral, the *Local* reported in early 2015 that the Italian government approved a plan to invest 260 million euros to promote Italian products globally.[60] According to the article, the country wants to increase exports of "Made in Italy" products by 50 billion euros over a three-year period.[61] Valerio Viale reported in *L'Italo Americano* that in 2014, the Google Cultural Institute along with the Italian government and the Italian Chamber of Commerce created an online display to promote "Made in Italy" products.[62] In November 2016, the Consulate General of Italy held its "First Italian Cuisine in the World Week" with cooking demonstrations, movies, and lectures on Italian food in 105 countries in hopes of promoting Italian food in the United States and worldwide, according to *L'Italo Americano*.[63] For example, in Los Angeles, during the week, restaurants with a "trademark of excellence distinction" created menus influenced by Italian movies.[64] The plan is to make the festival an annual event.[65]

While the Milan Expo 2015 was a place to showcase Italy's regional diversity and technological advancements in food production, it is a cause for concern in light of the larger global discussion on things like GMOs. Italy's reputation has always been one of fine taste in food, of holding fast to traditions in creating the best possible product, and that ideology doesn't jibe with mass marketing to increase sales in a global market. However, this is a struggle that many nations now face in this global landscape and in the United States; a foodie counter-revolution has sprung up where many young professionals are choosing to open their own small-batch food-related businesses to thwart BIG FOOD and control what goes into the nation's food. The problem with many of these American businesses is that they are new, without the time-tested traditions, and many lack in flavor, depth, and understanding of the ingredients and methods. For example, a popular modern ricotta maker adds sugar to the ricotta, thus changing the flavor of ricotta and subsequently, any products made with that ricotta. A modern butcher makes Italian sausage with nontraditional cheeses and spices, but calls it Italian sausage, thus changing the character of Italian sausage to new generations. Since Italians have been employing some of the same methods for centuries, sometimes even millennia depending on the products, it is difficult to sit and watch Italy take its place in the world's big supermarket and all that culture and tradition be lost. This fact was the impetus behind the Slow Food movement. So there is a worry that Italy will lose itself as it fights to expand its reach in the agrifood business.

There is no disputing, however, that pizza and spaghetti are the foods most synonymous with Italian cuisine and are popular the world over. Ed Levine said, "Everybody, from working class families to college kids to multibillionaires, loves pizza."[66] Because of the success of American pizza manufacturers, Italy sought to reclaim its product with an official designation of Neapolitan pizza. But it wasn't this Neapolitan pizza that the world fell in love with. That designation goes to the pizza created by the American immigrants of 100 years ago.

The Barilla cookbook says that spaghetti is "without doubt, the best-known pasta shape and the most representative of Italian cuisine in the world."[67] Why? Not because of Italians in Italy but because of Italians in America. It goes on to say, "*Pizza* and *spaghetti* still epitomize Italian culture for foreigners in their first encounter with Italy's culinary traditions."[68]

Italian food around the world includes the staples that became popular in the United States and that the United States exported in the past century. However, Italian immigrants to countries like the United Kingdom, Australia, Canada, Brazil, Argentina, and more brought traditional Italian cuisine with them.

Here, I will explore countries that have had Italian immigration in the past and how that has influenced the foodways of the country. If there was no historical Italian immigration to a particular country, I explore the Italian food culture that exists there now.

SOUTH AMERICA

Argentina

When one thinks of the cuisine of Argentina, one thinks of beef. However, the favorite food of the Argentinian people is pasta, according to a 2006 poll in Buenos Aires cited by MercoPress.[69] This statistic is not surprising, considering 60 percent[70] of the population of Argentina can claim Italian ancestry. During the great migration, about 2.5 million Italian immigrants settled in Argentina.[71] Most of these immigrants were from Northern Italy, according to Morreale and Carola.[72] The story of Italian immigration to Argentina is an interesting one detailed in Samuel L. Baily's *Immigrants in the Lands of Promise: Italians in Buenos Aires and New York City, 1870 to 1914*. According to him, there is much difference between the experience of immigrants to the United States and to Argentina. Argentinian immigrants were able to assimilate and to establish homes and communities faster and better for a number of reasons. These included that the dominant culture was a Latin one with the same dominant religion, Roman Catholicism. The language barrier was not as difficult as Spanish was similar to Italian and easier to learn than English. According to Baily, the government had a favorable outlook toward immigration in Argentina[73] whereas in the United States, it did not, and the immigrants met with much opposition and prejudice. In the United States, Italian immigrants had to compete with other immigrant groups, but in Argentina, Italians and Spanish were the only groups that immigrated there in great numbers. The economy was less developed there, creating a greater need for these workers. The workers going to Argentina also tended to be more highly skilled.[74] More Italians from Northern Italy settled in Argentina. This is evident in the cuisine of Argentina. For example, the use of gnocchi and polenta is more prevalent as are dishes like *milanese*.

The Italian food in Argentina is dissimilar from the Italian food in the United States. Why? The short answer is that the majority of Italian immigrants to Argentina were from Northern Italy and brought very different foodways with them from the Southern Italians who went to the United States. For example, the tomato isn't widely used in Northern Italian cooking, and on Argentinian Italian menus, there is often a dish for *milanese*, in the style of Milan. However, there is a dish in Argentina called *milanese napoletana* (also spelled *napolitana*), which is *milanese* with the addition of tomato and cheese. According to the Argentina Excepcion travel site, this dish is thought to have been created in Argentina by a chef at a restaurant called Napoli.[75] Another popular Christmas dish is *vitel toné*, or *vitello tonnato* in Italian, consisting of veal with a creamy tuna sauce, notes Mike Benayoun of the *196 Flavors* blog.[76] He says the dish is originally from the Piedmont region of Italy.[77] Caro says the Argentinian Christmas fruit bread *pan dulce* is *panettone*, from Northern Italy.[78] She also notes that every 29th of the month is *ñoquis* (gnocchi) day in Argentina, possibly in honor of a Venetian saint.[79] Gnocchi are potato pasta popular in Northern Italy. According to Maria Baez Kijac in *The South*

American Table: The Flavor and Soul of Authentic Home Cooking from Patagonia to Rio de Janeiro, With 450 Recipes, Sunday dinner is always pasta.[80] Argentines also eat the *tarta pascualina*, or Easter torte, which is a savory spinach and cheese pie[81] similar to the Italian *torta* or *pizza rustica/chiena*. Another example of Northern Italian cuisine in Argentina is the *fugazza*,[82] which is a focaccia, a pizza-type bread with onions and cheese on top. In the United States, focaccia has tomatoes with no cheese on top like it does in Southern Italy, while in Argentina, it does not have tomatoes but only onions, similar to the focaccia genoese of Genoa in Northern Italy that can be plain, with olive or onions, according to Leonardo Curti and James O. Fraioli in *Food Festivals of Italy: Celebrated Recipes from 50 Food Fairs*.[83] And pizza in Argentina has a thicker crust than traditional VPN.[84] I would say this is naturally expected if they created a focaccialike pizza. The Argentines also eat *faina*, a flat cake made from chickpeas that they sometimes put on top of pizza to make a *pizza a caballo*, according to the *Spruce* blog.[85] *Faina* is Genoese dialect for *farinata*, as it comes from Liguria[86] probably like the Argentinian immigrants who made it. In Argentina, there are ravioli, the filled pasta. However, they are called *ravioles*,[87] the Spanish word for ravioli. *Ravioles*, according to the *Food & Passion* blog, is also the name of small ravioli that come from the Rhone Alps, the French Alps that border with the Italian Alps of the Piedmont region of Italy.[88] Like the Waldensian dialect that had French and Italian elements to it, this word *ravioles* could be what the Northern Italian immigrants to Argentina called ravioli or it could just be the Spanish word for them. The early twentieth-century, thousand-page Argentinian cookbook Doña Lola's *El Arte de la Mesa,* lists twenty rice recipes, five cannelloni recipes, five spaghetti recipes, ten gnocchi recipes, five polenta recipes, ten ravioli recipes, and nine tagliatelle recipes, suggestive of Northern Italian cuisine.[89] The Italians also brought gelato-making to Argentina. Cadore, established in 1957, is one of the oldest shops in Buenos Aires, according to Claire of the *Authentic Foodquest* blog.[90] According to its website, its owners came from the Cadore region of Italy near Venice.[91] As they did elsewhere, Italians planted vegetables. Kijac says they dried the *chichocas de tomate* tomato to add to sauces and soups.[92] She adds they grew eggplant and made an eggplant and tomato relish from Italy known as *salsa de berenjenas con chichocas*.[93] Italians also brought their love of stuffed vegetables like zucchini to South America, she notes.[94] Veal tongue, according to Kijac, is an Italian dish that is popular throughout South America.[95] The tongue is prepared in an olive oil, garlic, and tomato sauce that she says she has also had in the United States served with fish.[96]

The longer answer is a sociological one. As mentioned earlier, the Italian Argentines were not marginalized and discriminated against like the Italian Americans. They were able to assimilate into society and adopt Spanish and Argentinian ways of doing things. The Italian Americans were "clannish" because they had to be. A positive outcome of this clannishness is that the old foodways of the great migration of 1880–1920 were preserved. A negative outcome is that Italian Americans still fight for acceptance in their homeland while Argentinian Italians never had that struggle.

Chile

Italians didn't immigrate to Chile in great numbers, but they did leave their mark. According to the "In the Shadow of the Volcanoes: Chile's Melting Pot," episode of *In the Americas with David Yetman*, 35 families from the Emilia-Romagna region in Northern Italy established a community in 1904 in the Chilean town of Capitán Pastene.[97] In 1907, they named the town "New Italy" but later changed the name to that of a Genoese captain, notes the website for Don Primo Trattoria Fabbrica.[98] Italians brought grapes and started wineries in Chile.[99] They have working wheat mills.[100] According to Stefano Ferrari in *Capitan Pastene: storia di un inganno*, they make pastas according to the Emilia-Romagna tradition.[101] Also, the Italians in Capitán Pastene continue to make prosciutto and salami just like their ancestors did in Italy.[102]

Peru

According to Janet E. Worrall in an article in *Italian America*, most Italians came to Peru during the nineteenth century, especially between 1840 and 1880, seeking a better life.[103] They were fishermen, merchants, and mariners from the Northern Italian regions of Liguria, Piedmont, Veneto, and Lombardy.[104] Many had trades or opened businesses, such as *panaderías*, or bread bakeries; pasta, chocolate, or oil factories; and restaurants.[105] According to Veronica Grimaldi Hinojosa, blogger for Rosetta Stone, Italian immigrants established communities and influenced Peruvian cuisine.[106] Looking through some Peruvian cookbooks, I see a diverse cuisine with many influences, including Creole, Chinese, and Japanese. There is a smidge of Italian in there too. Spaghetti with pesto called *tallerines en verde* (it's made with spinach and basil in Peru), green noodles (made from spinach in the Genoese style), *tagliatelles* with a prawn sauce of pisco with Parmesan, *muchame* (fish strips), cream-based and bolognese pasta sauces, a Peruvian version of minestrone, tripe a la italiana, duck *ravioles*, and Swiss chard pie are from the Genoese.[107] When comparing Peruvian minestrone from Gastón Acurio's *Peru* cookbook to Genoese minestrone in Maria Lo Pinto's *Art of Regional Italian Cooking*, one can see that both soups are made from a beef-based broth.[108] Interestingly, the Peruvian one has spinach and cabbage while the Genoese one has parsley and escarole.[109] Both have Parmesan cheese, although the Peruvian one adds queso.[110] The Genoese influence is evident although the minestrone has taken on a Peruvian flair. Apparently, early Italian immigrants suffered a bit of discrimination, as the word *bachiche* was a derogatory term for them equivalent to dago/wop/guinea and is now the name of a rice dish.[111] Ugo Plevisani is a contemporary Italian-Peruvian chef and restaurateur.[112] His wife, Sandra, is also a well-known chef and cookbook author.[113] Gabaccia notes that San Francisco's famous chocolatier, Domingo Ghirardelli, of Genoa, first made candy and imported in Peru before moving to the United States.[114]

Uruguay

Most Italian immigrants came to Uruguay in the mid- to late eighteen hundreds during the great migration.[115] The majority of Italian immigrants were from Genoa and Naples.[116] Scholar Renzo Pi Hugarte cites a 1992 study by Ricardo Goldaracena that says 38 percent of Uruguayans have an Italian surname.[117] Italians have had much influence on Uruguayan cuisine. Italians produced wine, much like they did in Argentina and the United States. Reinaldo de Lucca owns a winery in Uruguay that his grandparents started in the late eighteen hundreds, according to Luiz Alberto, on the *#winelover* blog.[118] Pasta is the most popular food in Uruguay.[119] Like Argentina, every 29th of the month is gnocchi day or *ñoqui* day.[120] Kijac notes Sunday dinner is always pasta, particularly ravioli, according to Hugarte.[121] According to the International Pasta Organisation, the most common pastas are *tallarines* (fettuccine), *ravioles* (ravioli), *ñoquis* (gnocchi), and *canelones* (cannelloni).[122] This makes sense, as these pasta types are more common in Northern Italy. However, Hugarte notes that many other pasta types are found like spaghetti and lasagna.[123] The Neapolitans brought their foods with them as well, including pizza, calzones, and mozzarella.[124] Foods from other regions of Italy are found also like polenta, risotto, spaghetti bolognese, salami, gorgonzola cheese, and osso bucco.[125] Caruso sauce is a creamy mushroom-ham-onion-meat extract pasta sauce originated in 1954 by Raimondo Monti of Mario and Alberto restaurant in Montevideo named for opera singer Enrico Caruso.[126] Kijac says the Uruguayan dish, *caldo de albondiguillas de pollo*, a chicken soup with meatballs, comes from Italian and Spanish immigrants.[127] *Milanese*-style sandwiches are a very popular street food, she notes.[128] And, she adds, *faina* is also very popular, as Hugarte notes, brought from Genoese immigrants.[129] The Christmas fruit bread *pan dulce* is like the Northern Italian *panettone*.[130] And Uruguayans make desserts using the *pasta frolla* dough, or pastry dough, the Italian immigrants used, notes Kijac.[131]

Paraguay

According to Antonella Cavallari, Italian ambassador to Paraguay, about 30 percent of people in Paraguay have Italian ancestry.[132] Because of the Italian influence, all types of pasta are common in Paraguay, according to

Myra Waldo in *The Art of South American Cookery*.[133] Here, they make a type of crepe called cannelloni, says Kijac.[134] Polenta in Paraguay is prepared with onion, cheese, and sour cream.[135] And, she notes, *milanese* is also popular.[136]

Brazil

Once, I suggested we go out for Brazilian food, but a friend protested, saying, "Brazilian food is Italian food." I didn't know if this was true, but when I perused the menu of the Brazilian restaurant, I found it listed a lot of Italian dishes.

This fact is no surprise, as Brazil played a major role in the Italian diaspora. Writing in 1925, Italian journalist Pietro Belli said, "Imagine you travel eight thousand nautic miles, across the Mediterranean and the Atlantic and suddenly find yourself in Italy. That's São Paulo. It seems paradoxical, but it is a reality, because São Paulo is an Italian city."[137] About 1.2 million Italians immigrated to Brazil.[138] And today, about 16 percent of Brazil's population is Italian, according to Gabriel Riel-Salvatore, writing in Panorama Italia.[139] That is about 25 to 30 million people.[140] No surprise, though. According to Angelo Trento in an essay in *Italian Workers of the World: Labor Migration and the Formation of Multiethnic States*, Brazil came in third after the United States and Argentina for number of Italian immigrants.[141] In 1888, Brazil abolished slavery, but workers were treated very poorly.[142] Italians worked on farms and coffee plantations.[143] Some created vineyards in southern Brazil.[144] In fact, says Kijac, Brazil was not a large producer of wine until the Italians arrived, bringing new grape varieties with them like Barbera, Moscato, and Trebbiano.[145] They were from the Veneto region and had arrived in the 1870s.[146] Today, they speak a dialect called Talian that is similar to the one spoken in Chipilo, Mexico.[147] In 1902, the Italian government banned subsidized immigration to Brazil.[148] Immigration tapered off at this time.[149] However, after World War II, Italians from the Southern regions of Italy immigrated to Brazil.[150] Many settled in São Paulo where there is a Neapolitan neighborhood called Mooca, according to Panorama Italia.[151]

The Italians more than left their mark on Brazilian foodways. Because of the Southern Italian immigrants, there is pizza and pasta as well as the Northern polenta (called *angu* by non-Italian Brazilians), risotto, *milanese*, and *panettone*.[152] According to Panorama Italia, Brazil is the third in the world for pasta production.[153] It also notes that Italian immigrants created pork sausages in a spicy version called *linguiça Calabrese* or non-spicy, *linguiça Toscana*.[154] The *Calabrese* is used on pizzas, which are a popular food in Brazil.[155] In São Paulo alone, there are over six thousand pizzerias, and residents eat about 1.4 million pizzas a *day*, according to the *Flavors of Brazil* blog.[156] It says Neapolitan immigrant Carmino Corvino, known as Dom Carmenielo, is credited with opening the first pizzeria, Santa Genoveva, in

1910.[157] And one hundred years later, in 2010, notes the blog, Brazilians celebrated the centennial of pizza within its borders.[158] Each year, São Paulo honors the best pizzaiolo during a competition on the Dia da Pizza.[159] Distinctively Brazilian pizza has a little sauce and mozzarella cheese, notes the blog.[160] A popular pizza includes chicken and creamy catupiry cheese, a cheese created in 1911 by Italian immigrant Mario Silvestrini.[161] Many Italians settled in the state of Espírito Santo, and today there are many dairy farms there that produce Italian cheese, according to *Flavors of Brazil*.[162] I suspect they are not Southern Italian, as they eat a turkey ragù with *polenta* the day after Christmas with leftover turkey.[163] The blog also mentions that mortadella is a popular cold cut in Brazil, although it is a bit different from its Italian counterpart.[164] In Brazil, it is made from beef and pork, whereas in Italy it is all pork.[165] It's also eaten as a cold cut on a sandwich.[166] In fact, the mortadella sandwich is quite popular in São Paulo and elsewhere, notes *Flavors of Brazil*.[167] *Frango com polenta* or *risotto* is a chicken and fried polenta dish,[168] most certainly from the Northern Italian immigrants. Another dish is *bife à parmigiana*,[169] similar in style to a chicken or veal parmesan. Maybe Emilia-Romagna immigrants contributed to this one, as there is a beef roast with *Parmigiano-Reggiano* cheese dish from Parma in Emilia-Romagna, although it's likely from Southern Italian immigrants, as it is similar to veal and eggplant parmesan.[170] The *chocotone* is a chocolate *panettone*.[171] Brazilians eat salt cod and bottarga from *tainha* fish, which could have come from the Italians and Portuguese as well as the Spanish, who eat both (bottarga in Italy is from mullet), as mentioned in the *Flavors of Brazil* blog.[172]

Italian Brazilians have festivals in honor of patron saints, as Italians do wherever they live. According to Panorama Italia, each year, the feast day of St. Vito draws large crowds.[173]

Venezuela

Italians went to Venezuela during the early part of the twentieth century and again to work in the oil industry in the 1950s and 1970s, according to an article by the BBC.[174] The article says there are about two million descendants of Italian immigrants in Venezuela.[175] Some opened bakeries called *panaderías*.[176] In fact, according to L. Fernando Gonzalez in *Criollo: A Taste of Venezuela*, they competed with the Portuguese immigrants to make different kinds of breads.[177] Gonzalez thinks the Venezuelan sticky bun called *golfeados* resulted from that competition.[178] According to the International Pasta Organisation, per capita, Venezuelans come in third in the world when it comes to eating pasta.[179] The potato gnocchi, *ñoquis*, are also popular here.[180]

NORTH AMERICA

Mexico

Italians didn't go to Mexico in great numbers. Venetian immigrants settled in the city of Chipilo in 1882 and still speak their dialect today.[181] But, generally, there isn't much Italian influence in foodways in Mexico. The Mexican sandwich known as *torta* is thought to have arrived with the nineteenth-century Italian immigrants from Northern Italy, or in particular one named Don Armando Martinez Centurion in 1892 in Mexico City.[182] It can have various fillings, including a *milanese*-style cutlet.[183] According to Cheryl Alters Jamison and Bill Jamison in *The Border Cookbook: Authentic Home Cooking of the American Southwest and Northern Mexico*, the *milanese*-style breaded beef cutlet is a dish that the Italian immigrants brought to Mexico.[184] And, food writer Nicholas Gilman mentions in his *Good Food in Mexico City* blog, there are many pizzerias and restaurants serving both Southern and Northern Italian cuisines.[185] He notes that the essentials of Italian cooking can be found like dried pastas in many shapes and imported cheeses like Parmesan, fontina, *pecorino*, mozzarella, and ricotta.[186] *Cucina moderna* has hit Mexico as well, according to his blog, as there are a number of Italian restaurants serving this style of Italian food.[187]

Central America & the Caribbean

Italians did not have a major presence in Central America and the Caribbean although they did move there in small numbers and left a mark. According to Regina Wagner in the *History of Coffee in Guatemala*, in the middle of the nineteenth century, an Italian living in Guatemala, Geronimo Mancinelli, gave seeds to the first man to own a coffee plantation there.[188] In 1873, a colony of Italians came to be farmers.[189] Later, Italians in skilled trades came.[190] Consuelo de Aerenlund documents his family's experience immigrating to Guatemala from Lombardy in *Voyage to an Unknown Land: The Saga of an Italian Family from Lombardy to Guatemala*.[191] He writes of the new immigrants being welcomed with spaghetti cooked by wives of established immigrants.[192] Also in Central America, Italians went to Costa Rica. About fifteen hundred Italians from Mantua arrived in Costa Rica in 1888 to work on the railroads, according to the *Italia Costa Rica* blog.[193] In the early nineteen hundreds, Calabrians came, and after World War II, more Italians came.[194] Now, there are about one hundred thousand Costa Ricans of Italian descent.[195] Alfredo Ingegno of *Italia Costa Rica* blog believes Italians own 30 percent of food and hospitality businesses like restaurants, pizzerias, ice cream shops, and bakeries.[196]

It seems that there were not as many Italians in the Caribbean. According to Josefina Maldonado in her cookbook, *Recipes my Grandmother*

Tomasa taste of Puerto Rico, the Italian legacy in Puerto Rico includes *funche*, a polenta porridge eaten for breakfast, brought by Italian immigrants.[197] The Italian immigrants also had their own version of *sofrito* and possibly brought the word "sofrito" to Puerto Rico.[198] In 1908, there were 160 Italians in Haiti, according to the Italian Commissariato dell'emigrazione.[199] They were jewelers, cobblers, carpenters, silversmiths, and other proprietors.[200] According to author Ann-Derrick Gaillot in an article for *Eater*, there is a breakfast dish called Haitian spaghetti, which is boiled spaghetti tossed in a frying pan with ketchup or tomato paste, spices, onion, garlic, and a protein like hot dogs, Vienna sausages, or herring.[201] She notes the dish originated pre-1934, while the Americans were occupying Haiti.[202] She says Americans "adopted this food from Italian immigrants in the United States" and subsequently introduced it to Haiti.[203] This example speaks to an earlier point of mine that Italian immigrants in the United States were responsible for bringing Italian food to a global audience.

EUROPE

Northern Europe

United Kingdom

According to Candida Martinelli in her Italophile Site, Italians have been immigrating to England for centuries; in the Middle Ages, she says, most were merchants and bankers from Northern Italy.[204] In the eighteenth and nineteenth centuries, she notes, they were artisans who made things like mirrors, frames, mosaics, barometers, thermometers, microscopes, telescopes, and medical instruments.[205] By the end of the nineteenth century to the early twentieth century, most Italian immigrants were working class employed in restaurants or as street vendors selling things like ice cream.[206] They also owned grocery stores and fish-and-chip shops.[207] In Chapter 4, I wrote about the prejudice the Italians experienced in Britain. Martinelli says after World War II, many moved to Australia, Canada, or New Zealand, and Britain deported some who were not citizens.[208]

The quintessential Anglo-Italian dish is spaghetti bolognese, but these days, Italian food in the United Kingdom is something different. There's a new interest in Italy's regional cuisine. As Mina Holland writes in her book, *The World on a Plate*, the trend is to serve "Mama's cooking with chef hats on."[209] Jacob Kenedy's concept for his London restaurant Bocca di Lupo was to create simple dishes from Italy's 20 regions meant for sharing.[210] What is on the menu? *Tagliatelle with ragú bolognese*, for one.[211] A sample menu I observed in November 2015 has 42 items, only six from Southern Italy.[212] While Southern Italian cuisine is the most popular in the world, it's only 14 percent of this menu. Other dishes on the menu include fried lamb chops and mustard peaches, and rosemary; venison tartare with Parmesan and capers; mallard—confit leg, roast breast marinated in amarone, treviso, and polenta; tripe with guanciale, chilli, and tomato; and roast suckling pig with uva fragola, chestnuts, white wine, and bay.[213]

Holland also mentions that at L'Anima in London, Chef Francesco Mazzei from Calabria, Italy, serves contemporary Italian food based on traditional Calabrian dishes.[214] Sample menu items include marinated black cod in prosecco and paprika served with palourde clams; butter and sage veal calf liver with pancetta and fig; beetroot *tortelli* with smoked *burrata*, ricotta, and aged balsamic vinegar; *fidelini* pasta with hand-picked crab, chilli, and Amalfi lemon.[215]

While some of these dishes sound appealing, they sound much more chef's hat than Mama's apron to me. I think they are chef-created dishes using Italian ingredients. And while I would appreciate dining at either restaurant, I don't think the dishes can compare to dishes made popular by Americans of Italian descent. And this is written by a person who enjoys fine dining and has eaten at restaurants like Thomas Keller's Per Se, Eric Ripert's Le Bernardin, Daniel Boulud's Daniel, and Mario Batali's Babbo, which by the way, started the trend in New York City restaurants of serving offal and unusual meats.

Also following the trend of regional Italian cuisine is London's Polpo, owned by Russell Norman and serving Venetian cuisine. This menu is tame compared with the others and less chef-influenced yet still contemporary. Cod cheeks, lentils and salsa verde; butternut squash, almond and ricotta salata bruschetta; stuffed fried olives; mortadella, gorgonzola and pickled radicchio pizzette.[216] The menu here sounds fabulous, but again, I don't think these dishes will ever have the worldwide appeal that the traditional cuisine of Southern Italy does.

An influential British-Italian chef and a favorite of mine is Antonio Carluccio. According to his autobiography and website, he got into the restaurant business after working as a wine merchant and opened Neal Street Restaurant in 1981.[217] His restaurant gave Jamie Oliver and British-Italian chef Gennaro Contaldo their start too.[218] He eventually built a successful brand, Carluccio's, with cafés and food shops, serving Italian food and importing Italian food products.[219] In addition to his shops, he has starred in BBC series on Italian food and has written numerous Italian cookbooks.[220] The Italian government honored him with the Commendatore OMRI, similar to British knighthood, for his work in Italian food.[221]

Sweden & Finland

According to Tomas Tengby and Ulrika Tengby Holm in *Viva Italia: 180 Classic Recipes*, Italians in Sweden opened restaurants and started importing food from Italy, as they were not so happy with the food in Sweden.[222] Taimi Previdi, in her *Best of Finnish Cooking*, notes that in Finland, there is a popular mayonnaise-based vegetable salad called Italian salad.[223] This salad exists in Russia as well. It is unclear how it got the name Italian salad in Finland.[224] However, according to Lorenza De' Medici, in *Italy: The Beautiful Cookbook*, it does exist in Italy as "Russian salad" because it's a haphazard mix of ingredients,[225] and Americans would know it as Russian salad as well.

AUSTRALIA

The immigration story to Australia is different because Italians didn't go to Australia in great numbers like they did to the Americas. Similar to Argentina, the early Italian immigrants to Australia were from Northern Italian regions. According to Cresciani, the first Italian settlement in Australia was in 1885 when 217 Italians from Friuli and Veneto settled in New South Wales and began growing grapes and making wine.[226] However, he notes, the settlement didn't last, as the Italians intermarried and the town was eventually abandoned.[227]

The Italians who came were a mix of educated and skilled and unskilled laborers.[228] They historically had a rough way to go. According to Cresciani, Australia had been taking the Kanaka people from the Solomon Islands to work the sugar cane fields in near slave labor.[229] As this practice became shunned because Australia wanted a white society, he notes, the government brought in Italians to work the fields.[230] In 1891, 335 laborers from Piedmont and Lombardy in Northern Italy went to Townsville, Australia, to work in agriculture, he says.[231] They eventually bought their own farms.[232]

Italian migrants worked as miners; Piedmontese, Lombard, and Tuscan migrants worked in agriculture, building railways, or as innkeepers; Sicilians worked in the fruit and fish industries; Friulians and Venetians worked as terrazzo workers; Aeolian Islanders worked as fruit and vegetable growers; and Neapolitans and Lucanians were barbers, traveling salesman, cobblers, shoemakers, florists, and organ grinders, according to Cresciani.[233] He notes that the Italian Consul of Perth complained that organ grinders were " . . . the plague of our emigration, and it would be a good thing to lose even the memory of them."[234] According to Matt Novak in "The Secret History of Whiteness," from 1901 to the mid-1970s, Australia's immigration policies admitted whites only.[235] He says Italians were seen as "other" and not white.[236] The prevailing attitudes about race in the late nineteenth century, discussed earlier, were also prevalent in Australia. These ideas influenced immigration policies. For example, there was a literacy requirement built into the 1901 Immigration Restriction Act.[237] Australia wanted people who adhered to British ways of living, says Novak—Protestant, English-speaking people with British customs and philosophies.[238] They thought that immigrants were working cheaper than natives and hurting wages and also that they were sending money home to Italy, not keeping it in Australia— similar fears used to justify dislike of immigrants in the United States 100 years ago and today.[239] Newspapers, according to Cresciani, reported that Italians were a "dirty Dago pest" and "that greasy flood of Mediterranean scum that seeks to defile and debase Australia."[240] He notes that Italians were often referred to as "wogs," "wops," or "dagoes."[241] It didn't help any that a Sicilian immigrant, Francesco Sceusa, who published the first Italian language newspaper in Australia in 1885, spoke out against other Italians, saying they needed to "use soap," assimilate, and not work for low wages, notes Novak.[242] While his intentions were good—he didn't want them to be pawns in a capitalist game, his words perpetuated a stereotype.[243]

Prior to 1922, there were only 8,500 Italians in Australia, according to Cresciani.[244] (He notes that a 1901 census record says 5,678.)[245] In 1921, the United States imposed a quota system, so Italian immigrants looked to other countries to settle, he says.[246] From 1922 to 1927, the number of Australian Italians grew to thirty-three thousand, a lot more but still not that many.[247] Some of these were workers and others were fleeing Fascism, notes Cresciani.[248] After World War II, Australia broadened its immigration policy. Cresciani says between 1947 and 1950, twenty thousand went to Australia.[249] In 1951, Italy and Australia entered into the Assisted Migration Agreement to pay for Italian migrants to move to Australia, he notes.[250] However, he says, when they got to Australia, there was no help for them with learning the language or using city services.[251] By 1973, 305,000 Italians had moved to Australia.[252] As of 2001, there were 218,718 Italian-born and over 800,000 claiming Italian ancestry, according to Cresciani.[253]

Despite Australia's early opinion of Italians, the Italians were productive members of society. Cresciani notes that in the 1920s, Italian laborers worked farmland in Griffith, New South Wales.[254] He says in 1921, there were 33 Italians there.[255] By 1940, he states, the Italians had worked to buy 23 percent of the farms and by 1954, almost half of them.[256] Some Italians became successful business owners, he says, like the Grollo brothers, whose father, Luigi, arrived poor in Australia.[257] The pair grew their business into a civil engineering company, Grocon Construction Pty Limited, building the Rialto building, the Crown Casino in Melbourne, and the Westin Hotel in Sydney.[258] In 1956, Franco Belgiorno-Nettis and Carlo Salteri created Transfield Pty Limited, and in 1987, built Sydney's Harbor Tunnel, notes Cresciani.[259] He adds that Sir Tristan Antico created the largest concrete business in Australia.[260] And Sir James Gobbo was Governor of Victoria from 1997-2000.[261]

While a number of Australian Italians achieved great success, Cresciani notes that it is a myth "that Italians in Australia have done well . . . ."[262] His data is based on a 1996 census survey.[263] At that time, he notes, many people did not speak English well (20.6 percent) and 42.4 percent of Italian-born women over 65 couldn't speak English well.[264] About 50 percent of the second generation tended to marry other Italians, thus not assimilating well.[265] The Italians also had a lower weekly income than the national average, notes Cresciani.[266]

Of course, the Australian Italians brought their foodways with them. Cresciani mentions Father Girolamo Davadi was a missionary to Australia in the 1870s and created vineyards and began making wine.[267] He says these early immigrants also created food factories such as a macaroni factory and restaurants.[268] In Melbourne, in the early 1920s, there were Italian restaurants, according to "Mediterranean Influence" by Tess Mallos in *The Food of Australia*.[269] In the 1940s, Italians opened produce markets, and in the next decade, began selling Italian products like salami and pasta.[270] Antonio Carluccio talks about present-day expat Italians in Australia growing prickly pears, chestnuts, walnuts, and olives; cultivating wine; and butchering their own meat and making sausage, salami, prosciutto, and lardons "in the Italian way" like all emigrants from Italy do wherever they go.[271]

A well-known Italian Australian in the restaurant business is Ronnie (Rinaldo) Di Stasio, who Carluccio calls a patron of the arts and architecture as well as vintner.[272] According to Australian journalist Ed Charles, Anthony Bourdain describes him in this way: "He's a fucking madman. And you have to be a fucking madman to be in the reastaurant [sic] business. There should be a statue of him in the neigbourhood [sic]. In all ways he is not bogus. He is passionate about food."[273] He opened Café di Stasio in 1988[274] and is referred to as the "godfather of Melbourne restaurateurs,"[275] according to Carluccio. Carluccio himself is often referred to as the "godfather" of Italian food in Britain.

Another "godfather" of Italian Australian cuisine is the late Beppi Polese, whose 2016 obituary in the *Australian* refers to him as "Sydney's 'godfather' of Italian restaurants."[276] Polese was originally from the Veneto region of Italy, where his family had humble beginnings—his father was a farm worker.[277] He had a tumultuous experience being imprisoned in a work camp during World War II.[278] The obituary says he escaped to Italy's Friuli region where he joined the Italian resistance movement against Mussolini.[279] He arrived in Australia in 1952, after having worked at fancy European hotels.[280] He opened his restaurant in Sydney in 1956, and it became the place to dine for the powerful—from politicians to celebrities, including Frank

Sinatra, notes the obituary.[281] His success garnered him the title of "godfather."[282]

These days, *cucina moderna* has made its way down under. Born in Australia, Maurice Terzini has created successful restaurants and bars in Australia.[283] His Icebergs Dining Room serves Italian dishes using Australian ingredients, for example, dishes like *Cavatelli e polipetti*—fresh *cavatelli*, braised Coffin Bay octopus, bone marrow, *gremolata* or *Agnello* con verdure—slow cooked Riverina lamb, Hispi cabbage, peas, garlic and anchovy vinaigrette.[284] According to an article in the *Australian*, Giovanni and Enrico Paradiso, brothers from Melbourne, and Marco Ambrosino have owned Fratelli Paradiso in Sydney for 15 years,[285] serving modern Italian fare like *tonnato*—veal, tuna mayo, and pickled shisito and dishes from Northern Italy like lasagna bolognese or Fiorentina steak.[286] Terzini and Giovanni Paradiso sponsored the Italo Dining and Disco Club, a hip event combining Italian food and music.[287]

AFRICA

Because the newly established Italian government wanted to get on the colonialism bandwagon in the late nineteenth century, there was an Italian presence in Libya, Eritrea, Ethiopia, and Somalia until the 1940s. This topic is a controversial one that has not been addressed much. In 2015, the documentary *If Only I Were That Warrior* was released, focusing on Fascist Italy's occupation of Ethiopia in 1935.[288] Italy's focus on colonialism in the late nineteen hundreds was one of a number of reasons why so many Italians left their country. They didn't like the choices the government was making and the direction the country was going. I would like to mention that Italian colonization of Africa was a goal of the Italian state, not one of the Italian people. It was during this time that Southern Italians left Italy because of the horrible conditions the government created there. According to Adolfo Rossi (1857–1921) cited in *Italoamericana: The Literature of the Great Migration, 1880-1943*, Italian emigration inspector and journalist, the Italian government spent money on its "so-called Colony of Eritrea" to the detriment of the Italians in North America.[289] Regardless, after unification and up to the Fascist regime, the Italian government decided to occupy parts of Africa. There are still Italian communities in some of these countries today. Therefore, Italian foodways have had some influence. For example, pasta is popular in Libyan and Somali cuisine.

Libya

Pasta is popular in Libya, according to James Beard award-winning author Clifford A. Wright.[290] According to Sarah Elmusrati in the *Food Libya* blog, Baretti e Scaletta opened the first pasta factory in Tripoli in 1915.[291] She notes others followed suit: Dando & Gherardi in 1934, La Pugliese Salpieto, and Castellano.[292] In Benghazi, she says, Scarpari and Vaudetto opened in 1930 and 1933, respectively.[293] *Macroona imbakbaka* is an Italian-influenced Libyan pasta and tomato stew dish made with either ditalini or broken spaghetti, notes Assia on the *Libyan Kitchen* blog.[294] *Amaretti* cookies popular in Italy made their way to Libya, known as *abambar*, notes Elmusrati who thinks *abambar* might originate in Libya.[295]

Ethiopia

In Ethiopia, traditional cuisine is very important. As mentioned in the previous chapter, there are many Orthodox Christians who do not eat animal products while fasting on certain occasions. They can get pizza sans dairy/meat. Coffee and macchiato are popular from Italian influence and can be made dairy-free with sunflower or soy milk, notes Miriam Berger in *BuzzFeed*.[296] According to Todd Kliman in "Can Ethiopian Cuisine Become Modern?" in the *Washingtonian*, a popular food TV personality in Ethiopia is Giordana Kebedom, who creates conservative fusion dishes of Italian and Ethiopian, such as creating an Italian dish and using *berbere* spice instead of red chili flakes.[297] Christopher Middleton of the *Telegraph* reports that Bono and Bob Geldof sing the praises of Castelli's in Addis Ababa, an Italian restaurant opened in 1948 by Francesco Castelli, an Italian soldier during World War II who did not want to return to Italy.[298] And today, the restaurant imports some things from Italy like salami but also uses locally made mozzarella and wine.[299]

Eritrea

Eritrea's capital, Asmara, is known as "Little Rome" because of the Italian influence seen in its architecture and heard in some of its words like "bicycletta" for bicycle or "piscina" for pool.[300] The city has art deco and futurist building styles.[301] According to Olivia Warren in *Taste of Eritrea: Recipes from One of East Africa's Most Interesting Little Countries*, when the Italians colonized in the late eighteen hundreds, they built roads, irrigation systems, water and sewage systems, railroads, and the longest aerial freight tramway in the world.[302] She notes they also planted cotton and vegetables; created businesses like a match company, a biscuit company, and wineries; and mined salt.[303] The Italians brought over fruits and vegetables that are still eaten today in the Italian way.[304] Tomatoes are called *commoderé*, the name obviously influenced by the Italian *pomodoro*, she notes.[305] Pasta was brought over from the Italians and has become a popular food.[306] *Lasagne* is popular, according to Rahawa Haile in an article for *Saveur*, and often served without ricotta.[307]

She says it is served for holidays.[308] Also noted is that because of the Italian influence, Eritrea has pizzerias, gelaterias, and coffee shops.[309] Other Italian dishes there include *milanese*, pizza, pastries, *panettone*, *frittata*, *capretto* (goat), crème caramel, and *macedonia di frutta* (fruit salad).[310]

Somalia

The Italian government also sent colonists to Somalia. Adriano Gallo writes that his family were farmers from Turin.[311] He says in 1940, the Italian population reached fifty thousand.[312] From the Italian influence, Somalian cuisine includes pasta.[313] According to Haile, in Somalia, pasta is called *baasto*.[314] Also, a variation of spaghetti bolognese is eaten.[315]

ASIA

East Asia

Slow Food Italy wants to bring Italian food to more of the Asian market. It showcased some of its purveyors at Slow Food Asia Pacific Festival in Seoul, Korea, in November 2015.[316] Products showcased include those from different regions of Italy like Di Martino pasta from Campania, Roi's extra-virgin olive oil from Liguria, Gli Aironi rice from Piedmont, and more.[317] (I thought a basic tenet of Slow Food was to eat locally.)

In the United States, there are some Asian-Italian restaurants gaining popularity like David Chang's latest venture, Momofuku Nishi, a fusion of Korean and Italian.[318] Basta Pasta in New York's Flatiron District is a Japanese Italian restaurant; however, it is not fusion. The cuisine is Italian; the chefs are Japanese. I myself thought the food was excellent and in keeping with Italian tradition.

There are VPN members in Asia as well but, besides those in Japan, not in great numbers. Currently, Taiwan has eight, China has two, the Philippines has one, and Korea has nine.[319]

Japan

A *Travel + Leisure* headline in 2015 says, "Italian Food is Hot in Japan Right Now."[320] But this trend has been popular for a few years. And it's not just Italian food that's popular. It's *cucina moderna*, the new Italian food. It's no surprise that the Japanese have bought the VPN hook, line, and sinker, as they are known for perfectionism and adhering to high standards when it comes to food preparation. If someone is telling them they have been doing Italian food wrong, they would listen. The fact that there are 68 VPN member pizzerias in Japan is a good indication they have believed the Italians who say VPN is the only real pizza.[321]

The Japanese have been eating spaghetti for about a century and are big fans of Italian cuisine.[322] What sparked this interest in *cucina moderna*? Well, an Eataly opened up in Tokyo in 2008.[323] But according to Corky White writing in the *Atlantic Monthly* in 2010, "Eataly has been a draw because of its uncompromising insistence on *la vera cucina italiana*."[324] *La vera cucina italiana*, the true cooking of Italy. Instead of coming up with the term *la vera cucina italiana* why don't the Italians just say, "Stop eating that red sauce slop of those Southern Italian *americani* we are trying so desperately to distance ourselves from." Of course, a Japanese interest in *la vera cucina italiana* means business for Italy. As White notes, the Japanese travel to Italy to take cooking classes and participate in *agriturismo*.[325] Another popular New York City gourmet shop carrying a lot of Italian items is Dean & DeLuca with 18 locations in Japan.[326]

China

For obvious reasons, Italy wants to appeal more to the Chinese market. While there are Italian restaurants in the major cities in China, the country has been a little slower to embrace Italian foods because, according to Wang, they don't know how to cook them.[327] He advocates more marketing in how to prepare Italian foods.[328] The Chinese have only gotten interested in cheese in the last ten years, but the market for it is growing especially among the young who want to try more Western foods.[329]

Southeast Asia

Vietnam

According to Uyen Luu in *My Vietnamese Kitchen: Recipes and Stories to Bring Vietnamese Food to Life on Your Plate*, Italian food is popular in Vietnam today. Spaghetti bolognese, or *mi Y*, as it is known in Vietnam, is a favorite dish.[330] Luu gives it Vietnamese flair with fish sauce.[331]

India

During the Roman Empire, the Romans visited India for trade, and later, so did Marco Polo and the Venetians.[332] Italians also went as Christian missionaries, mostly to South India.[333] The president of the Indian National Congress since 1998 is the Italian-born Sonia Gandhi.[334] Gandhi, whose birth name is Edvige Antonia Albina Maino, comes from the Veneto province of Italy.[335] The Italians are again doing business with India. For a number of years, Italy and India have been exporting and importing from each other in a brisk trade.[336] And, the modern pizzeria has also found its way to South India. In February 2016, 360 Degrees Pizza opened in Kochi, selling its version of modern pizza.[337] "Unlike the western brands of pizza (the ones we are more used to), this outlet offers you pizzas with a thin crust just like in Italy," writes Manorama Online.[338] Chef Aby Varghese says he uses ingredients from Naples and locally made fresh mozzarella.[339] The pizzeria covers all bases, from designer bbq chicken pizza, to classic Margherita and for the local palate, smoking tandoori pizza.[340] In July 2016, the *Indian Express* reported that JW Marriott's Italian restaurant, Oregano, in Chandigarh held a pizza festival, headed by the restaurant's Italian chef.[341] Chef Ritu Dalmia is a popular and well-known restaurateur, cookbook author, and TV host who demystifies Italian cuisine for the Indian home cook.[342] She owns a café at the cultural center at the Italian Embassy in New Delhi and has been honored by the Italian government with the *Cavalliere Stelle di Italia*, or Order of the Star of Italian Solidarity.[343] Her cookbook, *Italian Khana*, published by Random House India, is a collection of both classic Italian dishes and *cucina moderna*.[344] The recipes stick to Italian ingredients, the only variation for the Indian kitchen being the use of lamb instead of beef in her recipe for meat sauce.[345] According to NPR, the Vallombrosian Order of Benedictine monks, who came to India from the Vallombrosa abbey near Florence, have become famous for making and selling Italian cheeses like mozzarella, *burrata*, ricotta, and mascarpone to high-end restaurants in India where there is a demand for Western-style foods.[346]

C H A P T E R 9: Italian Food in Italy

Since its unification in 1861, Italy has had a hard time defining itself. The turmoil of the end of the nineteenth century and the subsequent loss of a third of its population left it flailing. The beginning rise of Fascism saw hope and prosperity and a resurgence of Roman ideals that was short-lived as Mussolini aligned himself with Hitler's insane mission. World War II saw terrible destruction in Italy and a time in which the people suffered once again. This would affect food traditions and foodways in Italy. In the early 1900s and again in the 1920s, Italy imported a lot of soybeans from China, according to William Shurtleff and Akiko Aoyagi of the Soyinfo Center.[1] They cite articles that said Italy studied giving infants soymilk to treat gastrointestinal problems.[2] In 1923, Shurtleff and Aoyagi note, Fulvio Bottari wrote the first book on soybeans. Interest in soy and its many applications was gaining ground.[3] They say that in 1922, Mussolini wanted to require soy flour be used to make polenta and bread.[4] The dictator founded a Soya Research Institute.[5] Soy flour was used in military rations.[6] During the war, people went without and food was rationed. As Montanari notes, newspapers and books printed budget recipes and articles on how to make mayonnaise without oil, etc.[7] An example of an Italian food born during this era of rationing and thrift is Nutella. During World War II and subsequent years, Pietro and Michele Ferrero made Nutella out of chocolate and ground hazelnuts to cut expenses because cocoa was scarce during the war and expensive after, according to *Daily Mail*.[8] After the war, Duggan says the government found that Southern Italian families could not afford to eat meat or sugar during those years.[9]

According to an article in the *Local*, the leadership in Italy has been a "revolving door" since then, without much stability.[10] Shurtleff and Aoyagi say soy*beans* weren't as prevalent during and after the war.[11] However, they note, in the 1950s, Italy was importing soy *oil* in great volume and it was being used as a cheaper alternative to olive oil.[12] (One has to wonder if some of it was being used to make counterfeit olive oil.) During the 1950s, there was an economic boom in Italy and by the mid-1960s, people stopped leaving, notes Montanari.[13] Everything Italian became fashionable, a second Italian Renaissance—Italian fashion, food, cars, wine, and attitude were the trends of the day. Duggan notes that in 1957, Italy became a member of the European Economic Community (EEC).[14] In the following years, he adds, exports rose and Italy became an industrial nation, turning out things like refrigerators and plastics products.[15]

Around this time, as mentioned before, Ancel Keys researched the low incidence of heart disease among Italians and said it was the healthy diet. The Mediterranean diet, including the diet of Southern Italians, consisted of vegetables, grains, and healthy fats. This diet became the standard of a healthy lifestyle.

In 1953, the Accademia Italiana Della Cucina was founded by a group of Italian intellectuals in Milan to study, celebrate, and promote the gastronomy of Italy, according to the *Oxford Companion to Italian Food*.[16] In 2003, the Italian government recognized the Accademia as a national cultural institution.[17] Ironically, during the 1950s and 1960s, Field wrote that bread was being commercially produced, as opposed to its production at privately owned bakeries, with highly refined flour that lacked in texture and nutrients.[18]

The economic success didn't last. A recession began in the 1970s and lasted into the 1980s. The birth rate in Northern Italy began to decline. In 1980, Italy imported three hundred thousand tons of soybean oil, the second-largest amount in Europe, according to Shurtleff and Aoyagi.[19] Luckily, Field notes, in the 1970s and 1980s, bakers set out to reclaim the breads of old using traditional methods and flours.[20] While the 1980s did see an economic boom in the North, the South continued to suffer. Duggan notes the unemployment rate among young men in the South was 45 percent in 1988.[21]

Today, Italians struggle with the same issues as the United States and Western cultures. And in Italy, it is much worse. Food in Italy today is not what it used to be. *Two Greedy Italians* starring British-Italian chefs Antonio Carluccio and Gennaro Contaldo is an excellent series detailing the competing forces of modernity versus antiquity in contemporary Italy. While the pair search their homeland to see what has changed and what has stayed the same, it is a bittersweet nostalgic journey. While they pull prickly pears and fruits from the trees as they pass them by and sample delicious olive oil, pizza, lemons, seafood, and more, they also see the negative effects that progress is having on their native country. In episode 2.1, an Italian doctor in Southern Italy says that children are more sedentary than they used to be, playing video games and watching TV.[22] Mothers work outside the home and children do still go home for lunches but they are eating food from machines more.[23] ANSA reports that Italy, along with Spain and Greece, have the most overweight children in the European Union.[24] It is a sad state of affairs in the country that originated the healthy Mediterranean diet. "It is a sign of our time as well that we have to copy everything that America sends us," Carluccio says.[25] Years ago, children were included in the family ritual of animal slaughter for food. They were taught to respect all parts of an animal. But this is changing, as Italy modernizes. According to an ANSA article on obesity in Italy, the reason Italy's obesity rate has tripled in the past 30 years includes the fact that Italy spends *less time* eating, such as a quicker lifestyle eating lunches on the go or while standing.[26] Interestingly enough, in 2015, the Mediterranean Diet Roundtable (MDR) was founded by Italians to promote the famous diet.[27] In April 2016, the MDR met in Los Angeles bringing together those with purchasing power in food service, academia, hospitals, schools, military, and the like to promote the healthy diet with the eventual goal of promoting Italian and Mediterranean products, according to Viale in *L'Italo Americano*.[28]

With women working outside the home since the 1950s, they are cooking less and less. Carluccio and Contaldo interview young women who don't want to be home cooking but instead enjoy career pursuits.[29] Italians themselves are taking cooking classes that are geared for tourists to relearn this forgotten art.[30]

The culture in Italy is not what it used to be. It is no longer so easy to find la dolce vita or the *Eat, Pray, Love* the media portrays. Italy is on the verge of a possible bankruptcy much like Greece because of unpaid bank loans, a 2.2 trillion-euro national debt, low productivity, an aging population, and high unemployment, according to Angela Giuffrida in the *Local*.[31] As mentioned before, there is currently a 42 percent unemployment rate, arguably more. (In Sardinia, it's 50 percent.)[32] ANSA says in the South, 62 percent of the people earn 40 percent of the national average earnings.[33] It adds since the economic crisis began in 2005, absolute poverty in Southern Italy has doubled from two million to four million in 2014.[34] ANSA also reports that basic services like water are not in regular supply.[35] It says 30 percent of all Italians and 40 percent of Southern Italians have problems with drinking water.[36] According to *Il Meridiano News*, the town where my grandmother is from has periodic water shutdowns that can last for days.[37] Lest people think the South is the only area suffering, according to the WHO list of the most polluted cities in the world from 2008 to 2013, 21 out of the first 500 were in Italy, all in northern Italy except for Napoli and one city in the Abruzzo region.[38] (To give perspective, most of the cities in the top ten were in India, Los Angeles ranked 605 on the list, and the New York City area was 918.)[39] Italy's largest bank, UniCredit, announced it was cutting 18,000 jobs, 6,900 of them in Italy, due to a 30 percent reduction in its third-quarter earnings from 2014 to 2015, according to an article in the *Rakyat Post*.[40] The birth rate is incredibly low. Italy is dependent upon tourism and its export business.

Former Prime Minister Matteo Renzi supported a free trade deal between the European Union and the United States called the Transatlantic Trade and Investment Partnership, according to Reuters.[41] The deal would have created new jobs in Europe and America, but the concern with such deals is the power they give big corporations in addition to concerns about food and the environment.[42] ANSA reports that in March 2016, he made a four-day visit to the United States to meet with President Obama and tour Enel's solar energy and geothermal power plant in Nevada and attend a Nuclear Security Summit in Washington, DC.[43] *Italian America* magazine says that the last state dinner that President Obama held at the White House celebrated Italy.[44] Renzi was in attendance, as well as prominent Italian Americans like Nancy Pelosi, Andrew Cuomo, Mario Andretti, and John Turturro.[45] Unfortunately for Renzi, Italy did not vote for his sweeping constitutional reforms, so he resigned in late 2016, according to CNN.[46] In an article in *EURACTIV*, Marta Bonucci writes that Italian representatives want to address the labeling of products to make them sound more Italian when the products themselves have no association with Italy.[47] The *Local* reports that in December 2014, Italy approved the Jobs Act, making hiring and firing easier for corporations.[48] The labor reform is controversial though, as it seems to benefit the corporations—not the workers. According to the World Bank, in an article by Marzio Bartoloni in *Il Sole 24 Ore*, the Jobs Act "simplified rules for firing and encouraged out-of-court settlements, reducing the time and the cost of labor-related cases."[49] However, some reform seems necessary to boost economic activity. According to Claudia Astarita in *This Is Italy*, in 2015, the European Commission also included 150 small- and medium-size businesses for SME Instrument funding.[50] The article says 25 of them are in Italy, the second most after Spain.[51] Bartoloni says foreign direct investments (FDI) were almost zero in 2012.[52] He adds that they grew from $0.09 billion in 2012 to $17 billion in 2013 and further growth is expected in the coming years.[53] Unfortunately for the South, most of the investments are in Lombardy.[54] In October 2015, China Daily reported that members of the Chinese Entrepreneur Club toured Lombardy for prospective infrastructure development.[55] Bartoloni says FDI investments in Italy are in industry, with one third in manufacturing.[56] Most of the investments, he notes, are from North America and Europe but investments from emerging markets like China, India, Russia, and other Asian countries are growing.[57] He also reports that with an 18 million-euro investment, the University of Salento in Lecce,

Puglia, has a new nanotechnology center.[58] According to the Ministry of Foreign Affairs and International Cooperation, the United States and Italy signed a joint declaration for a collaboration in the fields of science and technology for 2016–2017.[59] Arjun Kharpal reports for CNBC that there is more interest in technology start-ups in Italy now.[60] The *Italian Insider* says crowdfunding increased by 85 percent in 2015, generating close to 60 million euros.[61] Projects that were funded, it notes, include a documentary film, flood relief, and a journalism festival.[62] Apple's big news in January 2016 was that it is opening Europe's first iOS App Development Center in Naples to train students on developing iOS apps.[63] The *Local* says the government privatized 40 percent of the 153-year-old[64] state postal service with plans to do the same with railways, ANSA says, "opening them to the financial markets and to international investors."[65] This move, according to the *Local*, is said to bring in 3.4 billion euros.[66] The *Washington Times* reports that in May 2016, New York Governor Andrew Cuomo planned to visit Italy to bolster business ties.[67] Italy moved up 11 spots to number 45 in the World Bank's ranking of what countries are easiest in which to do business, according to Bartoloni.[68] Kharpal also notes 2015 saw a 12 percent increase in venture capital into the country from the previous year.[69] According to Ian Murphy in *Enterprise Times*, in April 2016, IBM announced its plan with the Italian government to invest $150 million to create the IBM Watson Health European Center of Excellence in Milan with the long-term goal of data-driven healthcare applications.[70] (Progress is defined by the definer. One can argue that this is a step in the wrong direction for a country that already has the second-highest rated healthcare system in the world, according to Bloomberg, and the second-highest life expectancy in Europe, according to the Organisation for Economic Co-operation and Development.[71] The old adage applies—if it ain't broke, don't fix it. As it is now, my relatives there say it is good. They still visit a knowledgeable family doctor who has an interest in their health.) The country is also interested in sustainable and green technologies and business methods. According to the Symbola Foundation and Unioncamere GreenItaly 2015 report, in the industry and services sector, 24.5 percent (372,000) of Italian businesses have invested in green technology.[72] In Europe, Italy produces less waste and uses less energy than other countries, according to *We the Italians*.[73] (However, it stands to reason that if the Italian economy is growing with many new investments, as it claims to be, that that energy use will be increasing.) ANSA reported that the Italian government has a long-term plan for the South funded by 95 billion euros through 2023.[74] Statistically, in 2015, ANSA reports that Italians themselves had more confidence in the economy than in prior years, up from 52.1 percent in 2014 to 57.3 percent.[75]

More is coming into Italy and more is going out. Luckily, the last quarter of 2014 saw a positive trend for Italian exports, according to ANSA.[76]

In fact, according to the European Digital Forum, since 2012, Italy is second in manufacturing in the European Union and fifth worldwide.[77] Elda Buonanno Foley notes in *We the Italians* that Italy has been the market leader in pasta exports, and it is recently expanding its reach to Russia, China, and India.[78] According to the *Local*, the European Commission estimated 0.6 percent economic growth in Italy for 2015 and 1.4 percent in 2016.[79] Italian exports of "beautiful and well-made products" (known as "Bello e Ben Fatto" or BBF in Italy) is expected to increase by 45 percent by 2020, according to Laura Cavestri in *Il Sole 24 Ore*.[80] BBF goods, according to *We the Italians*, include food and beverage products as well as furniture, apparel, home textiles, footwear, eyewear, and jewelry.[81] Cavestri estimates that by 2020, exports of these products will be 16 billion euros.[82] She says imports in China, Poland, and Russia are expected to grow, and in 2013, Italy supplied the most BBF products to China.[83] An article in *We the Italians* says that by 2020, there is expected to be 224 million people considered "new" wealth, meaning they earn over $35,000, i.e., have purchasing power.[84] The Italian Startup Act is new legislation to encourage new business endeavors. According to the European Digital Forum, the act includes things like free and online incorporation; certain fee exemptions and tax relief; free access to #ItalyFrontiers, a platform for national and foreign investors; and the first ad hoc regulation—where startups can raise money through equity crowdfunding in exchange for shares.[85] However, even with these progressive changes, it does seem a long way to go before Italy recovers from its recession. One reason is that much of Italy is still tied to tradition. According to native Italian Fabrizio Capobianco, founder and president of TOK.tv in an interview with Mucci in *We the Italians*, "... the promotion of the use of capital as an essential additive for their business, because even if you give away a piece of the company, the pie gets bigger and then you profit from that; and the thought that selling the company once brought to success is by no means a bad thing. These concepts are culturally distant from the traditional Italian mentality, and therefore very difficult to absorb."[86] It is important for me to note here that this ideology, while identified as an "American" one, is not one that all Americans subscribe to. In fact, many Americans feel that this is what has destroyed their country. If Italy embraces more capitalistic ideals, it leads to another question: what kind of changes will modernization bring?

Now, more women are in the workforce and they are not home cooking for the family. Parasecoli says most Italians shop at supermarkets like Americans do and stock up on food rather than shop at local markets daily.[87] Eataly, the Italian supermarket in New York City, first opened in Turin and is now also in Rome.[88] There are farmers' markets where people can still buy local goods.[89] Regionalism isn't what it used to be. Now, each region can get food from other regions, and they have been doing so for about 20–30 years.[90] As Mariani mentions, as early as the 1980s, Italians were importing hard-to-get products from other countries like Russian caviar because of the advancements in shipping technology such as overnight flights.[91] Because there are so many young unemployed Italians, they are choosing to remain single, says Parasecoli, and food manufacturers cater to this growing trend with frozen dinners and packaged meals.[92] As Severgnini notes, Italians are "increasingly tolerant of precooked and frozen meals."[93] Young Italians are not learning to cook from their families but from cooking schools.[94] This is a sad trend, as they will be learning the Italian food of their cooking school, not the Italian food traditions handed down from their grandparents and families.

According to the *Oxford Companion to Italian Food*, traditional meals at festivals and holidays (often religious observances) are changing as well with the times, using modern cooking methods and catering to new ingredients and tastes.[95] Eel, a staple in the cooking of Americans of Italian descent, is, it notes, no longer popular in Italy.[96] And due to globalization, it adds that Italians get fruit from all over the world, so desserts now include these types of fruits.[97]

Young Italian chefs are also inspired by this global cuisine. They create *nuova cucina*, which, according to the *Oxford Companion to Italian Food*, are more elaborate dishes with an Asian, particularly Japanese, influence.[98] In an episode of *Two Greedy Italians*, chefs Carluccio and Contaldo visit one such restaurant to sample the cuisine of a young up-and-coming chef.[99] The chef makes what she calls a risotto with Asian-inspired flavors.[100] Both Carluccio and Contaldo show appreciation for the young chef's effort but agree that her dish is not a risotto.[101]

Italians used to take pride in their gardens, but now they are not gardening as much as they used to or if they do, the gardens are smaller, and, as Severgnini says, more "utilitarian."[102] However, some tradition still remains. He notes that in Sardinia, the Camaldolese monks still grow the only citrus on the island, after eight centuries.[103]

Many Italians are resourceful and have found creative ways to earn a living such as starting their own bed and breakfasts. Agritourism is popular in Italy today where guests stay at a lodge that serves food from its own farm or has cooking classes with the food it grows, according to Parasecoli.[104] *Conde Nast Traveler* featured one, Agriturismo Dattilo, a store and bed and breakfast in Calabria where vineyards and olive groves abound.[105] My cousins and their families have opened bed and breakfasts.

Parasecoli says that in 2003, the European Union passed legislation requiring labeling of GMO food and feed if the GMO content is above 0.9 percent.[106] However, he adds, labeling is not required for meat of animals given GMO feed.[107] (One has to wonder if the animals used in DOP/DOC meat products were given this feed.) Of course, there are many people in Italy who do not like these changes and want food to keep its artisanal quality.

That is where movements like Slow Food began. These movements have reached other countries around the world as well.

Indeed, the owners of Domino's Pizza Inc. understand that Italians like to buy local. According to Ciara Linnane in *MarketWatch*, they opened their first store in Italy in Milan in October 2015 with plans to open three more by the end of 2015.[108] Unlike the pizza served in their American stores, the article says the tomato sauce and mozzarella will be Italian.[109] And they will offer products like prosciutto di Parma, gorgonzola, Grana Padano and *bufala* mozzarella.[110] Italians wouldn't have it any other way. It remains to be seen if they will have it at all.

In October 2015, the WHO announced that processed meat is carcinogenic.[111] According to an article by Isla Binnie for Reuters, Italian meat producers responded by saying Italy has one of the highest life expectancies in the world and that processed meats are eaten in moderation as part of a healthy Mediterranean diet.[112] The National Meat and Charcuterie Association noted that Italians eat about 25 grams daily, not the 50-gram-a-day portion cited in the WHO notice.[113]

One step up, two steps back could be the motto for progress in Italy. While the Italian government has offered generous subsidies in recent years to Sardinian farmers who employ green energy, a lot of that money goes to the wrong hands, according to an article by Ella Ide for AFP.[114] She mentions Rosetta Fanari, who owns a farm that makes an ancient ricotta using a solar steam generator, as being an example of how the subsidy system is supposed to work.[115] However, she contrasts a Chinese company that owns a plant in western Sardinia where 107,000 solar panels were installed to grow aloe plants but nothing is growing and the company has been getting subsidies for 20 years.[116]

Italian farmers are not giving up without a fight, though. The *Local* reports that in response to the Paris climate talks in late 2015, they asked the nation to forgo Alaskan salmon, Californian nuts, Brazilian watermelons, Egyptian green beans, Mexican blackberries, and Peruvian asparagus and instead, opt for locally grown produce like prickly pears and persimmons.[117]

There is some hope and good news for Italy, especially the South. In October 2015, ANSA reported that the GDP in Italy was predicted to grow, rising 1 percent in central and Northern Italy and 0.1 percent in the South.[118] While 0.1 percent is not much, it is the first sign of growth in the South in seven years, according to ANSA.[119] ANSA also says as of November 2015, the South will have 95 billion euros through the year 2023 from the European Regional Development Fund (ERDF), the European Social Fund (ESF), and European Union Cohesion Policy funding.[120]

Still, despite the challenges in Italy today, as of January 2016, Bloomberg ranked Italy as the second-healthiest country in the world and the healthiest in Europe.[121] Its healthcare system was ranked third in the world.[122]

As Finzi notes, the rankings take into account a number of factors—mortality rates, smokers, immunizations, access to healthcare, efficiency of healthcare, satisfaction with healthcare, and life expectancy.[123] He cites the Mediterranean diet as one of the reasons, along with the nightly *passeggiata*, when Italians walk throughout the town square with their families.[124] Finzi adds that Italians walk much more throughout the day.[125] Because many of the towns were built on hills and cliffs for protection during the Middle Ages, he says there are a lot of stairs and walkways for Italians to traverse daily.[126] In contrast, I would say people in the United States spend anywhere from eight to sixteen hours a day, five to seven days a week seated in front of a computer.

It remains to be seen as Italy continues to Westernize, as the political leaders continue to bring more foreign investors and business to Italy, whether it will remain the healthiest country in Europe. When Italians trade in long walks for long hours sitting at desks in corporate jobs like Americans do, will their health still be so good? Will they be as healthy when they can no longer take a break at lunch and must work the long hours demanded by most corporate jobs in the United States, well into the time, after dinner, when they would do their normal *passeggiata*? Given the state of the Italian economy in the twenty-first century, new Italian immigrants are coming to the United States and Europe and other countries where they can get work. These immigrants are not coming in as great numbers as the immigrants of yore, but they are bringing a new Italian culture with them—a modern one, the culture of contemporary Italy, its cuisine, its trends, and its values. Those values transfer also to food production and consumption.

CHAPTER 10: The Legacy of Italian Food

Modern Italian food writers, restaurateurs, and native Italians pontificate that Italian-American cuisine is American food created by Italian peasants over 100 years ago using American ingredients to remind these homesick peasants of their homeland. Nothing could be further from the truth.

Aprile notes that Italy was chosen as the European Authority on Nutrition with headquarters in Parma, in Northern Italy, "while the rest of the world identifies Italian food with Neapolitan pizza and spaghetti."[1] In fact, the world identifies Italian food with Neapolitan pizza and spaghetti because of the Italian immigrants in the United States—not the Italians in Europe.

I hope that, because of this book, the food world sees the discriminatory nature of the denunciation of the foodways of Americans of Italian descent, and in turn, rectifies this discrimination by recognizing the foodways of Americans of Italian descent. Doing anything less would be denying history. Truly, there is no way to dismiss and ignore the story of one third of Italy's population and its progeny. Their story started thousands of years ago on the Italian peninsula, and it continues on the American mainland, no less real, no less valid, no less Italian. Their story is one of a people who would not be taken, who lived for millennia under and with countless foreign invaders—who, once given the opportunity of freedom in the anomaly that is the United States—the government that Carlo Levi wrote about where the people feel that they have a share, they survived and many thrived in a way that they were prevented from doing in their home country. And, arguably, in some ways, especially in the food industry, in successful

155

Italian-American businesses noted throughout this book, these immigrants and their children have surpassed their Italian brothers and sisters back home, and this idea is probably the sting that native Italians feel when the culture of the Southern Italian immigrant is referred to as "Italian" the world over. The Southern Italian immigrant and his children—not the modern Italian born and bred in Italy—made pizza, made spaghetti and meatballs, made Italian food one of the two most popular ethnic cuisines on the planet.

However, the Italian-American struggle isn't over yet. The descendants of those early immigrants still suffer discrimination based on ethnicity, race, gender, and class, as I can attest to because I have experienced it both in North Carolina and New York. Recent census data shows that there are 17.5 million people of Italian descent in the United States with most of them living in the Northeastern states like New Jersey, New York, Pennsylvania, Connecticut, and Rhode Island.[2] Why do Italian Americans stay in the regions their ancestors settled? Do they feel it is more inclusive than the rest of the United States?

Just because the number of Italians are highest in the Northeast doesn't mean that that part of the country is immune to racism. This is the area, after all, where the *Jersey Shore* and the *Sopranos* were made and where MTV's and HBO's headquarters are. In an interview with Mucci in *We the Italians*, dean of the Calandra Institute, Anthony J. Tamburri, said that New York State Senator John D. Calandra investigated discrimination against Italians at The City University of New York where faculty and staff felt they had been the victims of discrimination, Italian Americans were not provided with needed counseling services, and the high school dropout rate for Italian Americans through the 1980s was high.[3] In 1978, Calandra published a report called "A History of Italian-American Discrimination at CUNY."[4] Mucci also interviews Joseph V. Scelsa, the founder and president of the Italian American Museum in New York, who was the director of the Italian American Institute at CUNY in 1984.[5] In 1992, the Institute (named the Calandra Institute in 1987) and the Italian-American community brought a successful civil rights suit against CUNY for discrimination.[6] Tamburri says the discriminatory practices continue to a "notably significant degree today."[7] (New York City is where, when I was young, I arranged *myself* to shadow a successful Italian-American professional who barely gave me the time of day. New York is also where I was told by an editor at a prestigious mainstream magazine [despite the fact that I had a recommendation from a respected and influential non-Italian person in the New York literary world] that an article written by me was good and would be published in the magazine "*if it was written by someone else*." I took this to mean someone whose name didn't end in "o," someone with a pedigree or an "acceptable" surname. I include these personal examples to illustrate the severity of the issue.)

Many Americans of Italian descent fought for their rights. They were instrumental in the labor movement 100 years ago. They fought for acceptance in American society. Columbus Day was first celebrated in the United States in 1792.[8] In 1892, President Harrison officially recognized the 400th anniversary of Columbus's voyage.[9] Due to the efforts of a Coloradan Italian originally from Genoa, Angelo Noce, Colorado became the first state to recognize Columbus Day in 1907.[10] According to the *Denver Post*, the parade stopped in the 1920s because of the Ku Klux Klan.[11] (By the way, it was an Italian judge, Alfred Paonessa, who outlawed the KKK in California in 1946.)[12] Noce worked to make the holiday a national one.[13] He died in 1922, and then the holiday was recognized in 35 states.[14] In 1934, President Franklin Roosevelt proclaimed it a federal holiday.[15] But today, Columbus Day is threatened. Seattle has changed it to Indigenous Peoples' Day. According to Randy Aliment, president of the Italian Chamber of Commerce in Seattle, the Italian Americans weren't even allowed to meet with city officials regarding their proposal for an alternate holiday.[16] This is especially interesting when one looks at the history of Italians in Washington State. According to an article in *Columbia Magazine*, those farmers who settled in the Walla Walla Valley often Anglicized their names to fit into the local society.[17] They weren't considered white and were often referred to as "foreign" or "Dagos" in the local newspapers.[18] One such paper reported, "In the vegetable industry, John Chinaman and the sons of Italy cut considerable figure. As gardeners, these two classes have few superiors . . . . Of late years, however, attracted by the profits of the business, many white men and those representing the best citizenship have become holders of valuable vegetable lands."[19] "John Chinaman" refers to the Chinese. So the Chinese and the Italians were inferior to the "white" farmers who were the "best citizenship." This history of prejudice should not be forgotten, and in fact, should be used as a reason to strengthen the celebration of Columbus Day for Italians in Washington State and elsewhere because the same historical prejudice existed in most municipalities in the United States at that time. Columbus Day was a source of pride for the early immigrants to Walla Walla. The article mentions that they commissioned a statue of Columbus and created a Columbus Day parade despite the negative feelings of the local "white" community.[20]

Twenty-first century Italy is also struggling, again, to define itself and to find its way in the modern world. Business leaders who want to compete in the global market may find it embarrassing that Puglian dancers still exorcise the poison from the spider bite in the *tarantella* or that flagellants still march the Calabrian streets as they did in early Christian times. But that is the beauty that is Italy. And it is also something that every country, including the United States, has—the old world and the new, the modern and the archaic, the rich and the poor. As any American will tell you, as any person from any industrialized country will tell you, Italy is not the only country living *la bella figura*.

Americans of Italian descent are only now starting to get recognized for their achievements. During the 2016 Academy Awards, Chris Rock hosted, addressing the need for more minority representation in Hollywood. Unfortunately, in his monologue, he poked fun at Sylvester Stallone with *Rocky*, said that Leonardo DiCaprio always gets good movie roles, and he poked fun at Paul Giamatti for his movie roles.[21] It was ironic that he would mention three Italian-American actors as if they represent the "white" race that has been dominating Hollywood. In fact, Italian-American actors are consistently bypassed and discriminated against unless they portray mafia-type characters. Sylvester Stallone wrote the screenplay for *Rocky* and was nominated for an Academy Award for best screenplay in 1977.[22] He was also nominated for best actor.[23] The film won best picture, best director, and best film editing.[24] Why didn't Stallone win? (Robert De Niro and Giancarlo Giannini were also up for best actor that year, as well as another Italian, Talia Shire, up for best actress.[25] Burt Young, who is of Italian descent, was nominated for best supporting actor.[26] They didn't win either.) Stallone created an iconic character in Rocky Balboa that speaks to man's inner struggle with himself and with societal forces. Everyone makes fun of the character of Rocky because of the way he talks, like he's a dumb Italian jock. However, his character is much more complex, speaking to Stallone's talent as a writer. Why didn't he win for best screenplay? The other actor Chris Rock mentioned was Leonardo DiCaprio. As his fans would note, his 2016 Oscar win was well overdue. Paul Giamatti is a fine actor who is a quarter Italian.[27] His family is from a city in Samnite territory near Benevento and his last name was Giammattei,[28] very similar to the last name of one of my great-grandparents and an uncommon last name originating in the Abruzzo region. At the same Oscar award ceremony, Whoopi Goldberg appeared in a joke clip about the lack of good roles for African American actors for the movie *Joy* starring Jennifer Lawrence.[29] The movie is based on the real life story of Joy Mangano, an entrepreneur and inventor. I understand and hear the argument about movie roles for African Americans, but the movie *Joy* also represents something unprecedented in Hollywood: a positive portrayal of an Italian American who is not involved in organized crime. It is a breakthrough movie for Italian Americans, and I think it was unfairly used to portray a typical "white" movie in Hollywood. The only other movie I can think of that portrays an Italian American in a positive light is *Unbroken* directed by Angelina Jolie about World War II veteran Louis Zamperini. I saw this film in a movie theater in North Carolina, and when the credits began to roll, I stood up and clapped. This was the first time in film I was seeing an Italian who represented us. Why wasn't it nominated for best picture in 2015? Why wasn't Angelina Jolie nominated for best director? She did more for the Italian-

American people with that one movie than anyone else in Hollywood has. The Emmy Awards are for television, not film, but why did it take Susan Lucci almost 20 years of nominations to finally win an Emmy? Was it the "i" at the end of her name? I don't know, but I do know that when she did, I cried, as if I had won, and I didn't even watch *All My Children*. I have to say the greatest Oscar moment for me was when Roberto Benigni climbed over the seats to get his award for *Life Is Beautiful*. And what better than to get it from Sophia Loren. A very Italian moment. I was proud and excited and felt like it was a win for Italians, as a people. Finally, why did it take the iconic Italian composer Ennio Morricone so long to win an Oscar? He has 500 movie credits to his name.[30] All of these Italian actors and musicians could have voiced discrimination, but they didn't. Being an Italian American, I understand the importance of inclusiveness in Hollywood and the need to represent all moviegoers and movie lovers. I just wish Chris Rock would have chosen a better way to express his feelings without picking on Sylvester Stallone, Leonardo DiCaprio, and Paul Giamatti. The good news is Ennio Morricone won, Leonardo DiCaprio won, Susan Lucci won, Roberto Benigni won, *Unbroken* was produced, *Joy* was produced . . . we are making inroads in Hollywood.

These examples I'm setting forth boil down to one issue—that all Italians must be a united Italian voice. Here is an example of what I'm talking about. My family are Neapolitan Italians from the New York City area. When I was in my twenties, I interviewed the older generation of Waldensians in Valdese, North Carolina, for an article on the community for the Italian-American magazine, *Primo*. The two men I talked to the most are now deceased. They told me about their experiences with prejudice in the area from the native North Carolinians because they were Italian. They told me about the horrible things the Waldensians endured throughout history in Italy. Southern Italians had been through so much as well. But as I sat with Joel Dalmas over a glass of wine and some cheese and bread, I thought, we are Italian. His family comes from a place in the Alps that borders France. The Italian foods his family ate were a tad different from the Italian foods my family ate, but the sentiment behind them was the same. I understood how comforting a bowl of polenta is. I understood how a glass of wine can bring people together and erase boundaries. And what I wanted to say to Joel Dalmas and John Bleynat and all the Waldensians, who are so kind and generous people, was that I am sorry, I am sorry for what happened in history. My family was in Southern Italy, also suffering, but somehow, I represented Roman Catholicism as I sat with these men. And I wanted them to know how sorry I was that something I represent could have hurt them and their families so much. As I sat there, I realized, they eat cabbage and potatoes, I eat macaroni with tomato sauce, but we are similar—there is something fundamental that I felt in that tiny town in North Carolina—a closeness, a familial connection, a connection that centuries and miles couldn't erase, that I didn't feel anywhere else in North Carolina ever—and that is being Italian.

It is also similar to what Lee felt and wrote about in her book on Chinese food, *The Fortune Cookie Chronicles*. The people of Chinese descent that she met in other countries may have danced salsa in Peru, or played reggae in Jamaica, but in "some sense," she says, "despite generations in other countries, we acknowledged each other as Chinese—even when we spoke no common languages."[31]

Unfortunately, this cross-cultural acceptance doesn't happen in the Italian community. The bias inherent in Collodi's description of pizza and in the word choice of contemporary food writers and chefs is alive and well today in various outlets of Italy denouncing Italian-American food as Italian food. And it comes from a deeper issue ingrained in the hearts of native Italians—that the Southern Italians (and working-class Northern Italians) who emigrated 100 years ago are not "really" Italian.

Molinari talks to an expat who says, "Italian Americans are not like us."[32] There's the "Other" again. This person goes on, "I lived in Queens for a while on a street that was full of them, they go around in sweats, they are vulgar, they say 'lobadroom' instead of 'bathroom' . . . in Italy we would say they are 'crude.'"[33] This person also says they "eat food that is all their own and has little to do with our cuisine."[34] Notice the word choice. Italian Americans eat "food," i.e. coarse, vulgar, basic. Italians eat "cuisine."

He also talks to Franco Zerlenga who came to New York from Italy in 1968 and worked for the Italian Cultural Institute on Park Avenue in the 1970s.[35] Zerlenga "winced" when he read a newsletter from the Ministry of Foreign Affairs that "suggested the Director of the Institute not have any association with Italian Americans."[36] What was the reason? According to Zerlenga, it was that the Italian government did not trust them because of the "hostility that had surrounded their mass departure."[37]

Today, according to the PBS documentary *The Italian Americans*, the majority of Americans of Italian descent work in blue-collar jobs.[38] At first glance, this fact would seem to support the statistics of illiteracy among their immediate ancestors. However, upon closer inspection, the lack of upward mobility is most likely a symptom of a larger problem—that Italians in the United States are subject to an inherent prejudice and bias transcending all aspects of society from social to educational to the workplace. It is directly related to their historical racial classification as "Other." Americans of Italian descent are considered white when it is convenient for the dominant white society. They are not white when it comes to fraternization—social mixing, country clubs, and other organizations. They are white when it comes to denying them access to affirmative action and scholarships for higher education. There are over 17 million Americans of Italian descent in the

United States, and with these numbers, they should have a higher impact on the country from an academic and professional standpoint. It can be assumed only that lack of opportunity is the culprit, a lack of opportunity stemming from an institutionalized bias that marginalized them as an "Other" group not worthy of time, attention, or investment.

Americans of Italian descent are synonymous with food in the United States, the opening of food-related businesses of all types, which is an important part of Italian culture, but they are not synonymous with education. In addition, Italian Americans themselves are to blame, as they do not do enough to help to rectify this past and present societal prejudice by mentoring the next generation of Italians, providing scholarships and internship programs to Americans of Italian descent, or assisting in job placement. As it stands, there is little community outreach in the Italian-American community.

Researchers have blamed the family structure of Italians as the problem for lack of upward mobility and assimilation. However, this is just not plausible. The Jewish and Greek cultures, for example, are very family oriented yet also community oriented. And Italians in the United States have been community oriented in the past. Take Roseto, Pennsylvania, for example, where health was discovered to be directly related to having a close-knit community, according to Malcolm Gladwell in *Outliers: The Story of Success*.[39] Some of the people of Roseto smoked cigars, were overweight, ate pizza and cookies, and drank wine, yet they did not suffer from heart disease like other communities.[40] An article by Dr. Rock Positano in the *Huffington Post* reports there was no crime and little public assistance.[41] As the community modernized, heart disease rose.[42] In my opinion, Roseto isn't just about heart disease. It's about a simpler lifestyle that is an all-around healthier one. The other Italy's *la dolce vita*—the one the Southern Italian immigrants lived—celebrating the good things in life without high fashion and fast cars. It's the one I grew up hearing about from my parents. The one where grandparents, aunts, uncles, and cousins lived under the same roof, in the same building, on the same block, in the same neighborhood. There were three, four, or five holiday dinners to attend. There was always someone there to care for a sick relative, give someone a ride, help someone move, lend a hand, lend an ear, cook a meal. The example of Roseto needs to be duplicated—not forgotten.

Lack of upward mobility and assimilation may have more to do with subtle discrimination. In some ways, Italian Americans have assimilated more through the generations. In the first generation of my family, born in Italy but living in the United States—my grandparents' generation—everyone, 100 percent, married other Italians. In my parents' generation, it was split evenly 50/50, 50 percent married Italians and 50 percent married non-Italians. In my generation, less than 20 percent are married to Italians. These non-Italian marriages are mostly to people of Irish descent, which is not unusual given that Italians and Irish went to the same Catholic churches. It would be interesting to study the rate of upward mobility and assimilation based on Italian-sounding name versus Anglo-sounding name. If I had grown up named Dina Smith in North Carolina, would my life experience have been different?

As Eleanor Roosevelt said, "No one can make you feel inferior without your consent." As an ethnicity, Italians have let American society view them as inferior without defending themselves or their progeny from this discrimination.

No offense to these fine actors, as I am a big fan of both, but as a culture, the Italian-American community needs to stop celebrating Robert De Niro and Al Pacino and start recognizing its lawyers, its doctors, its scientists, its writers, its teachers, and holding them up as the standard of Italian-American culture in the United States.

Successful CEOs, investors, entrepreneurs, doctors, scientists—what concrete thing have you done to help foster the next generation? What mentor programs, what internships have you provided? What financial aid or scholarships? There's an overabundance of lawyers in the United States who cannot find employment. Successful lawyers, what have you done to train them so they can take over your practice when you retire? Italian-American organizations, how much money have you raised for scholarships? I know that many Italian-American organizations, and I particularly mean the larger, more influential ones, say they are raising money for scholarships. Every little bit does help, but in today's world, where a year of college can reach almost $30,000, a thousand dollars will not help a working-class family send a child to college—it will probably pay only for books. What are they doing to provide full, needs-based scholarships to deserving young Italian Americans? Are they reaching out to Italian Americans in need who may not have the financial resources to join organizations? In 2010, LindaAnn Loschiavo wrote in "If Defamation Is Serious, Why Don't Italian American Organizations Take It Seriously?" that there are no nonprofit groups that solely fund and print the work of Italian-American writers and playwrights.[43] Why not?

There are some Italian-American studies programs in the United States exploring the much-needed documentation of the Italian-American experience, but what concrete things are they doing for the Italian-American community? Do they have job placement? Do they provide full- or at least half-tuition scholarships? Do they volunteer in the Italian-American community? What did Italian-American and Italian organizations do when Hurricane Sandy hit the working-class, largely Italian neighborhoods of Staten Island? I felt terrible when I saw an Italian-American woman pleading for help on the news. I used social media and contacted the Italian organizations I knew to try to help get aid to that area. I don't know what, if anything, came from that small gesture. What was done for the Italian-American community in New Orleans after Hurricane Katrina? Did Italian-American organizations raise money to help like they did for Italy during the devastating earthquakes in 2009 and 2016? Do Italian organizations in Italy and in the United States have the same consideration when a natural disaster hits Italian Americans? Sixty-nine of the 343 firefighters who perished in New York City on 9/11 were Italian.[44] A number of Italian Americans lost their lives that day, and countless more first responders suffer the toxic effects from providing aid. Are Italian-American organizations and organizations in Italy helping them? I don't know the answers to these questions, but I pose them less as a criticism and more as the idea for a solution. If these organizations are not supporting Italian Americans during times of crisis, perhaps they need to be.

What about Italian-American seniors? The Italian American Museum in Little Italy came under criticism for evicting an Italian-American senior. Is this what our progress and our assimilation leads us to? Is this what it means to become American?

Where is the Italian-American community? What is the Italian-American community? Who are they? If they are in the major cities where the early immigrants settled, do they provide any outreach to Italian Americans who do not live in those urban centers? Do they provide outreach to Italian Americans who do not have the financial resources to join groups like the Sons of Italy and the NIAF? Maybe instead of criticizing Italian youths like the ones who starred in *Jersey Shore*, the Italian community can reach out to them. Does the community care about the future? If so, they need to understand the past—the past is one that shouldn't be forgotten. With population numbers dwindling in Italy, Americans of Italian descent represent the descendants of the Kingdom of Naples and Sicily—of the old peninsula—of the place before "Italy." Forgetting that history is forgetting themselves. That is not the definition of becoming an American. They are a big piece of the cloth in the quilt that is the United States, and they deserve to be represented and portrayed as who they are. And that representation, that validation must first come from within. It's not just about tracing genealogy on Ancestry.com. It's about researching the history, learning the language, understanding the politics. That is the only way they can step into the future as a culture. Americans of Italian descent and Italians in Italy have a shared past with a rich culture. Without a shared future, what is the Italian culture?

Marco Mancassola is an Italian journalist and expatriate living in London.[45] In a 2015 *New York Times* article, he wrote about Italy's most recent emigrant crisis, of which he was a part.[46] He says that since the mid-1990s, highly skilled professionals and academics were leaving Italy to establish their careers and that the Italian government didn't do anything to keep them at home.[47] Since then, the numbers continue to grow, with about 94,000 Italians leaving in 2013.[48] (He mentions the Italian media says the real number is probably double or triple this.)[49] This phenomenon is evident in organizations like New York Italians in Manhattan, a non-profit organization devoted to Italian culture that started as a networking group for recent expat Italians. Why are bright young Italians leaving their homeland to seek work elsewhere? Low pay and high unemployment rates.[50] Mancassola says unemployment is 42 percent in Italy.[51] (In May 2015, a young man from Southern Italy made headlines when he jumped to his death from a building all because he couldn't find a job. Reports about his death estimated the unemployment rate at 60 percent.)[52] Also, while every country, including the United States engages in nepotism or some form of fraternal hiring/promoting/academic practices, in Italy, it seems to be worse.

New Italian immigrants sing the praises of the United States for its being a meritocracy. Vito M. Campese, president of the Italian Scientists and Scholars in North America Foundation, said, "Young Italians come to North America driven by the belief that they can make it in an open market, where intelligence, determination and ambition to succeed are the fundamental ingredients."[53] Native Italian Fabrizio Capobianco, founder and president of TOK.tv, praises the United States for its favorable stance on entrepreneurship, saying that meritocracy in Italy exists only in soccer, where the best players are chosen to play " . . . not those who had a famous surname or are paid more . . . ."[54] Mucci interviews Letizia Sirtori, the international tourism sales manager at Destination DC, in *We the Italians*, saying that the native Italian "found recognition [in the US] for her talent and skill—whilst back in Italy she lacked the recommendation of some or other powerful parasite."[55] In Sirtori's own words: "But America opened its doors to me, without me being the daughter of anyone important or powerful or rich; my dad is an electrician and my mum is a housewife, they taught me to study and work hard to earn satisfaction and success. And that's what it's like for lots of people here."[56] Mauro Galli, president of the Italian Chamber of Commerce in Chicago, Illinois, said, "The success of the Italian Americans is a sign of the high quality of the Italian DNA, that shines through in particular when we are given the opportunity to work well and express our creativity, as we are here in the US."[57] Are we?

A note on practices in the United States. There are safeguards in place to protect people from racial, gender, sexual orientation, disability, religious, ethnic, and age discrimination in the workplace and academic arenas. However, these and many other types of discrimination still exist that are not legally actionable because they are difficult to prove. (For example, if a company wants to fire someone who has a handicap or someone who has been sexually harassed, they will build a "paper trail" against that person so they blame the firing on employee performance, not the real reason, the handicap or the harassment.) Social class is one such separating factor in the United States. In addition, states and localities have their own systems of corruption that also marginalize or prevent the upward mobility of certain segments of society. The problem in the United States is that discrimination is so subtle yet so ingrained. It has to do with what church one goes to, what country club one belongs to, what zip code one lives in.

We are aware that historically, Americans of Italian descent have been subjected to this discrimination. According to UNICO Executive Director Andrè DiMino, the founder of UNICO, the largest Italian-American service and charity organization in the United States, Dr. Anthony Vastola, founded UNICO in 1922 because he wasn't allowed to join another service organization because he was Italian.[58] However, Italian Americans are still subjected to this discrimination because many of them are Roman Catholic in a predominantly Protestant country (and yes, it is 2018, but these biases still exist). Lamberto Andreotti, an Italian businessman who became CEO of Bristol-Myers Squibb, said "having an Italian passport is a rarity in the world in which I live that is populated by White Anglosaxon Protestants."[59] In a 2015 interview with Howard Stern, Madonna admitted she didn't fit in while in high school because it was predominantly "white" and "rich."[60] One has to wonder how much of the alienation and discrimination she felt was due to her Italian heritage. In the 1960s, my grandfather (who happened to be dark complected) wanted his family to join the lake beach club in his town and was told he could not for no valid reason other than the color of his skin. According to Salvatore J. LaGumina's essay "Prejudice and Discrimination," when seeking building contracts, contractors with Italian surnames were scrutinized as suspects of organized crime.[61] LaGumina notes that in 1993, John A. Segalla, a successful builder in Connecticut, sought to join a golf club and was denied because he had an Italian name.[62] In an article on Mario Batali, Jeff Biesold, the son of the owner of Mario Batali's great-grandfather's Italian import shop in Seattle, was talking about getting real San Marzano tomatoes.[63] "The Italians aren't very trustworthy, so you really have to find your good sources," says Biesold.[64] The author then notes "the room erupts with laughter."[65] I have heard people talk about Naples and its piles of garbage because of the "mafia." I heard people say the mafia controls present-day New York and keeps the garbage piled high. (I've never seen this in my years living there.) I have heard the languages of Southern Italy referred to as "low-class" because this ideology is the current programming coming from contemporary Italian sources. These are just a few examples among many and the reason Americans of Italian descent and Italians from Italy need to stand together to eradicate discrimination against them.

In fact, it can be argued that modern Italian expats are being treated better, as a whole, in the United States, than the descendants of the Italian immigrants of 100 years ago. They are able to work with work visas in the United States while many Americans of Italian descent are unemployed and marginalized in their birth country. In addition, they have a community of other expat Italians helping them to acclimate to the United States and helping them secure opportunities here in the form of scholarships and work study programs. Native Italian Gianluca De Novi, instructor at Harvard Medical School and co-founder of Triotech Ventures, told Mucci in an interview for *We the Italians* that he asked Basilicata, where he is from, to set aside one hundred thousand euros a year so he can host ten students at the university.[66] He's hoping to broaden this program to include other municipalities.[67] According to i-*Italy* NY, currently, the General Consulate of New York supports a program called "Meet the New Italians" designed for the new, young Italian immigrants to help them with career networking to introduce them to Italian employers.[68] The events explore different areas, such as fashion, finance, medicine, music, sports, etc.[69] Molinari says that Italians at Columbia University's business school make up 60 percent of the top 10 percent of students.[70] Most are company or family sponsored. (Where is the company sponsor for Italian Americans to attend Columbia's business school?) They do this so they can make double their salary in America, $125,000 as opposed to 68,000 euros.[71] (What about Italian-American business school grads who are not even making the dollar equivalent of 68,000 euros?) Mancassola says expat Italians are forming networks that the homeland could benefit from if it only took an interest.[72] He calls the networks the "other Italy" and says Italy needs to do something so that the citizens of this other Italy are not a "total, irrevocable loss to their country."[73] I am in agreement with this and would go further to include the descendants of the immigrants of 100 years ago—something Italy has been reluctant to do.

Italy has yet to embrace the children of its diaspora. Writer Candida Martinelli who runs the Italophile Site online writes, "The Italian diaspora, like most diaspora, is active abroad but largely ignored by the Italian government. The Ministry for Italians Abroad looks after the interests of only Italian citizens abroad. People of Italian origin are not considered Italian, and in the legal sense, the Ministry is correct. But for people who have all their lives been labeled 'Italian,' that can come as a surprise, if not a shock."[74] I am not a real Italian. Even though I have been labeled Italian all my life. There are 100 years between me and Concetto Farmica, but we share something in common. To Italy, I am spaghetti and meatballs.

Some expat Italians and Italians seeking to do business in the United States seem very quick to disassociate themselves from Italian Americans. They want to disassociate from mafia references in entertainment and popular culture like the *Sopranos*. They also want to disassociate from the ignorant-sounding portrayal of Italians in shows like MTV's *Jersey Shore* as well as the working-class Italian American who doesn't attend theater or read books. I do too. These portrayals are gross misrepresentations of Americans of Italian descent. While there are over 17 million Americans of Italian descent, according to Mucci in *We the Italians*, only 0.0068 percent are criminals.[75]

Expat Italians also want to disassociate from organized crime figures like Al Capone and Lucky Luciano. But when discussing Italian-American history, expat Italians should tread lightly. Al Capone, Lucky Luciano, and the like are part of Italian-American as well as American history—the history of Prohibition when a lot of Americans, not just Al Capone, were profiting from the creation and sale of illegal alcohol. There were many Irish and Jewish gangsters during this time and after, like Bugsy Siegel and Meyer Lansky, and many Anglo-Saxon outlaws throughout American history. I understand the critical difference between Italian gangsters and gangsters of other ethnicities. Anglo-Saxon, Jewish, and Irish Americans are celebrated for their accomplishments and are not likened to a handful of gangsters every time they do something, like Italians are.

This book is not about organized crime, but one has to wonder, how much of the Italian, Irish, and Jewish organized crime was due to the alienation and discrimination these groups faced when they came to the United States. In the 1920s, John Horace Mariano, an Italian-American scholar, noted that Italian immigrants were not in prison—only their children were, implying that the prejudice in the United States created the problem of organized crime in Italian-American communities.[76] According to Gianfranco Norelli and Suma Kurien, producers and directors of *Finding the Mother Lode*, interviewed in *We the Italians*, there was more incidence of organized crime in the Italian communities of the East Coast, Chicago, and New Orleans than the West Coast.[77] They say that historically, Italians in California/the West Coast were treated better and reached higher levels of success sooner than Italians in other parts of the country.[78] This success may have had something to do with the fact that California was part of Mexico and had a Latin culture and influence. The experience of the Italians in California probably had more in common with the experience of Italians in Argentina, to a lesser degree because California eventually became part of the United States. Especially for the early Italian immigrants, they had no police protection or American social services to aid them. In New York City, the Irish were the police force and if an Italian had a dispute with an Irish or American person, where could he turn? In fact, the mafia is thought to have its origins in the period of brigandage following Italy's unification. At this time, Southern Italians were fighting for their homeland—a fight in which the local landowning nobles, groups of brigands, and the working-class people colluded against the Italian army. According to Dickie, the earliest record of the Masonic-like rituals of the mafia date to the 1870s, a fact which would support the mafia's origins in post-unification Italy.[79] Writer Adolfo Rossi wrote in 1893, "our government [Italy] . . . has never done anything to protect the well-being and morality of the Italian colonies in North America, and it is no wonder that the Mafia and the Camorra flourish there as in the worst times of the Bourbons and that the Italian, illiterate, knife-wielding, exploited or exploiter, is despised more than the Irish and the Chinese."[80] Here, Rossi is putting blame on the Italian government for the Italian mafia in the United States because the Italian government did nothing to help the Italians in the United States. And, ironically, Italy now wants to take away the Italianness of Italian America, including the goodwill Italian Americans built in creating Italian products. Regardless, expat Italians should work to change media perception of Italians in the United States but without disassociating from the truth. As the Bible says, those without sin, cast the first stone. Italy as a whole, not just the South, does not have the most stellar reputation when it comes to organized crime, mafia, and corruption. As I recall, Berlusconi was Prime Minister of all of Italy, not just the South. And while criticizing Italian Americans of being ignorant, according to recent statistics, less than 50 percent of Italians read a book in 2015.[81]

While expat Italians may not be proud to be associated with the likes of Al Capone and Lucky Luciano, and while Americans of Italian descent may not be proud to either, they are part of our history. They belong to a time and a place that doesn't exist anymore. They represent a tiny percentage of Italian Americans, and they should not represent the only image of Italians in Chicago and New York. But they are a part of our history, a part that we must own, a part that cannot be rewritten because expats want to do business with the United States.

A man who is doing much to bridge the gap between Italian Americans and new Italian immigrants is Umberto Mucci, the founder of *We the Italians*, the tag line of which is "Two Flags, One Heart," which seems to say it all. According to his bio in *We the Italians*, he is a native Italian who works with the Italian American Museum in New York, who helped fundraise after the Abruzzo earthquake and who has worked on many programs fostering a relationship between Italy and the United States.[82] In my opinion, his most important contribution is his work with *We the Italians*, a newsletter and book he published with articles and interviews with Italians and Italian Americans who are working on projects that keep Italian-American history alive while also looking to the future of Italian culture in Italy and the United States.

I was fortunate to hear Mucci speak about his book at the Italian American Museum in New York in early 2016.[83] He told how his interviews with prominent Italian Americans throughout the country enlightened him about the Italian-American experience.[84] Prior to his research, he didn't have the knowledge of just how deep the prejudice had been for the early immigrants, and he also didn't know that they and their children had such an impact on so many fields and in so many states.[85] He said that the people of Italy have the "wrong idea" about Italian Americans.[86] He says that Italians in Italy do not know about the 300 Italian festivals in the United States or that there are Italian Americans in states like West Virginia.[87] Unfortunately, prior to his research, his view—and the view of other Italians—had been the same one perpetuated by entertainment of the ignorant mafioso.

I appreciate Mucci's work immensely—because he is the first to compile such an impressive list of interviewees in such diverse fields and organizations. But I am disappointed that an Italian-American group didn't think of this idea first. Why? Because Mucci's focus—and the focus of the talk I attended—was to discuss opportunities for expat Italians today or Italy in general to conduct business in the United States. Again, the United States being a land of opportunity—a meritocracy—was mentioned. What I heard here and what I hear often in the discourse of the modern, expat or native Italians is less of a mutual focus and more of how the Italian Americans can benefit the Italians in their goal of doing business in the United States. Italy continues to reach out to do business with the United States, as well it should. An article in *NJBIZ* mentioned that Maurizio Forte, trade commissioner and executive director for the United States of the Italian Trade Agency, met with business executives in New Jersey in April 2016 to discuss expanding business with the state.[88] The article says that currently, New Jersey imports $6.6 billion worth of Italian products.[89] Ironically, New Jersey Italians are the "kind" of Italians that Italian expats and Italians in Italy today are trying to disassociate from. *We the Italians* reports that the Consul General of Italy, Hon. Gloria Bellelli, met with various business and trade groups in South Carolina to expand trade between Italy and the state.[90] I wonder does she, and others seeking to do business, know the history of Italians in the South?

Mucci mentioned that Italy is making more money from its expats in the United States than it does from its own taxation.[91] Even in Mucci's book of interviews, his focus is on Italy doing business with the Italian-American community. Rosalba Maniaci, Italian consular agent of New Mexico, tells him that the people of New Mexico are interested in "Made in Italy" food products like imported pasta and cheeses, "high quality" olive oil, wine, coffee, ceramics, kitchenware, glassware, moka coffee pots, and espresso machines.[92] The president of the American Italian Museum in New Orleans, Frank Maselli, says that people in New Orleans want Italian food, wine, and clothing.[93] In Florida, people buy Italian-made boats.[94]

This *is* good. Many Italian products are high-quality and desirable products. However, I believe that any relationship established between Italy and Italian America needs to be a mutual one. And I do think Mucci's intent is to build that bridge between Italy and Italian Americans. He recently wrote about the New Orleans lynching and he is bringing similarly forgotten stories to the attention of Italians in Italy and Italian Americans who may not have known what their brothers and sisters endured in different parts of the country. Every day, *We the Italians* posts tidbits on Facebook of Italian and Italian-American history, and I do believe both are being given equal air time.

But this mutual relationship must be from all Italians doing business in the United States—not just Umberto Mucci.

The nonprofit organization New York Italians is an organization with similar goals to Mucci's. Their mission, on their website, is to preserve Italian and Italian-American traditions and culture.[95] They are doing a fabulous job in New York City with regular language classes and cultural events like movies and lectures celebrating Italians and Italian Americans. In 2016, the group organized what it called a "world bridge" between Naples and New York City to "strengthen the common thread between the Italian and Italian-American populations."[96] A great idea, however, while I did not attend, all of the events listed on the website for the event seemed to be about Italy, not Italian Americans, including photo exhibits, movies, musicians, and "Made in Italy" products.

It is important for me also to recognize outgoing Italian Consul General Natalia Quintavalle. According to an article in i-*Italy* NY, "Unlike some of her predecessors, Quintavalle understood that the historical and cultural heritage of the million-plus Italian Americans in New York is an asset to be cherished rather than snubbed."[97]

In August 2016, Palermo, Sicily, native Alberto Giuffre, a journalist at Fox News's sister network in Milan, wrote a book about his travels across the United States to lesser-traveled cities and towns with Italian counterparts like Naples, Florida, and Palermo, North Dakota.[98] He found out that the latter was named after Italians who built the railway there.[99] A town named Florence, Alabama, was named so because the man who surveyed it was from Tuscany.[100] This example is just one that there are Italians from Italy now who are trying to learn more about the United States and who are discovering the history of their cousins who moved here 100 years ago.

In June 2015, the *New York Times* reported that the mayor of Naples, Luigi de Magistris, visited Manhattan's Little Italy to create a connection between the two communities.[101] Msgr. Donald Sakano of the Basilica of St. Patrick's Old Cathedral on Mulberry Street orchestrated the visit. The article notes that the Church of the Most Precious Blood displayed Neapolitan *presépio* figures.[102] The mayor hopes that the two communities can connect in other ways like for destination weddings.[103] As part of his tour, he ate American buffalo mozzarella.[104] This visit is a good first start in bridging the gap that exists between native Italians and Americans of Italian descent. Instead of seeing each other as competitors of "Italian" culture, they need to see each other as they both are—Italian.

As John M. Viola, former president and COO of the National Italian American Foundation says, "We have to stop looking at Italy as 60 million people in a boot shaped peninsula who sent communities all around the world, and start thinking of Italy as 200 million people all over the world, most of them aware of being Italian. We can be doing business together, exchanging ideas and education, if we think of ourselves as 200 million Italians, well integrated in every country we live in, speaking multiple languages, engaged in all types of businesses and industries, and holding the highest ranking jobs—and all this while still feeling Italian!"[105] He goes on to say that with the diaspora of 100 years ago, "Italy missed something, lost a whole segment of the population. We are the offspring of that segment, and we feel that Italy becomes a whole again when we reattach to Italy. We still feel Italian."[106]

In December 2016, the *New York Times* profiled photographer Giuseppe Nucci regarding his work on documenting Italy's fading traditions and folkways.[107] Born in Italy in 1982,[108] Nucci felt it was necessary to record these folkways—religious processions, the slaughtering of pigs, and other rituals of Italian life—because Italy is modernizing and soon many of these old traditions will no longer exist.[109] Nucci says his grandmother moved from Italy to Pittsburgh and carried on Italian traditions as if she had never left Italy.[110] How can Italy not see that the immigrants of 100 years ago did *the same thing* in whatever country they went to? The religious processions like the San Gennaro Festival in New York City or the Giglio Festival in Brooklyn represent the carrying on of those traditions. Any Italian who has religious articles in his house, any Italian who has a garden, who makes her own wine, who has a family dinner on Sunday, who uses words of his Italian dialect, who keeps a lucky charm to ward off evil, who has no distinction between a first and third cousin—they're all family, who feels the stirrings in her heart of an operatic crescendo, who dances to a tarantella, who buys Italian pastries from an Italian-owned bakery, who has lemon with his espresso or a biscotti with her coffee, who drinks red wine with dinner and has olive oil and vinegar on his salad—no matter where we go, we carry Italy with us, some part of it is there through the generations. The young Italian expats, the native Italians look at each of us as someone different, but we are not different, we are you and you are us, the only distance is time and politics of place.

As Italy struggles to repair its image of corruption and complacency, it is looking for a sense of self. Will it find the power that it once had under the Roman Empire or the preeminence in art, science, gastronomy, and culture it had during the Middle Ages and the Renaissance? Will *la vita* be *dolce* again? I don't know. But one thing I do know. It will not find it by sweeping the history of the Southern Italians under the rug. It will not find it by claiming that everything made by an American of Italian descent is "American," i.e., inauthentic, not Italian. Italy has a history of greatness, but also one of pain—and the best thing about the history, it is over. It is time for Italy to atone for its past transgressions and then, with the proper acknowledgement and respect, its children around the world can forgive. (In 2011, Giuliano Amato, representing then-Italian President Giorgio Napolitano, apologized on behalf of the state to the citizens of Pontelandolfo and Casalduni for the "barbaric" actions of murder, rape, and destruction by the Italian army during its 1861 retaliation against the towns for their victory over an army troop.)[111] Only then will Italians in Italy and Americans of Italian descent truly be at peace with each other. Italy's future, its greatest strength, is here in the present—in the people the world over who call themselves Italian, born on its soil, or not.

Italy must act to show its interest in Italian America. Italian corporations promoting their "Made in Italy" products can donate money to save historic buildings and churches in Italian neighborhoods. How about an endowment to the American Italian Heritage Museum in Albany, New York? Or what about creating an Italian American Museum in Washington, DC, our nation's capital, to tell the true story of the Italian-American people to a worldwide audience. How about donating to the Romaggi Adobe in California for a Gold Country Family Museum[112] that will include information on Italians who settled in the area during the Gold Rush? What about the Mary Ann Esposito Foundation's Ciao Italia Italian Heritage and Education Resource Center for the research of Italian gastronomy?[113] What about reaching out to Americans of Italian descent who need financial assistance for college and who would benefit from mentorship and job placement programs? Italy could also make the process of dual citizenship easier for Americans of Italian descent, especially if they are Italian through both their maternal and paternal sides, or just their maternal side. (Interestingly, in June 2016, following Britain's Brexit from the European Union, Italian Prime Minister Matteo Renzi considered giving dual citizenship to British students in Italy.)[114] And given the historical butchering of Italian names in the early twentieth century, the Italian government should be understanding of name discrepancies on official documents. On September 19, 2016, the Italian Cultural Institute in New York hosted a talk on the future of the European Union after Brexit entitled "The European Union."[115] The same night at the same time, tens of blocks away downtown in Little Italy, the Figli di San Gennaro was holding the annual San Gennaro Mass, procession, and feast day celebration in honor of San Gennaro. To show support for the Italian-American community, the Italian Cultural Institute shouldn't have scheduled a talk on the night of the feast. In the heavily Italian-populated state of New Jersey, Senator Joe Pennacchio is proposing a resolution to preserve the Columbus Day holiday.[116] Other states should follow suit, especially those with significant Italian populations and history, and Italian organizations doing business in those states should support such a resolution. I have another suggestion that would help to save Columbus Day. I believe the celebration of Columbus Day was meant to bring together the native people of the Americas and the European settlers. If they haven't already done so, I think the organizers of the Columbus Day parades and celebrations should invite Native American tribes to participate and make the day a more inclusive one while still highlighting the Italian-American contribution to the United States. As Italians in the United States, we understand what it is like to be excluded. I experienced that in a more profound way than the average Italian American. And I witnessed firsthand the struggle of the Lumbee Indian population in North Carolina. I do not believe in an Indigenous Peoples' Day nor do I believe in an Italian American Day. I believe in Columbus Day. Columbus Day can be a great opportunity for these two groups—and all Americans—to come together and celebrate that we found each other—with all the pain that includes for the descendants of indigenous people, lower-class Europeans, African slaves, and all Americans whose ancestors experienced discrimination, genocide, prejudice, and marginalization—but with all the joy in being part of the ever-evolving yet steadfast nation with the most advanced, humanistic laws in the world.

These are only a few ideas of how Italians can bridge the gap with the Italian-American community and foster a mutually agreeable relationship for the future. Ultimately, the weight of the success of Americans of Italian descent falls on their own shoulders and whether or not, like Eleanor Roosevelt alluded to, they want someone else to rewrite their story. I don't, and that's why I wrote this book.

The message that I'd like to impart is that when you eat the foods of these Southern Italians, when you eat pizza or spaghetti with meatballs, you aren't eating some makeshift concoction—a round disk of dough topped with a "red sauce" and cheese or a plate of long threads of pasta topped with a "red sauce" and round balls of meat. You are eating the victory of the Southern Italian against oppression and marginalization. That, once given an opportunity—an opportunity that exists only in a country with a legal, financial, and political structure like the United States—could the Southern Italian prevail. While many have prevailed despite the flaws in the United States, many still struggle. Their success is partially dependent upon their brothers and sisters in Italy who are promoting "Made in Italy" products worldwide and the American people (of Italian heritage or not) who are consumers of those products. I understand why Italy is promoting its products. It is on the verge of economic collapse. And *many* of those "Made in Italy" products are exceptional, time-honored products that non-Italian Americans and Americans of Italian descent (myself included) want to and *should* consume. For the most part, I selectively buy olive oil and wine from Italy, as I do believe the quality supersedes any other. In general, I prefer European cheeses but also found a wonderful Italian cheese from Argentina at Zabar's. Again, I make selective purchases and read labels for everything I buy. I have come to love many products from Italy. I love Fabbri *amarena* (cherry) and *fragola* (strawberry) in syrup. I love cheeses like *caciocavallo, pecorino sardo,* and *toma.* I love different regional pasta shapes like *malloreddus, strascinati,* and *trofie.* I also love many of the products made by Italians in America. I love

Ferrara "Made in New York" cannoli, pastries, and torrone. I love Veniero's "Made in New York" pastries. I love Lombardi's "Made in New York" pizza. I love John's "Made on Bleecker Street" pizza. I love Raffetto's "Made in New York" ravioli. I love Mike's Pastry "Made in Boston" cannoli. I love Civitello's "Made in Schenectady" cannoli. I love Sally's Apizza "Made in New Haven" pizza. I love De Lillo's "Made in the Bronx" cannoli. I love Egidio's "Made in the Bronx" *sfogliatelle*. I know there is room in the market for "Made in Italy" and "Italian-Made in America" as well as "Made in Argentina" or any other locale where Italians produce quality products because those people and those products are *all* Italian. They *all* represent the history, ingenuity, and future of the people of the Italian peninsula.

NOTES

INTRODUCTION

1. Scotland County NC, "Cities & Towns," http://www.scotlandcounty.org/509/Cities-Towns; City of Laurinburg, NC, "History," http://www.laurinburg.org/history.

2. Laurinburg Presbyterian Church, "About LPC," http://laurinburgpres.com/about-lpc.

3. City of Laurinburg, NC, "History," http://www.laurinburg.org/history.

4. Ibid.

5. United States Census Bureau, 2010, https://factfinder.census.gov/faces/nav/jsf/pages/community_facts.xh tml.

6. Christine Quigley, *Modern Mummies: The Preservation of the Human Body in the Twentieth Century* (Michigan: McFarland & Company, 1998), 88-92.

7. Ibid.

8. "The Strange Case of Giuseppe Camiola," http://ourhamlet.org/forum/viewtopic.php?t=9527&p=28324.

9. Tim Bullard, "Spaghetti hung around Laurinburg a long time," *SCNow*, February 11, 2013, http://www.scnow.com/news/article_1c1d6d4c-7478-11e2-a34a-0019bb30f31a.html.

10. Peter Genovese, *Pizza City: The Ultimate Guide to New York's Favorite Food*, (New Brunswick, NJ: Rutgers University Press, 2013), 8. This statistic is changing as we speak, as North Carolina is now home to a number of Neapolitan-style pizzerias. In addition, more people from the Northeast are moving to North Carolina, and more pizzerias are popping up.

11. Scott Mason, "Carnival worker corpse kept for 61 years," January 14, 2009, http://www.wral.com/lifestyles/travel/video/4315576/.

12. Scott Mason, http://www.thetarheeltraveler.com/, accessed October 21, 2016.

13. Summer Whitford, "13 Things You Probably Didn't Know About Real Italian Food," *Daily Meal*, January 12, 2016, https://www.thedailymeal.com/travel/13-things-you-probably-didn-t-know-about-real-italian-food/slide-5, Slide 5, accessed October 21, 2016.

14. Consolato USA Napoli, https://twitter.com/USAnelSud/status/852430202923864065.

15. Simone Cinotto, *The Italian American Table: Food, Family, and Community in New York City* (Urbana, Chicago, and Springfield, IL: University of Illinois Press, 2013), 217.

16. Robert Sietsema, "10 Old-Fashioned Italian-American Restaurants to Try in New York and Jersey City," *Eater*, April 8, 2015, https://ny.eater.com/2015/4/8/8340057/old-school-italian-restaurants-ny-jersey-city-sietsema.

17. Maria Laurino, *The Italian Americans: A History*, (New York: W. W. Norton & Company, 2015), 23; Samuel L. Baily, *Immigrants in the Lands of Promise: Italians in Buenos Aires and New York City, 1870 to 1914*, (Ithaca, New York: Cornell University Press, 1999), 33; Jan Lahmeyer, "Italy population," Population Statistics, http://www.populstat.info/Europe/italyc.htm; Kath Mandile and Rita Mandile, "Italian Immigration: Why So Many Italians Live Outside Italy," *Italian Legacy* (blog), http://www.italianlegacy.com/italian-immigration.html. In the 1860s, Italy had a population of about 25 million. From 1861 to 1911, the population grew to about 35 million. From 1861 to 1900, about 7 million Italians left the country (about a third of the population). From 1900 to 1914, about 9 million left. Arguably, this 16 million is half of the Italian population at the time. Throughout my book, I say a third of the population left Italy, in order to account for the increasing birth rate through the range of years in question and for any repatriating Italians. It is a very unscientific number.

18. We the Italians, "A Study of Italians in the USA," https://www.facebook.com/WeTheItalians/posts/1155804047813551, Facebook post, July 18, 2016, accessed May 12, 2017.

19. Maurizio Molinari, *The Italians of New York*, trans. Louise Hipwell (Washington, DC: Vellum, an imprint of New Academia Publishing, 2012), 64.

20. Umberto Mucci, *We the Italians: Two flags, One heart, One hundred interviews about Italy and the US*, (Lexington, KY, 2016), 246.

21. Pete Hamill, interview, *New York: A Documentary Film*, PBS, 1999, https://www.youtube.com/watch?v=_8zv687Oqas.

CHAPTER 1: What Is "Italian" Food?

1. Alberto Capatti and Massimo Montanari, *Italian Cuisine: A Cultural History*, trans. Aine O'Healy (New York: Columbia University Press, 2003), 27.

2. Laurino, *The Italian Americans: A History*, 23.

3. Baily, *Immigrants in the Lands of Promise: Italians in Buenos Aires and New York City, 1870 to 1914*, 24.

4. Laurino, *The Italian Americans: A History*, 23.

5. Gianfranco Cresciani, *The Italians in Australia*, (Cambridge: Cambridge University Press, 2003), 18.

6. Jerre Mangione and Ben Morreale, *La Storia: Five Centuries of the Italian American Experience*, (New York: Harper Perennial, 1993), xiv.

7. Laurino, *The Italian Americans: A History*, 17, 39.

8. Ibid., 23.

9. Capatti, *Italian Cuisine: A Cultural History*, 86.

10. Cinotto, *The Italian American Table: Food, Family, and Community in New York City*, 38. Cinotto mentions the oral history tradition of food in the Mezzogiorno.

11. Christopher Duggan, *A Concise History of Italy*, (Cambridge: Cambridge University Press, 1984), 28.

12. Laurino, *The Italian Americans: A History*, 84.

13. Peter G. Vellon, *A Great Conspiracy Against Our Race: Italian Immigration Newspapers and the Construction of Whiteness in the Early 20th Century*, (New York: New York University Press, 2014), 10.

14. Francesco Durante and Robert Viscusi, eds., *Italoamericana: The Literature of the Great Migration, 1880-1943*, (New York: Fordham University Press, 2014), 88.

15. Vellon, *A Great Conspiracy Against Our Race: Italian Immigration Newspapers and the Construction of Whiteness in the Early 20th Century*, 10.

16. *Strangers in a Strange Land: A History of Italian-Language American Imprints, 1830-1945*, New York: Grolier Club, 2012, Press release. Organized in 1884, the Grolier Club is a club for bibliophiles.

17. Duggan, *A Concise History of Italy*, 156.

18. Ibid.

19. Barbara M. Kreutz, *Before the Normans: Southern Italy in the Ninth & Tenth Centuries*, (Philadelphia, PA: University of Pennsylvania Press, 1991), 139.

20. Carlo Ginzburg, *The Cheese and the Worms: The Cosmos of a Sixteenth-Century Miller*, (Baltimore, MD: The Johns Hopkins University Press, 1992), 31.

21. Arthur Schwartz, *Naples at Table: Cooking in Campania*, (New York: HarperCollins, 1998), 253.

22. Capatti, *Italian Cuisine: A Cultural History*, 157.

23. Ibid., 158.

24. Ibid., 186.

25. Donna R. Gabaccia, *We Are What We Eat: Ethnic Food and the Making of Americans*, (Cambridge, MA: Harvard University Press, 1998), 182.

26. Luisa Del Giudice, ed., *Oral History, Oral Culture, and Italian Americans*, (New York: Palgrave Macmillan, 2009), 5.

27. Ibid., 4.

28. Ibid.

29. Rossella Rago, *Cooking with Nonna*, http://cookingwithnonna.com, accessed May 14, 2017.

CHAPTER 2: The Italy They Left

1. Pino Aprile, *Terroni: All That Has Been Done to Ensure That the Italians of the South Became "Southerners,"* trans. Ilaria Marra Rosiglioni (New York: Bordighera Press, 2011).

2. Carlo Levi, *Christ Stopped at Eboli: The Story of a Year*, trans. Frances Frenaye (New York: Farrar, Straus and Giroux, 2006), 4. According to Levi, it's 5,000 years old.

3. UNESCO, "The Sassi and the Park of the Rupestrian Churches of Matera," http://whc.unesco.org/en/list/670.

4. Schwartz, *Naples at Table: Cooking in Campania*, xxx.

5. Duggan, *A Concise History of Italy*, 9, 32; George Holmes, ed., *The Oxford History of Italy*, (New York: Oxford University Press, 1997), 27-28.

6. Duggan, *A Concise History of Italy*, 32.

7. Tommaso Astarita, *Between Salt Water and Holy Water: A History of Southern Italy*, (New York: W. W. Norton & Company, 2005), 17.

8. Duggan, *A Concise History of Italy*, 34; Holmes, ed., *The Oxford History of Italy*, 33, 38, 47-48.

9. Massimo Montanari, *Italian Identity in the Kitchen, or Food and the Nation*, trans. Beth Archer Brombert (New York: Columbia University Press, 2013), 1.

10. Duggan, *A Concise History of Italy*, 34.

11. David Gilmour, *The Pursuit of Italy: A History of a Land, Its Regions, and Their Peoples*, (New York: Farrar, Straus and Giroux, 2011), 53; Kreutz, *Before the Normans: Southern Italy in the Ninth & Tenth Centuries*, 32.

12. Duggan, *A Concise History of Italy*, 35.

13. Ibid., 40.

14. Gilmour, *The Pursuit of Italy: A History of a Land, Its Regions, and Their Peoples*, 20.

15. John Hooper, *The Italians*, (New York: Viking, 2015), 275.

16. Kreutz, *Before the Normans: Southern Italy in the Ninth & Tenth Centuries*, 145.

17. Hooper, *The Italians*, 275.

18. "History," About us, Università degli Studi di Napoli Federico II, http://www.international.unina.it/contenuto.php?id_group=6&id_pag= 12.

19. Astarita, *Between Salt Water and Holy Water: A History of Southern Italy*, 94.

20. Ibid.

21. Ibid., 83.

22. Tommaso Astarita, *The Italian Baroque Table: Cooking and Entertaining from the Golden Age of Naples*, (Tempe, AZ: Arizona Center for Medieval and Renaissance Studies, 2014), 40.

23. John A. Marino, *Becoming Neapolitan: Citizen Culture in Baroque Naples*, (Baltimore: The Johns Hopkins University Press, 2011), 224-225.

24. Ibid., 216, 238.

25. Ibid., 220.

26. Astarita, *The Italian Baroque Table: Cooking and Entertaining from the Golden Age of Naples*, 41.

27. Montanari, *Italian Identity in the Kitchen, or Food and the Nation*, 16-17; Capatti, *Italian Cuisine: A Cultural History*, 21.

28. Henry Kamen, *Spain's Road to Empire: The Making of a World Power, 1492-1763*, (London: Allen Lane, 2002), 297.

29. Ibid., 381.

30. Ibid., 459.

31. Ibid., 460.

32. Ibid.

33. Ibid., 406.

34. Ibid.

35. Astarita, *Between Salt Water and Holy Water: A History of Southern Italy*, 198.

36. Ibid., 198-199; Valerio Lintner, *A Traveller's History of Italy*, (Northampton, Massachusetts: Interlink Books, 2008), 131; Pietro Colletta, *History of the Kingdom of Naples: 1734-1825, Volume 1*, trans. S. Horner (Edinburgh: T. Constable and Co., 1858), 13-14.

37. Astarita, *Between Salt Water and Holy Water: A History of Southern Italy*, 198, 200-201.

38. Ibid., 263-264.

39. Kamen, *Spain's Road to Empire: The Making of a World Power, 1492-1763*, 174.

40. Astarita, *Between Salt Water and Holy Water: A History of Southern Italy*, 219.

41. Ibid., 181, 187.

42. Ibid., 187.

43. Ibid., 186.

44. Ibid., 187.

45. Ibid., 218.

46. Ibid.

47. Ibid., 219.

48. Aprile, *Terroni: All That Has Been Done to Ensure That the Italians of the South Became "Southerners,"* 95, 106.

49. Astarita, *Between Salt Water and Holy Water: A History of Southern Italy*, 282.

50. Capatti, *Italian Cuisine: A Cultural History*, 21.

51. Sheryll Bellman, *America's Little Italys: Recipes & Traditions from Coast to Coast*, (Portland, ME: Sellers Publishing, 2010), 10.

52. John Mariani and Galina Mariani, *The Italian American Cookbook: A Feast of Food from a Great American Cooking Tradition*, (Boston: Harvard Common Press, 2000), 6.

53. Laurino, *The Italian Americans: A History*, 19.

54. Aprile, *Terroni: All That Has Been Done to Ensure That the Italians of the South Became "Southerners,"* 106.

55. Ibid., 108.

56. Ibid., 109.

57. Fabio Parasecoli, *Al Dente: A History of Food in Italy*, (London: Reaktion Books, 2014), 135.

58. Ibid.

59. Aprile, *Terroni: All That Has Been Done to Ensure That the Italians of the South Became "Southerners,"* 109.

60. Ibid.

61. Ibid., 178-179.

62. Marianna Izzo, "Luigi Giura e il ponte sospeso sul Garigliano. Un esempio di architettura industriale realizzato sotto i Borbone," *Il Giornale di Casoria*, June 20, 2014, http://www.ilgiornaledicasoria.it/luigi-giura-e-il-ponte-sospeso-sul-garigliano-un-esempio-di-architettura-industriale-realizzato-sotto-i-borbone/; Mille Anni di Scienza in Italia, Cronologie, Ministero dell'Università e della Ricerca Scientifica e Tecnologica, http://www.imss.fi.it/milleanni/cronologia/cronsca/isca1800.html.

63. Aprile, *Terroni: All That Has Been Done to Ensure That the Italians of the South Became "Southerners,"* 179.

64. Gilmour, *The Pursuit of Italy: A History of a Land, Its Regions, and Their Peoples*, 143.

65. Ibid.

66. Ibid.

67. Aprile, *Terroni: All That Has Been Done to Ensure That the Italians of the South Became "Southerners,"* 194.

68. Ibid.

69. Ibid., 134.

70. Ibid., 135.

71. Antonio Tirino, "Olio extravergine di oliva Sannio Caudino," Terre Sannite, August 23, 2015, http://www.terresannite.org/olio-extravergine-oliva-sannio-caudino/.

72. Gilmour, *The Pursuit of Italy: A History of a Land, Its Regions, and Their Peoples*, 142.

73. Aprile, *Terroni: All That Has Been Done to Ensure That the Italians of the South Became "Southerners,"* 178.

74. Ibid.

75. Ibid., 168.

76. Ibid.

77. Gilmour, *The Pursuit of Italy: A History of a Land, Its Regions, and Their Peoples*, 142.

78. Aprile, *Terroni: All That Has Been Done to Ensure That the Italians of the South Became "Southerners,"* 51.

79. Ibid., 95.

80. Ibid.

81. Ibid.

82. Ibid.

83. Ibid.

84. Ibid., 104-106.

85. Gilmour, *The Pursuit of Italy: A History of a Land, Its Regions, and Their Peoples*, 199.

86. Wikipedia, *Li chiamarono . . . briganti!*, https://en.wikipedia.org/wiki/Li_chiamarono..._briganti!; Alessandro Chetta, "Un film al giorno/Li chiamarono . . . Briganti!," *Corriere Della Sera*, February 4, 2016, http://corrieredelmezzogiorno.corriere.it/napoli/spettacoli/cards/film-giornoli-chiamaronobriganti/censura.shtml?refresh_ce-cp; Enrico Lancia, *Dizionario del cinema italiano vol. 6, dal 1990 al 2000*, (Rome, Italy: Gremese Editore, 2001), 359, https://books.google.com/books?id=sO8zxEhZbrMC&pg=PA359&lpg=PA359&dq=li+chiamarono+briganti+medusa&source=bl&ots=tq7_YDigvu&sig=sFFG5P1UsrlVZKF8ndhRHl-uWgw&hl=en&sa=X&ved=0ahUKEwj6z-ba_c_WAhVDYiYKHa7SBtcQ6AEIezAN#v=onepage&q&f=false.

87. Ibid.; Pasquale Squitieri, *Li chiamarono . . . briganti!*, Vidi, 1999.

88. Gilmour, *The Pursuit of Italy: A History of a Land, Its Regions, and Their Peoples*, 243, 245.

89. Ibid.

90. Ibid., 245.

91. Ibid.

92. John Dickie, *Darkest Italy: The Nation and Stereotypes of the Mezzogiorno, 1860-1900*, (New York: Palgrave, 1999), 25.

93. Ibid.

94. Holmes, ed., *The Oxford History of Italy*, 208.

95. Cresciani, *The Italians in Australia*, 16.

96. Aprile, *Terroni: All That Has Been Done to Ensure That the Italians of the South Became "Southerners,"* 67.

97. Ibid., 70.

98. Ibid.

99. Ibid., 72.

100. Ibid., 73.

101. Ibid., 72.

102. Ibid., 49.

103. Dickie, *Darkest Italy: The Nation and Stereotypes of the Mezzogiorno, 1860-1900*, 45.

104. Ibid., 46.

105. Aprile, *Terroni: All That Has Been Done to Ensure That the Italians of the South Became "Southerners,"* 48.

106. Ibid., 82.

107. Ibid., 84.

108. Mangione, *La Storia: Five Centuries of the Italian American Experience*, 60.

109. Ibid.

110. Ibid.

111. Ibid., 61.

112. Ibid., 73.

113. Ibid., 74.

114. Vellon, *A Great Conspiracy Against Our Race: Italian Immigration Newspapers and the Construction of Whiteness in the Early 20th Century*, 17.

115. Astarita, *Between Salt Water and Holy Water: A History of Southern Italy*, 274.

116. Ibid., 281.

117. Aprile, *Terroni: All That Has Been Done to Ensure That the Italians of the South Became "Southerners,"* 122.

118. Gilmour, *The Pursuit of Italy: A History of a Land, Its Regions, and Their Peoples*, 243.

119. Mangione, *La Storia: Five Centuries of the Italian American Experience*, 63.

120. I am using the term "peasant" because that is what scholars use.

121. Mangione, *La Storia: Five Centuries of the Italian American Experience*, 47.

122. Holmes, ed., *The Oxford History of Italy*, 209.

123. Capatti, *Italian Cuisine: A Cultural History*, 26.

124. Parasecoli, *Al Dente: A History of Food in Italy*, 140.

125. Astarita, *The Italian Baroque Table: Cooking and Entertaining from the Golden Age of Naples*, 62.

126. D. Mack Smith, *Cavour and Garibaldi 1860: A Study in Political Conflict*, (Cambridge: Cambridge University Press, 1986), 220-221; James Montgomery Stuart, *The History of Free Trade in Tuscany, With Remarks on Its Progress in the Rest of Italy*, (London, Paris, & New York: Cassell Petter & Galpin, 1876), Google Books, https://books.google.com/books?id=RuhM6ffvTUcC&pg=PA7&lpg=PA7&dq=history+of+free+trade+in+tuscany+stuart&source=bl&ots=C5Vl3ucuzl&sig=IRVDcP5_vYbWQumR3ipgy0zmiuY&hl=en&sa=X&ved=0ahUKEwiqvIyNpvLTAhXhh1QKHZ7QDqQQ6AEIKTAC#v=onepage&q=history%20of%20free%20trade%20in%20tuscany%20stuart&f=false, 119.

127. Charles Ulysses, *Travels through various provinces of the kingdom of Naples in 1789*, trans. Anthony Aufrere (London: Cadell, Jun. and W. Davies, 1795), 115.

128. Ibid., 75-76.

129. Ibid., 22.

130. Ibid., 64.

131. Ibid., 50.

132. Ibid., 430.

133. Ibid., 109.

134. Ibid., 98.

135. Ibid., 237.

136. Ibid., 411.

137. Astarita, *Between Salt Water and Holy Water: A History of Southern Italy*, 269.

138. Ibid.

139. Ibid.

140. Ibid., 288.

141. Aprile, *Terroni: All That Has Been Done to Ensure That the Italians of the South Became "Southerners,"* 76-77.

142. Ruth Ben-Ghiat and Stephanie Malia Hom, *Italian Mobilities* (London: Routledge, 2016), Introduction.

143. Laurino, *The Italian Americans: A History*, 81.

144. Aprile, *Terroni: All That Has Been Done to Ensure That the Italians of the South Became "Southerners,"* 86.

145. Ibid., 87.

146. Ibid., 125.

147. Ibid., 130-131.

148. Ibid., 141.

149. Ibid., 96.

150. Cresciani, *The Italians in Australia*, 47.

151. Mangione, *La Storia: Five Centuries of the Italian American Experience*, 76.

152. Ibid., 99.

153. Dickie, *Darkest Italy: The Nation and Stereotypes of the Mezzogiorno, 1860-1900*, 10.

154. Cresciani, *The Italians in Australia*, 21.

155. Dickie, *Darkest Italy: The Nation and Stereotypes of the Mezzogiorno, 1860-1900*, 15.

156. Levi, *Christ Stopped at Eboli: The Story of a Year*, 250.

157. Ibid.

158. Mangione, *La Storia: Five Centuries of the Italian American Experience*, 68.

159. Joseph Luzzi, *My Two Italies: A Personal and Cultural History*, (New York: Farrar, Straus and Giroux, 2014), 11.

160. David Yeadon, *Seasons in Basilicata: A Year in a Southern Italian Hill Village*, (New York: HarperCollins Publishers, 2004), 26.

161. Ibid.

162. Ibid., 27.

163. Ben Morreale and Robert Carola, *Italian Americans: The Immigrant Experience*, (New York: Metro Books, 2000), 13.

164. Ibid.

165. "Regional Pride," *Two Greedy Italians*, BBC, season 1, episode 3, May 18, 2011.

166. Anna Cento Bull and Mark Gilbert, *The Lega Nord and the Politics of Secession in Italy*, (New York: Palgrave, 2001), 105.

CHAPTER 3: Is *Cucina Moderna* the True Food of Italy?

1.   Molinari, *The Italians of New York*, 171.

2.   Ibid.

3.   Ibid., 171-172.

4.   Ibid., 172.

5.   Ibid.

6.   Ibid.

7.   Ibid.

8.   Robert Sietsema, "10 Old-Fashioned Italian-American Restaurants to Try in Brooklyn," *Eater*, December 1, 2014, https://ny.eater.com/2014/12/1/7315673/10-old-fashioned-italian-american-restaurants-to-try-in-brooklyn.

9.   Ibid.

10. Ibid.

11. Cinotto, *The Italian American Table: Food, Family, and Community in New York City*, 6.

12. Ibid.

13. Marcella Hazan, *The Classic Italian Cookbook: The Art of Italian Cooking and the Italian Art of Eating*, (New York: Ballantine Books, 1991), 1-4.

14. Marcella Hazan, *Amarcord: Marcella Remembers*, (New York: Gotham Books, 2008), 103.

15. Ibid., 81.

16. Ibid., 172.

17. Ibid., 219.

18. Dan Nosowitz, "How Capicola Became Gabagool: The Italian New Jersey Accent, Explained," *Atlas Obscura*, November 5, 2015, http://www.atlasobscura.com/articles/how-capicola-became-gabagool-the-italian-new-jersey-accent-explained.

19. Ibid.

20. Lavinia Pisani, "An excursus on the Italian-American language with Filomena Sorrentino," *L'Italo-Americano*, April 6, 2016, http://www.italoamericano.org/story/2016-4-6/italian-american-langiage. The word "language" is misspelled in the url.

21. Arthur Schwartz, *The Southern Italian Table: Authentic Tastes from Traditional Kitchens*, (New York: Clarkson Potter/Publishers, 2009), 55.

22. Luzzi, *My Two Italies: A Personal and Cultural History*, 119.

23. Hooper, *The Italians*, 28.

24. Ibid; Giulia Casati, "Italian Language: Dialects from Italy," *We the Italians*, #83, September 19, 2016, 30, http://wetheitalians.com/magazine#44/31.

25. Hooper, *The Italians*, 28.

26. Jody Scaravella and Elisa Petrini, *Nonna's House: Cooking and Reminiscing with the Italian Grandmothers of Enoteca Maria*, (New York: Atria Books, 2015), 77.

27. UNESCO Atlas of the World's Languages in Danger, http://www.unesco.org/culture/en/endangeredlanguages/atlas.

28. Tommasella Perniciaro, "Alghero: Where Catalan and Sardinian Cuisine Merge," Catavino, http://catavino.net/alghero-where-catalan-and-sardinian-cuisine-merge/.

29. Ibid.

30. Ibid.

31. Ibid.

32. Ibid.

33. James H. McDonald, "Italian-Mexicans," *Encyclopedia of World Cultures, Volume 8: Mesoamerican and the Caribbean*, (Hartford, CT: Human Relations Area Files, 1995), http://www.academia.edu/3569303/Italian-Mexicans, http://www.everyculture.com/Middle-America-Caribbean/Italian-Mexicans-Orientation.html; Karen Hursh Graber, "Immigrant Cooking in Mexico—Part Two: The Italians of Chipilo," Mexconnect, http://www.mexconnect.com/articles/2032-immigrant-cooking-in-mexico-part-two-the-italians-of-chipilo.

34. Ibid.

35. Ibid.; Daniel Hernandez, "Cruising in Chipilo, an Italian village in Mexico," *Intersections* (blog), August 16, 2010, http://danielhernandez.typepad.com/daniel_hernandez/2010/08/chipilo-puebla.html.

36. Carolyn MacKay, e-mail message to author, September 27-29, 2017.

37. *Tra Ponente e Levante*, So What Pictures, 2016, http://www.traponenteelevante.com/.

38. "La Barranca Park," Westside Santa Cruz, http://westsidesantacruz.org/la-barranca-park.html; "History," Stagnaro Bros., http://stagnarobros.com/history/.

39. R. B., "Hyphenated Italian R.B. grew up in the States, then lived many years in Brazil and Argentina," Candida Martinelli's Italophile Site, http://italophiles.com/rb.htm.

40. Cresciani, *The Italians in Australia*, 7.

41. Schwartz, *The Southern Italian Table: Authentic Tastes from Traditional Kitchens*, 161.

42. Rocco DiSpirito, *Rocco's Italian American*, (New York: Hyperion, 2004), 52.

43. Ibid., 54.

44. Romeo Salta, *The Pleasures of Italian Cooking*, (New York: Macmillan Publishing Co., Inc., 1977), xi.

45. Ibid., xiii.

46. Ibid., 76.

47. John Scialdone, *A Neapolitan Peasant's Cookbook*, (Norfolk/Virginia Beach, VA: The Donning Company, 1987), xii.

48. John F. Mariani, *How Italian Food Conquered the World*, (New York: St. Martin's Press, 2011), 201; Stefania Spatti, "Lidia Bastianich: A story of food, love and nostalgia," *Il Sole 24 Ore*, February 7, 2017, https://translate.google.com/translate?hl=en&sl=it&u=http://america2 4.com/news/lidia-bastianich-una-storia-di-cibo-amore-nostalgia&prev=search.

49. Mucci, *We the Italians: Two flags, One heart, One hundred interviews about Italy and the US*, 31.

50. Lidia Matticchio Bastianich and Tanya Bastianich Manuali, *Lidia's Italy: 140 Simple and Delicious Recipes from the Ten Places in Italy Lidia Loves Most*, (New York: Alfred A. Knopf, 2007), 40.

51. Ibid., 4; "About Istria," Official tourist website of Istria, http://www.istra.hr/en/about-istra/about-istra; "Croatia," http://istra.hr/en/about-istra/croatia.

52. Wikipedia, "Istria," https://en.wikipedia.org/wiki/Istria.

53. Bastianich, *Lidia's Italy: 140 Simple and Delicious Recipes from the Ten Places in Italy Lidia Loves Most*, 40.

54. "The Long Way Home," *Finding Your Roots with Henry Louis Gates, Jr.*, PBS, season 3, episode 9, March 1, 2016, http://www.pbs.org/weta/finding-your-roots/.

55. Ibid.; Gianfranco Cresciani, "A Clash of Civilisations? The Slovene and Italian Minorities and the Problem of Trieste from Borovnica to Bonegilla," *Italian Historical Society Journal*, Volume 12, Number 2, July-December 2004, https://drive.google.com/file/d/0B1aAzmXBjZO5eFQySUlrdTBYRkk /view.

56. Ibid.

57. "The Long Way Home," *Finding Your Roots with Henry Louis Gates, Jr.*, PBS, season 3, episode 9, March 1, 2016, http://www.pbs.org/weta/finding-your-roots/.

58. Ibid.

59. Bastianich, *Lidia's Italy: 140 Simple and Delicious Recipes from the Ten Places in Italy Lidia Loves Most*, 4.

60. Ibid.

61. Ibid.

62. "Population by Ethnicity, By Towns/Municipalities, 2011 Census," Croatian Bureau of Statistics, https://www.dzs.hr/Eng/censuses/census2011/results/htm/E01_01_0 4/e01_01_04_zup18.html.

63. Hooper, *The Italians*, 11.

64. Bastianich, *Lidia's Italy: 140 Simple and Delicious Recipes from the Ten Places in Italy Lidia Loves Most*, 6-33.

65. Ibid., 40-66.

66. Ibid., 72-92.

67. Ibid., 98-126.

68. Lidia Matticchio Bastianich, *Lidia's Italian-American Kitchen*, (New York: Alfred A. Knopf, 2001).

69. Ibid., xiv.

70. Ibid.

71. Ibid., xv.

72. Ibid., xvi.

73. Bastianich, *Lidia's Italy: 140 Simple and Delicious Recipes from the Ten Places in Italy Lidia Loves Most*, 244.

74. Louis Zamperini and David Rensin, *Devil at My Heels: A Heroic Olympian's Astonishing Story of Survival as a Japanese POW in World War II*, (New York: Harper, 2003), 104, 206.

75. Bastianich, *Lidia's Italian-American Kitchen*, xvi.

76. Ibid.

77. Ibid.

78. Ibid.

79. Ibid.

80. Ibid.

81. Mariani, *How Italian Food Conquered the World*, 212.

82. "Mission statement," International Olive Council,
     http://www.internationaloliveoil.org/estaticos/view/100-mission-
     statement; "Basic texts," International Olive Council,
     http://www.internationaloliveoil.org/estaticos/view/101-basic-texts;
     "International Agreement on Olive Oil, 1956" United Nations Treaty
     Collections,
     https://treaties.un.org/pages/ViewDetails.aspx?src=TREATY&mtdsg_
     no=XIX-1&chapter=19&clang=_en.

83. Bellman, *America's Little Italys: Recipes & Traditions from Coast to Coast*, 10.

84. "Hope Cemetery," *Atlas Obscura*,
     http://www.atlasobscura.com/places/hope-cemetery.

85. Bellman, *America's Little Italys: Recipes & Traditions from Coast to Coast*, 10.

86. Durante, *Italoamericana: The Literature of the Great Migration, 1880-1943*, 57.

87. Paul Moses, *An Unlikely Union: The Love-Hate Story of New York's Irish and
     Italians*, (New York: New York University Press, 2015), 116-117.

88. Ibid., 219; Jonathan Gill, *Harlem: The Four Hundred Year History from Dutch
     Village to Capital of Black America*, (New York: Grove Press, 2011), 204;
     Constantine N. Katsoris, "A Tribute to the Fordham Judiciary: A
     Century of Service," *Fordham Law Review*, Volume 75, Issue 5, 2007,
     2310,
     http://ir.lawnet.fordham.edu/cgi/viewcontent.cgi?article=4254&contex
     t=flr.

89. Walter Grutchfield, "Avignone Pharmacy," *Walter Grutchfield* (blog),
     http://www.waltergrutchfield.net/avignone.htm, accessed May 17, 2017;
     Jeremiah Moss, "Avignone Chemist," *Jeremiah's Vanishing New York*
     (blog), January 21, 2015,
     http://vanishingnewyork.blogspot.com/2015/01/avignone-
     chemist.html.

90. Cinotto, *The Italian American Table: Food, Family, and Community in New
     York City*, 134.

91. Miles Ryan Fisher, "It's a Wonderful (Italian-American) Life: The American Tale of the Italian Banker," *Italian America*, Volume XX, Number 4, Fall 2015, 22-24.

92. Ibid.

93. Ibid.

94. Ibid.

95. Ibid.

96. Ibid.

97. Joseph P. Kahn, "The Immigrant Prince," *Inc.*, July 1, 1986, https://www.inc.com/magazine/19860701/786.html.

98. Ibid.

99. Molinari, *The Italians of New York*, 154.

100. Ibid.

101. Bellman, *America's Little Italys: Recipes & Traditions from Coast to Coast*, 41.

102. Andy Boy, "Company History," http://www.andyboy.com/the-company/the-company-today/.

103. "Our Founder," Generoso Pope Foundation, http://gpfny.org/our-founder/.

104. Ibid.

105. Ibid.

106. Ibid.

107. Ibid.

108. Daniela Gioseffi, *Word Wounds and Water Flowers*, (VIA Folios, 1995), dedication, http://capa.conncoll.edu/gioseffi.ww&wf.html.

109. Anton Evangelista, *Author and Activist: The Daniela Gioseffi Story*, Comprehensive Films, Inc., http://www.authorandactivist.com/about.html.

110. Ibid.

111. Ibid.

112. "Ten 'Italian' Dishes That Don't Actually Exist in Italy," *Local*, August 4, 2016, https://www.thelocal.it/20160804/ten-italian-dishes-that-dont-exist-in-italy.

113. Ibid.

114. Morreale, *Italian Americans: The Immigrant Experience*, 85.

115. Bethany Jean Clement, "A Look Inside Merlino Foods, Supplier to Seattle's Best Restaurants," *Seattle Times*, February 27, 2015, http://www.seattletimes.com/life/food-drink/a-look-inside-merlino-foods-supplier-to-seattles-best-restaurants/.

116. Ibid; "About Us," Merlino Foods, http://www.merlino.com/aboutus/.

117. Arthur Schwartz, *New York City Food: An Opinionated History and More Than 100 Legendary Recipes*, (New York: Stewart, Tabori & Chang, 2004), 156.

118. Mariani, *The Italian American Cookbook: A Feast of Food from a Great American Cooking Tradition*, 7.

119. Cinotto, *The Italian American Table: Food, Family, and Community in New York City*, 161.

120. Ibid., 156.

121. Ibid.

122. Ibid., 161.

123. Ibid.

124. Gruppo Lactalis Italia, http://www.gruppolactalisitalia.com/Locator.cfm?sectionid=950&CFID=8260784&CFTOKEN=80068484&jsessionid=f0306763dbbe40346be5507c101158556658.

125. Cinotto, *The Italian American Table: Food, Family, and Community in New York City*, 163.

126. Ibid., 164.

127. Ibid.

128. Mariani, *The Italian American Cookbook: A Feast of Food from a Great American Cooking Tradition*, 8.

129. Gabaccia, *We Are What We Eat: Ethnic Food and the Making of Americans*, 50-54.

130. Ibid.

131. Ibid.

132. Ibid., 52-53.

133. Ibid., 52.

134. Adriana Trigiani, *Cooking with My Sisters: One Hundred Years of Family Recipes, from Bari to Big Stone Gap*, (New York: Random House, 2004), 29.

135. Jane Ziegelman, *97 Orchard: An Edible History of Five Immigrant Families in One New York Tenement*, (New York: Smithsonian Books, 2010), 194.

136. Jacob Riis, *How the Other Half Lives: Studies Among the Tenements of New York*, 49.

137. Oretta Zanini De Vita, *Encyclopedia of Pasta*, trans. Maureen B. Fant (Berkeley and Los Angeles, CA: University of California Press, 2009), 260.

138. Mariani, *How Italian Food Conquered the World*, 53.

139. Cinotto, *The Italian American Table: Food, Family, and Community in New York City*, 142.

140. Joel Denker, *The World on a Plate: A Tour Through the History of America's Ethnic Cuisine*, (Lincoln, NE: University of Nebraska Press, 2003), 16-18, https://books.google.com/books?id=S_x6nrkcoUkC&pg=PA16&lpg=PA16&dq=vaccaro+1867+contessa+entellina&source=bl&ots=TnzBNM3U9_&sig=C85mdtW8MOhcO5uJ81IOlZPwrXQ&hl=en&sa=X&ved=0ahUKEwi00JuxlsfWAhUDSiYKHZo2DUIQ6AEIRDAH#v=onepage&q=vaccaro%201867%20contessa%20entellina&f=false.

141. Ibid.

142. National Italian American Foundation (NIAF) Facebook post, January 12, 2016, https://www.facebook.com/niaf.org/.

143. "Dole Timeline," Dole, http://www.dole.com/en/AboutDole.

144. Bellman, *America's Little Italys: Recipes & Traditions from Coast to Coast*, 118.

145. Gabaccia, *We Are What We Eat: Ethnic Food and the Making of Americans*, 67.

146. Ibid., 114.

147. Ibid.

148. James and Karla Murray, "The Urban Lens: Documenting Gentrification's Toll on the Mom-and-Pops of Greenwich Village," *6sqft*, February 2, 2016, https://www.6sqft.com/the-urban-lens-documenting-gentrifications-toll-on-the-mom-and-pops-of-greenwich-village/.

149. Paul Biasco, "Amazing History of City's 1st Italian Importer Found in Teardown Building," *DNAinfo*, July 29, 2016, https://www.dnainfo.com/chicago/20160729/river-west/amazing-history-of-citys-1st-italian-importer-found-teardown-building.

150. Ibid.

151. Ibid.

152. Ibid.

153. Ibid.

154. Bellman, *America's Little Italys: Recipes & Traditions from Coast to Coast*, 29.

155. Ibid., 35.

156. Moses, *An Unlikely Union: The Love-Hate Story of New York's Irish and Italians*, 142.

157. Gabaccia, *We Are What We Eat: Ethnic Food and the Making of Americans*, 68.

158. Bellman, *America's Little Italys: Recipes & Traditions from Coast to Coast*, 32.

159. Mezzetta, "Our History," http://www.mezzetta.com/about-us/our-history.

160. Ibid.

161. Bellman, *America's Little Italys: Recipes & Traditions from Coast to Coast*, 33.

162. Ibid., 66.

163. Gabaccia, *We Are What We Eat: Ethnic Food and the Making of Americans*, 69.

164. Bellman, *America's Little Italys: Recipes & Traditions from Coast to Coast*, 150.

165. Ernest Dollar, "Shop Local," *Walter Magazine*, http://www.waltermagazine.com/art_and_culture/shop-local/.

166. Mariani, *How Italian Food Conquered the World*, 57.

167. Cinotto, *The Italian American Table: Food, Family, and Community in New York City*, 3.

168. Jim Heimann, Steven Heller, and John Mariani, eds., *Menu Design in America: A Visual and Culinary History of Graphic Styles and Design 1850-1985*, (Cologne, Germany: Taschen, 2011), 207.

169. Hugh Shankland, *Out of Italy: The Story of Italians in North East England*, (Leics, UK: Troubador Publishing Ltd., 2014), 99.

170. Gillian Riley, *The Oxford Companion to Italian Food*, (New York: Oxford University Press, 2007), 261.

171. Cinotto, *The Italian American Table: Food, Family, and Community in New York City*, 112.

172. Aprile, *Terroni: All That Has Been Done to Ensure That the Italians of the South Became "Southerners,"* 178.

173. Cinotto, *The Italian American Table: Food, Family, and Community in New York City*, 164.

174. Frank Bruni, *Born Round: A Story of Family, Food and a Ferocious Appetite*, (New York: The Penguin Press, 2009), 41.

175. Trigiani, *Cooking with My Sisters: One Hundred Years of Family Recipes, from Bari to Big Stone Gap*, 18.

176. Ibid.

177. Pollio Dairy Products Corp., 1961, 1.

178. Ibid.

179. Alleva Dairy, https://www.allevadairy.com/.

180. Florence Fabricant, "DiPalo Chooses Wine to Go With Its Cheese," *New York Times*, November 25, 2008, http://www.nytimes.com/2008/11/26/dining/26store.html.

181. Cinotto, *The Italian American Table: Food, Family, and Community in New York City*, 170, 177-178.

182. Ibid.

183. Ibid.

184. Ibid., 142.

185. Ibid., 165.

186. Ibid., 167.

187. Ibid., 147; Gabaccia, *We Are What We Eat: Ethnic Food and the Making of Americans*, 69.

188. Gabaccia, *We Are What We Eat: Ethnic Food and the Making of Americans*, 69.

189. Cinotto, *The Italian American Table: Food, Family, and Community in New York City*, 147.

190. Ibid.

191. Gabaccia, *We Are What We Eat: Ethnic Food and the Making of Americans*, 111.

192. Ibid., 154.

193. Ibid., 154-155.

194. Mariani, *The Italian American Cookbook: A Feast of Food from a Great American Cooking Tradition*, 5.

195. Ibid., 8.

196. Ibid., 9.

197. Parasecoli, *Al Dente: A History of Food in Italy*, 61-62.

198. Carol Helstosky, *Pizza: A Global History*, (London: Reaktion Books, 2008), 22; Antonio Mattozzi, *Inventing the Pizzeria: A History of Pizza Making in Naples*, trans. Zachary Nowak (London: Bloomsbury, 2009), 47.

199. Mattozzi, *Inventing the Pizzeria: A History of Pizza Making in Naples*, 15.

200. Ibid., 25.

201. Ibid.

202. Ibid.

203. Ibid., 49.

204. Ibid., 40.

205. Capatti, *Italian Cuisine: A Cultural History*, 186.

206. Mattozzi, *Inventing the Pizzeria: A History of Pizza Making in Naples*, 50.

207. Ibid.

208. Bastianich, *Lidia's Italian-American Kitchen*, xvii.

209. Bellman, *America's Little Italys: Recipes & Traditions from Coast to Coast*, 27; Dante & Luigi's Corona di Ferro, http://www.danteandluigis.com/.

210. Gabaccia, *We Are What We Eat: Ethnic Food and the Making of Americans*, 115.

211. Ibid.

212. Ibid.

213. Moses, *An Unlikely Union: The Love-Hate Story of New York's Irish and Italians*, 142.

214. Mariani, *The Italian American Cookbook: A Feast of Food from a Great American Cooking Tradition*, ix.

215. Ibid., 1.

216. Ibid., 2.

217. Ibid., ix.

218. Bruni, *Born Round: A Story of Family, Food and a Ferocious Appetite*, 257.

219. Ibid.

220. Ziegelman, *97 Orchard: An Edible History of Five Immigrant Families in One New York Tenement*, 223.

221. Beppe Severgnini, *Ciao, America!: An Italian Discovers the U.S.*, (New York: Broadway Books, 2002), 193.

222. Gabaccia, *We Are What We Eat: Ethnic Food and the Making of Americans*, 198.

223. Mariani, *The Italian American Cookbook: A Feast of Food from a Great American Cooking Tradition*, x.

224. Mariani, *How Italian Food Conquered the World*, 211.

225. Mariani, *The Italian American Cookbook: A Feast of Food from a Great American Cooking Tradition*, x.

226. Douwe Yntema, *The Archaeology of South-East Italy in the First Millennium BC*, (Amsterdam: Amsterdam University Press, 2013), 165, 226.

227. Alfredo Viazzi, *Alfredo Viazzi's Italian Cooking*, (New York: Random House, 1979), 12.

228. Valerio Viale, "Mediterranean Diet Roundtable: More Than Food, It's a Way of Life," *L'Italo-Americano*, April 28, 2016, http://www.italoamericano.org/story/2016-4-28/mdr-la.

229. Elisabetta Povoledo, "Italy Growers Wary of Olive Oil Fraud as New Law Is Weighed," *New York Times*, February 27, 2016, https://www.nytimes.com/2016/02/28/world/europe/italy-growers-wary-of-olive-oil-fraud-as-new-law-is-weighed.html?_r=0.

230. Galbani, http://galbanicheese.com/our-cheeses/dairy-aisle/.

231. Mariani, *How Italian Food Conquered the World*, 153.

232. Ibid.

233. Parasecoli, *Al Dente: A History of Food in Italy*, 50.

234. Ibid. 50-51.

235. Mariani, *How Italian Food Conquered the World*, 153.

236. Kreutz, *Before the Normans: Southern Italy in the Ninth & Tenth Centuries*, 114.

237. Burton Anderson, *The Wines of Italy*, (New York: The Italian Trade Commission, 2002), 7.

238. Ulysses, *Travels through various provinces of the kingdom of Naples in 1789*, 216.

239. Anderson, *The Wines of Italy*, 7.

240. Dina Di Maio, "Valdese, North Carolina," *F & L Primo*, Volume 3, Issue 4, 2003, 52.

241. Mucci, *We the Italians: Two flags, One heart, One hundred interviews about Italy and the US*, 36.

242. Frank J. Prial, "Robert Mondavi, Napa Wine Champion, Dies at 94," *New York Times*, May 17, 2008, http://www.nytimes.com/2008/05/17/business/17mondavi.html?pagewanted=all&_r=0; Eric Pace, "Julio Gallo, 83, Wine Industrialist, Dies," http://www.nytimes.com/1993/05/04/obituaries/julio-gallo-83-wine-industrialist-dies.html.

243. Mariani, *How Italian Food Conquered the World*.

244. Ibid., 166.

245. Ibid.

246. Ibid.

247. "Researchers have found 6,000-year-old Italian wine in a Sicilian cave," *Local*, August 28, 2017, https://www.thelocal.it/20170828/researchers-found-6000-year-old-italian-wine-in-a-sicilian-cave.

248. Mariani, *How Italian Food Conquered the World*, 166-7.

249. Gilmour, *The Pursuit of Italy: A History of a Land, Its Regions, and Their Peoples*, 21; Lintner, *A Traveller's History of Italy*, 2-3.

250. Riley, *The Oxford Companion to Italian Food*, 208.

251. Ibid.

252. MIPAAF, "Italian Flavors: Calabria Salami," *We the Italians*, #69, October 2015, http://wetheitalians.com/magazine-news/italian-flavors-calabria-salami.

253. Louis Inturrisi, "Sicily/Sardinia," in *Savoring Italy*, ed. Alexandra Arrowsmith (New York: HarperCollins Publishers, 1992), 226.

254. Schwartz, *Naples at Table: Cooking in Campania*, xlii.

255. Ibid., 21.

256. Ibid.

257. Ibid., 182.

258. Summer Whitford, "13 Things You Probably Didn't Know About Real Italian Food," *Daily Meal*, January 12, 2016, http://www.thedailymeal.com/travel/13-things-you-probably-didn-t-know-about-real-italian-food.

259. Mariani, *How Italian Food Conquered the World*, 155.

260. Ibid.

261. Ibid.

262. Mariani, *The Italian American Cookbook: A Feast of Food from a Great American Cooking Tradition*, xi.

263. Capatti, *Italian Cuisine: A Cultural History*, 283-284.

264. Merriam-Webster, "Peasant," https://www.merriam-webster.com/dictionary/peasant.

265. Ibid.

266. Ibid.

267. *Webster's New World Dictionary of the American Language*, "Peasant," (New York: Warner Books, 1987), 440.

268. Capatti, *Italian Cuisine: A Cultural History*, 95.

269. Ibid.

270. Ibid., 96.

271. Kahn, "The Immigrant Prince," *Inc.*, July 1, 1986.

272. Prince, "Our Story," https://www.princepasta.com/en-us/content/27448/OurStory.aspx.

273. Kahn, "The Immigrant Prince," *Inc.*, July 1, 1986.

274. Zanini De Vita, *Encyclopedia of Pasta*, 260.

275. Gabaccia, *We Are What We Eat: Ethnic Food and the Making of Americans*, 68.

276. Zanini De Vita, *Encyclopedia of Pasta*, 121; Academia Barilla, ed., *I Love Pasta: An Italian Love Story in 100 Recipes*, (Newtown, CT: The Taunton Press, 2013), 88.

277. Zanini De Vita, *Encyclopedia of Pasta*, 121.

278. Cinotto, *The Italian American Table: Food, Family, and Community in New York City*, 134.

279. Academia Barilla, ed., *I Love Pasta: An Italian Love Story in 100 Recipes*, 18.

280. Glenn Collins, "At Eataly, the Ovens and the Cash Registers Are Hot," *New York Times*, August 28, 2012, https://mobile.nytimes.com/2012/08/29/dining/eataly-exceeds-revenue-predictions.html.

281. "The Alps and Arrangiarsi," *Two Greedy Italians*, BBC, season 2, episode 3, May 10, 2012.

282. Mottolini, "Who We Are," http://www.mottolini.eu/en/.

283. MIPAAF, "Italian Flavors: Valtellina Bresaola," *We the Italians*, #56, March 2015, http://www.wetheitalians.com/.

284. Ibid.

285. Ibid.

286. Ibid.

287. Parasecoli, *Al Dente: A History of Food in Italy*, 18.

288. Liz Barrett, *Pizza: A Slice of American History*, (Minneapolis, MN: Voyageur Press, 2014), 24.

289. Riley, *The Oxford Companion to Italian Food*, 160.

290. Ibid.

291. Ibid.

292. Ibid.

293. Ibid.

294. MIPAAF, "Italian Flavors: Calabria Salami," *We the Italians*, #69, October 2015.

295. Ibid.

296. Riley, *The Oxford Companion to Italian Food*, 161-162. On page 154, Riley mentions that the European Economic Commission regulates dairy products, and regulations often come into conflict with traditional methods.

297. "History," Slow Food USA, https://www.slowfoodusa.org/history.

298. "Liguria and La Bella Figura," *Two Greedy Italians*, BBC, season 2, episode 2, April 26, 2012.

299. David Gentilcore, *Pomodoro!: A History of the Tomato in Italy*, (New York: Columbia University Press, 2010), 81.

300. Ibid.

301. Ibid., 83.

302. Capatti, *Italian Cuisine: A Cultural History*, 69.

303. Ibid., 82.

304. Jim Yardley, "Fear of Ruin as Disease Takes Hold of Italy's Olive Trees," *New York Times*, May 11, 2015, https://www.nytimes.com/2015/05/12/world/europe/fear-of-ruin-as-disease-takes-hold-of-italys-olive-trees.html?action=click&contentCollection=Europe&module=RelatedC overage&region=Marginalia&pgtype=article.

305. Ibid.

306. Ibid.

307. Mucci, *We the Italians: Two flags, One heart, One hundred interviews about Italy and the US*, 59.

308. "Friarielli tossici a Casoria, scoperta maxi discarica sotterranea," Fanpage.it, September 24, 2015, http://napoli.fanpage.it/friarielli-tossici-a-casoria-scoperta-maxi-discarica-sotterranea/.

309. Nicholas Blechman, "Food Chains," *New York Times*.

310. Nicholas Blechman, "Extra Virgin Suicide," *New York Times*, January 1, 2014, https://www.nytimes.com/interactive/2014/01/24/opinion/food-chains-extra-virgin-suicide.html.

311. Nicholas Blechman, "The Mystery of San Marzano," *New York Times*, August 16, 2015, https://www.nytimes.com/interactive/2015/08/16/opinion/sunday/fo od-chains-mystery-of-san-marzano.html?_r=0.

312. Ibid.

313. Cecilia Anesi, Giulio Rubino, and Lorenzo Bodrero, "Pulp fiction: Asda's 'made in Italy' tomato puree hails from China," *Guardian*, February 27, 2013, http://www.theguardian.com/world/2013/feb/27/asda-italy-tomato-puree-china.

314. Ibid.

315. Ibid.

316. Ibid.

317. Ibid.

318. Nicholas Blechman, "Code Name Parmigiano," *New York Times*, June 6, 2014,

https://www.nytimes.com/interactive/2014/06/06/opinion/food-chains-code-name-parmigiano.html.

319. Nicholas Blechman, "Planet Pasta," *New York Times*, March 14, 2014, https://www.nytimes.com/interactive/2014/03/14/opinion/food-chains-planet-pasta.html.

320. Ibid.

321. "Italy Exports Wine, But Drinks Less," *Italian America*, Volume XX, Number 1, Winter 2015, 4.

322. Ibid.

323. Ibid.

324. Vinepair, "United States of Alcohol," January 14, 2015, http://vinepair.com/wine-blog/united-states-of-alcohol-map/.

325. Mariani, *The Italian American Cookbook: A Feast of Food from a Great American Cooking Tradition*, xi.

326. Beppe Severgnini, *La Bella Figura: A Field Guide to the Italian Mind*, (New York: Broadway Books, 2006), 22.

327. Schwartz, *The Southern Italian Table: Authentic Tastes from Traditional Kitchens*, 10.

328. Mariani, *The Italian American Cookbook: A Feast of Food from a Great American Cooking Tradition*, 22.

329. Astarita, *The Italian Baroque Table: Cooking and Entertaining from the Golden Age of Naples*, 184.

330. Mariani, *The Italian American Cookbook: A Feast of Food from a Great American Cooking Tradition*, 22.

331. Ibid.

CHAPTER 4: They Came to America

1. Dona De Sanctis, "It's 'Only' a Movie…," *Italian America*, Volume XX, Number 2, Spring 2015, 15.

2. Ibid.

3. Ibid.

4. Russ Frushtick, "Take-Two Chairman Responds to 'Mafia 2' Complaints from Italian-American Group, UNICO," MTV, August 19, 2010, http://www.mtv.com/news/2461704/take-two-chairman-responds-to-mafia-2-complaints-from-italian-american-group-unico/.

5. Nick Summers, "'Mafia III' drops you in a '60s gang war this October," Engadget, April 19, 2016, https://www.engadget.com/2016/04/19/mafia-3-trailer-october-7/.

6. Sam Roberts, "An Immigrant's Contribution to Mount Rushmore Is Recognized, 75 Years Later," *New York Times*, June 28, 2016, http://www.nytimes.com/2016/06/29/nyregion/luigi-del-bianco-mount-rushmore.html?_r=1.

7. Ibid.

8. "H. Res. 269," Congress.gov, https://www.congress.gov/bill/107th-congress/house-resolution/269/actions.

9. Bonnie Heather McCourt, *Antonio Meucci: The TRUE Inventor of the Telephone, April 13, 1808-October 18, 1889*, Garibaldi-Meucci Museum pamphlet.

10. Julia Marsh, "Judge Accused of Making Anti-Italian Remarks," *New York Post*, March 23, 2015, http://nypost.com/2015/03/23/judge-accused-of-making-anti-italian-remarks/.

11. Ibid.

12. Dave Collins, "Connecticut lawmakers subpoena deported former residents," Associated Press, March 1, 2016, https://www.apnews.com/8b52574135174c55b717b2ad4999050d.

13. Ibid.

14. Ibid.

15. Maria Teresa Cometto, "'Iron Lady' Italian Style," i-*Italy* NY, Year 4, Issue 1-2, February-March 2016, 21.

16. Severgnini, *Ciao, America!: An Italian Discovers the U.S.*, 129-130.

17. Ibid., 129.

18. Ibid., 130.

19. Ibid.

20. Vellon, *A Great Conspiracy Against Our Race: Italian Immigration Newspapers and the Construction of Whiteness in the Early 20th Century*, 17.

21. Baily, *Immigrants in the Lands of Promise: Italians in Buenos Aires and New York City, 1870 to 1914*, 86.

22. Laurino, *The Italian Americans: A History*, 82.

23. Ibid.

24. Shankland, *Out of Italy: The Story of Italians in North East England*, 91.

25. Ibid.

26. Ibid., 90.

27. Baily, *Immigrants in the Lands of Promise: Italians in Buenos Aires and New York City, 1870 to 1914*, 86.

28. Riis, *How the Other Half Lives: Studies Among the Tenements of New York*, 41.

29. Durante, *Italoamericana: The Literature of the Great Migration, 1880-1943*, 21.

30. Ibid., 57.

31. Riis, *How the Other Half Lives: Studies Among the Tenements of New York*, 47.

32. Ibid., 41.

33. Mangione, *La Storia: Five Centuries of the Italian American Experience*, 213.

34. Susan Taylor Block, "The MacRae Farm Colonies: Surprises in St. Helena," *Susan747* (blog), May 7, 2010, https://susan747.wordpress.com/; J. Vincent Lowery, "Hugh MacRae, Southern Agriculture, and the Question of Selective Immigration," *Southeastern Immigration*, August 22, 2014, http://www.southeasternimmigration.org/research/hugh-macrae-southern-agriculture-and-the-question-of-selective-immigration/.

35. J. Vincent Lowery, "Hugh MacRae, Southern Agriculture, and the Question of Selective Immigration," *Southeastern Immigration*, August 22, 2014, http://www.southeasternimmigration.org/research/hugh-macrae-southern-agriculture-and-the-question-of-selective-immigration/.

36. Ibid.

37. Ibid.

38. Ibid.

39. Ibid.

40. "Recipes From America's Italian Communities, Part 6," *Jovina Cooks Italian* (blog), May 1, 2015, https://jovinacooksitalian.com/2015/05/01/recipes-from-americas-italian-communities-part-6/.

41. Ibid.

42. Vellon, *A Great Conspiracy Against Our Race: Italian Immigration Newspapers and the Construction of Whiteness in the Early 20th Century*, 81.

43. Ibid., 81-82.

44. Peter Vellon, "'Between White Men and Negroes': The Perception of Southern Italian Immigrants through the Lens of Italian Lynchings," in *Anti-Italianism: Essays on a Prejudice*, eds. William J. Connell and Fred Gardaphe (New York: Palgrave MacMillan, 2010), 27.

45. Ibid., 28.

46. Ibid.

47. Vellon, *A Great Conspiracy Against Our Race: Italian Immigration Newspapers and the Construction of Whiteness in the Early 20th Century*, 83.

48. Cinotto, *The Italian American Table: Food, Family, and Community in New York City*, 78.

49. Vellon, *A Great Conspiracy Against Our Race: Italian Immigration Newspapers and the Construction of Whiteness in the Early 20th Century*, 84.

50. Ibid.

51. Ziegelman, *97 Orchard: An Edible History of Five Immigrant Families in One New York Tenement*, 193.

52. Baily, *Immigrants in the Lands of Promise: Italians in Buenos Aires and New York City, 1870 to 1914*, 86.

53. Morreale, *Italian Americans: The Immigrant Experience*, 152.

54. Ibid.; "Prohibition: Speakeasies, Loopholes and Politics," NPR, June 10, 2011, http://www.npr.org/2011/06/10/137077599/prohibition-speakeasies-loopholes-and-politics.

55. Dick Rosano, "The Italian-American Pioneers of the California Wine Industry," Cal-Italia.com, 2003-2011, http://www.cal-italia.com/history.html.

56. "People of Charles Krug," Charles Krug Winery, https://www.charleskrug.com/estate/people; Grace Hwang Lynch, "Chinese Laborers Built Sonoma's Wineries. Racist Neighbors Drove Them Out," *The Salt*, NPR, http://www.npr.org/sections/thesalt/2017/07/13/536822541/the-forgotten-chinese-who-built-sonoma-s-wineries; "Gustave Niebaum," Inglenook, https://www.inglenook.com/.

57. Dick Rosano, "The Italian-American Pioneers of the California Wine Industry," Cal-Italia.com, 2003-2011, http://www.cal-italia.com/history.html.

58. Ibid.

59. Baily, *Immigrants in the Lands of Promise: Italians in Buenos Aires and New York City, 1870 to 1914*, 87.

60. Ibid., 88.

61. Ibid., 89.

62. Vellon, "'Between White Men and Negroes': The Perception of Southern Italian Immigrants through the Lens of Italian Lynchings," in *Anti-Italianism: Essays on a Prejudice*, 25; Mangione, *La Storia: Five Centuries of the Italian American Experience*, 272.

63. Donna R. Gabaccia, *Italy's Many Diasporas*, (Routledge, 2013, and Google Books), 65, https://books.google.com/books?id=DS-MAQAAQBAJ&pg=PA58&source=gbs_toc_r&cad=2#v=onepage&q&f=false; "Slavery v. Peonage," PBS, http://www.pbs.org/tpt/slavery-by-another-name/themes/peonage/.

64. Ibid.

65. Mangione, *La Storia: Five Centuries of the Italian American Experience*, 271.

66. Ibid., 272.

67. Ibid.

68. Ibid.

69. Ibid.

70. Ibid., 208-211.

71. Ibid.

72. Moses, *An Unlikely Union: The Love-Hate Story of New York's Irish and Italians*, 118.

73. Vellon, *A Great Conspiracy Against Our Race: Italian Immigration Newspapers and the Construction of Whiteness in the Early 20th Century*, 86.

74. Ibid., 93.

75. Cresciani, *The Italians in Australia*, 23.

76. Ibid.

77. Mangione, *La Storia: Five Centuries of the Italian American Experience*, 299-301.

78. Ibid., 299-300; Bruce Watson, *Sacco & Vanzetti*, (New York: Viking, 2007), 331.

79. "The Story of a Proletarian Life—Bartolomeo Vanzetti," Libcom.org, January 14, 2012, https://libcom.org/library/story-proletarian-life.

80. Ibid.

81. Ibid.

82. Ibid.

83. Ibid.

84. Ibid.

85. Watson, *Sacco & Vanzetti*, 304-305.

86. Bellman, *America's Little Italys: Recipes & Traditions from Coast to Coast*, 59.

87. Ibid.

88. Mangione, *La Storia: Five Centuries of the Italian American Experience*, 37-38.

89. Ziegelman, *97 Orchard: An Edible History of Five Immigrant Families in One New York Tenement*, 189.

90. Riis, *How the Other Half Lives: Studies Among the Tenements of New York*, 47.

91. Ibid., 49.

92. Ibid.

93. Laurino, *The Italian Americans: A History*, 78.

94. Moses, *An Unlikely Union: The Love-Hate Story of New York's Irish and Italians*, 81.

95. Ziegelman, *97 Orchard: An Edible History of Five Immigrant Families in One New York Tenement*, 162-165.

96. Ibid., 164.

97. Ibid., 164-165.

98. Ibid., 186.

99. Ibid.

100. Baily, *Immigrants in the Lands of Promise: Italians in Buenos Aires and New York City, 1870 to 1914*, 111.

101. Parasecoli, *Al Dente: A History of Food in Italy*, 154.

102. Baily, *Immigrants in the Lands of Promise: Italians in Buenos Aires and New York City, 1870 to 1914*, 110.

103. Morreale, *Italian Americans: The Immigrant Experience*, 142.

104. Ziegelman, *97 Orchard: An Edible History of Five Immigrant Families in One New York Tenement*, 216.

105. Eileen Tighe, ed., *Woman's Day Encyclopedia of Cookery, Volume 2*, (New York: Fawcett Publications, Inc., 1966), 243.

106. Ibid.

107. Gabaccia, *We Are What We Eat: Ethnic Food and the Making of Americans*, 66.

108. Ibid.

109. David Kamp and Marion Rosenfeld, *The Food Snob's Dictionary: An Essential Lexicon of Gastronomical Knowledge*, (New York: Broadway Books, 2007), 18.

110. Jens Lund, "Walla Walla Sweets: Onions and Ethnic Identity in a Pacific Northwest Italian Community," *Columbia Magazine*, Volume 8, Number 3, Fall 1994, http://www.washingtonhistory.org/files/library/walla-walla-sweets.pdf.

111. Ibid.

112. Taylor Block, "The MacRae Farm Colonies: Surprises in St. Helena," *Susan747* (blog), May 7, 2010, https://susan747.wordpress.com/.

113. Gary Kamiya, "Odd Arch Is Last Remnant of Bustling Produce Market built in 1874," *San Francisco Chronicle*, February 27, 2015, http://www.sfchronicle.com/bayarea/article/Odd-arch-is-last-remnant-of-bustling-produce-6106142.php.

114. Ibid.

115. Andy Boy, "Company History," http://www.andyboy.com/the-company/the-company-today/.

116. Bellman, *America's Little Italys: Recipes & Traditions from Coast to Coast*, 59.

117. Burt Wolf, "Ellis Island," *Travels & Traditions*, #213, http://www.burtwolf.com/program-blog/tt-213.

118. Moses, *An Unlikely Union: The Love-Hate Story of New York's Irish and Italians*, 299.

119. Ibid.

120. Rita Cipalla, "Joe Desimone: From Produce Farmer to Owner of Seattle's Pike Place Market," *L'Italo Americano*, April 29, 2016, http://www.italoamericano.org/story/2016-4-29/desimone.

121. Ibid.

122. Ibid.

123. Betty Boyd Caroli, *Italian Repatriation From the United States, 1900-1914*, (Lincoln, NE: iUniverse, Inc., 2008), 64.

124. Mariani, *How Italian Food Conquered the World*, 53.

125. Ibid., 56.

126. Elizabeth Vallone, "Food! Glorious Food! Italians Are What They Eat," *L'idea Magazine*, January 13, 2015, http://www.lideamagazine.com/food-glorious-food-italians-eat/.

127. Ziegelman, *97 Orchard: An Edible History of Five Immigrant Families in One New York Tenement*, xiii.

128. Schwartz, *New York City Food: An Opinionated History and More Than 100 Legendary Recipes*, 158.

129. DiSpirito, *Rocco's Italian American*, 37.

130. Hazan, *Amarcord: Marcella Remembers*, 72.

131. Ibid., 81.

132. Ibid.

133. Ibid.

134. Ibid., 109.

135. Parasecoli, *Al Dente: A History of Food in Italy*, 249.

136. Schwartz, *The Southern Italian Table: Authentic Tastes from Traditional Kitchens*, 10.

137. Ibid.

138. Ibid., 109.

139. United States Census Bureau, https://www.census.gov/, accessed May 23, 2017.

140. "This is what Italy's population will look like in 50 years," *Local*, April 26, 2017, https://www.thelocal.it/20170426/this-is-how-italys-population-will-look-in-50-years-time; "Anno 2013 Bilancio Demografico Nazionale," Istat, Istituto nazionale di statistica, June 16, 2014, http://www.istat.it/it/files/2014/06/Bilanciodemografico_2013_def.pdf?title=Bilancio+demografico+nazionale+-+16%2Fgiu%2F2014+-+Testo+integrale.pdf.

141. Hazan, *Amarcord: Marcella Remembers*, 109.

142. Parasecoli, *Al Dente: A History of Food in Italy*, 228.

143. Gabaccia, *We Are What We Eat: Ethnic Food and the Making of Americans*, 52.

144. Cinotto, *The Italian American Table: Food, Family, and Community in New York City*, 129.

CHAPTER 5: Spaghetti and Meatballs

1. Robert Sietsema, "Battle of the New York City Heroes," *Eater*, October 29, 2014, https://ny.eater.com/2014/10/29/7101407/battle-of-the-new-york-city-heroes.

2. Pellegrino Artusi, *Science in the Kitchen and the Art of Eating Well*, trans. Murtha Baca and Stephen Sartarelli (Toronto, CAN: University of Toronto Press, 2011), 55.

3. Cinotto, *The Italian American Table: Food, Family, and Community in New York City*, 109.

4.   Carol Field, *The Italian Baker*, (Berkeley: Ten Speed Press, 2011), 76-77.

5.   Ibid., 251.

6.   Ibid., 8.

7.   Jane and Michael Stern, *500 Things to Eat Before It's Too Late*, (Boston, Houghton Mifflin Harcourt, 2009), 58; Jane and Michael Stern, "Now, That's an Italian," *Gourmet*, April 2005, http://www.gourmet.com/magazine/2000s/2005/04/now-thats-an-italian.html; "Our Story," Amato's, http://www.amatos.com/story/.

8.   "10 'Italian' Dishes That Don't Exist in Italy," *Local*, Slide 6, August 4, 2016, https://www.thelocal.it/galleries/Culture/10-italian-dishes-that-dont-exist-in-italy/6.

9.   Judy Buchenot, "Italian Chef Brings Authentic Tastes of Home to Batavia," *Chicago Tribune*, *Aurora-Beacon News*, February 27, 2015, http://www.chicagotribune.com/suburbs/aurora-beacon-news/lifestyles/ct-abn-gaetano-dibenedetto-st-0301-20150227-story.html.

10. Ibid.

11. Ibid.

12. Eva Sandoval, "Ten 'Italian' Foods You Won't Find in Italy," *Fodor's Travel*, February 27, 2013, http://www.fodors.com/news/ten-italian-foods-you-wont-find-in-italy-6510.html.

13. Shaylyn Esposito, "Is Spaghetti and Meatballs Italian?," *Smithsonian Magazine*, June 6, 2013, http://www.smithsonianmag.com/arts-culture/is-spaghetti-and-meatballs-italian-94819690/?no-ist.

14. Alessia Gargiulo, "17 Italian Foods That Aren't Italian at All," *Swide*, Dolce & Gabbana, September 6, 2013, http://www.swide.com/food-travel/, (Reblogged at https://peekingintoitaly.wordpress.com/2014/05/09/17-italian-foods-that-arent-italian-at-all-reblogged-post/.)

15. Schwartz, *The Southern Italian Table: Authentic Tastes from Traditional Kitchens*, 172.

16. Ibid.

17. Schwartz, *New York City Food: An Opinionated History and More Than 100 Legendary Recipes*, 170.

18. Schwartz, *Naples at Table: Cooking in Campania*, 269.

19. Capatti, *Italian Cuisine: A Cultural History*, 67.

20. Artusi, *Science in the Kitchen and the Art of Eating Well*, 251.

21. Bastianich, *Lidia's Italian-American Kitchen*, xv, 134.

22. Vera Abitbol, "Romania: Chiftele," *196 Flavors* (blog),
     http://www.196flavors.com/romania-chiftele/, accessed May 23, 2017.

23. Artusi, *Science in the Kitchen and the Art of Eating Well*, 238.

24. Robert Sietsema, "10 Old-Fashioned Italian-American Restaurants to
     Try in Brooklyn," *Eater*, December 1, 2014,
     https://ny.eater.com/2014/12/1/7315673/10-old-fashioned-italian-
     american-restaurants-to-try-in-brooklyn.

25. Montanari, *Italian Identity in the Kitchen, or Food and the Nation*, 45.

26. Gentilcore, *Pomodoro!: A History of the Tomato in Italy*, 71.

27. Ibid.; "Cerlone, Francesco." Treccani Enciclopedia,
     http://www.treccani.it/enciclopedia/francesco-cerlone_(Dizionario-
     Biografico)/; Domenico Scafoglio and Luigi M. Lombardi Satriani,
     Pulcinella: il mito e la storia, (Milano: Leonardo, 1992), 170; Francesco
     Cerlone, "La forza della bellezza," in *Commedie*, (Napoli, 1828), 62,
     https://archive.org/details/bub_gb_9aMelnWzZ0UC/page/n61.

28. Alessandro Magnasco, *The Supper of Pulcinella and Colombina*, 1725-1730,
     (Raleigh, NC: North Carolina Museum of Art).

29. Ibid.

30. Gentilcore, *Pomodoro!: A History of the Tomato in Italy*, 46.

31. Ibid.

32. Parasecoli, *Al Dente: A History of Food in Italy*, 79.

33. Ibid.

34. Gentilcore, *Pomodoro!: A History of the Tomato in Italy*, 51.

35. Astarita, *The Italian Baroque Table: Cooking and Entertaining from the Golden
     Age of Naples*, 51.

36. Parasecoli, *Al Dente: A History of Food in Italy*, 135.

37. Ulysses, *Travels through various provinces of the kingdom of Naples in 1789*, 17.

38. Ibid., 237.

39. Ibid., 248.

40. Ibid., 257.

41. Colletta, *History of the Kingdom of Naples: 1734-1825, Volume 1*, 335.

42. Emilio Sereni, *History of the Italian Agricultural Landscape*, trans. R. Burr Litchfield (Princeton, NJ: Princeton University Press, 1997), xxvii; Zanini De Vita, *Encyclopedia of Pasta*, 20.

43. Zanini De Vita, *Encyclopedia of Pasta*, 20.

44. Ibid.

45. Lintner, *A Traveller's History of Italy*, 121; Astarita, *Between Salt Water and Holy Water: A History of Southern Italy*, 84.

46. Claudia Roden, *The Food of Spain*, (New York: HarperCollins, 2011), 38.

47. Ibid., 38.

48. Gentilcore, *Pomodoro!: A History of the Tomato in Italy*, 54.

49. Roden, *The Food of Spain*, 422.

50. "Recipe—Meatballs in Tomato Sauce," *Flavors of Brazil* (blog), March 3, 2010, http://flavorsofbrazil.blogspot.com/2010/03/recipe-meatballs-in-tomato-sauce.html.

51. "Território brasileiro e povoamento, italianos, regiões de origem," Instituto Brasileiro de Geografia e Estatística, https://brasil500anos.ibge.gov.br/territorio-brasileiro-e-povoamento/italianos/regioes-de-origem.

52. "Recipe—Meatballs in Tomato Sauce," *Flavors of Brazil* (blog), March 3, 2010, http://flavorsofbrazil.blogspot.com/2010/03/recipe-meatballs-in-tomato-sauce.html.

53. Astarita, *The Italian Baroque Table: Cooking and Entertaining from the Golden Age of Naples*, 91.

54. Gentilcore, *Pomodoro!: A History of the Tomato in Italy*, 61-62.

55. Ibid., 64.

56. Ibid.

57. Arturo Iengo, *Cucina Napoletana: 100 Recipes from Italy's Most Vibrant City*, (Northampton, MA: Interlink Books, 2008), 7.

58. Ibid.; Gentilcore, *Pomodoro!: A History of the Tomato in Italy*, 57.

59. Iengo, *Cucina Napoletana: 100 Recipes from Italy's Most Vibrant City*, 84.

60. Ibid.

61. Roden, *The Food of Spain*, 38.

62. Ibid.

63. Astarita, *The Italian Baroque Table: Cooking and Entertaining from the Golden Age of Naples*, 114.

64. Gentilcore, *Pomodoro!: A History of the Tomato in Italy*, 73.

65. Astarita, *The Italian Baroque Table: Cooking and Entertaining from the Golden Age of Naples*, 131.

66. Artusi, *Science in the Kitchen and the Art of Eating Well*, 93-94.

67. Ibid.

68. Ibid., 94.

69. Iengo, *Cucina Napoletana: 100 Recipes from Italy's Most Vibrant City*, 55.

70. Ibid.

71. Matthew Pantaleno, "Grandma Marie 1913-2013," Youtube, https://www.youtube.com/watch?v=j33odebMuNA, 1:00, accessed May 24, 2017.

72. Lyn Stallworth and Rod Kennedy, Jr., *The Brooklyn Cookbook*, (New York: Alfred A. Knopf, Inc., 1991), 84.

73. Esposito, "Is Spaghetti and Meatballs Italian?," *Smithsonian Magazine*, June 6, 2013, http://www.smithsonianmag.com/arts-culture/is-spaghetti-and-meatballs-italian-94819690/?no-ist, percynjpn and keltcrusader.

74. Schwartz, *New York City Food: An Opinionated History and More Than 100 Legendary Recipes*, 170.

75. DiSpirito, *Rocco's Italian American*, 40.

76. Mariani, *How Italian Food Conquered the World*, 57.

77. DiSpirito, *Rocco's Italian American*, 26.

78. Eligio Bucciarelli, "What, You Can't Order Spaghetti and Meatballs in Italy?," *Così Italiano* (blog), http://www.cosiitaliano.com/407/what-you-cant-order-spaghetti-and-meatballs-in-italy/, accessed May 24, 2017.

79. Ziegelman, *97 Orchard: An Edible History of Five Immigrant Families in One New York Tenement*, 196-197.

80. Ada Boni, *The Talisman Italian Cook Book*, trans. Matilde La Rosa (New York: Crown Publishers, Inc., 1978), xix.

81. Ibid.

82. Gennaro Contaldo, *Gennaro's Italian Year*, (London: Headline Publishing Group, 2006), 121; Jamie Oliver, Jamie Oliver's Food Tube, Twitter, June 7, 2017, https://twitter.com/JamiesFoodTube/status/872521303135207426.

83. Mariani, *How Italian Food Conquered the World*, 68.

84. Ziegelman, *97 Orchard: An Edible History of Five Immigrant Families in One New York Tenement*, 224.

85. Andreas Viestad, "Potato Sausages," New Scandinavian Cooking, http://www.newscancook.com/recipes-by-chef/potato-sausages/, accessed May 24, 2017.

86. Ibid.

87. Ibid.

88. Boni, *The Talisman Italian Cook Book*, 154-155.

89. Ibid., v.

90. Maria Luisa Taglienti, *The Italian Cookbook*, (New York: Random House, 1955), About the Author.

91. Ibid.

92. Ibid., viii.

93. Ibid., About the Author.

94. Ibid., vi.

95. Ibid., 73.

96. Ibid., 55.

97. Heimann, *Menu Design in America: A Visual and Culinary History of Graphic Styles and Design 1850-1985*, 158.

98. Ibid., 169.

99. Ibid., 202.

100. Ibid., 182.

CHAPTER 6: Italian Food in America

1. Severgnini, *La Bella Figura: A Field Guide to the Italian Mind*, 30.

2. Ibid.

3. Ibid.

4. Ibid.

5. Capatti, *Italian Cuisine: A Cultural History*, 69.

6. Ibid.

7. L. Volosciuc and V. Josu, "Ecological Agriculture to Mitigate Soil Fatigue," David Dent, ed., *Soil as World Heritage*, (Netherlands: Springer, 2014), 431-435, https://link.springer.com/chapter/10.1007%2F978-94-007-6187-2_45#page-1.

8. MIPAAF, "Italian Flavors: Ispica New Carrot," *We the Italians*, #83, September 2016, 26-28, https://www.joomag.com/magazine/we-the-italians-september-19-2016-83/0049492001474195687?page=26.

9. Capatti, *Italian Cuisine: A Cultural History*, 156, 162, 165.

10. Montanari, *Italian Identity in the Kitchen, or Food and the Nation*, 20-25.

11. Ibid., 21.

12. Ibid., 25.

13. Ibid.

14. Parasecoli, *Al Dente: A History of Food in Italy*, 132.

15. Ibid.

16. Capatti, *Italian Cuisine: A Cultural History*, 27.

17. Claudia Baroncelli, "Feast of the Seven Fishes: the Italian American tradition not all Italians know," *Swide*, Dolce & Gabbana, December 17,

2014, http://www.swide.com/art-culture/feast-of-seven-fishes-the-italian-american-christmas-tradition-not-all-italians-know/2014/12/17.

18. Domenick Rafter, "Feast of Seven Fishes: A Look at the Popular Italian-American Christmas Tradition," *Queens Tribune*, November 12, 2015, http://queenstribune.com/feast-of-seven-fishes-a-look-at-the-popular-italian-american-christmas-tradition/.

19. Ibid.

20. Riley, *The Oxford Companion to Italian Food*, 193.

21. Bastianich, *Lidia's Italian-American Kitchen*, 378.

22. Bob Batz Jr., "Restaurant, Chef Perpetuate the Italian Tradition of the Feast of St. Joseph," *Pittsburgh Post-Gazette*, March 18, 2010, http://www.post-gazette.com/food/2010/03/18/Restaurant-chef-perpetuate-the-Italian-tradition-of-the-Feast-of-St-Joseph/stories/201003180502.

23. Ibid.

24. Ibid.

25. Maria C. Montoya, "Learn more on 'Cuccidatta' and St. Joseph Day altars at SoFAB," *Times-Picayune*, March 2, 2009, http://blog.nola.com/judywalker/2009/03/learn_more_on_cuccidatta_and_s.html; "St. Joseph's Day Altars," New Orleans Official Guide, New Orleans Tourism Marketing Corporation, http://www.neworleansonline.com/neworleans/seasonal/stjosephsday.html.

26. Ruth Schuster, "8,000-year Old Olive Oil Found in Galilee, Earliest Known in World," Haaretz, December 17, 2014, https://www.haaretz.com/jewish/archaeology/.premium-1.632310; Marc Guitteny, *Olive Tree*, (Monaco, Monaco Press, 2001), 1.

27. E. N. Frankel, R. J. Mailer, S. C. Wang, et. al., "Evaluation of Extra-Virgin Olive Oil Sold in California," (Davis, California: UC Davis Olive Center, 2011), http://olivecenter.ucdavis.edu/research/files/report041211finalreduced.pdf.

28. Cinotto, *The Italian American Table: Food, Family, and Community in New York City*, 172.

29. Mattia Locatelli, *A Collection of Genuine Italian Recipes*, (New York: Costa & Aliani Press, 1939), 41.

30. Cinotto, *The Italian American Table: Food, Family, and Community in New York City*, 172.

31. Antonio Tirino, "Olio extravergine di oliva Sannio Caudino," Terre Sannite, August 23, 2015, http://www.terresannite.org/olio-extravergine-oliva-sannio-caudino/.

32. "China Food Giant Buys into Italian Olive Oil," *Local*, October 8, 2014, https://www.thelocal.it/20141008/china-food-giant-buys-into-italian-olive-oil-maker.

33. Ibid.

34. Schwartz, *Naples at Table: Cooking in Campania*, 5.

35. Schwartz, *The Southern Italian Table: Authentic Tastes from Traditional Kitchens*, 11.

36. "Losing 'Virginity': Olive Oil's 'Scandalous' Fraud," NPR, December 12, 2011, http://www.npr.org/2011/12/12/143154180/losing-virginity-olive-oils-scandalous-industry.

37. Ibid.

38. Bill Whitaker, "Agromafia," *60 Minutes*, CBS, January 3, 2016, http://www.cbsnews.com/news/60-minutes-agromafia-food-fraud/.

39. Jerry Finzi, "All About Italian Olive Oil: The Good, the Bad, and the Amazing," *Grand Voyage Italy* (blog), January 11, 2016, http://www.grandvoyageitaly.com/piazza/all-about-italian-olive-oil-the-good-the-bad-and-the-amazing.

40. Whitaker, "Agromafia," *60 Minutes*, CBS, January 3, 2016, http://www.cbsnews.com/news/60-minutes-agromafia-food-fraud/.

41. Finzi, "All About Italian Olive Oil: The Good, the Bad, and the Amazing," *Grand Voyage Italy* (blog), January 11, 2016, http://www.grandvoyageitaly.com/piazza/all-about-italian-olive-oil-the-good-the-bad-and-the-amazing.

42. "Extra-virgin olive oil ID system launched in Bari," ANSA, March 21, 2016, http://www.ansa.it/english/news/2016/03/17/extra-virgin-olive-oil-id-system-launched-in-bari_28ea3665-be99-49cc-bff4-aa7150d62bea.html.

43. Ibid.

44. Ibid.

45. Ibid.

46. Hannah Howard, "Italy Triumphs at 2016 NYIOOC," *Olive Oil Times*, April 16, 2016, http://www.oliveoiltimes.com/olive-oil-basics/italy-triumphs-at-2016-nyiooc/51193.

47. Capatti, *Italian Cuisine: A Cultural History*, 1.

48. Parasecoli, *Al Dente: A History of Food in Italy*, 35.

49. Ibid., 37.

50. Salma Hage, *The Lebanese Kitchen*, (London: Phaidon Press, 2012), 63, 438.

51. Bastianich, *Lidia's Italy: 140 Simple and Delicious Recipes from the Ten Places in Italy Lidia Loves Most*, 280.

52. Pollio Dairy Products Corp., 1961, 1.

53. Ibid., 2.

54. Capatti, *Italian Cuisine: A Cultural History*, 10-11.

55. Ibid., 37.

56. Ibid., 40.

57. Ibid.

58. Ibid., 41, 90.

59. Ibid., 41-42.

60. Ibid., 42.

61. Ibid.

62. Ibid., 55.

63. Gentilcore, *Pomodoro!: A History of the Tomato in Italy*, 66.

64. Astarita, *The Italian Baroque Table: Cooking and Entertaining from the Golden Age of Naples*, 242.

65. Burt Wolf, "Ellis Island," *Travels & Traditions*, #213, http://www.burtwolf.com/program-blog/tt-213.

66. Bellman, *America's Little Italys: Recipes & Traditions from Coast to Coast*, 18.

67. Dina Di Maio, "Hoboken Ice Cream," Hobokeni.com, 2002, http://www.hobokeni.com/blogs/ddimaio/hoboken-ice-cream; Jane Marchiony Paretti, "The Man Who Invented the Ice Cream Cone Italo Marchiony Created the Dish You Could Eat—and He Created it in Hoboken," *Hudson Reporter*, September 14, 2005, http://www.hudsonreporter.com/view/full_story/2405732/article-The-man-who-invented-the-ice-cream-cone-Italo-Marchiony-created-the-dish-you-could-eat---and-he-created-it-in-Hoboken?instance=more_page.

68. Ibid.

69. Ibid.

70. Capatti, *Italian Cuisine: A Cultural History*, 112.

71. Ibid., 45, 50, 75, 80.

72. Ibid., 45.

73. Ibid., 80.

74. Ibid., 81.

75. "Brazilian Bottarga—Tainha Roe Is Golden," *Flavors of Brazil* (blog), December 29, 2010, http://flavorsofbrazil.blogspot.com/2010/12/brazilian-bottarga-tainha-roe-is-golden.html.

76. Ibid.

77. Ibid.

78. Zanini De Vita, *Encyclopedia of Pasta*, xiv.

79. Bellman, *America's Little Italys: Recipes & Traditions from Coast to Coast*, 16.

80. Capatti, *Italian Cuisine: A Cultural History*, 51; Julia Della Croce, *Pasta Classica*, (San Francisco, CA: Chronicle Books, 1992), 11; Mark Grant, *Roman Cookery: Ancient Recipes for Modern Kitchens*, (London: Serif, 2008), 60-61; Field, *The Italian Baker*, 250. It's unclear whether *lagana* was more breadlike or pastalike. I think the words "lagana" and "lasagna" look similar, but I'm not sure the dishes were. Grant says Horace wrote about eating it with leeks and chickpeas, which suggests it is more of a pasta. But then it was used to scoop up ingredients, reminding me of

the Ethiopian *injera*, which is more like a bread. Field says it was a likely predecessor of pizza.

81. Bellman, *America's Little Italys: Recipes & Traditions from Coast to Coast*, 16.

82. Capatti, *Italian Cuisine: A Cultural History*, 52.

83. Astarita, *Between Salt Water and Holy Water: A History of Southern Italy*, 162.

84. Capatti, *Italian Cuisine: A Cultural History*, 54, 104.

85. Ibid., 117.

86. Ibid., 54.

87. Ibid.

88. Ibid., 55.

89. Ibid., 57.

90. Ibid.

91. Phyllis Macchioni, "Auntie Pasta: Scrippelles," *This Italian Life* (blog), October 17, 2013, http://thisitalianlife.blogspot.com/2013/10/auntie-pasta-scrippelles.html, accessed May 26, 2017.

92. Ibid.

93. Capatti, *Italian Cuisine: A Cultural History*, 65-66.

94. Ibid., 66.

95. Ibid., 129.

96. Ibid., 128-129.

97. Ibid., 148.

98. Ibid.

99. Vallone, "Food! Glorious Food! Italians Are What They Eat," *L'idea Magazine*, January 13, 2015, http://www.lideamagazine.com/food-glorious-food-italians-eat/.

100. Ibid.

101. "Cosa 'sta sotto' i cibi? 7 Italiani su 10 controllano l'origine degli alimenti e privilegiano il Made in Italy," Polli Cooking Lab, September 25, 2015, http://pollicookinglab.it/?p=641, accessed May 26, 2017.

102. Ibid.

103. Ibid.

104. Severgnini, *La Bella Figura: A Field Guide to the Italian Mind*, 22.

105. Matt Blitz, "History of the Caesar Salad," *Food & Wine*, June 22, 2017, http://www.foodandwine.com/fwx/food/we-can-thank-tijuana-and-prohibition-caesar-salad.

106. Bastianich, *Lidia's Italian-American Kitchen*, 108.

107. Sandoval, "Ten 'Italian' Foods You Won't Find in Italy," *Fodor's Travel*, February 27, 2013, http://www.fodors.com/news/ten-italian-foods-you-wont-find-in-italy-6510.html.

108. "Harry Olivieri, 90, Co-Inventor of Cheese Steak in Philadelphia, Dies," *New York Times*, July 22, 2006, http://www.nytimes.com/2006/07/22/us/22olivieri.html?mcubz=0.

109. Bellman, *America's Little Italys: Recipes & Traditions from Coast to Coast*, 43.

110. Central Grocery & Deli, http://www.centralgrocery.com.

111. Elena, "La moffoletta palermitana del 2 novembre (o muffuletta)," *La Montagna Incantata* (blog), November 2, 2012, http://lamontagnaincantata.blogspot.com/2012/11/la-moffoletta-palermitana-del-2.html, accessed May 26, 2017.

112. Ibid.

113. Ibid.

114. "Muffuletta o moffoletta?," RAI TV, March 11, 2014, http://www.rai.it/dl/RaiTV/programmi/media/ContentItem-29b25144-fc9d-4f13-a266-ebfad8e5eb8d.html, accessed May 26, 2017.

115. Ibid.

116. "Spaghetti Primavera," *Food & Wine*, http://www.foodandwine.com/recipes/spaghetti-primavera, accessed May 26, 2017; Amanda Hesser, "Le Cirque's Spaghetti Primavera," *New York Times*, May 14, 2009, http://www.nytimes.com/2009/05/17/magazine/17food-t.html, accessed May 26, 2017.

117. Serena Renner, "Where to Taste San Francisco's Most Iconic Dish," *AFAR*, October 8, 2015, November/December 2015 issue,

https://www.afar.com/magazine/where-to-taste-san-franciscos-most-iconic-dish, accessed May 26, 2017.

118. Ines Di Lelio, Comment, *Hunting for the Very Best* (blog), April 29, 2015, https://huntingfortheverybest.wordpress.com/2015/04/28/the-real-fettuccine-alfredo/.

119. Ibid.

120. Ibid.

121. Gargiulo, "17 Italian Foods That Aren't Italian at All," *Swide*, Dolce & Gabbana, September 6, 2013, http://www.swide.com/food-travel/, (Reblogged at https://peekingintoitaly.wordpress.com/2014/05/09/17-italian-foods-that-arent-italian-at-all-reblogged-post/.)

122. Bita, "Golden Breakfast Porridge with Cinnamon & Sugar (Kaachi)," *Honest & Tasty* (blog), September 4, 2014, http://honestandtasty.com/golden-porridge-with-cinnamon-sugar-kaachi/, accessed May 26, 2017.

123. Kimberly Kohatsu, "The Origins of Fettuccine Alfredo," *Huffington Post*, January 13, 2014, http://www.huffingtonpost.com/Menuism/the-origins-of-fettuccine_b_4590831.html, accessed May 26, 2017.

124. Sara Rimer, "Teressa Bellissimo, Inventor of Spicy Buffalo Wings, Dies," *New York Times*, November 6, 1985, http://www.nytimes.com/1985/11/06/nyregion/teressa-bellissimo-inventor-of-spicy-buffalo-wings-dies.html, accessed May 26, 2017.

125. Mariani, *The Italian American Cookbook: A Feast of Food from a Great American Cooking Tradition*, x.

126. Calvin Trillin, "An Attempt to Compile a Short History of the Buffalo Chicken Wing," *New Yorker*, August 25, 1980, http://www.newyorker.com/magazine/1980/08/25/an-attempt-to-compile-a-short-history-of-the-buffalo-chicken-wing, accessed May 26, 2017.

127. Scaravella, *Nonna's House: Cooking and Reminiscing with the Italian Grandmothers of Enoteca Maria*, 47.

128. "How It All Started," Tropicana, http://www.tropicana.com/our-story.

129. "Amedeo Obici and Bay Point Farm History," The Obici House, http://theobicihouse.com/-history.html.

130. Mariani, *How Italian Food Conquered the World*, 93.

131. Ibid.

132. Ibid., 18.

133. Ibid., 59.

134. Ibid., 145.

135. Ibid., 145-146.

136. Ibid., 129.

137. Ibid., 151.

138. Iengo, *Cucina Napoletana: 100 Recipes from Italy's Most Vibrant City*.

139. Ibid.

140. Astarita, *The Italian Baroque Table: Cooking and Entertaining from the Golden Age of Naples*, 147-148.

141. Schwartz, *The Southern Italian Table: Authentic Tastes from Traditional Kitchens*, 187.

142. Schwartz, *Naples at Table: Cooking in Campania*.

143. Ibid.

144. Di Maio, "Valdese, North Carolina," *F & L Primo*, Volume 3, Issue 4, 2003, 49.

145. Ibid.

146. Ibid., 50.

147. Ibid.

148. Ibid.

149. Ibid.

150. Ibid.

151. Ibid.

152. Ibid.

153. Ibid.

154. Ibid., 51.

155. Ibid., 49.

156. *Cooking with the Waldensians*, (Kearney, NE: Morris Press, 2001).

157. Antonio Carluccio, *Italia: the recipes and customs of the regions*, (London: Quadrille Publishing Limited, 2005), 8-21.

158. Ibid., 17.

159. *Cooking with the Waldensians*, 38.

160. Carluccio, *Italia: the recipes and customs of the regions*, 17.

161. *Cooking with the Waldensians*, 100-101.

162. Carluccio, *Italia: the recipes and customs of the regions*, 19.

163. *Cooking with the Waldensians*, 120.

164. Parasecoli, *Al Dente: A History of Food in Italy*, 128.

165. *Cooking with the Waldensians*, 57.

166. Dina Di Maio, "Soutisso: The Journey of an Italian Sausage from the Valleys of the Alps to the Valleys of North Carolina," *Primo*, 2nd edition, 2016, 58-59.

167. Ibid.

168. "Silvio Ursini," Brummell Blog, http://www.brummellmagazine.co.uk/brummell-blog-silvio-ursini/; "Our Story," Obica, http://www.obica.com/portal/US/en/about-us/our-story/.

169. Ibid.

170. Astarita, *The Italian Baroque Table: Cooking and Entertaining from the Golden Age of Naples*, 230.

171. "Poor Man's Food," *Two Greedy Italians*, BBC, season 1, episode 2, May 11, 2011.

172. Ibid.

173. Mariani, *How Italian Food Conquered the World*, 124.

174. Ibid., 211.

175. Carrie Vasios Mullins, "International Face Off: Nutella," *Serious Eats*, March 2012, http://sweets.seriouseats.com/2012/03/international-face-off-nutella.html#comments-195384.

176. David Robinson, "Sorrento Cheese name ages out as owner rebrands product as Galbani," *Buffalo News*, September 6, 2013, http://buffalonews.com/2013/09/06/sorrento-cheese-name-ages-out-as-owner-rebrands-product-as-galbani/; "About Lactalis American Group, Inc.," http://www.lactalisamericangroup.com/company/.

177. Robinson, "Sorrento Cheese name ages out as owner rebrands product as Galbani," *Buffalo News*, September 6, 2013, http://buffalonews.com/2013/09/06/sorrento-cheese-name-ages-out-as-owner-rebrands-product-as-galbani/.

178. Assocamerestero sull'Italian Sounding, "Mapping the IT," *We the Italians*, #86, December 19, 2016, 34, http://www.wetheitalians.com.

179. Ibid.

180. Ibid.

181. Ibid.

182. Ibid., 36, 38.

183. BelGioioso, "The 9 Secrets of BelGioioso," https://www.belgioioso.com/Secret.

184. Stella D'oro, "History," http://www.stelladoro.com/about/; Josh Kosman, "Not the Original Recipe," *New York Post*, May 10, 2009, http://nypost.com/2009/05/10/not-the-original-recipe/.

185. Beth Borzone, "'We Won't Work for Crumbs': Stella D'Oro Workers Set Precedent for Fighting Back!," *Huffington Post*, July 19, 2009, http://www.huffingtonpost.com/beth-borzone/we-wont-work-for-crumbs-s_b_216587.html; Daniel Beekman, "CT Owner Sells Stella D'oro Brand," *New York Post*, September 25, 2009, http://nypost.com/2009/09/25/ct-owner-sells-stella-doro-brand/.

186. Mama Francesca, http://www.mamafrancescacheese.com/; Cheese Merchants of America, http://www.cheesemerchants.com/.

187. Mama Francesca, http://www.mamafrancescacheese.com/.

188. Assocamerestero sull'Italian Sounding, "Mapping the IT," *We the Italians*, #86, December 19, 2016, 36-38, http://www.wetheitalians.com.

189. Eataly, "Order In An Eatalian with Eataly," https://www.eataly.com/us_en/stores/nyc-flatiron/amazon-order-eatalian/.

190. Ibid.

191. Degrado Italo-Americano, https://www.facebook.com/Degrado-Italo-Americano-1541013436145195/.

192. Ibid.

193. Schwartz, *New York City Food: An Opinionated History and More Than 100 Legendary Recipes*, 176.

194. Scaravella, *Nonna's House: Cooking and Reminiscing with the Italian Grandmothers of Enoteca Maria*, 192.

195. Degrado Italo-Americano, https://www.facebook.com/Degrado-Italo-Americano-1541013436145195/.

196. Ibid.

197. Ibid.

198. Ibid.

199. Ibid.

200. Ibid.

201. Ibid.

202. Ibid.

203. "Marchio Ospitalità Italiana Award Ceremony," IACC-Miami, May 25, 2016, http://iacc-miami.com/marchio-ospitalita-italiana/.

204. "25 Restaurants in New York City Get the 'Italian Hospitality' Quality Seal," *L'Italo Americano*, April 29, 2016, http://www.italoamericano.org/story/2016-4-29/italian-food.

205. "Marchio Ospitalità Italiana Award Ceremony," IACC-Miami, May 25, 2016, http://myemail.constantcontact.com/Marchio-Ospitalita-Award-Ceremony---May-25th.html?soid=1105311588597&aid=xnhWGEUy6n8.

206. Zona Blu, http://zonabluweston.com/our-story/.

207. Sette Bello, http://www.settebellofla.com/.

208. Preamble, Ospitalità Italiana, http://www.10q.it/progetto_rim.php?lang=en.

CHAPTER 7: Pizza

1. Helstosky, *Pizza: A Global History*, 23-24.

2. Ibid., 7.

3. Ibid.

4. Ibid.

5. "The King of Romance," *Guardian*, April 16, 2003, https://www.theguardian.com/books/2003/apr/16/alexandredumaspere; "Biography of Alexandre Dumas," Alexandre Dumas, http://www.alexandredumasworks.com/alexandre-dumas-biography/.

6. Helstosky, *Pizza: A Global History*, 17.

7. Ibid.

8. Ibid.

9. Field, *The Italian Baker*, 251.

10. Barrett, *Pizza: A Slice of American History*, 14; "The History of Brick Ovens," Forno Bravo, https://www.fornobravo.com/pompeii-oven/the-history-of-brick-ovens/, accessed May 28, 2017.

11. Field, *The Italian Baker*, 250.

12. Anna Pernice, "Dove mangiare la pizza a Napoli," *Travel Fashion Tips* (blog), http://www.travelfashiontips.com/2016/01/dove-mangiare-la-pizza-a-napoli.html, January 27, 2016, accessed May 28, 2017; Enrico Volpe, *I Piatti Tipici della Cucina Napoletana e Lucana*, (Naples, Italy: Cuzzolin, 2015), 80.

13. Volpe, *I Piatti Tipici della Cucina Napoletana e Lucana*, 81.

14. Ibid.

15. Helstosky, *Pizza: A Global History*, 18.

16. Schwartz, *Naples at Table: Cooking in Campania*, 67.

17. Helstosky, *Pizza: A Global History*, 18.

18. Ibid.; Schwartz, *Naples at Table: Cooking in Campania*, 67.

19. Helstosky, *Pizza: A Global History*, 18.

20. Volpe, *I Piatti Tipici della Cucina Napoletana e Lucana*, 78.

21. Ibid., 78-79; Martin Maiden, "Pizza is a German(ic) Word!," Your Dictionary, https://web.archive.org/web/20030115224054/http://www.yourdictio nary.com/library/pizza.html.

22. Field, *The Italian Baker*, 251.

23. Cristian Bonetto and Helena Smith, *Naples, Pompeii & the Amalfi Coast*, (London: Lonely Planet Publication Pty Ltd, 2016), 89.

24. Ibid.

25. *Collezione di Tutti I Poemi in Lingua Napoletana, Volume 26*, 1789, 247, https://books.google.it/books?id=Mm8tAAAAMAAJ&pg=PA247&lpg =PA247&dq=pezzulo+pozzuoli&source=bl&ots=04epS_dMYT&sig= TtOLqFAwJ5yKv6gkHlJZ6RfFa7w&hl=it&sa=X&ved=0ahUKEwjrj5 Tet8jWAhWIQiYKHYlVCDUQ6AEIVDAF#v=onepage&q=pezzulo &f=false; Wikipedia Italy, "Pozzuoli," https://it.wikipedia.org/wiki/Pozzuoli.

26. Dale Erwin and Tessa Fedele, *Dictionary: English-Neapolitan; Neapolitan-English*, (Middletown, Delaware: 2015), 307; R. Siddall, "Lime Cements, Plasters, Mortars and Concretes," 2000, http://www.ucl.ac.uk/~ucfbrxs/limes/G123notes.htm.

27. R. Siddall, "Lime Cements, Plasters, Mortars and Concretes," 2000, http://www.ucl.ac.uk/~ucfbrxs/limes/G123notes.htm.

28. Ed Levine, *Pizza: A Slice of Heaven*, (New York: Universe Publishing, 2005), 51.

29. Nancy Verde Barr, *We Called It Macaroni: An American Heritage of Southern Italian Cooking*, (New York: Alfred A. Knopf, 1990), 277.

30. Levine, *Pizza: A Slice of Heaven*, 50; Wikipedia Italy, "Codex diplomaticus cajetanus," https://it.wikipedia.org/wiki/Codex_diplomaticus_cajetanus.

31. Maiden, "Pizza is a German(ic) Word!," Your Dictionary, https://web.archive.org/web/20030115224054/http://www.yourdictio nary.com/library/pizza.html; "Professor Martin Maiden," University of Oxford, http://www.ling-phil.ox.ac.uk/people/martin-maiden.

32. Helstosky, *Pizza: A Global History*, 22; Associazione Verace Pizza Napoletana, http://www.pizzanapoletana.org/272-e_la_burocrazia_entra_in_cucina_una_legge_per_la_vera_pizza__neapol itan_pizza_has_everyone_agree.htm, accessed May 28, 2017.

33. "Regulations for obtaining use of the collective trade mark 'Verace Pizza Napoletana' - (Vera Pizza Napoletana)," Associazione Verace Pizza Napoletana, http://www.pizzanapoletana.org/public/pdf/VPN%20disciplinare%20english.pdf, accessed May 28, 2017.

34. Helstosky, *Pizza: A Global History*, 22; Pernice, "Dove mangiare la pizza a Napoli," *Travel Fashion Tips* (blog), http://www.travelfashiontips.com/2016/01/dove-mangiare-la-pizza-a-napoli.html, January 27, 2016, accessed May 28, 2017.

35. Barrett, *Pizza: A Slice of American History*, 14.

36. Helstosky, *Pizza: A Global History*, 26.

37. Artusi, *Science in the Kitchen and the Art of Eating Well*, 427.

38. Helstosky, *Pizza: A Global History*, 26.

39. Field, *The Italian Baker*, 199.

40. "History and meaning of the Italian Tricolour flag," Keep in Touch with Your Italian Roots, http://www.italyheritage.com/magazine/articles/history/tricolore-storia.htm.

41. Pernice, "Dove mangiare la pizza a Napoli," *Travel Fashion Tips* (blog), http://www.travelfashiontips.com/2016/01/dove-mangiare-la-pizza-a-napoli.html, January 27, 2016, accessed May 28, 2017.

42. Helstosky, *Pizza: A Global History*, 28.

43. Ibid.

44. Genovese, *Pizza City: The Ultimate Guide to New York's Favorite Food*, 84.

45. Ibid.

46. Ibid., 83; "History," John's of Bleecker Street, http://www.johnsbrickovenpizza.com/history.html; "About Totonno's," Totonno's, http://www.totonnosconeyisland.com/about-us.html; Jane Black, "How Patsy Grimaldi, the 81-Year-Old New York Pizza Legend, Is Getting His Good Name Back," *Grub Street*, October 21, 2012, http://www.grubstreet.com/2012/10/pizza-legend-patsy-grimaldi-gets-his-good-name-back.html.

47. Genovese, *Pizza City: The Ultimate Guide to New York's Favorite Food*, 12.

48. "Regulations for obtaining use of the collective trade mark 'Verace Pizza Napoletana' - (Vera Pizza Napoletana)," Associazione Verace Pizza Napoletana, http://www.pizzanapoletana.org/public/pdf/VPN%20disciplinare%20 english.pdf, accessed May 28, 2017.

49. Barrett, *Pizza: A Slice of American History*, 20.

50. Wolfgang Puck, *Pizza, Pasta, and More!* (New York: Random House, 2000), 73.

51. "About Us," O'Scugnizzo's Pizzeria, https://uticapizza.com/about-us/.

52. Ibid.

53. Barrett, *Pizza: A Slice of American History*, 34.

54. Ibid.

55. Levine, *Pizza: A Slice of Heaven*, 128.

56. Frank Pepe Pizzeria Napoletana, http://www.pepespizzeria.com/.

57. Genovese, *Pizza City: The Ultimate Guide to New York's Favorite Food*, 7.

58. "About Us," Marra's of Philadelphia, http://www.marrasone.com/about-us/4578717307.

59. "History," Santora's Pizza and Catering, http://www.santoraspizzaandcatering.com/about/.

60. "Our Pizza," Aloy's Italian Restaurant, http://www.aloysrestaurant.com/#.

61. "About Us," Zuppardi's Apizza, http://www.zuppardisapizza.com/.

62. Ibid.

63. John Lynds, "Second slice—Santarpio's will open another location in Peabody Family hopes to open new restaurant in May at old Bennigan's site," *East Boston Times-Free Press*, January 28, 2010, http://www.santarpiospizza.com/images/EBtimes.pdf.

64. "About Us," Alongi's Italian Restaurant, http://www.alongis.com/about-us/.

65. "History," Pizzi Café, http://www.pizzicafe.com/history/.

66. Ibid.

67. Ibid.

68. Genovese, *Pizza City: The Ultimate Guide to New York's Favorite Food*, 7.

69. "The Modern Story," Modern Apizza http://modernapizza.com/the-modern-story/.

70. "History," DeLucia's Brick Oven Pizza, http://deluciasbrickovenpizza.com/history.html.

71. "Our Story," Jennie's Pizzeria, https://www.jenniespizzeria.com/our-story/.

72. "History," Tommaso's, http://www.tommasos.com/history.html.

73. Ibid.

74. Ibid.

75. "About Us," Reservoir Tavern, https://therestavern.com/about-us/.

76. Barrett, *Pizza: A Slice of American History*, 34.

77. Sally's Apizza, http://www.sallysapizza.com/index.html.

78. Adam Kuban, "Do You Know These Regional Pizza Styles?," *Serious Eats*, 2008, http://slice.seriouseats.com/archives/2008/01/a-list-of-regional-pizza-styles.html.

79. The Slice Team, "Gallery: Eight Styles to Add to Your Pizza Lexicon," *Serious Eats*, http://slice.seriouseats.com/archives/2012/05/eight-styles-to-add-to-your-pizza-lexicon-slideshow.html#show-241336.

80. Ibid.

81. "Menu," Papa's Tomato Pies, https://www.papastomatopies.com/menu.php.

82. Barrett, *Pizza: A Slice of American History*, 63.

83. Ibid., 64.

84. Schwartz, *The Southern Italian Table: Authentic Tastes from Traditional Kitchens*, 43.

85. Helstosky, *Pizza: A Global History*, 61.

86. Barrett, *Pizza: A Slice of American History*, 106.

87. Ibid.

88. Ibid.

89. Joe Bonwich, "Provelology: The study of a made-up cheese with a made-up name," *St. Louis Post-Dispatch*, May 15, 2012, http://www.stltoday.com/lifestyles/food-and-cooking/provelology-the-study-of-a-made-up-cheese-with-a/article_d033b816-b856-5d5c-a8ca-a3c6592db4f0.html.

90. "The Story," DiCarlo's Pizza, http://www.dicarlospizza.com/story/.

91. Rebecca Caro, "Argentinean Deep Dish Pizza," *From Argentina With Love* (blog), May 30, 2008, http://www.fromargentinawithlove.typepad.com/from_argentina_with_love/page/36/.

92. Eileen Tighe, ed., *Woman's Day Encyclopedia of Cookery, Volume 9*, (New York: Fawcett Publications, Inc., 1966), 1411.

93. Helstosky, *Pizza: A Global History*, 57.

94. Bob Orkand, "A Slice of History—Pizza in America," *The Huntsville Item*, May 18, 2014, http://www.itemonline.com/opinion/orkand-a-slice-of-history-pizza-in-america/article_177fdbdb-aa47-508b-bac4-e0fe16c4cee7.html.

95. Moses, *An Unlikely Union: The Love-Hate Story of New York's Irish and Italians*, 296.

96. Ibid.

97. Mariani, *How Italian Food Conquered the World*, 63.

98. Ibid.; Orkand, "A Slice of History—Pizza in America," *The Huntsville Item*, May 18, 2014, http://www.itemonline.com/opinion/orkand-a-slice-of-history-pizza-in-america/article_177fdbdb-aa47-508b-bac4-e0fe16c4cee7.html.

99. Orkand, "A Slice of History—Pizza in America," *The Huntsville Item*, May 18, 2014, http://www.itemonline.com/opinion/orkand-a-slice-of-history-pizza-in-america/article_177fdbdb-aa47-508b-bac4-e0fe16c4cee7.html.

100. Barrett, *Pizza: A Slice of American History*, 27.

101. Ibid.

102. Ibid.

103. Ibid., 54.

104. Ibid., 123-124.

105. Ibid.

106. Ibid.

107. Ibid., 124.

108. Ibid., 27.

109. Helstosky, *Pizza: A Global History*, 61.

110. Ibid.

111. Gabaccia, *We Are What We Eat: Ethnic Food and the Making of Americans*, 169-170; "Our History," Totino's, http://www.totinos.com/History.

112. Gabaccia, *We Are What We Eat: Ethnic Food and the Making of Americans*, 170.

113. Barrett, *Pizza: A Slice of American History*, 142.

114. Ibid.

115. Ibid., 144.

116. Ibid., 144-145.

117. Jan Uebelherr, "Joseph Simek was a founder of Tombstone Pizza," *Milwaukee Journal Sentinel*, February 20, 2013, http://archive.jsonline.com/news/obituaries/simek-a-founder-of-tombstone-pizza-has-died-g08rrao-192103331.html/.

118. Ibid.

119. Levine, *Pizza: A Slice of Heaven*, 277.

120. Ibid., 280.

121. Ibid., 269.

122. Ibid.

123. Ibid.

124. Ibid.

125. Ibid.

126. Ibid., 270-276.

127. Ibid.

128. Helstosky, *Pizza: A Global History*, 74.

129. "About Us," Pizza Hut, http://blog.pizzahut.com/our-story/.

130. Helstosky, *Pizza: A Global History*, 84.

131. Ibid., 85, 87.

132. Barrett, *Pizza: A Slice of American History*, 145.

133. Helstosky, *Pizza: A Global History*, 73.

134. Ibid., 76.

135. Toto's Pizza House, http://totospizzahouse.com.au/; Karl Quinn, "The lowdown on Lygon: how a street became famous," *Sydney Morning Herald*, November 12, 2013, http://www.smh.com.au/entertainment/movies/the-lowdown-on-lygon-how-a-street-became-famous-20131112-2xe8b.html.

136. Samantha Oster, *Cardinal Points: Mapping Adelaide's Diversity—People, Places, Points of View*, (Kent Town, South Australia: Wakefield Press, 2001), 20. Other sources said the pizzeria opened in 1956, 1957, or 1959.

137. John Mackie, "Bringing the first pizza ovens to Canada in the 1950s," *Vancouver Sun*, October 15, 2008, http://www.calgaryherald.com/Bringing+first+pizza+ovens+Canada+1950s/882493/story.html.

138. Amy Pataki, "They'll always be first, if not best," *Toronto Star*, May 19, 2007, https://www.thestar.com/entertainment/2007/05/19/theyll_always_be_first_if_not_best.html.

139. Ibid.

140. "History," Pizzeria Napoletana, http://www.napoletana.com/.

141. Helstosky, *Pizza: A Global History*, 33.

142. Ibid., 29-33.

143. Mattozzi, *Inventing the Pizzeria: A History of Pizza Making in Naples*, xxv, xxvi.

144. Ibid., xxv.

145. Ibid., xxxi.

146. Ibid.

147. Helstosky, *Pizza: A Global History*, 37.

148. Ibid., 38.

149. Levine, *Pizza: A Slice of Heaven*, 322. (Other sources say 1996.)

150. Lucas Leigh, "The Mother of All Pizzas," *PMQ*, November-December 2005, http://www.pmq.com/November-December-2005/The-Mother-of-All-Pizzas/.

151. Ibid.; Helstosky, *Pizza: A Global History*, 38.

152. Helstosky, *Pizza: A Global History*, 38.

153. Ibid.

154. "Regulations for obtaining use of the collective trade mark 'Verace Pizza Napoletana' - (Vera Pizza Napoletana)," Associazione Verace Pizza Napoletana, http://www.pizzanapoletana.org/public/pdf/VPN%20disciplinare%20english.pdf, accessed May 28, 2017.

155. Helstosky, *Pizza: A Global History*, 38.

156. Ibid.

157. Barrett, *Pizza: A Slice of American History*, 21.

158. Levine, *Pizza: A Slice of Heaven*, 328.

159. Leigh, "The Mother of All Pizzas," *PMQ*, November-December 2005, http://www.pmq.com/November-December-2005/The-Mother-of-All-Pizzas/.

160. Helstosky, *Pizza: A Global History*, 39.

161. Levine, *Pizza: A Slice of Heaven*, 330.

162. Ibid., 329.

163. Ibid., 46.

164. Schwartz, *Naples at Table: Cooking in Campania*, 5.

165. L'Antica Pizzeria Da Michele, http://damichele.net/index.php?lang=uk.

166. Ibid.

167. Ibid.

168. Claudia Ausilio, "Antica Pizzeria da Michele: 'Vi sveliamo i segreti e la ricetta per fare la nostra pizza,'" *Vesuvio Live*, April 5, 2016, http://www.vesuviolive.it/ultime-notizie/142418-antica-pizzeria-michele-vi-sveliamo-segreti-la-ricetta-la-nostra-pizza/.

169. Ibid.

170. Ibid.

171. Ibid.

172. Schwartz, *The Southern Italian Table: Authentic Tastes from Traditional Kitchens*, 43.

173. Ibid.

174. Ibid.

175. Ibid.

176. Levine, *Pizza: A Slice of Heaven*, 46-48.

177. Ibid., 44.

178. "About," Frank Pepe Pizzeria Napoletana, http://www.pepespizzeria.com/index.php#about.

179. Levine, *Pizza: A Slice of Heaven*, 46.

180. Vesi, http://www.vesi.it/.

181. Scott Reitz, "Cavilli Pizza Is Now Certified by APN, the New Italian Arbiters of Pizza Greatness," *Dallas Observer*, July 22, 2014, http://www.dallasobserver.com/restaurants/cavilli-pizza-is-now-certified-by-apn-the-new-italian-arbiters-of-pizza-greatness-7025201. The pizzeria is named Cavalli. It is misspelled in the headline and url.

182. Ibid.

183. Ibid.

184. Alberto Nardelli and George Arnett, "Italy puts Neapolitan Pizza-making forward for Unesco recognition," *Guardian*, March 4, 2016, https://www.theguardian.com/lifeandstyle/2016/mar/04/italy-neapolitan-pizza-unesco-cultural-heritage-naples-food; "UNESCO: Art of the Neapolitan Pizza inscribed on the Representative List of the

Intangible Cultural Heritage of Humanity," OnuItalia.com, December 7, 2017, http://www.onuitalia.com/2017/12/06/unesco-art-neapolitan-pizza-inscribed-representative-list-intangible-cultural-heritage-humanity/.

185. UNESCO, Intangible Cultural Heritage of Humanity, https://ich.unesco.org/en/lists.

186. Ibid.

187. "Italy senators call for pizza-maker qualification," BBC, June 22, 2016, http://www.bbc.com/news/blogs-news-from-elsewhere-36596090.

188. Genovese, *Pizza City: The Ultimate Guide to New York's Favorite Food*, 5.

189. Helstosky, *Pizza: A Global History*, 70.

190. Ibid.

191. Ibid.

192. Levine, *Pizza: A Slice of Heaven*, 296.

193. Helstosky, *Pizza: A Global History*, 95.

194. Ibid.

195. Ibid.

196. Dinfin Mulupi, "Pizza vs injera: Selling Italian food in Ethiopia," *How we made it in Africa*, April 8, 2015, http://www.howwemadeitinafrica.com/pizza-vs-injera-selling-italian-food-in-ethiopia/.

197. Ibid.

198. "City Super Group: China is a new frontier for Italian food," Italian Food, July 23, 2015, http://www.italianfood.net/blog/2015/07/23/china-closer-word-buyers/.

199. Ibid.

200. Associazione Verace Pizza Napoletana, http://www.pizzanapoletana.org/shownaz.php?n=Cina.

201. Ibid., http://www.pizzanapoletana.org/associati.php.

202. Cara Giaimo, Pizza Ovens That Almost (Never) Cool Off," *Atlas Obscura*, September 11, 2015, http://www.atlasobscura.com/articles/pizza-ovens-that-never-cool-off.

203. Associazione Verace Pizza Napoletana, http://www.pizzanapoletana.org/eng_forno_gas_avpn.php.

204. "Ingredients," Papa John's, http://www.papajohns.com/company/papa-johns-ingredients.html.

205. Ibid.

206. Ibid.

207. "Nutrition," Pizza Hut, https://m.nutritionix.com/pizza-hut/portal/.

208. Ibid.

209. "Nutrition," Domino's Pizza, https://www.dominos.com/en/pages/content/nutritional/ingredients.jsp.

210. Ibid.

211. Ibid.

212. "Nutritional Guide," Little Caesars, https://littlecaesars.com/Portals/0/PDF/Nutrition/59441_aa_Nutri_Flyer_LJobi_4c_WEB.pdf?ver=2017-04-24-073451-940.

213. Pizza Today's 2016 Top 100 Pizza Companies, *Pizza Today*, November 1, 2016, http://www.pizzatoday.com/pizzeria-rankings/2016-pizza-today-top-100-pizza-companies/.

214. Levine, *Pizza: A Slice of Heaven*, 54.

CHAPTER 8: Italian Food Around the World

1. Mariani, *How Italian Food Conquered the World*.

2. Montanari, *Italian Identity in the Kitchen, or Food and the Nation*, 20.

3. Severgnini, *La Bella Figura: A Field Guide to the Italian Mind*, 33.

4. Schwartz, *The Southern Italian Table: Authentic Tastes from Traditional Kitchens*, 10.

5. Mariani, *How Italian Food Conquered the World*, 196.

6. Ibid., 68; Mucci, *We the Italians: Two flags, One heart, One hundred interviews about Italy and the US*, 82-85; "About IWFI," Italian Wine & Food Institute, https://iwfinews.com/about-us/the-institute/.

7. Mariani, *How Italian Food Conquered the World*, 198.

8. Ibid.

9. Ibid., 228.

10. Ibid., 260.

11. Ibid., 261.

12. Ibid., 241.

13. Hazan, *Amarcord: Marcella Remembers*, 222.

14. Ibid.

15. Hazan, *The Classic Italian Cookbook: The Art of Italian Cooking and the Italian Art of Eating*, 89-91. Her book lists three tomato sauces. While this one became the most famous, the first one she lists has olive oil, not butter, and she recommends it going well with all macaroni.

16. Schwartz, *The Southern Italian Table: Authentic Tastes from Traditional Kitchens*, 84.

17. Oretta Zanini De Vita and Maureen B. Fant, *Sauces & Shapes: Pasta the Italian Way*, (New York: W. W. Norton & Company, 2013), 70-71.

18. Antonio Carluccio, *Antonio Carluccio's Italian Feast*, (London: BBC Books, 1996), 81.

19. Ibid.

20. Ibid.

21. Hazan, *The Classic Italian Cookbook: The Art of Italian Cooking and the Italian Art of Eating*, 121.

22. Ibid., 120.

23. Patrick Browne, "Eataly shows its bite in Forbes top brand list," *Local*, December 3, 2015, http://www.thelocal.it/20151203/eataly-shows-its-bite-in-forbes-top-brand-list.

24. Ibid.

25. Molinari, *The Italians of New York*, 174.

26. Tom Kingston, "Osama bin Laden's family buy historic Italian marble quarries," *Telegraph*, July 31, 2014, http://www.telegraph.co.uk/news/worldnews/europe/italy/11004295/Osama-bin-Ladens-family-buy-historic-Italian-marble-quarries.html.

27. "ChemChina makes €7.1bn bid for Pirelli," *Guardian*, March 23, 2015, https://www.theguardian.com/business/2015/mar/23/chemchina-makes-71bn-bid-for-italy-pirelli-tyre-maker.

28. Parasecoli, *Al Dente: A History of Food in Italy*, 233.

29. Ibid., 245.

30. Academia Barilla, ed., *I Love Pasta: An Italian Love Story in 100 Recipes*, 14-19.

31. Ibid., 19-20.

32. Ibid.

33. Academia Barilla, http://www.academiabarilla.com/; Academia Barilla, ed., *I Love Pasta: An Italian Love Story in 100 Recipes*, 9.

34. Academia Barilla, http://www.academiabarilla.com/.

35. Jennifer 8. Lee, *The Fortune Cookie Chronicles: Adventures in the World of Chinese Food*, (New York: Hachette Book Group, 2008), 244.

36. Ibid.

37. Erika Kinetz, "Correction: China-Italy-Money Laundering Story," Fox News, June 5, 2015, http://www.foxnews.com/world/2015/06/06/correction-china-italy-money-laundering-story.html.

38. Ibid.

39. The White House Office of the Press Secretary, "FACT SHEET: United States-Italy Cooperation, U.S. Embassy & Consulates in Italy," October 18, 2016, https://it.usembassy.gov/fact-sheet-united-states-italy-cooperation/.

40. SACE, "Italian good news: Is € 50 billion a realistic goal for Italian agrifood exports?," *We the Italians*, #57, April 3, 2015, http://wetheitalians.com/.

41. Ibid.

42. Expo Milano 2015, http://www.expo2015.org/archive/en/learn-more.html.

43. Ibid.

44. Ibid.

45. Stephanie Kirchgaessner, "Expo 2015 in Milan is—for the hopeful—a sign that Italy is back on its feet," *Guardian*, April 29, 2015, http://www.theguardian.com/travel/2015/apr/29/expo-2015-milan-ready-no-what-more-italian-corruption.

46. Aprile, *Terroni: All That Has Been Done to Ensure That the Italians of the South Became "Southerners,"* 163.

47. Ibid.

48. Kirchgaessner, "Expo 2015 in Milan is—for the hopeful—a sign that Italy is back on its feet," *Guardian*, April 29, 2015, http://www.theguardian.com/travel/2015/apr/29/expo-2015-milan-ready-no-what-more-italian-corruption.

49. Ibid.

50. Ibid.

51. "Cantone denies 'irregularities' in Eataly Expo contract," ANSA, April 9, 2015, http://www.ansa.it/english/news/lifestyle/food_wine/2015/04/09/eataly-asked-for-expo-explanations_50222f33-e11d-4d66-9195-269590c00c98.html.

52. Ibid.

53. "Police fire tear gas at Milan Expo protesters," RT, May 1, 2015, https://www.rt.com/news/254933-milan-expo-protest-clashes/.

54. Ibid.

55. Ibid.

56. Marco Mancassola, "Embracing the Other Italy," *New York Times*, March 9, 2015, https://www.nytimes.com/2015/03/10/opinion/embracing-the-other-italy.html.

57. Aprile, *Terroni: All That Has Been Done to Ensure That the Italians of the South Became "Southerners,"* 100.

58. Ibid., 171.

59. SACE, "Italian good news: Is € 50 billion a realistic goal for Italian agrifood exports?," *We the Italians*, #57, April 3, 2015, http://wetheitalians.com/.

60. "'Made in Italy' gets €260 m to go global," *Local*, February 27, 2015, https://www.thelocal.it/20150227/government-invests-256-million-in-italian-exports.

61. Ibid.

62. Viale, "Mediterranean Diet Roundtable: More Than Food, It's a Way of Life," *L'Italo-Americano*, April 28, 2016, http://www.italoamericano.org/story/2016-4-28/mdr-la. This information appeared in an earlier version of this article that has since been deleted from the current online version. However, it appears at the Google site, https://www.google.com/culturalinstitute/beta/project/made-in-italy.

63. "The International Week of Italian Cuisine Is Coming This November," *L'Italo Americano*, November 10, 2016, http://www.italoamericano.org/story/2016-11-10/italian-cuisine-world.

64. Ibid.

65. Ibid.

66. Mariani, *How Italian Food Conquered the World*, 287; Levine, *Pizza: A Slice of Heaven*, 10.

67. Academia Barilla, ed., *I Love Pasta: An Italian Love Story in 100 Recipes*, 37.

68. Ibid.

69. "Argentina, spaghetti or beef country?," MercoPress, January 12, 2006, http://en.mercopress.com/2006/01/12/argentina-spaghetti-or-beef-country.

70. "Italian Heritage," Argentina Food Wine Culture Festival, Consulate General of the Argentine Republic, 2017, https://www.argentinafestival.org.hk/about-argentina.

71. Maria Baez Kijac, *The South American Table*, (Boston, MA: The Harvard Common Press, 2003), 26.

72. Morreale, *Italian Americans: The Immigrant Experience*, 58.

73. Baily, *Immigrants in the Lands of Promise: Italians in Buenos Aires and New York City, 1870 to 1914*, 220.

74. Ibid., 75, 100.

75. "The Italian Cuisine in Argentina," Argentina Excepcion, http://www.argentina-excepcion.com/en/travel-guide/gastronomy/italian-cuisine-argentina, accessed May 30, 2017.

76. Mike Benayoun, "Argentina: Vitel Toné," *196 Flavors* (blog), https://www.196flavors.com/argentina-vitel-tone/, accessed May 30, 2017.

77. Ibid.

78. Rebecca Caro, "Pan Dulce—Panettone," *From Argentina With Love* (blog), December 25, 2009, http://www.fromargentinawithlove.typepad.com/from_argentina_with_love/2009/12/pan-dulcepanettone-1.html.

79. Rebecca Caro, "National Ñoquis (Gnocchi) Day," *From Argentina With Love* (blog), February 28, 2008, http://fromargentinawithlove.typepad.com/from_argentina_with_love/2008/02/national-oquis.html.

80. Kijac, *The South American Table*, 229.

81. Rebecca Caro, "Tarta Pascualina—Spinach and Ricotta Tart with Peppers," *From Argentina With Love* (blog), June 29, 2009, http://www.fromargentinawithlove.typepad.com/from_argentina_with_love/2009/06/tarta-pascualina--spinach-and-ricotta-tart-with-peppers.html.

82. Mina Holland, *The World on a Plate: 40 Cuisines, 100 Recipes, and the Stories Behind Them*, (New York: Penguin Books, 2014), 341-348.

83. Leonardo Curti and James O. Fraioli, *Food Festivals of Italy: Celebrated Recipes from 50 Food Fairs*, (Layton, UT: Gibbs Smith, 2008), 40.

84. Marian Blazes, "How to Make Fugazza: Argentinian Focaccia," *The Spruce* (blog), May 3, 2017, https://www.thespruce.com/fugazza-argentinian-style-focaccia-3029456.

85. Marian Blazes, "Fainá: Garbanzo Flatbread," *The Spruce* (blog), August 21, 2017, https://www.thespruce.com/faina-garbanzo-flatbread-3029673; Chris, "Farinata," *Roadtripping Vegan* (blog), June 27, 2016, https://roadtrippingvegan.com/2016/06/27/farinata/.

86. Ibid.

87. Claire, "The Italian influence in Argentina's cuisine," *Authentic Foodquest* (blog), August 28, 2015, https://www.authenticfoodquest.com/the-italian-influence-in-argentinas-cuisine/.

88. "Ravioles du Royans," *Food & Passion . . . The Diary of a Food Enthusiast* (blog), April 19, 2009, http://foodandpassion.blogspot.com/2009/04/ravioles-du-royans.html.

89. Rachel Laudan, "Lasagne in Early 20th-Century Italo-Argentinian Cuisine," http://www.rachellaudan.com/2010/06/lasagne-in-early-20th-century-italo-argentinian-cuisine.html, accessed May 30, 2017.

90. Claire, "The Italian influence in Argentina's cuisine," *Authentic Foodquest* (blog), August 28, 2015, https://www.authenticfoodquest.com/the-italian-influence-in-argentinas-cuisine/.

91. Cadore, http://heladeriacadore.com.ar/.

92. Kijac, *The South American Table*, 124.

93. Ibid.

94. Ibid., 293-294.

95. Ibid., 238.

96. Ibid.

97. "In the Shadow of the Volcanoes: Chile's Melting Pot," *In the Americas with David Yetman*, season 2, episode 2, January 11, 2014, http://intheamericas.org/works/202-in-the-shadow-of-the-volcanoes-chiles-melting-pot/; "Historia Capitán Pastene," Don Primo Trattoria Fabbrica, http://www.donprimo.cl/.

98. "Historia Capitán Pastene," Don Primo Trattoria Fabbrica, http://www.donprimo.cl/.

99. "In the Shadow of the Volcanoes: Chile's Melting Pot," *In the Americas with David Yetman*, season 2, episode 2, January 11, 2014, http://intheamericas.org/works/202-in-the-shadow-of-the-volcanoes-chiles-melting-pot/.

100. Ibid.

101. Stefano Ferrari, *Capitan Pastene: storia di un inganno*, 2014, 21, https://books.google.cl/books?id=lMjoAwAAQBAJ&pg=PA21&lpg=PA21&dq=capitan+pastene+italianos+ricette&source=bl&ots=04wBHQ0oOs&sig=_BOAvk7DyRB6xkWApeiSNcMytE0&hl=es-

419&sa=X&ved=0ahUKEwii9dqJusnWAhXDQSYKHdPyBB0Q6AEI
YjAM#v=onepage&q=capitan%20pastene%20italianos%20ricette&f=f
alse.

102. "In the Shadow of the Volcanoes: Chile's Melting Pot," *In the Americas
with David Yetman*, season 2, episode 2, January 11, 2014,
http://intheamericas.org/works/202-in-the-shadow-of-the-volcanoes-
chiles-melting-pot/.

103. Janet E. Worrall, "Italians Immigrants in the Peruvian Economy, 1860-
1914," *Italian Americana*, Volume 2, Number 1, Autumn 1975, 51-52,
http://www.jstor.org/stable/29775863; David Knowlton, "Peruvian
and Italian Met and Wed," *Cuzco Eats* (blog), November, 3, 2013,
http://cuzcoeats.com/peruvian-and-italian-met-and-wed/.

104. Ibid.

105. Ibid., 56, 59; Ibid.

106. Veronica Grimaldi Hinojosa, "Where Peruvian and Italian Cuisine
Meet," Rosetta Stone, December 23, 2013,
http://www.rosettastone.co.uk/blog/where-peruvian-and-italian-
cuisine-meet/.

107. Knowlton, "Peruvian and Italian Met and Wed," *Cuzco Eats* (blog),
November, 3, 2013, http://cuzcoeats.com/peruvian-and-italian-met-
and-wed/; Gastón Acurio, *Peru: The Cookbook*, (London: Phaidon Press
Limited, 2015), 12, 256, 270.

108. Acurio, *Peru: The Cookbook*, 155; Maria Lo Pinto, *The Art of Italian
Cooking*, (New York: Doubleday & Company, Inc., 1969), 16.

109. Ibid.

110. Ibid.

111. Acurio, *Peru: The Cookbook*, 192.

112. Sandra Plevisani, https://www.facebook.com/sandraplevisani1/.

113. Ibid.

114. Gabaccia, *We Are What We Eat: Ethnic Food and the Making of Americans*,
67-68.

115. Renzo Pi Hugarte, "Elementos de la cultura italiana en la cultura del
Uruguay," UNESCO, October 9, 2001, 17,

http://www.unesco.org.uy/shs/fileadmin/templates/shs/archivos/anua
rio2001/1-pihugarte.pdf.

116. Ibid.

117. Ibid.

118. Luiz Alberto, "A new discovery in Uruguay: De Lucca. Wines made for
#winelover-s," *#winelover* (blog), December 30, 2015,
http://www.winelover.co/a-new-discovery-in-uruguay-de-lucca-wines-
made-for-winelover-s/

119. "Uruguay Pasta Traditions," Pasta For All,
http://www.pastaforall.info/wordpress/what-is-pasta/pasta-around-
the-world/uruguay/; Hugarte, "Elementos de la cultura italiana en la
cultura del Uruguay," UNESCO, October 9, 2001, 18,
http://www.unesco.org.uy/shs/fileadmin/templates/shs/archivos/anua
rio2001/1-pihugarte.pdf.

120. Ibid.

121. Kijac, *The South American Table*, 229; Hugarte, "Elementos de la cultura
italiana en la cultura del Uruguay," UNESCO, October 9, 2001, 18,
http://www.unesco.org.uy/shs/fileadmin/templates/shs/archivos/anua
rio2001/1-pihugarte.pdf.

122. "Uruguay Pasta Traditions," Pasta For All,
http://www.pastaforall.info/wordpress/what-is-pasta/pasta-around-
the-world/uruguay/.

123. Hugarte, "Elementos de la cultura italiana en la cultura del Uruguay,"
UNESCO, October 9, 2001, 18,
http://www.unesco.org.uy/shs/fileadmin/templates/shs/archivos/anua
rio2001/1-pihugarte.pdf.

124. Ibid.

125. Ibid.

126. "Uruguay Pasta Traditions," Pasta For All,
http://www.pastaforall.info/wordpress/what-is-pasta/pasta-around-
the-world/uruguay/; Ángel Ruocco, "Los Capeletis a la Caruso
cumplieron 60 años," La Fonda del Ángel,
http://www.elobservador.com.uy/los-capeletis-la-caruso-cumplieron-
60-anos-n751562.

127. Kijac, *The South American Table*, 147.

128. Ibid., 214.

129. Ibid., 352; Hugarte, "Elementos de la cultura italiana en la cultura del Uruguay," UNESCO, October 9, 2001, 18, http://www.unesco.org.uy/shs/fileadmin/templates/shs/archivos/anua rio2001/1-pihugarte.pdf.

130. Caro, "Pan Dulce—Panettone," *From Argentina With Love* (blog), December 25, 2009, http://www.fromargentinawithlove.typepad.com/from_argentina_with_ love/2009/12/pan-dulcepanettone-1.html; Hugarte, "Elementos de la cultura italiana en la cultura del Uruguay," UNESCO, October 9, 2001, 18, http://www.unesco.org.uy/shs/fileadmin/templates/shs/archivos/anua rio2001/1-pihugarte.pdf.

131. Kijac, *The South American Table*, 367.

132. "Italianos en el Paraguay elegirán representantes," ABC Color, December 1, 2014, http://www.abc.com.py/edicion-impresa/internacionales/italianos-en-el-paraguay-elegiran-representantes-1311493.html.

133. Myra Waldo, *The Art of South American Cookery*, (New York: Hippocrene Books, 1996), 180.

134. Kijac, *The South American Table*, 191.

135. Ibid., 321.

136. Ibid., 214.

137. Wikipedia, "Italian Brazilians," https://en.wikipedia.org/wiki/Italian_Brazilians.

138. Kijac, *The South American Table*, 26.

139. Gabriel Riel-Salvatore, "Samba Italiana—The historical journey of Italians in Sao Paulo," Panorama Italia, July 2, 2014, https://www.panoramitalia.com/en/arts-culture/history/samba-italiana-historical-journey-italians-sao-paulo/2542/.

140. Ibid.

141. Angelo Trento, "'Wherever We Work, The Land Is Ours': The Italian Anarchist Press and Working-Class Solidarity in São Paulo," Donna R. Gabaccia, ed., *Italian Workers of the World: Labor Migration and the Formation of Multiethnic States*, (Chicago, Illinois: University of Illinois, 2001), 102,

https://books.google.com/books?id=cKS9MNlIv7gC&pg=PA2#v=on epage&q=brazil&f=false.

142. Ibid., 103.

143. Ibid.

144. Gabriel Riel-Salvatore, "'Mèrica, Mèrica' The Italian journey in Brazil," Panorama Italia, July 2, 2014, http://www.panoramitalia.com/en/arts-culture/history/merica-merica-italian-journey-brazil/2543/.

145. Kijac, *The South American Table*, 41.

146. Riel-Salvatore, "'Mèrica, Mèrica' The Italian journey in Brazil," Panorama Italia, July 2, 2014, http://www.panoramitalia.com/en/arts-culture/history/merica-merica-italian-journey-brazil/2543/; Amanda Fulginiti, "Parlemo Talian," Panorama Italia, July 2, 2014, https://www.panoramitalia.com/en/arts-culture/history/parlemo-talian-discovering-unique-venetian-brazilian-language/2541/.

147. Ibid.

148. Riel-Salvatore, "'Mèrica, Mèrica' The Italian journey in Brazil," Panorama Italia, July 2, 2014, http://www.panoramitalia.com/en/arts-culture/history/merica-merica-italian-journey-brazil/2543/.

149. Ibid.

150. Ibid.

151. Ibid.; Riel-Salvatore, "Samba Italiana—The historical journey of Italians in Sao Paulo," Panorama Italia, July 2, 2014, https://www.panoramitalia.com/en/arts-culture/history/samba-italiana-historical-journey-italians-sao-paulo/2542/.

152. "Angu—the Polenta of Brazil," *Flavors of Brazil* (blog), May 20, 2010, http://flavorsofbrazil.blogspot.com/2010/05/angu-polenta-of-brazil.html.

153. Amanda Fulginiti, "Eating Italian Style in Brazil," Panorama Italia, July 2, 2014, https://www.panoramitalia.com/en/food-wine/article/eating-italian-style-brazil/2540/.

154. Ibid.

155. Ibid.

156. "Pizza—the 100th Anniversary in Brazil," *Flavors of Brazil* (blog), October 6, 2010, http://flavorsofbrazil.blogspot.com/2010/10/pizza-100th-anniversary-in-brazil.html.

157. Ibid.

158. Ibid.

159. Ibid.

160. Ibid.

161. Fulginiti, "Eating Italian Style in Brazil," Panorama Italia, July 2, 2014, https://www.panoramitalia.com/en/food-wine/article/eating-italian-style-brazil/2540/.

162. "Christmas Leftovers—Espírito Santo Style," *Flavors of Brazil* (blog), December 26, 2012, http://flavorsofbrazil.blogspot.com/2012/12/christmas-leftovers-espirito-santo-style.html.

163. Ibid.

164. "That's No Baloney! Brazilian Mortadela," *Flavors of Brazil* (blog), January 26, 2012, http://flavorsofbrazil.blogspot.com/2012/01/thats-no-baloney-brazilian-mortadela.html.

165. Ibid.

166. Ibid.

167. Ibid.

168. "Chicken Risotto (Risoto de Frango)," *Flavors of Brazil* (blog), July 1, 2010, http://flavorsofbrazil.blogspot.com/2010/07/recipe-chicken-risotto-risoto-de-frango.html; Fulginiti, "Eating Italian Style in Brazil," Panorama Italia, July 2, 2014, https://www.panoramitalia.com/en/food-wine/article/eating-italian-style-brazil/2540/.

169. Fulginiti, "Eating Italian Style in Brazil," Panorama Italia, July 2, 2014, https://www.panoramitalia.com/en/food-wine/article/eating-italian-style-brazil/2540/.

170. Christopher Steighner, ed., *La Cucina: The Regional Cooking of Italy*, (New York: Rizzoli Publications, Inc., 2009), 637.

171. Fulginiti, "Eating Italian Style in Brazil," Panorama Italia, July 2, 2014, https://www.panoramitalia.com/en/food-wine/article/eating-italian-style-brazil/2540/.

172. "Brazilian Bottarga—Tainha Roe Is Golden," *Flavors of Brazil* (blog), December 29, 2010, http://flavorsofbrazil.blogspot.com/2010/12/brazilian-bottarga-tainha-roe-is-golden.html.

173. Riel-Salvatore, "Samba Italiana—The historical journey of Italians in Sao Paulo," Panorama Italia, July 2, 2014, https://www.panoramitalia.com/en/arts-culture/history/samba-italiana-historical-journey-italians-sao-paulo/2542/.

174. Caterina Notargiovanni, "Por qué tantos en Venezuela están eligiendo Italia para huir de la crisis," BBC, August 16, 2017, http://www.bbc.com/mundo/noticias-america-latina-40899539.

175. Ibid.

176. L. Fernando Gonzalez, *Criollo: A Taste of Venezuela*, (CreateSpace Independent Publishing Platform, January 30, 2016), 36.

177. Ibid.

178. Ibid.

179. "The World Pasta Industry Status Report 2013," International Pasta Organisation, http://www.internationalpasta.org/resources/World%20Pasta%20Industry%20Survey/IPOstatreport2014low.pdf; "Venezuela Pasta Traditions," Pasta For All, http://www.pastaforall.info/wordpress/what-is-pasta/pasta-around-the-world/venezuela/.

180. "Venezuela Pasta Traditions," Pasta For All, http://www.pastaforall.info/wordpress/what-is-pasta/pasta-around-the-world/venezuela/.

181. Hernandez, "Cruising in Chipilo, an Italian village in Mexico," *Intersections* (blog), August 16, 2010, http://danielhernandez.typepad.com/daniel_hernandez/2010/08/chipilo-puebla.html.

182. Nicholas Gilman, "Mangia! Italian Food in Mexico City," *Good Food in Mexico City* (blog), September 17, 2016, http://goodfoodmexico.com/mangia-italian-food-in-mexico-city/; Ibid.,

"Tortas in La Capital," May 24, 2009,
http://goodfoodmexico.com/tortas-in-la-capital/; "Conoce el
verdadero origen de la torta," Chilango, December 8, 2011,
http://www.chilango.com/ciudad/el-inventor-de-las-tortas/.

183. Ibid.

184. Cheryl Alters Jamison and Bill Jamison, *The Border Cookbook: Authentic
Home Cooking of the American Southwest and Northern Mexico*, (Boston, MA:
The Harvard Common Press, 1995), 190.

185. Gilman, "Mangia! Italian Food in Mexico City," *Good Food in Mexico City*
(blog), September 17, 2016, http://goodfoodmexico.com/mangia-
italian-food-in-mexico-city/.

186. Ibid.

187. Ibid.

188. Regina Wagner, *The History of Coffee in Guatemala*, (Bogotá, Colombia,
Villegas Editores, 2001), 26, 62,
https://books.google.com/books?id=trfs8E0EdbUC&pg=PA62&lpg=
PA62&dq=geronimo+mancinelli&source=bl&ots=fMVXtkRAOK&sig
=C3263QaT5itnhjHZ7JTF8xpOGTY&hl=en&sa=X&ved=0ahUKEwj
FzImjkcvWAhXKQCYKHcpSCKAQ6AEIRTAI#v=onepage&q=man
cinelli&f=false.

189. Informe Nacional de Desarrollo Humano, Guatemala, 2005, 61,
http://www.url.edu.gt/PortalURL/Archivos/49/Archivos/ca4.pdf.

190. Rigoberto Bran Azmitia, "History of the Italian influence in Guatemala,"
Journal of Central America, June 17, 1961,
http://cultura.muniguate.com/index.php/component/content/article/8
6-laloba/538-influencia.

191. Consuelo de Aerenlund, *Voyage to an Unknown Land: The Saga of an Italian
Family from Lombardy to Guatemala*, (Xlibris, 2006),
https://books.google.com/books?id=XvZmBgAAQBAJ&pg=PT1&lpg
=PT1&dq=Consuelo+de+Aerenlund,+Voyage+to+an+Unknown+Lan
d:++The+Saga+of+an+Italian+Family+from+Lombardy+to+Guatem
ala&source=bl&ots=FPtjJobMsz&sig=6ihtpuL8LWy6B5O58oS9sTQKl
-A&hl=en&sa=X&ved=0ahUKEwjRi-
iqmcvWAhULySYKHViVBI8Q6AEIKzAB#v=onepage&q=Consuelo
%20de%20Aerenlund%2C%20Voyage%20to%20an%20Unknown%20
Land%3A%20%20The%20Saga%20of%20an%20Italian%20Family%20
from%20Lombardy%20to%20Guatemala&f=false.

192. Ibid., 37.

193. "Immigrazione italiana," *Italia Costa Rica* (blog),
     http://www.italiacostarica.com/costa-rica/immigrazione-italiana/.

194. Ibid.

195. Ibid.

196. Alfredo Ingegno, "La comunità italiana a Puerto Viejo osservata dai
     costaricensi," *Italia Costa Rica* (blog), January 18, 2017,
     http://www.italiacostarica.com/la-comunita-italiana-a-puerto-viejo-
     osservata-dai-costaricensi/.

197. Josefina Maldonado, *Recipes my Grandmother Tomasa taste of Puerto Rico*,
     Amazon Digital Services, May 8, 2015, 29.

198. Ibid., 74.

199. *Emigrazione e colonie, Volume 3*, Commissariato dell'emigrazione, 1908,
     https://books.google.com/books?id=B6o9AAAAYAAJ&pg=RA1-
     PA343&dq=emigrazione+italiana+in+haiti&hl=en&sa=X&ei=XugZV
     ZC2ErfIsASqvIDwDg&ved=0CDYQ6AEwAw#v=onepage&q=emigr
     azione%20italiana%20in%20haiti&f=false.

200. Ibid.

201. Ann-Derrick Gaillot, "How Italian Spaghetti Became a Haitian Breakfast
     Staple," *Eater*, March 2, 2017,
     https://www.eater.com/2017/3/2/14780710/haitian-spaghetti.

202. Ibid.

203. Ibid.

204. "Italian Immigrants in London," Candida Martinelli's Italophile Site,
     http://italophiles.com/london_italians2.htm.

205. Ibid.

206. Ibid.

207. Shankland, *Out of Italy: The Story of Italians in North East England*, 99.

208. "Italian Immigrants in London," Candida Martinelli's Italophile Site,
     http://italophiles.com/london_italians2.htm.

209. Holland, *The World on a Plate: 40 Cuisines, 100 Recipes, and the Stories Behind
     Them*, 101.

210. Ibid.; Bocca di Lupo, http://www.boccadilupo.com/.

211. Bocca di Lupo, http://www.boccadilupo.com/food-and-wine.php.

212. Ibid.

213. Ibid.

214. Holland, *The World on a Plate: 40 Cuisines, 100 Recipes, and the Stories Behind Them*, 101.

215. L'Anima, http://www.lanima.co.uk/our-menus.

216. Polpo, http://www.polpo.co.uk/.

217. Antonio Carluccio, *A Recipe for Life*, (London: Hardie Grant Books, 2012), 37; "About Comm. Antonio Carluccio OBE," http://antonio-carluccio.co.uk/about/.

218. David Stephenson, "Top chef lifts lid on rift with TV partner: 'Greedy chef stole my lines,' says Carluccio," *Express*, November 29, 2015, http://www.express.co.uk/showbiz/tv-radio/622867/Top-Italian-chef-rift-with-TV-partner-Greedy-stole-lines-Antonio-Carluccio.

219. "About Comm. Antonio Carluccio OBE," http://antonio-carluccio.co.uk/about/.

220. Ibid.

221. Ibid.; Carluccio, *A Recipe for Life*, 229-230.

222. Tomas Tengby and Ulrika Tengby Holm, *Viva Italia: 180 Classic Recipes*, (New York: Skyhorse Publishing, 2012), 40.

223. Taimi Previdi, *The Best of Finnish Cooking*, (New York: Hippocrene Books, Inc., 2000), 118.

224. Ibid.

225. Lorenza De' Medici and Patrizia Passigli, *Italy: The Beautiful Cookbook*, (San Francisco, CA: Collins Publishers Inc., 1989), 54.

226. Cresciani, *The Italians in Australia*, 36.

227. Ibid.

228. Ibid., 37.

229. Ibid., 45.

230. Ibid.

231. Ibid., 47.

232. Ibid.

233. Ibid., 58.

234. Ibid., 59.

235. Matt Novak, "The Secret History of Australian Whiteness," Gizmodo, November 19, 2015, http://www.gizmodo.com.au/2015/11/the-secret-history-of-whiteness/.

236. Ibid.

237. Ibid.

238. Ibid.

239. Ibid.

240. Cresciani, *The Italians in Australia*, 57.

241. Ibid., 134.

242. Novak, "The Secret History of Australian Whiteness," Gizmodo, November 19, 2015, http://www.gizmodo.com.au/2015/11/the-secret-history-of-whiteness/.

243. Ibid.

244. Cresciani, *The Italians in Australia*, 24.

245. Ibid., 49.

246. Ibid., 78.

247. Ibid., 24.

248. Ibid., 79.

249. Ibid., 125.

250. Ibid.

251. Ibid., 128.

252. Ibid., 125.

253. Ibid., 141.

254. Ibid., 64.

255. Ibid.

256. Ibid.

257. Ibid., 137.

258. Ibid.,

259. Ibid., 137-138.

260. Ibid., 139.

261. Ibid., 138.

262. Ibid., 142.

263. Ibid.

264. Ibid.

265. Ibid., 143.

266. Ibid., 142.

267. Ibid., 31.

268. Ibid., 35.

269. Tess Mallos, "Mediterranean Influence," in *The Food of Australia*, ed. Wendy Hutton (Singapore, Periplus Editions [HK] Ltd., 1996), 18.

270. Ibid., 17.

271. Carluccio, *A Recipe for Life*, 5.

272. Ibid.

273. Ed Charles, "Bourdain on Ronnie di Stasio," Tomato, 2005, https://tomatom.com/2006/08/bourdain-on-ronnie-di-stasio/.

274. Larissa Dubecki, "Café di Stasio," *Sydney Morning Herald*, August 13, 2011, http://www.smh.com.au/entertainment/restaurants-and-bars/cafe-di-stasio-20110810-1in8i.html.

275. Carluccio, *A Recipe for Life*, 5.

276. John Lethlean, "Beppi Polese: Sydney's 'godfather' of Italian restaurants dies at 90," *Australian*, March 22, 2016, http://www.theaustralian.com.au/news/nation/beppi-polese-sydneys-

godfather-of-italian-restaurants-dies-at-90/news-
story/e47cd3dbbea3a5cc3efbd461c485e2be.

277. Ibid.

278. Ibid.

279. Ibid.

280. Ibid.

281. Ibid.

282. Ibid.

283. "Maurice Terzini," General Thinking,
http://generalthinking.com/profileview.cfm?pk_person=1130.

284. Icebergs, http://idrb.com/, December 2015.

285. Milanda Rout, "For Fratelli Paradiso in Potts Point, it's front of house
that counts," *Australian*, September 4, 2015,
http://www.theaustralian.com.au/life/food-wine/for-fratelli-paradiso-
in-potts-point-its-front-of-house-that-counts/news-
story/3da8dcd2861a69907ab0374d88181078.

286. Fratelli Paradiso, http://fratelliparadiso.com/, December 2015.

287. Anna Harrison, "Italo Dining and Disco Club," *Russh Magazine*,
http://www.russh.com/destination/italo-dining-disco-club-sydney/.

288. Valerio Ciriaci, *If Only I Were That Warrior*, Awen Films, 2017,
http://ifonlyiwerethatwarrior.com/.

289. Durante, *Italoamericana: The Literature of the Great Migration, 1880-1943*,
145.

290. Clifford A. Wright, "Libyan Soup," October 9, 2007,
http://www.cliffordawright.com/caw/recipes/display/bycategory.php/
recipe_id/865/id/36/.

291. Sarah Elmusrati, "World Pasta Day," *Food Libya* (blog), October 25,
2010, https://foodlibya.wordpress.com/2010/10/25/world-pasta-day/.

292. Ibid.

293. Ibid.

294. Assia, "Macroona Imbakbaka," *The Libyan Kitchen* (blog), October 31, 2011, http://thelibyankitchen.blogspot.com/2011/10/macroona-imbakbaka.html.

295. Sarah Elmusrati, "A Likely Story," *Food Libya* (blog), December 31, 2011, https://foodlibya.wordpress.com/2011/12/31/a-likely-story/.

296. Miriam Berger, "17 Delicious Ethiopian Dishes All Kinds Of Eaters Can Enjoy," *BuzzFeed*, June 19, 2014, http://www.buzzfeed.com/miriamberger/ethiopian-food.

297. Todd Kliman, "Can Ethiopian Food Become Modern?," *Washingtonian*, February 12, 2015, http://www.washingtonian.com/2015/02/12/why-hasnt-ethiopian-food-gone-upscale/.

298. Christopher Middleton, "Star rating for an Addis trattoria," *Telegraph*, June 4, 2005, http://www.telegraph.co.uk/foodanddrink/restaurants/3319726/Star-rating-for-an-Addis-trattoria.html.

299. Ibid.

300. Olivier Laurent, "Exploring Eritrea's Italian Past," *Time*, June 27, 2016, http://time.com/4373937/eritrea-italy/; Natasha Stallard, "Africa's 'Little Rome,' the Eritrean city frozen in time by war and secrecy," *Guardian*, August 18, 2015, https://www.theguardian.com/world/2015/aug/18/eritrea-asmara-frozen-in-time-africas-little-rome.

301. Stallard, "Africa's 'Little Rome,' the Eritrean city frozen in time by war and secrecy," *Guardian*, August 18, 2015, https://www.theguardian.com/world/2015/aug/18/eritrea-asmara-frozen-in-time-africas-little-rome.

302. Olivia Warren, *Taste of Eritrea: Recipes From One of East Africa's Most Interesting Little Countries*, (New York: Hippocrene Books, Inc., 2000), 4-5.

303. Ibid., 4.

304. Ibid., 13.

305. Ibid.

306. Ibid.; Rahawa Haile, "How Lasagne Landed in Africa," *Saveur*, October/November 2017, 14.

307. Haile, "How Lasagne Landed in Africa," *Saveur*, October/November 2017, 14.

308. Ibid.

309. Ibid.

310. Ibid.; Warren, *Taste of Eritrea: Recipes From One of East Africa's Most Interesting Little Countries*, 13.

311. Adriano Gallo, "Memories from Somalia—Part one," Hiiraan Online, July 12, 2011, https://www.hiiraan.com/op2/2011/july/memories_from_somalia_part_one.aspx.

312. Ibid.

313. Ligaya Mishan, "Safari Brings Somali Cuisine to Harlem," *New York Times*, October 1, 2015, https://www.nytimes.com/2015/10/07/dining/hungry-city-safari-somali-restaurant-harlem.html?mcubz=0.

314. Haile, "How Lasagne Landed in Africa," *Saveur*, October/November 2017, 14.

315. Ibid.

316. "A Little Italy in Seoul," Slow Food, November 19, 2015, https://www.slowfood.com/a-little-italy-in-seoul/.

317. Ibid.

318. Momofuku Nishi, *New York Magazine*, http://nymag.com/listings/restaurant/momofuku-nishi/; Momofuku Nishi, https://nishi.momofuku.com/.

319. Associazione Verace Pizza Napoletana, http://www.pizzanapoletana.org/associati.php.

320. Scott Haas, "Italian Food is Hot in Japan Right Now," *Travel + Leisure*, http://www.travelandleisure.com/articles/italian-food-in-japan.

321. Associazione Verace Pizza Napoletana, http://www.pizzanapoletana.org/shownaz.php?n=Giappone.

322. Corky White, "Italian Food: Japan's Unlikely Culinary Passion," *Atlantic Monthly*, October 6, 2010, https://www.theatlantic.com/health/archive/2010/10/italian-food-japans-unlikely-culinary-passion/64114/.

323. Ibid.

324. Ibid.

325. Ibid.

326. Scott Haas, "12 Restaurants Forging the Delicious Bond Between NYC and Japan," *Travel + Leisure*, June 10, 2015, http://www.travelandleisure.com/articles/japan-outposts-new-york-city-restaurants.

327. "City Super Group: China is a new frontier for Italian food," Italian Food, July 23, 2015, http://www.italianfood.net/blog/2015/07/23/china-closer-word-buyers/.

328. Ibid.

329. Ibid.

330. Uyen Luu, *My Vietnamese Kitchen: Recipes and Stories to Bring Vietnamese Food to Life on Your Plate*, (London: Ryland Peters & Small, 2013), 123.

331. Ibid.

332. "Gli Italiani in India: Viaggi e Memoriali," Storia, Ambasciata d'Italia New Delhi, http://www.ambnewdelhi.esteri.it/ambasciata_newdelhi/it/i_rapporti_bilaterali/cooperazione_politica/storia; Wikipedia, "Italians in India," https://en.wikipedia.org/wiki/Italians_in_India.

333. Ibid.

334. Wikipedia, "Italians in India," https://en.wikipedia.org/wiki/Italians_in_India; "AICC Office Bearers," Indian National Congress, http://inc.in/AICC-Office-Bearers.

335. Geetika Mantri, "As Sonia Gandhi turns 69, here are 7 lesser known facts about the Congress supremo," Catch News, February 14, 2017, http://www.catchnews.com/national-news/as-sonia-gandhi-turns-69-here-are-7-lesser-known-facts-about-the-congress-supremo-1449648017.html.

336. "Italian Companies in India," India Brand Equity Foundation, February 13, 2007, https://www.ibef.org/pages/14793.

337. Divya P., "360 Degrees Pizzeria—Italian it is!," On Manorama, June 21, 2016, http://travel.manoramaonline.com/travel/eatouts/360-degrees-pizzeria-italian-panampilly-nagar-kochi.html.

338. Ibid.

339. Ibid.

340. Ibid.

341. Jagmeeta Thind Joy, "Pizza festival, Hyderabadi dawat, monsoon menu on platter for food lovers this weekend in Chandigarh," *Indian Express*, July 9, 2016, http://indianexpress.com/article/cities/chandigarh/pizza-festival-hyderabadi-dawat-monsoon-menu-on-platter-for-food-lovers-this-weekend-in-chandigarh-2902559/.

342. Niharika Krishna, "A Chat In The Café With Ritu Dalmia On The Perks Of Being A Celebrity Chef," *Polka Cafe*, April 20, 2015, http://www.polkacafe.com/interview-with-celebrity-chef-ritu-dalmia-of-italian-khana-fame-1239.html; Ritu Dalmia, *Italian Khana*, (New Delhi, Random House India, 2008).

343. Amy Kazmin, "A Taste for Italian in New Delhi," *Financial Times*, March 26, 2013, https://www.ft.com/content/7ab87234-9214-11e2-851f-00144feabdc0.

344. Dalmia, *Italian Khana*.

345. Ibid., 48.

346. Aarthi Gunnupuri, "These Monks Have A Calling: Making Fresh Italian Cheese — In India," NPR, January 25, 2017, http://www.npr.org/sections/thesalt/2017/01/25/510254472/these-monks-have-a-calling-making-fresh-italian-cheese-in-india.

CHAPTER 9: Italian Food in Italy

1. William Shurtleff and Akiko Aoyagi, *History of Soybeans and Soyfoods: 1100 B.C. to the 1980s*, Soyinfo Center, 2007, http://www.soyinfocenter.com/HSS/europe4.php.

2. Ibid.

3. Ibid.

4. Ibid.

5. Ibid.

6. Ibid.

7. Montanari, *Italian Identity in the Kitchen, or Food and the Nation*, 56.

8. Jenny Awford, "Mr Nutella Michele Ferrero who became Italy's wealthiest man with £14.4billion chocolate empire dies aged 89 after a long illness," *Daily Mail*, February 14, 2015, http://www.dailymail.co.uk/news/article-2954096/Michele-Ferrero-dies-aged-89.html.

9. Duggan, *A Concise History of Italy*, 262.

10. "Five reasons why Italy is on the up," *Local*, May 6, 2015, http://www.thelocal.it/20150506/five-reasons-why-italy-is-on-the-up.

11. Shurtleff and Aoyagi, *History of Soybeans and Soyfoods: 1100 B.C. to the 1980s*, Soyinfo Center, 2007, http://www.soyinfocenter.com/HSS/europe4.php.

12. Ibid.

13. Montanari, *Italian Identity in the Kitchen, or Food and the Nation*, 59.

14. Duggan, *A Concise History of Italy*, 263.

15. Ibid.

16. Riley, *The Oxford Companion to Italian Food*, 7.

17. "Istituzione culturale," Accademia Italiana Della Cucina, https://www.accademiaitalianadellacucina.it/it/content/istituzione-culturale.

18. Field, *The Italian Baker*, x.

19. Shurtleff and Aoyagi, *History of Soybeans and Soyfoods: 1100 B.C. to the 1980s*, Soyinfo Center, 2007, http://www.soyinfocenter.com/HSS/europe4.php.

20. Field, *The Italian Baker*, x-xi.

21. Duggan, *A Concise History of Italy*, 287.

22. "Calabria and Bambinone," *Two Greedy Italians*, BBC, season 2, episode 1, April 19, 2012.

23. Ibid.

24. "Fight against obesity starts at table, says 'Eating Planet,'" ANSA, March 21, 2016, http://www.ansa.it/english/news/2016/03/21/fight-against-obesity-starts-at-table-says-eating-planet_d3315e39-14c5-4a44-aa97-db1e8b884994.html.

25. "Calabria and Bambinone," *Two Greedy Italians*, BBC, season 2, episode 1, April 19, 2012.

26. "Fight against obesity starts at table, says 'Eating Planet,'" ANSA, March 21, 2016, http://www.ansa.it/english/news/2016/03/21/fight-against-obesity-starts-at-table-says-eating-planet_d3315e39-14c5-4a44-aa97-db1e8b884994.html.

27. Viale, "Mediterranean Diet Roundtable: More Than Food, It's a Way of Life," *L'Italo-Americano*, April 28, 2016, http://www.italoamericano.org/story/2016-4-28/mdr-la.

28. Ibid.

29. "The Family," *Two Greedy Italians*, BBC, season 1, episode 1, May 4, 2011.

30. Ibid.

31. Angela Giuffrida, "Five reasons why the world is worried about the state of Italy," *Local*, February 17, 2016, https://www.thelocal.it/20160217/five-reasons-why-the-world-is-worried-about-the-state-of-italy.

32. Ella Ide, "Mafia and multinationals milk Italy's green energy boom," AFP, July 27, 2015, https://www.yahoo.com/news/mafia-multinationals-milk-italys-green-energy-boom-145245277.html.

33. "62% in south earn up to 40% of average," ANSA, October 27, 2015, http://www.ansa.it/english/news/general_news/2015/10/27/62-in-south-earn-up-to-40-of-average_4118fb9d-8b61-490c-8ef8-215c27596bc9.html.

34. Ibid.

35. "Italians satisfied at growth return," ANSA, November 19, 2015, http://www.ansa.it/english/news/business/2015/11/19/italians-satisfied-at-growth-return_b75dabfe-c7b9-4216-947c-2a6e866589e5.html.

36. "18.3% in South have poor water supplies," ANSA, November 19, 2015, http://www.ansa.it/english/news/2015/11/19/18.3-of-families-in-south-have-poor-water-supplies-2_e91aa1d5-8b76-4268-bb72-37af004981f9.html.

37. Daniela Devecchi, "Festività 'asciutte' a Casoria: cittadini a tre giorni senza acqua," *Il Meridiano News*, December 26, 2016,

http://www.ilmeridianonews.it/2016/12/festivita-asciutte-a-casoria-cittadini-da-tre-giorni-senza-acqua/.

38. Wikipedia, "List of most polluted cities by particulate matter concentration," July 2016, https://en.wikipedia.org/w/index.php?title=List_of_most_polluted_cities_by_particulate_matter_concentration&oldid=731594537.

39. Ibid.

40. "Italian bank axing over 18,000 jobs," *Rakyat Post*, November 12, 2015, http://www.therakyatpost.com/business/2015/11/12/italian-bank-axing-over-18000-jobs/.

41. James Mackenzie, "Italy's Renzi presses for EU-U.S. trade deal," Reuters, May 8, 2015, http://www.reuters.com/article/us-eu-usa-trade-italy/italys-renzi-presses-for-eu-u-s-trade-deal-idUSKBN0NT1P720150508.

42. Ibid.

43. Paul Virgo, "Renzi sees US-Italian energy cooperation," ANSA, March 29, 2016, http://www.ansa.it/english/news/politics/2016/03/29/renzi-sees-us-italian-energy-cooperation_6c527ec0-c24a-4a8d-a51d-fbd252a30dd8.html. Enel is a multinational electric and gas company based in Italy. The plant in Nevada is a part of a U.S. subsidiary of the company.

44. "Italy Honored at Final State Dinner," *Italian America*, Volume XXII, Number 1, Winter 2017, 5.

45. Ibid.

46. Ibid.; Angela Dewan and Lorenzo D'Agostino, "Italy's Matteo Renzi officially resigns after crushing referendum defeat," CNN, December 7, 2016, http://www.cnn.com/2016/12/07/europe/italy-pm-renzi-resignation/index.html.

47. Marta Bonucci, "Italian farmers want to seize TTIP opportunity," *EURACTIV*, November 9, 2015, http://www.euractiv.com/section/agriculture-food/news/italian-farmers-want-to-seize-ttip-opportunity/.

48. "Five reasons why Italy is on the up," *Local*, May 6, 2015, http://www.thelocal.it/20150506/five-reasons-why-italy-is-on-the-up.

49. Marzio Bartoloni, "Business-friendly reforms are making Italy more competitive, World Bank says," *Il Sole 24 Ore*, October 28, 2015, http://www.italy24.ilsole24ore.com/art/business-and-economy/2015-10-27/investimenti-esteri-132332.php?uuid=ACxVMBOB.

50. Claudia Astarita, "Italy among the most successful countries for Horizon 2020 SME Instrument," *This Is Italy*, December 5, 2015, http://www.thisisitaly-panorama.com/investment-news/italy-among-the-most-successful-countries-for-horizon-2020-sme-instrument/.

51. Ibid.

52. Marzio Bartoloni, "Foreign direct investment stages a comeback, but continues to elude the South," *Il Sole 24 Ore*, May 15, 2015, http://www.italy24.ilsole24ore.com/art/business-and-economy/2015-05-14/foreign-direct-investment-stages-comeback-but-continues-to-elude-the-south-134650.php?uuid=AB3oIGgD.

53. Ibid.

54. Ibid.

55. "Italian entrepreneurs eye collaboration with China on infrastructures," *China Daily*, October 23, 2015, http://www.chinadaily.com.cn/business/2015-10/23/content_22264178.htm.

56. Bartoloni, "Foreign direct investment stages a comeback, but continues to elude the South," *Il Sole 24 Ore*, May 15, 2015, http://www.italy24.ilsole24ore.com/art/business-and-economy/2015-05-14/foreign-direct-investment-stages-comeback-but-continues-to-elude-the-south-134650.php?uuid=AB3oIGgD.

57. Ibid.

58. Marzio Bartoloni, "CNR opens research center in a new 'Nanotech Valley' near Lecce," *Il Sole 24 Ore*, May 16, 2015, http://www.italy24.ilsole24ore.com/art/business-and-economy/2015-05-11/the-nanotech-valley-that-speaks-pugliese-160739.php?uuid=ABmZFKeD.

59. "Italia e Stati Uniti rinnovano la cooperazione scientifica—Firmata la Dichiarazione congiunta per il biennio 2016-2017," Ministry of Foreign Affairs and International Cooperation, January 14, 2016, http://www.esteri.it/mae/en/sala_stampa/archivionotizie/approfondimenti/2016/01/italia-e-stati-uniti-rinnovano.html.

60. Arjun Kharpal, "Italy: Europe's next big start-up hub?," CNBC.com, October 12, 2015, http://www.cnbc.com/2015/10/12/italy-europes-next-big-tech-start-up-hub.html.

61. Ivana Pais, "Crowdfunding in Italy generated almost 60 million euros," *Italian Insider*, November 19, 2015, http://www.italianinsider.it/?q=node/3393.

62. Ibid.

63. "Apple Opening Europe's First iOS App Development Center in Italy," Apple, January 21, 2016, http://www.apple.com/pr/library/2016/01/21Apple-Opening-Europes-First-iOS-App-Development-Center-in-Italy.html.

64. "Poste Italiane IPO to generate €3.4bn for Italy," *Local*, October 23, 2015, http://www.thelocal.it/20151023/poste-italiane-ipo-to-generate-34bn-for-italy?utm_medium=twitter&utm_source=twitterfeed.

65. "Privatizations 'improve competitiveness,'" ANSA, December 4, 2015, http://www.ansa.it/english/news/politics/2015/12/04/privatizations-improve-competitiveness_44af8790-803d-4ed8-8245-f87a6bd3c556.html.

66. "Poste Italiane IPO to generate €3.4bn for Italy," *Local*, October 23, 2015, http://www.thelocal.it/20151023/poste-italiane-ipo-to-generate-34bn-for-italy?utm_medium=twitter&utm_source=twitterfeed.

67. "NY Gov. Cuomo planning trade trips to China, Italy," *Washington Times*, March 29, 2016, http://www.washingtontimes.com/news/2016/mar/29/ny-gov-cuomo-planning-trade-trips-to-china-italy/.

68. Bartoloni, "Business-friendly reforms are making Italy more competitive, World Bank says," *Il Sole 24 Ore*, October 28, 2015, http://www.italy24.ilsole24ore.com/art/business-and-economy/2015-10-27/investimenti-esteri-132332.php?uuid=ACxVMBOB.

69. Kharpal, "Italy: Europe's next big start-up hub?," CNBC.com, October 12, 2015, http://www.cnbc.com/2015/10/12/italy-europes-next-big-tech-start-up-hub.html.

70. Ian Murphy, "Italy gets European healthcare centre," *Enterprise Times*, April 4, 2016, http://www.enterprisetimes.co.uk/2016/04/04/italy-gets-european-healthcare-centre/.

71.   Jerry Finzi, "Italy: Healthiest Country in Europe!," *Grand Voyage Italy* (blog), January 19, 2016, http://www.grandvoyageitaly.com/piazza/italy-healthiest-country-in-europe; "How does Italy compare?" Health at a Glance: Europe 2016, Organisation for Economic Co-operation and Development, 2016, https://www.oecd.org/els/health-systems/Health-at-a-Glance-EUROPE-2016-Briefing-Note-ITALY.pdf.

72.   "Italian good news: GreenItaly 2015," *We the Italians*, #72, November 13, 2015, http://www.wetheitalians.com/index.php/web-magazine/italian-good-news-greenitaly-2015.

73.   Ibid.

74.   "Govt says 95bn available for Masterplan," ANSA, November 4, 2015, http://www.ansa.it/english/news/politics/2015/11/04/govt-says-95bn-available-for-masterplan_a5b38624-b663-4f6c-aceb-679527fb656f.html.

75.   "Italians' economic satisfaction up," ANSA, November 19, 2015, http://www.ansa.it/english/news/general_news/2015/11/19/italians-economic-satisfaction-up_e54f1e0f-635a-497b-9b0c-1b6fcf6c57d4.html.

76.   "Italian enterprises upbeat abt exports," ANSA, March 11, 2015, http://www.ansa.it/english/news/business/2015/03/11/italian-enterprises-upbeat-abt-exports_4063a786-67a1-460d-9545-6a39da67f034.html.

77.   European Digital Forum, http://www.europeandigitalforum.eu/scale-up-manifesto-policy-tracker//country/IT.

78.   Elda Buonanno Foley, "The Italian way: Addressing the Italian Stereotypes, Myth 1 'La Pasta,'" *We the Italians*, #59, May 1, 2015, http://www.wetheitalians.com/.

79.   "Five reasons why Italy is on the up," *Local*, May 6, 2015, http://www.thelocal.it/20150506/five-reasons-why-italy-is-on-the-up

80.   Laura Cavestri, "Exports to emerging markets of Italian 'beautiful and well-made' products to increase by 45% by 2020," *Il Sole 24 Ore*, May 12, 2015, http://www.italy24.ilsole24ore.com/art/business-and-economy/2015-05-11/export-made-italy-130535.php?uuid=ABkdU2dD.

81.   Confindustria/Prometeia, "Italian good news: Exporting La Dolce Vita," *We the Italians*, #60, May 15, 2015, http://www.wetheitalians.com/.

82. Cavestri, "Exports to emerging markets of Italian 'beautiful and well-made' products to increase by 45% by 2020," *Il Sole 24 Ore*, May 12, 2015, http://www.italy24.ilsole24ore.com/art/business-and-economy/2015-05-11/export-made-italy-130535.php?uuid=ABkdU2dD.

83. Ibid.

84. Confindustria/Prometeia, "Italian good news: Exporting La Dolce Vita," *We the Italians*, #60, May 15, 2015, http://www.wetheitalians.com/.

85. European Digital Forum, http://www.europeandigitalforum.eu/scale-up-manifesto-policy-tracker//country/IT.

86. Mucci, *We the Italians: Two flags, One heart, One hundred interviews about Italy and the US*, 80.

87. Parasecoli, *Al Dente: A History of Food in Italy*, 203.

88. Ibid., 204.

89. Ibid., 205.

90. Ibid., 203-204.

91. Mariani, *How Italian Food Conquered the World*, 210.

92. Parasecoli, *Al Dente: A History of Food in Italy*, 211.

93. Severgnini, *La Bella Figura: A Field Guide to the Italian Mind*, 31.

94. Parasecoli, *Al Dente: A History of Food in Italy*, 212; "The Family," *Two Greedy Italians*, BBC, season 1, episode 1, May 4, 2011.

95. Riley, *The Oxford Companion to Italian Food*, 194.

96. Ibid.

97. Ibid.

98. Ibid., 344.

99. "Regional Pride," *Two Greedy Italians*, BBC, season 1, episode 3, May 18, 2011.

100. Ibid.

101. Ibid.

102. Severgnini, *La Bella Figura: A Field Guide to the Italian Mind*, 169.

103. Ibid., 166.

104. Parasecoli, *Al Dente: A History of Food in Italy*, 214.

105. David Prior, "Paradise Regained," *Condé Nast Traveler*, April 2015, 106.

106. Parasecoli, *Al Dente: A History of Food in Italy*, 208.

107. Ibid.

108. Ciara Linnane, "Domino's brings American pizza to . . . Italy," *MarketWatch*, October 5, 2015, http://www.marketwatch.com/story/dominos-brings-american-pizza---to-italy-2015-10-05.

109. Ibid.

110. Ibid.

111. Isla Binnie, "No prosciutto panic, please: Italian producers respond to WHO meat alarm," Reuters, October 27, 2015, http://www.reuters.com/article/us-health-meat-italy-idUSKCN0SL1W120151027.

112. Ibid.

113. Ibid.

114. Ide, "Mafia and multinationals milk Italy's green energy boom," AFP, July 27, 2015, https://www.yahoo.com/news/mafia-multinationals-milk-italys-green-energy-boom-145245277.html.

115. Ibid.

116. Ibid.

117. "Farmers want polluting Christmas food blacklist," *Local*, November 30, 2015, https://www.thelocal.it/20151130/italy-farmers-call-for-christmas-blacklist-of-planet-polluting-food.

118. "South Italy's GDP set to rise," ANSA, October 27, 2015, http://www.ansa.it/english/news/business/2015/10/27/south-italys-gdp-set-to-rise_586637a9-3eba-4d27-8ad2-e3a75daf8d55.html.

119. Ibid.

120. "Govt says 95bn available for Masterplan," ANSA, November 4, 2015, http://www.ansa.it/english/news/politics/2015/11/04/govt-says-

95bn-available-for-masterplan_a5b38624-b663-4f6c-aceb-679527fb656f.html.

121. Finzi, "Italy: Healthiest Country in Europe!," *Grand Voyage Italy* (blog), January 19, 2016, http://www.grandvoyageitaly.com/piazza/italy-healthiest-country-in-europe.

122. Ibid.

123. Ibid.

124. Ibid.

125. Ibid.

126. Ibid.

CHAPTER 10: The Legacy of Italian Food

1. Aprile, *Terroni: All That Has Been Done to Ensure That the Italians of the South Became "Southerners,"* 162.

2. Liz O'Connor, Gus Lubin, and Dina Spector, "The Largest Ancestry Groups in the United States," *Business Insider*, August 13, 2013, http://www.businessinsider.com/largest-ethnic-groups-in-america-2013-8; Ana Swanson, "Amazing maps show where Americans come from and who we really are today," *Washington Post*, June 19, 2015, https://www.washingtonpost.com/news/wonk/wp/2015/06/19/amazing-maps-show-where-americans-come-from-and-who-we-really-are-today/?utm_term=.4ce282acae78.

3. Mucci, *We the Italians: Two flags, One heart, One hundred interviews about Italy and the US*, 380.

4. Ibid., 381.

5. Ibid., 359.

6. Ibid.

7. Ibid., 381.

8. "Columbus Day," Today in History - October 12, Library of Congress, https://www.loc.gov/item/today-in-history/october-12.

9. Ibid.

10. Tom Noel, "Columbus Day started in Colorado," *Denver Post*, September 26, 2010, http://www.denverpost.com/ci_16158140.

11. Ibid.

12. Mucci, *We the Italians: Two flags, One heart, One hundred interviews about Italy and the US*, 169; Marianna Gatto and Hayley Moore, *Judge Alfred Paonessa and The Early Civil Rights Movement in California*, Italian American Museum of Los Angeles, http://italianhall.org/docs/Paonessa%20-%20Students.pdf.

13. Noel, "Columbus Day started in Colorado," *Denver Post*, September 26, 2010, http://www.denverpost.com/ci_16158140.

14. Ibid.

15. "Columbus Day," Today in History - October 12, Library of Congress, https://www.loc.gov/item/today-in-history/october-12.

16. Mucci, *We the Italians: Two flags, One heart, One hundred interviews about Italy and the US*, 9.

17. Lund, "Walla Walla Sweets: Onions and Ethnic Identity in a Pacific Northwest Italian Community," *Columbia Magazine*, Volume 8, Number 3, Fall 1994, http://www.washingtonhistory.org/files/library/walla-walla-sweets.pdf.

18. Ibid.

19. Ibid.

20. Ibid.

21. "Transcript: Read Chris Rock's 2016 Oscars Opening Monologue," *L.A. Times*, February 28, 2016, http://www.latimes.com/entertainment/envelope/oscars/la-et-transcript-chris-rock-opening-monologue-20160228-story.html.

22. "The 49th Academy Awards," The Oscars, 1977, https://www.oscars.org/oscars/ceremonies/1977.

23. Ibid.

24. Ibid.

25. Ibid.

26. Ibid.

27. Eric Martone, ed., *Italian Americans: The History and Culture of a People*, (Santa Barbara, California: ABC-CLIO, 2017), 284.

28. Lawrence Baldassaro, *Beyond DiMaggio: Italian Americans in Baseball*, (Lincoln, Nebraska: University of Nebraska Press, 2011), 415, https://books.google.com/books?id=YkcqDwAAQBAJ&pg=PA415&l pg=PA415&dq=Angelo+Giammattei&source=bl&ots=uhB37lFpmr&si g=MswKb7nLmdVlsTYHHicOXCPUhd8&hl=en&sa=X&ved=0ahUK Ewjumtqj6cjWAhVhiFQKHUgUDEEQ6AEIOjAF#v=onepage&q=A ngelo%20Giammattei&f=false.

29. Loren Gush, "Oscars 2016: Chris Rock and Whoopi Goldberg add diversity to Joy, The Martian and The Revenant," *Verge*, February 28, 2016, https://www.theverge.com/2016/2/28/11130602/chris-rock-whoopi-goldberg-parody-video-academy-awards-2016.

30. Angus MacKinnon, "After over 500 film scores, Oscar at last for Ennio Morricone," GMA News Online, March 1, 2016, http://www.gmanetwork.com/news/showbiz/showbizabroad/557361/after-over-500-film-scores-oscar-at-last-for-ennio-morricone/story/.

31. Lee, *The Fortune Cookie Chronicles: Adventures in the World of Chinese Food*, 252.

32. Molinari, *The Italians of New York*, 45.

33. Ibid.

34. Ibid.

35. Ibid., 87-88.

36. Ibid.

37. Ibid.

38. *The Italian Americans*, PBS, February 2015; Tom Verso, "To Educate Italian American Children . . . or Not?," i-*Italy*, April 27, 2009, http://www.iitaly.org/magazine/focus/op-eds/article/educate-italian-american-childrenor-not.

39. Malcolm Gladwell, *Outliers: The Story of Success*, (New York: Little, Brown and Company, 2008), 9-10.

40. Ibid., 3-11.

41. Dr. Rock Positano, "The Mystery of the Rosetan People," *Huffington Post*, March 28, 2008, http://www.huffingtonpost.com/dr-rock-positano/the-mystery-of-the-roseta_b_73260.html.

42. Ibid.

43. LindaAnn Loschiavo, "If Defamation Is Serious, Why Don't Italian American Organizations Take It Seriously?," in *Anti-Italianism: Essays on a Prejudice*, eds. William J. Connell and Fred Gardaphe (New York: Palgrave MacMillan, 2010), 152.

44. Moses, *An Unlikely Union: The Love-Hate Story of New York's Irish and Italians*, 325.

45. Mancassola, "Embracing the Other Italy," *New York Times*, March 9, 2015, https://www.nytimes.com/2015/03/10/opinion/embracing-the-other-italy.html.

46. Ibid.

47. Ibid.

48. Ibid.

49. Ibid.

50. Ibid.

51. Ibid.

52. Pino Neri, "Gennaro senza lavoro si toglie la vita," *Il Mattino*, 2015, http://www.ilmattino.it; "Gennaro si toglie la vita perché senza lavoro," Leggo, http://www.leggo.it/news/italia/pomigliano_ragazzo_senza_lavoro_suicidio-1032553.html.

53. Mucci, *We the Italians: Two flags, One heart, One hundred interviews about Italy and the US*, 67.

54. Ibid., 81.

55. Ibid., 377.

56. Ibid., 379.

57. Ibid., 162.

58. Ibid., 124.

59. Molinari, *The Italians of New York*, 142.

60. Madonna interview, Howard Stern Show, March 11, 2015, https://www.youtube.com/watch?v=BGHrYS-1IWo.

61. Salvatore J. LaGumina, "Prejudice and Discrimination: The Italian American Experience Yesterday and Today," in *Anti-Italianism: Essays on*

a Prejudice, eds. William J. Connell and Fred Gardaphe (New York: Palgrave MacMillan, 2010), 113.

62. Ibid., 111.

63. Clement, "A Look Inside Merlino Foods, Supplier to Seattle's Best Restaurants," *Seattle Times*, February 27, 2015, http://www.seattletimes.com/life/food-drink/a-look-inside-merlino-foods-supplier-to-seattles-best-restaurants/.

64. Ibid.

65. Ibid.

66. Mucci, *We the Italians: Two flags, One heart, One hundred interviews about Italy and the US*, 121.

67. Ibid.

68. R.C., "Meet the New Italians of New York," i-*Italy NY*, Year 4, Issue 1-2, February-March 2016, 33-34.

69. Ibid.

70. Molinari, *The Italians of New York*, 145-147.

71. Ibid.

72. Mancassola, "Embracing the Other Italy," *New York Times*, March 9, 2015, https://www.nytimes.com/2015/03/10/opinion/embracing-the-other-italy.html.

73. Ibid.

74. "Hyphenated Italians, the Italian Diaspora," Candida Martinelli's Italophile Site, http://italophiles.com/hyphenated_italians.htm.

75. Mucci, *We the Italians: Two flags, One heart, One hundred interviews about Italy and the US*, 112.

76. Durante, *Italoamericana: The Literature of the Great Migration, 1880-1943*, 9.

77. Mucci, *We the Italians: Two flags, One heart, One hundred interviews about Italy and the US*, 271.

78. Ibid.

79. Dickie, *Darkest Italy: The Nation and Stereotypes of the Mezzogiorno, 1860-1900*, 79.

80. Durante, *Italoamericana: The Literature of the Great Migration, 1880-1943*, 145.

81. "Less than 50% Italians read book last yr," ANSA, January 14, 2016, http://www.ansa.it/english/news/lifestyle/arts/2016/01/14/less-than-50-italians-read-book-last-yr_9c012844-af2f-40b1-a8f7-b527739c087d.html.

82. Mucci, *We the Italians: Two flags, One heart, One hundred interviews about Italy and the US*, 404-405.

83. Italian American Museum, 2016.

84. Ibid.

85. Ibid.

86. Ibid.

87. Ibid.

88. Tom Bergeron, "New Jersey and Italy: Perfect together—Italian trade head eager to expand business ties," NJBIZ.com, April 25, 2016, http://www.njbiz.com/article/20160425/NJBIZ01/160429913/new-jersey-and-italy-perfect-together--italian-trade-head-eager-to-expand-business-ties.

89. Ibid.

90. "The IACC Chapter in South Carolina hosted a delegation from Miami leaded by Hon. Gloria Bellelli, Consul General of Italy," *We the Italians*, May 14, 2016, http://www.wetheitalians.com/business-lifestyle-south-east/the-iacc-chapter-in-south-carolina-hosted-a-delegation-from-miami-leaded-by-hon-gloria-bellelli-consul-general-of-italy.

91. Italian American Museum, 2016.

92. Mucci, *We the Italians: Two flags, One heart, One hundred interviews about Italy and the US*, 235.

93. Ibid., 243.

94. Ibid., 147.

95. "Mission," New York Italians, http://www.newyorkitalians.org/mission/.

96. "NY Italians and The World Bridge New York: Donate Now," New York Italians, November 1, 2016,

http://www.newyorkitalians.org/2016/11/01/ny-italians-and-the-world-bridge-new-york-donate-now/.

97. Cometto, "'Iron Lady' Italian Style," i-*Italy NY*, Year 4, Issue 1-2, February-March 2016, 21.

98. Amy Kellogg, "Journalist discovers stories behind US cities and towns with Italian names," Fox News, August 5, 2016, http://www.foxnews.com/us/2016/08/05/journalist-discovers-stories-behind-us-cities-and-towns-with-italian-names.html.

99. Ibid.

100. Ibid.

101. Sarah Maslin Nir, "An Italian Mayor Makes His First Trip to Manhattan, and Likes What He Tastes," *New York Times*, June 4, 2015, https://www.nytimes.com/2015/06/05/nyregion/an-italian-mayor-makes-his-first-trip-to-manhattan-and-likes-what-he-tastes.html.

102. Ibid.

103. Ibid.

104. Ibid.

105. Mucci, *We the Italians: Two flags, One heart, One hundred interviews about Italy and the US*, 402.

106. Ibid., 403.

107. Ania Bartkowiak, "Documenting Rural Italy's Vanishing Traditions," *New York Times*, December 8, 2016, https://lens.blogs.nytimes.com/2016/12/08/documenting-rural-italys-vanishing-traditions-giuseppe-nucci/.

108. Ibid.

109. Ibid.

110. Ibid.

111. Dickie, *Darkest Italy: The Nation and Stereotypes of the Mezzogiorno, 1860-1900*, 41; "A nome del presidente della Repubblica vi chiedo scusa per quanto qui è successo. Così Giuliano Amato a Pontelandolfo," *Gazzeta Benevento*, August 15, 2011, http://www.gazzettabenevento.it/Sito2009/dettagliocomunicato.php?Id=34589.

112. "Save the Romaggi Adobe," *Primo*, 4th edition, 2016, 52-53.

113. Tammy Minn, "Mary Ann Esposito," *Tastes of Italia*, March/April 2017, 24-25.

114. "Italy 'wants to give citizenship to UK students,'" *Italian Insider*, June 27, 2016, http://www.italianinsider.it/?q=node/3999.

115. "The European Union," Italian Cultural Institute, September 19, 2016, http://www.iicnewyork.esteri.it/iic_newyork/en/gli_eventi/calendario/2016/09/the-european-union-a-challenge.html.

116. "New Jersey legislator fighting to save Columbus Day," *We the Italians*, January 19, 2017, http://www.wetheitalians.com/art-heritage-east/new-jersey-legislator-fighting-to-save-columbus-day.

ACKNOWLEDGEMENTS

Special thanks to the following colleagues and friends for reading earlier drafts of this manuscript: Michael Gross, the director of the legal department at the Authors Guild; Rhona Whitty, writer and editor for the New York chapter of the Women's National Book Association; Donna Kerrigan; ND; and Carmine Sarracino, professor of English at Elizabethtown College.

For their research and/or publishing help, thanks to Stephanie Lundegard and Saul Porter at the Garibaldi-Meucci Museum, Carolyn MacKay, Francesco Grisanzio at the Authors Guild, Becky Stinnett, Tara Macomber, Fatima Shaik, Brad and Carolyn Manuel, the staff at the Duke University Library Service Center, and Vincenzo Forgione.

Thank you to my friend, Patrick Reilly.

Much love to my dear late friends, Barnard and Florence Seligman.

This book was written with thoughts of all those who came before me, to family and friends I have lost, including Stephanie DeLorenzo.

Thank you, scholar and food writer Michael W. Twitty, for coining the term "culinary justice." When people ask me what area of law I specialize in, this is going to be my response.

And finally, thank you to the Sicilian man I met while shopping. You said the cookbook about Italian food in New York didn't represent your foodways. This one's for you.

AUTHOR BIO

One day, I was eating lunch at the delightful and much-missed Ennio & Michael, a popular Italian spot in the Village. It was a beautiful sunny day and I was alone. An older gentleman—at least in his eighties—was sitting at the table next to mine. He was talking to the waiter about monkfish. I'd never had monkfish, so I inquired about it. He invited me to sit with him, an invitation that started a years-long friendship. The man was Hans Schindler, a brilliant Jewish chemist who worked for the United States during World War II and helped defeat the Nazis. He was a "Doctor" but preferred to be called "Mister." When I asked Mr. Schindler why, he said, "Titles mean nothing." I was deeply moved by this exceptional man's humility.

For those who *do not* share Mr. Schindler's sentiments, I have an Esq. at the end of my name and an MFA in creative writing from NYU. I've written and/or edited for *Glamour, Family Circle, Time Out New York*, the American Bar Association, Scholastic, Vault.com, *USA Boxing News, David Kherdian's Forkroads: A Journal of Ethnic American Literature*, and *Voices in Italian Americana*. I wrote about Italian-American personalities, food, and Little Italys for *Primo* magazine. My interview with poet Daniela Gioseffi is included in *Pioneering Italian American Culture: Escaping La Vita Cucina*, Via Folios, 2013. I have interviewed novelist Louisa Ermelino and cartoonist Mark Tatulli. For Hobokeni.com, I wrote about Italian bread, pastries, and pizza, including an interview with Cake Boss Buddy Valastro. Hailing from a line of restaurateurs, my parents included, I currently have a food blog at http://huntingfortheverybest.wordpress.com. I took food writing and blogging classes at the New School University and the Institute of Culinary Education in NYC. I won a CASE (Council for Advancement and Support of

283

Education) award to study marine sciences in Maine where I toured a lobster wharf and halibut hatchery and ate fresh oysters from the Damariscotta River.

For those who *do* share Mr. Schindler's sentiments, I am Dina. When it comes to delicious food, I don't discriminate. There's room in my heart (and my stomach) for pizza, pasta, polenta, and pork bbq. I'm equally happy at Di Fara's in Brooklyn, Del Posto in Chelsea, Da Michele in Naples, or Hursey's BBQ in Burlington, North Carolina.

Made in the USA
Middletown, DE
03 September 2021